1976

ook may be kept

JOSIAH ROYCE
An Intellectual Biography

The historic connection which exists between mathematics and exact science on the one hand and conceptions of knowledge on the other, needs no emphasis: from Plato to the present day, all the major epistemological theories have been dominated by, or formulated in the light of, accompanying conceptions of mathematics. Nor is the reason for this connection far to seek; mathematics, of all human affairs, most clearly exhibits certitude and precision. If only one could come at the basis of this ideal character, the key-conceptions of epistemology might be disclosed. Thus every major discovery of theoretical mathematics, and every fundamental change in the manner in which this subject is conceived, is sure to find its sequel, sooner or later, in epistemology.

C. I. Lewis, *Mind and the World Order*

Also muss auf Kant zurückgegangen werden.

Otto Liebmann, *Kant und die Epigonen*

Bruce Kuklick

JOSIAH ROYCE

An intellectual biography

THE BOBBS-MERRILL COMPANY, INC.

Indianapolis and New York

FOR MURRAY MURPHEY

ACKNOWLEDGMENTS

Both Yale University and the American Philosophical Society provided summer grants for the research and writing of this book, and I am particularly grateful for the Society's expression of confidence in the results of my work. The staffs of Harvard's University Archives and Houghton Library facilitated my examination of the Royce, James, and Peirce papers; and the librarian at Merton College, Oxford, was equally helpful in regard to the Bradley papers. The Reverend A. H. M. Kempe was more than kind in giving me access to Alfred Bray Kempe's papers, as were Grace and Frederika de Laguna in giving me access to those of Theodore de Laguna. All three were generous with their time and information.

My students at Yale, especially Larry Stewart, John Van Scoyoc, and Robert Brandom, have often stimulated my thinking when I was resting most content with preconceptions. My bursary assistant, Emmet McLaughlin, doesn't really appreciate my gratitude to him for doing so much of the typing and all of the ransacking of Sterling Library's shelves. Sydney Ahlstrom, Kenneth Blackwell, Michael Dunn, Robert Imbelli, Karl Otto Liebmann, R. M. Martin, and Rich Thomason have been of service at various stages in my work. Everyone who studies Royce is indebted to John Smith, and I was more than fortunate in having him close at hand during most of the time I was working on this project; everyone who studies the history of American philosophy must sooner or later be impressed by the scholarship and kindness of Max Fisch, and I am no exception.

As my dedication should make clear, my study owes the most to Murray Murphey, one of the few gifted men I have met. Had I not known him when I was a student I doubt whether this book would ever have been written. To an extent greater than I would like to admit, it reflects his thinking. (I have had the use of his own work on Royce in

Murphey and Flower's forthcoming *History of American Philosophy*.) But much more than that he has been a model for me of what a teacher and scholar should be. I affectionately acknowledge my professional and personal debt to him.

My wife is a very secular young woman, and although she gradually grew tolerant of my enterprise, her initial reaction to my plan to study Royce was uncomprehending disdain. At one point in my research, however, she went off to Britain to examine the papers of colonial civil servants. The extensive research and writing I did in those two months is much more a tribute to her than thanks for free editorial work.

CONTENTS

INTRODUCTION

This book is an exercise in the logic of the history of ideas; the essay tries to avoid the two methods which characterize studies of the "Golden Age" of American thought. On the one hand, philosophers have attempted to extract what is "still living" in a past thinker.* The strategy is to reconstruct the argument a man has presented for a position, or to give the position a coherence it does not appear to have, or to demonstrate that the man has "something to say" on a currently important topic. These studies have two striking features: they show us that even contemporary philosophy needs a usable past; and they frequently make contributions to recent philosophical controversy. Unfortunately we learn little of the thought of the man under scrutiny for his ideas are often distorted beyond recognition. I have tried to rescue Royce from the condescension of the present.

On the other hand, intellectual historians have usually not written anachronistic history, but they have generally been unconcerned with philosophy altogether. They approach late nineteenth- and early twentieth-century American thinkers with a set of concepts only negligibly connected to the data and with little concern for philosophic argument. They often equate pragmatism with the politics of Franklin Roosevelt's Brains Trust. Just as often, however, there is a statement of the history of the technical doctrines: more or less clearly, we have been told that to trace the story of American thought is to trace a peculiar version of experimental Anglo-American empiricism from Peirce, to James, to Dewey; if we wish to examine a secondary theme, we may examine the Hegelian Royce who stands outside this tradition, influenced by German thought,

---

* For example: A. J. Ayer, *The Origins of Pragmatism* (London, 1968); Peter Fuss, *The Moral Philosophy of Josiah Royce* (Cambridge, Mass., 1965); W. B. Gallie, *Peirce and Pragmatism* (Dover ed., New York, 1966); John Wild, *The Radical Empiricism of William James* (New York, 1969).

the leading U.S. expositor of a different philosophic style, absolute idealism.*

This picture is wrong not merely in detail but in principle. I have indicated that the Cambridge pragmatists—Royce among them—were part of a major philosophical movement. Their pragmatism is a form of neo-Kantianism which draws from a set of connected doctrines: a constructionalist epistemology stressing the changing character of our conceptual schemes; a commitment to a variety of voluntarism; a Kantian concern with the nature of possible experience; an adherence to the idealist principle that existence does not transcend consciousness; a distrust of traditional British empiricism; a recognition of the importance of logic for philosophy; an uncomfortableness with the dichotomy between the conceptual and the empirical; a refusal to distinguish between questions of knowledge and of value; an emphasis on the relation of philosophy to practical questions; and a desire to reconcile science and religion.[1]

The Harvard philosophers conducted a dialogue with major figures in the western tradition. They have little relation to the analyses the historian has made of them; nor were they influenced by Franklin, Jefferson, Emerson, and the Adamses; nor by Beard and Veblen.

In offering an alternative to these two varieties of intellectual history, I have tried to sort out the issues which led Royce to the views he defended and to show how his position changed over the years as he refined it and faced new difficulties. He begins his philosophical career as a neo-Kantian puzzled by the same sorts of problems which perplexed William James. The idealistic arguments of Royce's first major work, *The Religious Aspect of Philosophy,* are advanced only after several years as a "pure pragmatist." Through 1900 he elaborates this idealism along both metaphysical and ethical lines. But after the 1885 book the

---

* For example: Paul Conkin, *Puritans and Pragmatists* (New York, 1968); Merle Curti, *The Growth of American Thought* (3rd ed., New York, 1964); Ralph Henry Gabriel, *The Course of American Democratic Thought* (2nd ed., New York, 1940); Richard Hofstadter, *Social Darwinism in American Thought* (rev. ed., New York, 1955); Perry Miller, ed., *American Thought: Civil War to World War One* (New York, 1954).

principal question confronting him is the connection between the world of the absolute and our world of everyday experience. During the nineties he explores various resolutions of this problem, concentrating on psychological ones. By the end of the century—in *The World and the Individual* and what follows it—he turns to symbolic logic to effect a reconciliation between the two worlds, and mathematical studies dominate his thinking until 1910. His last writings, notably *The Problem of Christianity*, attempt to translate his technical conclusions into more comprehensible language, while preserving the insights of his more popular twentieth-century work. In short, I have learned my way around the main trails of Royce's system, and I have tried to map them accurately. But I am sure that there are side trails I have missed and fear that even important ones are unexplored because of my own lack of understanding.

By contemporary standards a lack of clarity pervades Royce's work, but I have not read into his language more exactness than it will bear. I have simply attempted to make intelligible what I think he was saying. Undoubtedly vagueness is one of his major failings, but if we are to understand his philosophy it is pointless to demand of him standards which he had no intention of meeting. To interpret him with them in mind would be an ahistoric enterprise. Aside from discussing the major tensions in his writing, I have also muted my internal criticism of Royce's thought. Although I have been much concerned with philosophic argument, I am not sure that appraisals of the correctness of a position are part of the task of the intellectual historian, and I am dubious, at any rate, about our ability to specify what is philosophically right or wrong. Although I have tried to show Royce's relation to the intellectual life around him and his connection to the tradition of philosophy at Harvard which extends from at least 1870 to the present, I have not tried to make him "relevant." I am not convinced that *any* of our present philosophic tastes provide or should provide a canon for judging past thinkers; and I am convinced that if a man is worth studying, he is worth studying for what *he* had to say. I am sure that in some sense Royce thought as he did because he was "an American" and, indeed, "a Californian." I am also sure that his personal life influenced his writing. But I have found little evidence which would allow me to interpret his work in these terms; and I would suggest that no one else has such evidence. Of course, I would not deny that thought must be understood within the social context in which it arises, and for the purposes of this book I have assumed that the limits of Royce's thinking were defined by his culture's concern with the doctrine of evolution and, in particular, its relation to religion. But the major stimulus to work in philosophy has always been previous or contemporary work in philosophy. Consequently, in interpreting Royce's large output, I have been conscious of the influence and writing of his fellow scholars.

Three central themes ought to shape much of the history of twentieth-century American philosophy and have shaped my narrative: the impact of logic on philosophy; the relationship between pragmatism and idealism; and the significance of Kant.

If we ignore Royce's interest in the foundations of mathematics—especially after 1900—we are bound to get a distorted picture of his thought. His first published book was a short primer on Boolean algebra, and he introduced symbolic logic into the Harvard curriculum. After Charles Peirce he was the foremost logician in the country and a formative influence on C. I. Lewis. By the turn of the century logic was the spine of Royce's philosophy, and we can understand little of what he wrote without reference to it. Like Peirce, who was his senior, and those philosophers at Harvard who succeeded him—Lewis, Nelson Goodman, and Willard Quine—Royce sought the ground for all philosophical speculation in logic. Although he maintained that the end of this speculation was a solution to moral, social, and religious problems, they had to be approached from a logico-mathematical base. In fact, from this perspective James stands outside the customary concerns of Harvard thinking, although for some it may contribute to his greatness.

Both James and the Cambridge logicians have been pragmatic in their epistemology, and from Peirce to the present this pragmatism has had an affinity for metaphysical idealism. Peirce was always an idealist of some kind; in *Mind and the World Order* Lewis tilts for pages against idealism, and despite his form of "realism" often lapses into ambiguous

forms of expression and states that there may be no issue between him
and idealists. Later pragmatic analysts have also advocated idiosyncratic
doctrines which are different from other contemporary empiricisms.
Since guilt by association must suffice in lieu of an extended study, we
ought to note that Quine's denial of the analytic-synthetic distinction and
his espousal of what some have called a coherence theory of truth are
moves idealists traditionally make. When Royce and James taught at
Harvard the issues between pragmatism and idealism were perhaps most
muddied because the two men were pictured as opponents. I shall try to
show, however, that Royce was a pragmatist as early as 1880 and that it
was easy for him to develop an idealistic ontology *because* he was a pragmatist. As Royce later called his doctrine Absolute Pragmatism, we may
interpret James as a pluralistic idealist. The epistemological disputes between the two men were over specific and highly technical points, but
they shared certain peculiar beliefs whose central feature we may label
pragmatic and whose affinities to idealism we ought to recognize.

The affinity of pragmatism for an idealistic metaphysic is not difficult to explain once we realize that pragmatism is a neo-Kantian development, and the third theme which runs through this essay is an
account of the Kantian sources of Royce's philosophizing. He initially
approached epistemology and metaphysics with a disdain for post-
Kantian speculation and embraced the neo-Kantian attempt to build
directly on the first *Critique*. Throughout his career it was Kant's work—
and particularly the problem of the deduction of the categories—which
guided Royce's thinking. But in singling out Kant as a major "influence"
on the American, I do not wish to dismiss other influences. Royce read
omnivorously and had a capacity for using all sorts of information to
buttress his position. He was willing to appropriate whatever good ideas
were about, and it may be foolish to sort out the strands of the nineteenth-century fabric of scholarship that were most significant for him.
But if I have made Royce dependent on the views of any of his contemporaries, it is on the following: Baldwin, Bradley, James, Kempe, and
Peirce.

In writing this book, I have realized how secular my friends are,

philosophers and non-philosophers, and I have been asked many times
what perversity attracted me to a man identified with religious thinking,
and indeed its genteel side. As I hope to show, this categorization is a
mistake. But let me add that I have found Royce's moralism almost always conventional and trite. His popular philosophy is thin in substance
and overblown in rhetoric. Nonetheless, at his best Royce is a powerful,
consistent, and intriguing thinker. I have been struck by the ingenious
and complex maneuvers he is able to make in elaborating his position.
In reading through his published and unpublished work I have come to
feel that he was an extraordinary human being with an incredible drive
and a wide range of talents. Royce has stimulated and fascinated me for
six years; I hope I have conveyed this stimulation and fascination to the
reader.

1

EARLY PRAGMATISM
1877–1884

Josiah Royce was born in Grass Valley, California, in November, 1855, six years after his parents migrated there as "forty-niners." When his family moved to San Francisco in 1866, he enrolled in his first formal school, and attended local institutions until his graduation from the University of California at Berkeley in 1875. Royce so impressed local businessmen that they agreed to send him to Germany for a year of study. On his way to Leipzig and Göttingen he stopped in Boston and briefly met William James. The nineteen-year-old again made a favorable impression, and when he returned from Germany to study for a Ph.D. in the new graduate program at The Johns Hopkins University, he began a real acquaintance with the Harvard psychologist. Royce received his doctorate in philosophy from Hopkins in 1878, but although the acquaintance with James developed into friendship, there were no teaching positions of any sort at Harvard; in fact, there were no positions in philosophy anywhere, and the young man traveled back to Berkeley where he became an Instructor in Literature and Composition.

Even before he returned to the west coast, Royce wrote that he would grow spiritually consumptive in its metaphysical climate. After six months there he told James there was "no philosophy in California." "From Siskiyou to Ft. Yuma and from the Golden Gate to the Summit of the Sierras," Royce lamented, "there could not be found brains enough [to] accomplish the formation of a single respectable idea that was not a manifest plagiarism. Hence the atmosphere for the study of metaphysics

is bad. And I wish I were out of it."[1] His chance came in the spring of
1882: Harvard offered him a job replacing James, who was to be on leave
in 1882–1883. Royce was so discontented with Berkeley that he gave
little regard to his future prospects in Cambridge and made the difficult
continental trip with a wife and infant son for a one-year appointment
which paid $1250. He arrived in Boston in the fall of 1882 to lecture in
James's courses in psychology.

Teaching psychology was not yet metaphysics, but it was closer to
metaphysics than literature and composition. Actually, Royce's interests
were not so unrelated as they appear. As an undergraduate he studied both
philosophy and literature, and during his graduate training spent a great
deal of time on the German romantics. During the seventies his study of
them paralleled his study of nineteenth-century German philosophy. In
the four years he spent at Berkeley his own work increasingly stressed
the technical developments in German intellectual history, and teaching
psychology at Harvard did not require much of a shift: it was still the
science of mind, and his superiors also gave Royce other congenial
assignments.[2]

At Hopkins and Berkeley Royce offered courses of lectures that
expounded his own thought. His dissertation was also an attempt at
original philosophy, and with its acceptance he started to contribute to
philosophical journals. In his classes at Cambridge he does not seem to
have elaborated his own ideas, but soon after he arrived he delivered
some evening talks entitled "The Religious Aspect of Philosophy." In
them he continued to work out the position which he espoused more fully
in the book of the same name published in 1885. The doctrines formulated there were consequently the result of seven years of reflection; and
if we are able to understand his first book, we must explore Royce's attempts to account for the nature of knowledge, the pervasive theme in
his early writings.

Kant's influence on Royce was enormous; the young man wrote of
him as "the good father,"[3] and in *The Religious Aspect of Philosophy*,
which Royce described as belonging to the "wide realm of post-Kantian

Idealism," he announced that he felt his debt to Kant "most of all."[4]
Prior to 1885 Royce's Kantianism is more striking. He came to philosophy as a neo-Kantian troubled by the status of the *Ding an sich;* as he
struggled with the problems which Kant's view generated, he elaborated
a position which was idealistic but simultaneously voluntaristic and even
pragmatic. The result of the first *Kritik,* Royce wrote in 1881, is that
"we all now live, philosophically speaking, in a Kantian atmosphere";
the problems of the critical philosophy are fundamental, and the philosophy of the future must be the critical one. Although Royce was to become
one of the leading exponents of post-Kantian Idealism, his road to this
position was not through the post-Kantians. We should study them because "with all their extravagances" they never lost sight of Kant. Even
Schopenhauer, whose voluntarism, rather than any Hegelian doctrine,
was later cited as an influence on Royce, in no way challenges Kant. In
his formative years Royce considered Schopenhauer an unsatisfactory
expositor of Kant and an inadequate speculator in his own right;
Schopenhauer's significance was that he led younger students "to look for
themselves" into Kant.[5]

It is in the more exact thinking of the German neo-Kantian movement that the battle "to grasp and to perfect the critical idea in all its
meaning and consequence begins afresh. . . ." But if Royce believed the
neo-Kantians were the true heirs to Kant, and if his own early work was
in this tradition, Royce was no mere expositor of his master. He was concerned with a "needed reform" in the critical philosophy, a reform connected with the status of the things in themselves. Royce stated the need
to go "back to Kant,"[6] and in his doctoral dissertation of 1878, "On the
Principles of the Interdependence of Knowledge," he attempted a reinterpretation of the Kantian doctrine of the *Ding an sich.* The absolute idealism of *The Religious Aspect of Philosophy,* seven years later, is the
culmination of this reinterpretation.

The central problem in his dissertation is to rebut a self-imposed
skepticism. He begins by analyzing judgments. A judgment is expressed
in a proposition of subject-predicate form which brings two ideas together in a way designed to indicate their relationship. But, Royce asserts,

what one knows in a judgment can only be the relation of the ideas in
one's mind, at the particular moment one joins them: "Every judgment
is relative to the momentary insight of the thinker."[7]

Suppose I state that cherries are red. We cannot assume that there
are external objects whose real relations are "represented" by the judgment. To do this is simply to make another assumption, a higher order
judgment: " 'Cherries are red' represents the fact that cherries are red."
We are left with analyzing why or how this judgment can be true.[8] If
we argue that it "represents" the real relations of some external objects,
we are making another assumption, and are plunged into an infinite
regress.

The skeptical account does not rest here. If I like and you dislike
cherries, my idea of them will differ from yours; similarly, if I have just
been stabbed and you have not, my idea of redness will differ from yours.
We can never be sure that our ideas are identical.[9] Hence our judgments
cannot even be about common ideas. A judgment's sole significance is in
the relation between its subject and predicate for the individual at the
time he makes the judgment. Royce maintains that his relation is the complete or partial identification of the subject idea with the predicate idea.
When an individual judges, the mind simply takes the two ideas and
"unite[s] them by a definite identifying activity": "the act of judgment
is an act of identification."[10]

Judgments for Royce are acts, expressions of our wills, and only
in judging can we make a claim to knowledge; if we are to know, we can
know only in judging. Before we judge, we cannot say that the two ideas
identified in the judgment are like one another in any respect. "What
may be the likeness or unlikeness of our ideas before we judge of them,
we can never know." In fact, because knowledge comes about only in
judging, it is improper even to consider likeness or unlikeness as belonging to the ideas in themselves. To speak of ideas being alike or unlike is to presuppose that we have compared them, that is, in some way
judged. The act of judgment in effect creates the whole or partial identity of the subject and predicate ideas in a judgment. Thus, Royce
emerges with a more complete definition of 'judgment': a judgment is an

expression of will, an act whose subject is the identification of the subject and predicate ideas.[11]

Individual judgments are indubitable, and because of that fact give us a myriad of absolute truths. Unfortunately, this doctrine is also skeptical since Royce so far admits no truths outside of the immediately personal present. He has guaranteed truth by making error impossible. Blaming this on Kant, Royce admits the skeptical conclusion:

> . . . with Kant we find the great result to hold, that one greatest of all philosophic results in the history of thought, and the one that will always be recognized as Kant's greatest among his many great services—the principle namely that all Knowledge is creative, that its objects such as they are, exist and must exist in, through, and for itself. One hears much now-adays about Knowledge as relative. It is well to remember that Knowledge is relative only because it is creative, because, in other words, if the creative activity of Knowledge were other than it is, the objects and content of Knowledge would be other than they are . . . it creates its own ideas, it is relative indeed, but full of life.[12]

Obviously, however, human beings engage in what Royce calls "reasoned discourse," do behave as if their judgments are true of something beyond themselves, and do try to show that their fellows sometimes err. The point of the dissertation is to investigate "reasoned discourse" and to seek a justification for it. A further examination of individual judgments leads Royce to his positive results.

What can it mean to say "that the ideas in themselves are not identical, but are not only made so in the act of willing? What were these ideas in themselves?" The ideas which we identify in judging are ideas as they momentarily are in the mind when we judge. Ideas in themselves are ideas capable of analysis and connection with one another in a whole series of judgments; they are realized only partially and symbolically in any one judgment: "The ideas in themselves are abstractions of our own, and express the fact that we desire to be able to introduce one and the same idea into a whole series of acts of willing, that we ought to be able to do so, that we ideally must be able to do so."

We have various ways of ascertaining that our ideas are identical.

The first way, Royce claims, is by acting—by "actual examination in common of objects." For example, we may verify that we all have the same idea of a cherry by bringing one in and looking at it. But this process of direct verification may be difficult or even impossible, and we have another expedient: we make in common other judgments in which the idea of cherry enters. If we agree in these judgments, we become more sure that we have the same idea in common, that we have "a community of ideas." Scientific discourse stands as our best attempt to insure that we are dealing with the same ideas. Even so, Royce concludes, we are left with a degree of indefiniteness—a "personal equation." In all this verification,

> . . . we seem to ourselves to be aiming at the realization of a single idea as separate and apart from every individual judgment, and as entering into each judgment with its nature already fixed. In fact we never attain such an independent idea. In fact in every one of our judgments about it we have but a momentary and onesided view of it, or rather it is for the time being but a single side of an act of identification. Nevertheless, to attain such an independent idea is our wish, our ideal, the object of our definitions. And to these unattainable ideals of fixed and stable notions, we give the name of Ideas in themselves. By the term we mean not that which enters into any judgment, or that which is known in its nature as such apart from judgment; we mean only that which one desires to have enter into every reflective judgment, and that one postulates as pre-existent to each such judgment. . . . [The Ideas in themselves are] the ideals of reflective thought, the independent and stable elements we postulate but never can know, and that we define only by means of individual judgments, although they are assumed as *de jure* before all individual judgments about them . . .[13]

This constructive argument is based on the thought of the first *Critique*. The explicit intention is "no other than to substitute those Ideas in themselves for the term Things in themselves as Kant uses it in the chapter on Phenomena and Noumena, i.e., in the sense of *Grenzbegriffe*."[14] The notion of the Ideas in themselves

> . . . is framed in accordance with the spirit of Kant's true critical definition of the concept of the *Ding an sich*—not to be sure in

accordance with the concept as Kant himself sometimes loosely defines it, not in accordance with the notion that certain uncritical interpreters and judges of Kant have always been willing to find in it. Kant's *Ding an sich*, in its purely critical sense, is as little the cause of the *Erscheinung*, as our above-defined Ideas in themselves are the cause of the individual ideas. Hence all the profound wisdom that, from Jacobi to the latest defender of the faith, has been expressed in pointing out a certain famous and obvious difficulty in the application of the Category of Causality to the *Ding an sich*, is as little formidable to the true critical thought as it is in itself cheap and threadbare.[15]

This conception plays a major role in grounding empirical knowledge, or reasoned discourse. We suppose that our judgments may oppose one another. How is this possible, given the nature of judgments? Whatever Royce says of the Ideas in themselves, he claims that there can never be "direct opposition" between two actual judgments, and the reason for this is easy to see. Direct opposition between two judgments would imply that, for example, the subject ideas involved were the same while the predicate ideas were different. Yet Royce has already urged that the ideas in any judgment are unique; our judgments are always about different things and can never really conflict. Suppose I say 'It is Tuesday' and you say 'It is Wednesday'. Each is "an independent identification of two momentary subjective notions. . . . Each is as such a perfectly true judgment."

Royce does want to allow what he calls "indirect opposition" of two judgments: one may *conceive* that the theoretical or practical consequences of the first would finally directly oppose the formation of some theoretical or practical consequences of the other, and so would nullify or tend to nullify the latter. As he is fond of saying, judgments are acts of will, and his doctrine seems to be that while no two acts of will can conflict, it is possible that the acts of will implied by one judgment can oppose some *attempt* to form acts of will implied by the other. "The memory of a judgment consequent upon one of the original judgments opposes in the mind the attempt to form a judgment consequent upon the other original judgment. . . ." The opposition is not—as it might seem—

direct and therefore inconsistent with the position of no "direct opposition." Direct resistance to *incomplete acts of will* yields what Royce calls indirect opposition.[16]

But how can even the consequences of judgments result in indirect opposition? The consequences, the dissertation argues, could never become opposed except through the strange impression that identical ideas are involved in the two original judgments:

> . . . there is no true opposition among judgments as judgments at all; . . . all opposition arises through a practical demand of our own that whole series of our judgments shall be made upon the same ideas, or upon partly the same, and through the fact that from the nature of judgments themselves this demand can never be fully realized. In other words, all opposition of judgments belongs, not to the judgments as they actually are, but to the judgments considered as judgments about the Ideas in themselves.[17]

Because we believe that our judgments involve Ideas in themselves, we are led to believe that our judgments may be indirectly opposed. Upon analysis, this opposition proves illusory but is still demanded: the opposition has a "practical justification":

> judgments themselves are not in themselves considered opposed or harmonious, but completely independent, only receiving connection through our practical activity about them. This practical activity has its form in the assumption that the ideas in two or more judgments are the same, or in the intention that in a series of judgments the ideas shall be the same. But when the ideas in two or more judgments are the same, or are assumed to be, we have arising the notion previously described, the notion of Ideas in themselves. Only in view of and in respect to the Ideas in themselves, can propositions agree or differ, harmonize or oppose, be identical with or contradictory to one another.*

---

* "On the Principles of the Interdependence of Knowledge," Royce Papers, Harvard University Archives, pp. 83–84. Reasoned discourse presupposes another principle on which Royce elaborates in a striking passage:

> When two propositions have one Idea in common, the truth of one can follow from the truth of the other only through the mediation of a third, which has an Idea in common with both, and which so substituting for the Idea peculiar

Our reasoned discourse involves an extraordinary paradox. There is no opposition among judgments. But, constrained for some reason to believe that there is opposition, we conjure up a second arbitrary belief—the Ideas in themselves—to account for the first belief.

Royce defines individual judgments in terms of will, and the justification he gives for reasoned discourse follows this voluntaristic analysis. The goal of reasoned discourse is to put an end to strife, where strife is "the expression of obstructed Intention or Purpose." The function of reasoned discourse is universal harmony. Our justification for reasoning about the world is practical. The Ideas in themselves express "*a likeness among judgments made or demanded for a given purpose.*"[18] Ideas in themselves are constructs designed to serve our purposes; they are "necessary" constructs in that other attempts to secure commonality of ideas fail.

But why ought we to accept these results as an answer to Royce's skepticism? What real grounding does he offer for the basis of our knowledge of the world? Actually, none. The principles elaborated, he admits, "are satisfactory, because as rational beings we find ourselves satisfied with them. . . . Useless it is to give any final metaphysical basis to our procedure as reasoning beings. . . ." The assumptions which he has delineated are just that—"arbitrary," "unprovable" assumptions. It is impossible to give an ultimate warrant to the "final mystery" of these assumptions.[19]

"On the Principles of the Interdependence of Knowledge" is the Ph.D. dissertation of a twenty-two-year-old, and it has the defects of the genre: passages are obscure and much of the argument is unclear. But the thrust of the work is unmistakable. Royce is concerned with the foundations of our knowledge beyond what is momentarily presented to the

---

to the first proposition the same Idea expressed in terms of the Idea peculiar to the second, reduces the first to likeness with the second (p. 106).

I think we can understand the cryptic remarks Royce made toward the end of his life about the centrality of the community to his thought only if we consider this early work. See Chapter 11.

self. His examination of Kantian doctrines leads him to assert that the
only foundation is the practical needs of individuals. We postulate the
Ideas in themselves and act on this postulation because we relieve strife
and remove obstructions to the fulfillment of our purposes. Even so, the
Ideas in themselves are postulates, and we ascertain their meaning by
experimentation, direct and indirect verification, and by examining the
practical and theoretical consequences to which we are led in holding the
ideas.

He does not base this voluntarism on Schopenhauer. In an essay
written about this time, "Of the Will as the Principle in Philosophy,"
Royce rejects this interpretation. His explanation of the function of the
will has "transgressed [the] reasonable limits" which would allow any
identification with Schopenhauer. "Our agreement with his doctrine,"
Royce says, "is little more than verbal."[20] Rather, Royce is a neo-Kantian
espousing a variety of pragmatism.* As he writes James in 1880, "The
final basis of our thought is ethical, practical." And some of this, Royce
adds, he has learned from James himself.[21] Years later Royce made this
same judgment on his earlier work. In his 1903 Presidential Address to
the American Philosophical Association, he apologized to his colleagues
for his youthful outlook. "Before I fell a prey to that bondage of absolutism," he confessed,

> . . . there was a time when I was not a constructive idealist of any
> sort, and when, if I understand the meaning of the central conten-
> tion of pragmatism, I was meanwhile a very pure pragmatist. . . .
> for a time at least, I did seriously struggle not only to be what is
> now called a pragmatist, but also to escape falling into the clutches
> of any Absolute.[22]

Within two years of writing his dissertation, however, Royce found this
pragmatism unsatisfactory. To believe that the final justification for our

---

* The most interesting evidence for this assertion is Royce's later attacks on
James. The doctrine Royce attributes in the early 1900s to James bears extraordinary
similarities to the one Royce was in the process of rejecting before he wrote *The
Religious Aspect of Philosophy*, and his arguments against James are precisely the
ones Royce was bringing against his own pragmatism in the early 1880s. See Chapter 6.

knowledge is arbitrary is to give, he concedes, no justification at all. By 1880 he was formulating a different position.

We posit the Ideas in themselves to insure a rational basis for action. This positing, Royce reflects, in no way guarantees or renders it probable that our action *will be* rational. The postulates cannot "dictate" that experience be orderly, that our lives be harmonious, or that we have grounded knowledge about the world. Ideas in themselves express in part an "innocent wish" that these things are so, but this wish cannot justify their existence.[23] As he conceptualizes his dilemma, he relates it to a familiar problem: how are Kant's categories related to experience? Mind is to make a contribution to knowledge. But if, for example, the mind's category of causality is applicable to experience, then experience itself furnishes instances of uniform succession, and the category is superfluous. If experience has no regular succession, the category is useless. To meet this kind of objection, Royce says in his dissertation that the category of causality, like Ideas in themselves, is a pragmatic construct. After contemplation, he believes this to be no answer at all. This kind of postulate does not ground our knowledge, does not justify our beliefs. Kant had urged that "the understanding is to give laws to nature." The question is still *how*.[24]

Royce starts this time by reformulating the critical position. He is concerned with the *purpose* of thought, which is to learn the laws of phenomena and to predict experience. Experience, however, has a dual nature. First, something is given to us, "something that I passively receive and cannot at this time alter. . . . I cannot resist the force that puts it into my consciousness."[25] Royce defines the given no further and is satisfied to treat it as whatever is the momentarily present content of consciousness. Second, we contribute something to experience. Every judgment which enables us to learn the laws of phenomena goes beyond the given. The notions of past and future are necessary to all these judgments. For example, the judgment 'Cherries are red' does not help us understand empirical phenomena unless we assume that cherries exist in time, i.e., are entities with a past and probably a future. But the past and future are never included in the given. Royce concludes that the notions of past and future are constructs which we make up to reduce the given to coherence. The given is interpreted as a sign of something *not* given. For instance, we imply that some aspects of the given are memories indicating that something not present was once present: "To declare that there has been a past time at all, is to attribute to some element of the present a reality that does not belong to it as present."[26] This active construction is definitive of mind. It expresses the interest that we have in "reality," and is subservient to our practical inclinations. Knowing—determined equally by what is given and what we add by anticipation and completion of the given—is still in a deep sense acting.[27]

In spite of the greater lucidity of expression, Royce has made no advance on the thought of his dissertation. Like Kant he urges that in consciousness there is both a given and the spontaneous activity of thought. Unlike Kant Royce does not believe that we can divorce the two and then have thought organize the given; rather, thought *constructs* from the given what is not given; the thinking activity does not infuse sense with form, but from present sense projects the past and future.[28] Yet if our knowledge is just our own construct which depends on practical needs, what basis have we for accepting it? In what sense can we justify our claim to knowledge?

Royce's answer to these questions for the first time brings a dialectical argument into his philosophizing. Consider the sentence 'There is no future'. The acceptance of this assertion leads to its denial. To conceive a condition in which time has ceased is to introduce a time element into the assumed condition, i.e., a future time. To conceive of a non-future is to conceive of something after the present and, therefore, as future. We have a conception (the assumption that there will be a future) which in Royce's terminology is absolutely true. A dialectical argument demonstrates the conception's truth: its denial implies its assumption. In an analogous fashion we can make the same argument for the absoluteness of the past. There are thus some constructs of ours, e.g., the future and the past, which are absolutely true. To put the position in another way, the notion of the momentarily present which is given necessarily involves the notions of past and future. These constructs are not merely constructs, but constructs which express the essence of thought itself. The time flow, Royce contends, is not some independent thing-in-itself but indicates that our constructs determine the nature of experience: we cannot conceive that experience could be other than it is.[29]

When he made this discovery in 1880, he was jubilant:

> I work on Kant in the evening. I reflect on the analogy between Kant's 'Ich denke' and the doctrine of the active present moment to which I find myself driven in my efforts.
>
>   * * *
>
> I see Kant as I never saw him before. But we must put our problem differently. Thus says Kant: What is the relation of knowledge to its object? Thus say we: What is the relation of every conscious moment to every other? Our question may be more fundamental, and can be made so only through study of him.[30]

The belief that some postulates are necessary as well as practically justified was a major advance, but his argument has a weakness. The future and the past are our constructions, however much they are necessary constructions, i.e., aspects of the activity of thought itself. We mean by past and future what we conceive as past and future. Given this position, we can solve the problem of induction, for example, by fiat: the future resembles the past because we determine it to be so. Royce's logic has done too much. It is now impossible to doubt anything, for what we posit to be true must be true. Royce puts just this complaint into the mouth of an objector in what was to prove a prescient fashion:

> But, says the objector, all this leaves open no place for a difference between truth and error. If by past and future, and by the content of past and future one means only what is conceived as past and future and as the content thereof, then an error in prediction or in history is impossible. And with error disappears whatever is worth calling truth.

As Royce saw later, his handling of this difficulty was inadequate. We mean by error, he claims, that an expectation is disappointed when we find a present content of experience contrasting with the expectation *conceived* as past: error depends on remembering that a past expectation has been disappointed. But Royce defines the reality of the past as our present consciousness of the past, and for error to disappear we need only suppose an appropriate spontaneity of memory. As Royce admits, error becomes the *consciousness* of error.[31] For a conveniently forgetful person error would not exist. But without an adequate explanation of error, any theory of truth remains unsatisfactory. If he cannot distinguish error from truth in any coherent manner, Royce's attempt to set out the purpose of thought as learning the laws of phenomena fails: prediction exempt from error is no prediction at all.

It is perhaps unfair to leave Royce in this situation, but before we can understand how he resolves the problem, we must turn to another aspect of his work.

While writing his dissertation at Hopkins in 1877, Royce delivered a series of lectures on "The Return to Kant"; in them he took up at length the postulational basis of our knowledge. He cannot explain why the assumptions of thought turn out to be satisfactory; although experience verifies them, we cannot inquire why this is so. It is an inexplicable fact that "our sensations do occur with such a degree of regularity that the activity of thought has the power of making enough valid hypotheses for practical use." The "critical doctrine" has to rest with this analysis of the nature of knowledge. But as a Kantian, Royce states that if mind is removed from the universe, "the order of inanimate Nature" might still exist, although there would be no knowledge of it, no truth or error.[32] In his dissertation written a year later, he goes further, proclaiming that his philosophy is a brand of idealism. By this he does not necessarily mean that consciousness *constitutes* existence; rather, existence is "not external or foreign to Consciousness," a position consistent with his Kantianism. What he calls the Ideas in themselves can also be considered what we normally speak of as "external things": constructs of ours which unify our experience but which we never fully verify. They are "independent" of this or that mode of consciousness, and "relatively or absolutely stable as a . . . permanently possible content of Knowledge." Ideas in themselves, or as we may view them, external objects, do not depend on our individual consciousness. Human selves, Royce declares, "are transient in Consciousness; the individual passes; Existence remains." In addition to these mystifying comments, he concludes his dissertation with further remarks on the arbitrary nature of his findings, that is to say, that we merely posit the Ideas in themselves for practical purposes. But how can this be true? If the Ideas in themselves are *our* postulates, how can they be independent of us and not depend on our consciousness? How does Royce explain this anomaly? He does not. The Ideas in themselves "are perfectly inexplicable, total mysteries." Although they depend on consciousness, "we cannot in the least determine what and how various kinds of consciousness may exist. . . ."[33]

In two essays published in 1880 and 1881, "The Nature of Voluntary Progress" and "Doubting and Working," the tension between individual consciousness and "Consciousness" becomes explicit. In relation to any given individual, he writes,

> beliefs are always the satisfaction of individual wants. . . . The adjective 'true' is applied to a belief by the one whose intellectual wants it satisfies, at the time when it satisfies them. . . . A system of beliefs is held, just as a system of government endures, so long as it seems to the men concerned advantageous to cling to it.

But this does not mean that what is acceptable to *my* needs must be true. "My needs are narrow and changing. It is humanity in its highest development to which the truth will be acceptable." So in order to analyze truth we must substitute the broader social view of mankind for the individual's personal view: there must be some "measure" of truth outside any individual's ideas.[34]

By 1882 Royce had convinced himself that some truths are necessary as well as pragmatically demanded, and he again returned to the relation between his theory of truth and the status of external objects. The distinct individual and social elements in his formulation led him to admit nonpragmatic considerations: if our ideas are true, reality cannot be a creation of ours but must be independent of our ideas; we can justify them, it seems, only if they correspond to this reality. But this reality must simultaneously have a relation to consciousness. The outcome of these insights is a first attempt to harmonize two distinct notions of 'idea': the first, that an idea fulfills the purpose for which it is called forth; the second, that an idea corresponds to an external object. In 1882 the result is a tentative adherence to a Berkeleyan theory.[35]

There are some past, present, and future experiences which none of us experiences; yet we require them to make sense of the reality of the world. We want to say that the cherries on the tree exist when no one of us is experiencing them. Moreover, this "possible experience" cannot be "merely possible"; it cannot consist of "empty possibilities." When no one is about, the cherries are on the tree; a piece of green cheese is not. I can imagine green cheese on the tree, but the possible experiences which define the external world have a different status; they have a reality beyond my conception of them. We are led, Royce says,

> to the conception of one uniform absolute experience. This absolute experience, to which all facts would exhibit themselves in their connexion as uniformly subject to fixed law is conceived as "possible". But once again, what does that mean? Is the meaning only the empty tautology that if all the gaps and irregularities of individual experience were got rid of by means of connecting links and additional experience, these gaps and irregularities would disappear? Is the meaning only this, that if there were an absolute experience of an absolutely regular series of facts, this experience would be absolute and uniform? . . . Here then is our dilemma. Matter as a mere possibility of experience is more than any animal's known actual experience. And yet this matter is to be real for consciousness. Nor is it to be real for consciousness simply in so far as the possible experience is represented or conceived. The reality consists not merely in the representation in present consciousness of a possible experience, but in the added postulate that this conception is valid beyond the present consciousness. How is this postulate to be satisfied?

If we postulate an actual absolute experience, and if we are to be consistent "idealists," we must also claim that this experience *is* consciousness, or *for* some consciousness. Moreover, the consciousness involved cannot simply be an individual consciousness, for example, mine. Royce meets this problem by postulating a "hypothetical subject."

This hypothetical subject we shall postulate only as an hypothesis. That is, its existence is not a necessary result of the postulate that there is an external reality [i.e., absolute experience]. One can form other hypotheses [to account for this, e.g., panpsychism]. But this hypothesis has the advantage of being simple and adequate. . . . [We have, however, postulated] what of course never can be proven, that all the conceived "possible experiences" are actual in a Consciousness of which we suppose nothing but that it knows these experiences, or knows facts corresponding in number and in other relations to these experiences. This Consciousness is the Universal Consciousness. . . .[36]

By the early 1880s Royce's thought was in a curious state. Our ideas exist in order to fulfill our needs, but because they must refer beyond us if they are to be true, he supposes an "impersonal experience" to which our true ideas will correspond. To explain the special status of this possible experience which defines reality, he postulates a hypothetical subject for this experience; yet he maintains that we cannot give a proof of this subject's existence. Epistemological research had so far denied Royce a firm basis for his metaphysics; *it* must proceed by hypothesis. We cannot expect to have an "Absolute vision of truth, free from all taint of postulate."[37] Finally, there is still no way for human knowers to be in error about the reality which the hypothetical subject defines beyond their consciousness.

In the 1883 lectures at Harvard, Royce took a new step. The external consciousness is still an assumption. But it is now a *necessary* assumption "which I make because I want to think clearly. . . . I know no other view that offers any chance of a philosophy." In elaborating the meaning of his assumption, he approaches "the position which some call absolute or objective idealism." He does not ask that his audience accept this idealism as dogma, but argues that it follows from the possibility of agreement between thought and object, that is, that it is the outcome of any discussion of how error is possible. Regarded in itself, the mind of any individual is concerned only with its own ideas; sincerity and truth are identical, error inconceivable. But if we are to have error, Royce concludes this analysis,

> my thought is related to a higher thought even as the parts of one
> of my thoughts are related to the whole thought . . . [and] then
> comparison is possible between my thought and its object, for my
> thought, its object both as I know this object and as it is, are to-
> gether in an universal thought, of which they form parts, and in
> which they live and move and have their being. As my thoughts
> are an unity more or less complete in themselves, so all thoughts
> and objects must be postulated as an unity in that thought for
> which is the whole universe.[38]

With the publication of *The Religious Aspect of Philosophy* in 1885 the
universal thought ceases to be a construct. Using the dialectical argument
in an extended fashion, Royce shows to his satisfaction that error is
logically necessary; thereafter, he goes on to *prove* the actuality of the
absolute experience. As he later recalled, in preparing *The Religious
Aspect of Philosophy*, he "had definitely passed over from . . . [the]
earlier skeptical position. . . ."[39]

2

ABSOLUTE IDEALISM
1885–1897

Royce arranged parts of *The Religious Aspect of Philosophy* as an intellectual autobiography outlining the transition we have traced.[1] The book's most important job, however, was to present his "synthetic idealism," and this was done in his famous chapter eleven—"The Possibility of Error." Here Royce sets out the most significant argument he makes in his entire career; it is the "steadfast rock"[2] on which he builds for over twenty-five years, and a topic to which he refers for the next twelve. We must consequently examine his analysis with care, but before we undertake this task we must consider a few details.

We ought first to note Royce's priorities. He devotes a large portion of *The Religious Aspect of Philosophy* to a survey of religious problems because they first drove him to philosophy and because they deserve "our best efforts and our utmost loyalty." Even so, he urges that his philosophy depends in no way on his personal concerns. The system expounded for its own sake, Royce asserts, would not be based on the religious, and it is clear from his preface that the foundation for religious thinking has "nonreligious" grounds. That is, other philosophical speculation—call it for the moment theoretical—is for Royce "logically prior" to religious speculation. In *The Religious Aspect of Philosophy* he calls it "the *technical* statement of the proof" of his doctrine.[3] In *The Spirit of Modern Philosophy*, written seven years later, he terms this argument a "metaphysical discussion" of which his religious doctrines are a consequence.[4] In the introduction to *Studies of Good and Evil*, consisting

75389

LIBRARY
College of St. Francis
JOLIET, ILL.

mainly of essays in ethics, he stresses the importance of practical philosophizing, but reiterates that it is an *application* of his "fundamental convictions."[5] It is perhaps impossible to find an adequate description of
these convictions, and throughout Royce's early career they are amor-
phous. But even in *The Religious Aspect of Philosophy*, he claims three
times that the point of the argument in "The Possibility of Error" is to
determine *"the logical conditions"* which make error possible.[6] In re-
stating his position in *The Spirit of Modern Philosophy* he declares that
the road to the Absolute is "a product of dry logic,"[7] and when he
becomes a devotee of symbolic logic at the end of the century, this formulation is explicit. Religious—perhaps more broadly social and ethical—
concerns remain predominant but they are "conceptually subordinate" to
logic. In a wider sense the "thorny," "stony," and "arid" way—but the
only way—which leads to the Absolute is the way of logic. As *The Spirit
of Modern Philosophy* expresses his view, one purpose of his work is "to
remove from idealism . . . this reproach of being a mere poem of moral
enthusiasm." "We do not," he says, "believe in the world of the absolute
Self because we merely long for something spiritual"; the doctrine is "the
outcome of a rigid logical analysis."[8]

There is a second preliminary point which may be clear but which
I take up to clarify my own confusions. Like many who followed him and
James at Harvard, Royce was committed to a version of phenomenalism.
The finite knower is directly aware *not* of a physical object but of what
is momentarily present.[9] We can best, if inadequately, speak about this
"given"—what is directly before the mind—by using locutions like 'This
appears white to me' or 'It seems as if there is a white paper in front of
me' or perhaps even 'White spot, here, now.' From this slender basis
Royce proposes to demonstrate that we can have knowledge of a more
extensive realm—the external world. Often he is content to express his
theses by saying that this external world consists of contents of consciousness or, equivalently, of actual and possible experience. And he contrasts
ideas and experience—what is before my mind when I close my eyes and
imagine the desk in front of me and what I see when I open my eyes.
But, of course, his cardinal principle is that in experience we are given

ideas, internal data, and that it is of these ideas that the external world is made. The external world is some sort of arrangement, combination, or synthesis of these ideas. It goes beyond any of the ideas we have or can be directly aware of at any time, but we must account for the external world in ideal terms, that is, in terms which rule out an independently existing externality. As Royce expresses himself in *The Religious Aspect of Philosophy,*

> Popular belief about an external world is for the first an active assumption or acknowledgment of something more than the data of consciousness. What is directly given in our minds is not external. All direct data are internal facts; and in the strictest sense all data are direct. . . . the external world . . . is actively accepted as being symbolized or indicated by the present consciousness, not as being given in the present consciousness.[10]

This classical idealist doctrine sometimes leads Royce into an obscurity which I have tried to eliminate in my explication. On his view my ideas presumably refer to a real, although still ideal, world beyond them. But it is statements which are true or false: statements about my present ideas will be true if they "correspond" to the real world. Although Royce sometimes puts his doctrine in these words—substituting 'judgment' for 'statement'—he is confusing in his usage. Sometimes he considers ideas or perceptions—the present content of someone's consciousness—to be true or false of their objects when he means statements (or judgments) about these ideas. And he often makes judgments themselves intend or refer to their objects without noting the role of the judger. Although he clearly makes the distinction, he sometimes conflates two separate notions which the term 'idea' brings together. If I see that the cat is on the mat, I may state that the cat is on the mat and my statement will be correct if my perception (idea) is an accurate one. I may also believe that Caesar crossed the Rubicon. Then the statement 'Caesar crossed the Rubicon' will be true if Caesar crossed the Rubicon, that is, if my belief is true. Because Royce believes that whatever is before the mind is an idea, he often treats both these cases as cases of my having true or false ideas, assimilating "states of belief" to perceptual states. Of course, this assimilation is justifiable in his system; nonetheless, his language can be puzzling, and I have tried to make the terminology unambiguous.

Royce correctly traces aspects of his heritage to Berkeley and sets up the argument for his absolutism by formulating the Berkeleyan claims for idealism as he did three years before. We begin our explication of Royce's principal doctrine here.

There are, he claims, two aspects of idealism. The first, which Berkeley made famous, has no "absolute character" about it, but attempts only to show that our world is an ideal one. It

> . . . undertakes, in a fashion that might be acceptable to any skeptic, to examine what you mean by all the things, whatever they are, that you believe in or experience. This idealistic analysis consists merely in a pointing out, by various devices, that the world of your knowledge, whatever it contains, is through and through such stuff as ideas are made of, that you never in your life believed in anything definable *but* ideas, that, as Berkeley put it, "this whole choir of heaven and furniture of earth" is nothing for any of us but a system of ideas which govern our belief and our conduct.[11]

This argument proceeds in a familiar fashion, and after making a Berkeleyan analysis of secondary qualities Royce asks the expected questions about the nature of primary qualities.[12] What is philosophically interesting is his discussion of the result of this argument.

We are directly presented only with our own ideas. Let us assume that they "correspond" to the real world outside ourselves although we will not discuss this correspondence. Given that in our consciousness a and b are related, we assume a similar relation A:B in the external world. What is the most plausible hypothesis concerning the nature of the terms A and B in this assumed external world? Berkeley contends that there corresponds to finite consciousness a higher and farther reaching consciousness, "containing all that is abiding in our consciousness and much more besides." There is no external world but this other consciousness; the statements we make about it are true, for example, if our present experiences correspond to the experiences of this higher consciousness which ours are about. Each possible and actual experience of every moment in our lives and all the possible and actual experiences which comprise our universe will be "represented" by some momentarily present fact in the external consciousness. The relations of these facts will be similar in nature and in complexity to the relations among the facts of our actual or possible experiences. And the consciousness of this "universal Knowing One" will determine the limits of possible experience:

> this supposed universal knowing consciousness, this "Not-Our-selves," has, under the conditions stated, all the essential characteristics of a real world. It is beyond us; it is independent of us; its facts have a certain correspondence to our sensations. Under the supposition that by nature we tend to be in agreement with this consciousness, progress in the definiteness and extent of our agreement with it may be both possible and practically useful. This agreement would constitute truth. No other real world need be supposed behind or above this consciousness.[13]

This consciousness is not a creator but a seer. It does not make or unmake individual beings; on the contrary, they are made or unmade when data that we call organic living bodies arise or disappear in the universal consciousness. These data pass and with them passes the individual consciousness with which they co-existed. The growth and decay is a "law of experience"—"an ultimate and inexplicable sequence." We make no claims about the dependence or independence of the finite consciousness on the external consciousness, but assert only the one-to-one relationship.

This analysis is only a hypothesis. It is merely an elaboration and clarification of Royce's thought as it had developed prior to *The Religious Aspect of Philosophy*. He claims that it is simple, intelligible, and plausible.[14] But his commitment to it as anything other than hypothesis depends on more far-reaching considerations, the other aspect of idealism which we must explore.

This second aspect is a product of the speculation of the post-Kantians, and here Royce makes his own contribution. His initial point is a negative one against a position which he conceives as a major impediment to absolutism. He has not attempted to specify what the "correspondence" relation is between the real world and my ideas—immediate experience—but, according to Royce, Berkeley argues that it was their *cause*.[15] On the one hand, Royce sometimes feels that this view implies polytheism: if the external consciousness causes our ideas, it and they must be distinct, each independent centers of consciousness. On the other hand, we might construe causality as a relation independent of thought; or, to put this analysis another way, the external consciousness would not be a consciousness but a "power," a cause.[16] Against both of these positions, Royce urges that the external world cannot *cause* our ideas (or perceptions) about it; the correspondence relation must be something deeper.

If I should say that the external world causes my ideas, this belief necessitates something prior to the principle of causation: my thought demands that my *idea* of causality and my *idea* of the specific causal relation involved *correspond* to the truth of things. I cannot conceive of a cause of my ideas except insofar as I postulate that my conception of the cause is similar to the cause itself.[17] Royce makes this argument more than once, and perhaps makes it most neatly in an article written in 1892. Suppose I define the real object as the cause of my present ideas, my experience; I must still ask what I mean by causation: it is a relation between facts, and I must have some idea of this relation before I attribute it to the outer object which I never experience myself. I must, therefore, first believe that my notion of causation *corresponds* to an objective truth beyond me, that is, an objective truth about the relation between the real object and my ideas.

> . . . this means that there is here at least *one* external truth, and so one "object" (viz.:—the external fact of the causation itself), which I believe in, not because it is itself the cause of my idea of the causation, but because I trust that my idea of causation is valid, and corresponds to the truth. And it is only by *first* believing in this objective truth, viz., the causation, that I come to believe in *x* the cause. Hence it follows that even in case of immediate sense-perception, my belief in the external object is always primarily not so much a belief that my experiences need causes, as an assurance

that certain inner beliefs of mine are as such, valid, i.e., that they
correspond with that which is beyond them.[18]

In *The Religious Aspect of Philosophy* Royce concludes that the conception of reality which the search for causes entails is always subordinate
to another conception. This conception is that our ideas have something
beyond them and *like* them.

It is not difficult to understand the point. If causality is a logically
primary concept, metaphysical realism might be a tenable position. Although it is not for Berkeley, the cause of our ideas might be something
different in kind from them. But if the real world is *similar* to our ideas,
we can more easily accept its ideal nature; as Royce will show, our ideas
are fragments of the real world.

Linked to the view that causation is a secondary notion is a view
which, as we have seen, plays a large role in Royce's thought. At each
moment of our lives we postulate a past and future like our own present
consciousness but external to it. The purpose of Kant's critical philosophy
was to define the forms of this postulation. Although as yet unestablished,
the general law of the postulation is that the real world is conceived
"after the pattern of the present data, with such modification as is necessary to bring the conception into harmony with already established
habits of thought, and with the conceived results of previous experience."
The aim is to reach as complete and unified a conception of reality as
possible, combining the greatest fullness of data with the greatest simplicity of conception.[19]

Royce is left with three questions: the first, which he will not entirely answer, has a catalytic effect on his thinking: What is the exact
nature of this correspondence between our ideas and the real world; the
second, which is left over from his earlier ruminations, will be definitely
answered: What is the status of the hypothetical external consciousness
which he has called in to do service as the real world; the third, which
he believed he had dissolved earlier, now takes primacy of place: How
is error possible? To answer these questions Royce went to "the very
heart of skepticism itself."[20] Extreme skepticism would bring him to
absolute truth.

What guarantee have we that our ideas, our experiences, in any way correspond to the real world? What basis have we for saying that what we take to be true is in fact so? The skeptic urges that everything is doubtful and that we may always be mistaken. But even this skepticism implies that error exists. Is there any way to avoid this assumption? Suppose we argue that what is true, is true *for us*, that two assertions meet on no common ground, so that neither is "really true" or "really false." This position goes further than skepticism and declares the belief that we are in error itself erroneous. Royce calls this view that of the total relativity of truth; it is the doctrine of the Ph.D. dissertation for which he now has a counterargument. Consider the statement 'There is error'. If it is true, there is error. If it is false, then there is, *ipso facto*, error.[21] We cannot escape the conclusion that error exists; to deny its existence is contradictory. The dialectical argument Royce discovered five years before at last rescues him from relativism. We have, at least, one ultimate truth—that there is error, and Royce asks, how is error possible, what are the logical conditions which enable us to err?[22]

Error is commonly defined as a judgment that does not agree with its object. In an erroneous judgment we combine subject and predicate as the corresponding elements in the world are not combined:

> Now, in this definition, nothing is doubtful or obscure save the one thing, namely, the *assumed relation between the judgment and its object*. The definition assumes as quite clear that a judgment has an object, wherewith it can agree or not agree. And what is meant by the agreement would not be obscure, if we could see what is meant by the object, and by the possession of this object implied in the pronoun *its*. What then is meant by *its object?*[23]

Royce is again investigating thought's "correspondence" to the real world. My statement that the cat is on the mat is not true because the cat on the mat *causes* my perceptions (ideas) of the animal; rather a statement will be true if my perceptions correspond to the real world in some noncausal sense of 'correspond'. What is this sense?

Royce claims his analysis is an account of the "common sense" view of this notion. Although he feels the analysis is correct, it allows little room for error, and will push us nearer to absolute idealism. In order to think about an object—even if falsely, even in error—I must do more that have an idea that resembles the object. I must *mean* to have my idea resemble the object. To make the point in another way, I must aim at the object, pick it out; that is, I must possess the object enough to identify it as what I mean. For example, suppose I have burned my fingers; I experience (i.e., have an idea of) my fingers being burned. Another man may also have burned fingers; my idea will then be *like* his idea, i.e., his experience. But I am not necessarily thinking of *his* fingers when I say 'This thumb is burned'. To think of an object I must not merely have an idea which resembles the object, but I must *mean* to have the idea resemble just *that* object.[24]

The intention of the speaker, Royce urges, must pick out the object, and here we have a paradox. If, in judging, I mean or intend the object to which the judgment will refer, to which a perception may correspond, then I know the object. But if I know the object, how can I err about it? If I say falsely that the cat is on the mat, I must knowingly refer to some aspect of the situation about which I make the judgment. There must be a mat in the room, or a cat on the sofa, and I must in some fashion intend to refer to these facts. If I have no knowledge like this, my judgment may just as well refer to the cat on the mat in another room, and then my judgment would be true and not false. But given that I know all this, how can I err?

> As common sense conceives the matter, the object of a judgment is not as such the whole outside world of common sense, with all its intimate interdependence of facts, with all its unity in the midst of diversity. On the contrary, the object of any judgment is just that portion of the then conceived world, just that fragment, that aspect, that element of a supposed reality, which is seized upon for the purpose of just this judgment. Only such a momentarily grasped fragment of the truth can possibly be present in any one moment of thought as the object of a single assertion. Now it is hard to say how within this arbitrarily chosen fragment itself there can still be room for the partial knowledge that is sufficient to give

to the judgment its object, but insufficient to secure to the judgment its accuracy.[25]

Error is possible if an object, on the one hand, is *not* wholly present to mind and, on the other, is yet partially present.[26] But however difficult it is to account for the nature of error on this "common sense" analysis of correspondence and reference, it proves impossible to account for specific erroneous judgments. Let us try to explain errors about matters of fact. These errors are about actual or possible experiences: we expect or postulate an experience that at a given time or under given conditions turns out to be other than we expected or postulated it to be. But the two ideas, actual experience and expectation (or postulation), are separate, apart in time; they can never both be present to me at once. How can I bring them together to compare them? In the case of an erroneous prediction, says Royce,

> . . . we have supposed two different ideas, one of an expected future, the other of an experienced present, and we have supposed the two ideas to be widely separated in time, and by hypothesis they are not together in one consciousness at all. Now how can one say that in fact they relate to the same moment at all? How is it intelligible to say that they do? How, in fine, can a not-given future be a real object of any thought; and how when it is once the object thereof, can any subsequent moment be identified with this object. . . . Each one means the object that it thinks. How can they have a common object? Are they not once for all different thoughts, each with its own intent? But in order to render intelligible the existence of error about matters of fact, we must make the unintelligible assumption, so it would seem, that these two different thoughts have the same intent, and are but one.[27]

If Royce points out the difficulties in explaining factual errors, his greatest fame as a dialectician derives from his skill in urging that errors about the mental states of others are equally inexplicable. If two people, John and Thomas, are talking together we must really consider *four* people: the real John, the real Thomas, John as Thomas conceives him, and Thomas as John conceives him. When John makes judgments about Thomas, of whom does John judge? Plainly of *his* Thomas, for nothing else can be an object of John's judgments. But can he err about his Thomas? It would seem not, for *his* Thomas is not outside his thoughts: John's conception of Thomas *is* John's conception, and what he asserts it to be, that for him it *must be*. Moreover, John cannot err about the real Thomas, because—so far as John is concerned—the real Thomas is unknown.

The only way to resolve the dilemmas in this class of cases, and in all cases, is to regard the matter from the viewpoint of a third person. Suppose I make a judgment about an idea. If another being knows my judgment, "sees" the real object that I cannot see, and "sees" that my conception is unlike the object in some critical respect, this being could say that my assertion was an error. If Thomas could "see" himself as he really is and see John's conception about him—that is, if Thomas could in some way "get outside himself"—then he could possibly "see" John's error. Of course, in this case Thomas would have present to his consciousness what we normally think of as an external object as well as the consciousness of another. Moreover, mere disagreement of thought with an object will not make a thought erroneous. The judgment must disagree with the object to which the judger *means* it to refer. If John never has the real Thomas "in mind," how can John choose the real Thomas as his object? Once again we may solve this puzzle by supposing that a being exists to whom the real Thomas and John's conception of him are both directly present. Under appropriate circumstances this being could see that John's conception of Thomas *meant* the real Thomas; or rather because the being has directly present to him Thomas and John's conception of Thomas, it would be possible for this being to *mean* Thomas by John's conception. The being could compare the one to the other; if John's conception of Thomas agreed with the real Thomas, then John's ideas could be declared true; otherwise, erroneous.[28]

Although it solves our problems, we might reject this suggestion because it contradicts the presupposition that John and Thomas are separate self-existent beings. But we can account for error on no other supposition, and it is necessary that we do so. Suppose then, Royce declares in a famous and provocative passage, we drop the natural presupposition, and say that John and Thomas are both actually present to and included in a third and higher thought. To explain the possibility of error about matters of fact seemed hard, because of the natural postulate that time is a pure succession of separate moments, so that the future is now as future non-existent, and so that judgments about the future lack real objects, capable of identification. Let us then drop this natural postulate, and declare time once for all present in all its moments to an universal all-inclusive thought. And to sum up, let us overcome all our difficulties by declaring that all the many beyonds, which single significant judgments seem vaguely and separately to postulate are present as fully realized intended objects to the unity of an all-inclusive, absolutely clear, universal, and conscious thought, of which all judgments, true or false, are but fragments, the whole being at once Absolute Truth and Absolute Knowledge. Then all our puzzles will disappear at a stroke, and error will be possible, because any one finite thought, viewed in relation to its own intent, may or may not be seen by this higher thought as successful and adequate in this intent.[29]

Royce defines an error as an "incomplete thought": a higher thought which includes the error and its intended object knows the error to have failed in the purpose that it more or less clearly had.[30]

Before we investigate the nature of this absolute thought and its relation to finite individuals—a task which Royce does not undertake in *The Religious Aspect of Philosophy*—it is well to examine "the only outwardly plausible objection" to his view. A critic might urge that an error is an error to a *possible* critical thought that should undertake to compare the erroneous judgment with its object. The critical thought need not be real and actually include the erroneous thought, but need only be a possible judge of its truth. The "infinite all-knower" is no reality, but simply a "logical possibility."

Royce answers this objection by elaborating a notion of possibility which precludes the state of affairs described above. His conception of possible experience was important in forcing him to absolute idealism, and his explication develops that notion in a manner significant for his later work. "Bare" or "empty" possibilities, all unactualized possibilities for Royce, are impossibilities or unintelligible entities. He tolerates only what he later would call "valid possibilities." In this legitimate sense, for x to be possible is for x to be actual *or* for us to have confirmed the occurrence of x given the realization of other conditions. For the Absolute to be possible is for it to be actual; or for us to know it to be actual provided other conditions hold. Here these other conditions concern the nature of error. We know that *if* there is error, then the Absolute exists. Only in this sense can we speak of a "possible all-knower." But our dialectical argument shows that there is error: by *modus ponens* our "possible all-knower" *is* actual. Whether Royce has any notion of possibility distinct from actuality is unclear, and perhaps he does not need it. It is not until some time later that the ramifications of his doctrines become plain and his view of possibility becomes critical. For the time, he has met this "only plausible objection";[31] his epistemological study finally generates an adequate metaphysics.

Royce spent his second year at Harvard substituting for George Herbert Palmer, who went on leave at James's return; nonetheless, Royce still had temporary status, and was able to remain in Cambridge for a third year (1884–1885) only by accepting part-time work teaching English. After *The Religious Aspect of Philosophy* appeared in January of 1885, the situation became more encouraging. Royce was rewarded with a five-year appointment as Assistant Professor to begin in September of 1885.[32] Thereafter he was indispensable. In 1892 he became a full professor, and until his death twenty-four years later was a member of the great Harvard department that did so much to shape the development of twentieth-century American pragmatism. In addition to Royce, James, and Palmer, the philosophic talent assembled in Cambridge in those years included, among others, Hugo Münsterberg, George Santayana, Ralph Barton Perry, and William Ernest Hocking. Throughout the period Royce stood out as a major figure.

The argument from the possibility of error did much to make his reputation: it established the young Harvard instructor as one of the leading proponents of philosophical idealism. James thought the book "one of the very freshest, profoundest, solidest, most human bits of philosophical work I've seen in a long time."[33] James was so impressed that he accepted Royce's doctrine, and did not come up with an alternative to it until eight years later, in 1893.[34] It is not surprising that Royce himself continuously repeats the argument over the next decade in order to convert any who still might be skeptical. His 1892 *Spirit of Modern Philosophy* elaborates the same formulations, stressing that the notions of wondering and doubting are also keys to the proof of absolute idealism.[35] In an article written about the same time, "The Implications of Self-Consciousness," he puts forward identical reasoning, urging that we can arrive at the Absolute from the necessity of error or illusion.[36]

In 1895 Royce traveled to California to make a significant address entitled "The Conception of God." Once more he makes the same case, emphasizing that *ignorance* implies the existence of the Absolute.[37] In the proof given in "The Conception of God" there is—as we should expect at this point—a crispness in the movement of Royce's thought which makes it worthwhile to summarize the argument again. Suppose we wish to deny absolutism, and stress our finite limitations, our ignorance. We assert that only our finite fragments of experience exist. But if that is a fact, then it must be experienced: on an assumed Berkeleyan analysis, whatever is, must be *for* a consciousness. The supposition that there is no experience beyond our finite experiences proves contradictory; in its entirety experience must constitute one self-determined and consequently absolute and organized whole:

> If every reality has to exist just in so far as there is experience of its existence, then the determination of the world of experience to be this world and no other, the fact that reality contains no other facts than these, is, as the supposed final reality, itself the object of one experience, for which the fragmentariness of the finite world appears as a presented and absolute fact, beyond which no reality is to be viewed as even genuinely possible. For this final experience, the conception of any possible experience beyond is known as an ungrounded conception, as an actual impossibility. But so, this final experience is by hypothesis forthwith defined as One, as all-

inclusive, as determined by nothing beyond itself, as assured of the complete fulfillment of its own ideas concerning what is,—in brief, it becomes as absolute experience. The very effort to deny an absolute experience involves, then, the actual assertion of such an absolute experience.[38]

This position solves two of the three puzzles which plagued Royce in the late seventies and early eighties: the status of the hypothetical external consciousness and the nature of error. Through the nineties Royce spends little time on these issues. Rather, he examines the relation between the finite individual and the Absolute, a question which involved specifying the way finite ideas "correspond" to their objects. His doctrine enabled him to make intelligible the common sense view that even an erroneous judgment about an object can partially intend its object: the idea which prompts the judgment and the intended object are fragments of a more inclusive thought which compares the idea to its intended object. Although this position explains error, it was a long time before Royce could explain the relation between ideas and object, finite and infinite. In *The Spirit of Modern Philosophy*, however, he does draw an analogy to make the connection clearer. Even in error I cannot mean an object, he says, unless it is "already present in essence" to "my larger self," "my complete consciousness." The Absolute is the only real or complete self; and I and all my finite fellows are fragments of him. Suppose I have forgotten someone's name; when I try to remember it, I am sure all the while that I mean just one particular name, and no other. If I find it, I immediately *recognize* it—it is the name I *meant* all along. In one sense I knew it all the while: my present self presupposes in its hunt that the "deeper self" of which the name is a part already possesses what was sought. Similarly the finite selves with their fragments of experience are parts of the one larger self. Our search for truth is a search for what we already possess, and our deepest doubts and profoundest ignorance entail the larger self.[39] Consider, Royce says elsewhere, what it means to be either the self of "this moment" or the being who thinks about "this world of objects." We must be organically related to a com-

plete reflective person whom our finite consciousness implies: only one
existent person is logically possible, namely, the one complete self.[40]

We have already documented that Royce was a pragmatist like
James prior to writing *The Religious Aspect of Philosophy*. Even the
doctrine advanced there is pragmatic in its emphasis on the intentionality
of judgment, in the idea that a judgment chooses, picks out, or means its
object. But Royce was so enchanted with some aspects of his argument
that he pushed the pragmatic, voluntaristic elements into the background.
Consequently, James's enthusiasm for Royce's "pantheistic monism"[41]
turned to disdain for the "barren intellectualism" and the "block universe" of absolute thought. George Holmes Howison, an important idealist in his own right who held the chair of philosophy at Berkeley, was
also vehement in his attacks on the same Roycean tenets. When Royce
delivered "The Conception of God" at Berkeley, Howison was his chief
opponent, and Royce showed that he was not immune to these criticisms.
The address itself answers some of the criticisms James and Howison
expressed; more far-reaching emendations appear in "The Absolute and
the Individual," a supplementary essay Royce prepared to "The Conception of God" and to the comments Howison and two other academics
made on it. "The Absolute and the Individual" grew out of a series of
papers written for private discussion in California and out of Royce's
attempt "to expound some further developments" of his position.[42] It was
not published until two years after "The Conception of God," and its 220
pages constitute the first major indication of a shift in Royce's thought
and a reassertion of his earlier voluntarism. *

The two charges to which Royce responds are those of pantheism
and determinism, and there is much in his work to substantiate these
charges. *The Religious Aspect of Philosophy* proclaims that the world of
life is "an organic total"; the individual selves are "drops in this ocean
of the absolute truth." The world is no "mass of separate facts," but
everything is "fully present in the unity of one eternal moment."

* These two essays along with the essays of his critics, were published by Royce et al.,
in New York in 1897 as *The Conception of God*.

The finite individual is *in* the organic life of God, the "all-pervading thought."[43] This conception is not *prima facie* one in which there is room for individual freedom. Even in 1885 when James was a Roycean, he thought the difficulties in *The Religious Aspect of Philosophy* lay in the question of freedom.[44] Moreover, to Royce it is a matter of indifference "whether anybody calls all this Theism or Pantheism." He deprecates those who enunciate a doctrine of "Universal Thought" and try to foist it on plain people as the "God of our Fathers." He does not care if his notion of God agrees with anyone else's and acknowledges that his is not the one of much traditional theology.[45] It is not surprising that some philosophers took Royce at his word. By 1895 his concern for these questions reveals the Harvard idealist as more a Christian thinker. His conception of God, he believes, is "distinctly theistic, and not pantheistic." Finite individuals are not to lose their "ethical independence." "What the faith of our fathers has genuinely meant by God," Royce insists, is "identical with the inevitable outcome of a reflective philosophy."[46]

The fundamental argument for the existence of the Absolute in "The Conception of God" is the same as that of *The Religious Aspect of Philosophy*. Royce cared more for that book's "critical argument" than anything else he had ever done,[47] and still maintained that every estimate of the place of the finite individual in the universe must be made "*subject to the validity*" of this kind of argument.[48] With this limitation in mind he proceeds to define the nature of individuality more closely, and the change in doctrine reflects a change in his analysis of the categories describing the Absolute. In *The Religious Aspect of Philosophy* he defines the Absolute as thought, as the absolute knower. *The Spirit of Modern Philosophy* stresses this conception; in the "Implications of Self-Consciousness" written later in 1892 Royce makes the point bluntly:

> I have accordingly laid stress upon this character of the divine World-Self as a Thinker, and have labored to distinguish between this his fullness of Being, as idealism is obliged to define it, and those customary notions which define God first of all in "dynamic," rather than in explicitly rational terms. . . . in insisting upon thought as the first category of the divine Person, I myself am not

at all minded to lose sight of the permanent, although, in the order of logical dependence, secondary, significance of the moral categories, or of their eternal place in the world of the completed Self. That they are thus logically secondary does not prevent them from being, in the order of spiritual worth and dignity, supreme.[49]

In "The Conception of God" this emphasis is not so strong. The attribute central to God or the Absolute is omniscience, "all logically possible knowledge, insight, wisdom." To have all wisdom the Absolute must possess the answer to every rational question. To question means to have ideas of what is not present and to ask if these ideas do express or could express what some experiences *not present* would verify. For the Absolute these two elements—ideas and experience—would be fully and universally joined: "all genuinely significant, all truly thinkable ideas would be seen as directly fulfilled, and fulfilled in his own experience." Although Royce defines the Absolute as the union of absolute thought *and* absolute experience, the two factors "still remain distinguishable." The Absolute thinks or has ideas, and he experiences, that is, he has what we might call feeling, a world of immediate data of consciousness presented as fact.[50] The Absolute is still a knower; knowledge, however, is not defined only in terms of thinking, but as a union of what the ordinary man takes to be ideas and what he takes to be the external world—what Royce designates as experience.*

In "The Absolute and the Individual" published two years later, he sometimes wrote of the absolute experience instead of the Absolute; it was still the union of two distinct facets—thought and experience. In investigating the experiential facet, Royce first appears to give it the name *will*. The essential element of will is attention, the favoring of one conscious content as against a dimly recognized background of other contents; will involves a preference for data attended to, as against data that remain, relatively speaking, merely ideal or possible objects of attention.[51] Finite beings constantly exercise will when they concentrate, as they must, on one or another aspect of what is before their minds. To

---

* These two elements are both, of course, ideal. But that Royce thinks them distinguishable even in the Absolute indicates the difficulties in assimilating experience to thought.

attend to the work in front of me is to blot out, as it were, the sounds of the automobiles in the street below, or not to notice the color of the paper on which I write or the lack of heat in the room. This attention is a display of will.

Royce wishes to define the relation of will to the Absolute. The Absolute has present to it all our contents of consciousness and all validly possible contents of consciousness; this experience yields answers to all the questions posed by absolute thought. But having this experience present involves will: the Absolute attends to what is before it; it excludes from actuality the "barely possible"; it chooses. The Absolute (or, as Royce urges at this point, the absolute consciousness) has an individuating aspect in addition to Thought and Experience. This aspect determines that the content of consciousness—the absolute experience—present to absolute thought shall be *this* world "rather than any other of the abstractly possible but not genuinely possible worlds."[52] Royce has brought a voluntarist element into his notion of the Absolute. As he writes to Howison, who arranged the California meeting, the interpretation of the Absolute is "more obviously teleological."[53] By this redefinition Royce hopes to make a place for finite individuals, to defend himself from the imputation of pantheism. He also wants to assert the freedom of these individuals and of the Absolute. The first task requires a further analysis of will; the second, of possibility. The first proves a major advance; the second, I think, a major stumbling block.

What is an individual? Royce takes uniqueness as the *definiens* of individuality, and he holds, accordingly, that thought—discursive language—can never individualize. For example, no matter how extensively we describe a man, we cannot do so uniquely: we only define a type. This type may have only one exemplification, but only further experience can persuade us of this. Can experience individuate? Royce's answer is *no*: it only presents us with a mass of data. Experience usually comes to us individualized, into experiences of this moment, this place, and of this desk and this pen; but in these cases we assume a previous knowledge of an individual whole or of a determinate fact within which or in relation to which the "this" of passing experience becomes definable as *individual*.

Most of these *this*'s are so because of one constantly presupposed individual of daily life: I, the self. The question ultimately becomes how we define the individuality of the self.[54]

An individual is an object of exclusive interest: for something to be an individual is for us to regard it as irreplaceable by any other object. Our exclusive interest is a feeling such that we find repugnant the idea of two objects simultaneously satisfying the feeling. Individuality is a teleological category. But this principle of individuation is identical with the analysis of selective attention or will, and what Royce also calls love. We human individuals are such because God's love, his choice, his selective attention, his will have made us the objects of his exclusive interest. In fact, the absolute experience contains those objects which are the unique expressions of Divine Will. [55] God's love which makes *this* world is

> . . . an exclusive love,—a love that only one world, one Whole, could fulfill. Such a being [like the Absolute] would say: "There shall be but this one world." And for him this world would be fact. The oneness would be the mere outcome and expression of his will. This would then be an individual world, that is, the sole instance of its universal idea or type. In this individual world, every finite fact, by virtue of its relations to the whole, would be in its own measure individual. And individuality, in such a world, would neither be absorbed in one indistinct whole, nor yet be opaque fact. For the exclusive love of the Absolute for this world would render the individuality of the fact secondarily intelligible, as being the fulfilment of the very exclusiveness of the love.[56]

The finite individual is a part, a fragment, of the Absolute. The elements of any moment of our consciousness unite to form the whole of that moment. Similarly, our consciousnesses form the "one luminously transparent conscious moment" of the Absolute. But our experiences are unique constituents of the Absolute. They are nowhere else capable of representation in God's universe and are therefore "metaphysically necessary" to the fulfillment of God's "life." Without those unique experiences which constitute us, God's life would be different; God would not be God, the precise individual *He* is. Finally, from our perspective—the only one in which it is intelligible to speak of human individuals—God in no way "determines" our individuality; rather, in expressing our wills, we shape what is—from the absolute perspective—the will of God:

> In my grade of reality, I am unique as this element in and of the Divine Will. Nothing else than my will gives my will its essential character. From this point of view, the individual will . . . can say to God in his wholeness: "Were I not, your Will would not be"; for had I not this my unique attentive choice . . . God's Will would be incomplete. He would not have willed just what I, and I alone, as this fragment of his life, as this member of the Divine Choice, will in him, and as this unique portion of his complete Will.[57]

The individual self, so defined, is free. He possesses the same kind of freedom which characterizes God and which his individual uniqueness defines.

From our point of view, there is in individual consciousness an element determined by nothing in the whole of God's life except the individual. This element Royce calls the ethically organizing interests of a man's life, his exclusive interests; they make a man one self. Royce views these exclusive interests as expressive of what he calls a man's ideal, life-ideal, or plan of life—what a man most clearly proposes to be:

> the true or metaphysically real Ego of a man . . . is simply the totality of his experience *in so far* as he consciously views this experience as, in its meaning, the struggling but never completed expression of his coherent plan in life, the changing but never completed partial embodiment of his one ideal. His empirical ego, or collection of egos, is constituted by his relatively self-conscious moments just as they chance to come. His metaphysically real Ego is constituted by his experiences in so far as they mean for him the struggle towards his one ideal. . . . Whoever has not yet conceived of such an ideal is no *one* Ego at all . . . but is a series of chance empirical selves, more or less accidentally bound together by the processes of memory.[58]

The exclusive interests which express an ideal insure that individuality and self-hood are fundamentally moral notions. And because these interests define freedom, our notion of ourselves as moral creatures and our notion of freedom are one: "in choosing the ideal, which is the one means of giving his life the unity of Self, the individual is free."[59]

We share, as it were, in the freedom of the Absolute: if we are not free, it is not free.[60] And we must ask if it is free. Of course, Royce will answer yes. In order to do so he examines—in his longest discussion of the subject—the notion of possibility.

Royce regards the idea of "bare," "abstract," or "fantastic" possibilities with contempt. The possible is intelligible only if it is actual or if we confirm that it would exist given the existence of other conditions. Royce elaborates this doctrine in *The Religious Aspect of Philosophy* against the argument that the Absolute might be possible and invokes it thereafter on appropriate occasions, including his paper "The Conception of God." This view leads him to a novel account of counterfactual conditionals of the sort 'If wishes were horses, beggars could ride'. We might think that these hypotheticals express "bare possibilities" and that we may declare them false or nonsensical. But we often feel they express something true. Royce asserts that we label these hypotheticals true *if* we can "translate" them into some true categorical statement. If something like 'Beggars are unrealistic' is true, then the hypothetical will be true; otherwise not.[61] What we justifiably construe as possible we still "ground" in the actual. By 1897, however, Royce argues for the freedom of the Absolute because in attending to *this* world, it is (freely) able to exclude "barely possible" worlds. By definition we cannot ground these barely possible worlds in the actual: lack of divine attention excludes them from it. How are they intelligible? How do they represent *real* alternatives to what is?

In "The Absolute and the Individual" Royce recognizes this problem and formulates it by supposing a disparity between absolute thought and absolute experience. There can be no experience which realizes all that thought could and would regard as possible. But since the actual grounds all "valid" possibilities, to the extent that "bare possibilities" express what is the case, some aspect of actual experience in the Absolute will fulfill them. So far, this is a restatement of his former position: we reduce "bare possibilities" to aspects of the actual if we make sense of them. "If," he says, "hypotheses contrary to fact can be present as expressions of concrete truth to an experience that faces truth, the presence of such hypotheses contrary to fact is not excluded from an Absolute Experience, even in so far as it is absolute." But, Royce adds,

> . . . the presence of such hypotheses as elements of an Absolute Experience would, in the next place, reconcile our two conflicting views as to the relation of idea and content in such an Absolute Experience. Ideas must always transcend content, even in an Absolute Experience? Yes, as abstract or unreal ideas, for the reason before pointed out. No actual experience could adequately fulfill, or present contents adequately express, the infinite regresses, the infinitely infinite groups of possible examples of every universal, whose abstract possibility a merely abstract thought demands. Ideas, then, must indeed in one sense transcend data even in an Absolute Experience. But how? Answer: *As hypotheses contrary to fact,* not as expressions of genuine and unfulfilled truth.[62]

What this means is difficult to say. Royce consistently maintains that we must ground "bare possibilities" in the actual if they are to be intelligible, and "The Absolute and the Individual" initially affirms this idea. The ideas of the barely possible do *not* transcend absolute experience; insofar as they are true—and Royce apparently means and sometimes uses 'legitimate'—they can be "translated" into aspects of actual experience. Then, however, he *allows* the "barely possible" ideas to transcend experience; they exist as hypotheses contrary to fact which are acceptable but which no actual experience fulfills.[63]

The rationale of this move is plain. Attention or will enables the Absolute to exclude barely possible experience. This exercise of will "cannot be conceived as determined by any of the ideas, or by the thought-aspect of the Absolute in its wholeness, or as necessitated by thought, to attend thus or so. In this sense the attentive aspect of the Absolute . . . appears as itself possessed of Absolute Freedom."[64] The Absolute is free because its will excludes barely possible but intelligible experience. And because the Absolute is free, we are free.

I do not think Royce can have it both ways. His analysis of the

barely possible in "The Absolute and the Individual" preserves the freedom of each of them, but it is inconsistent with his other remarks on
possiblility. To defend his proof for the existence of the Absolute, he
roots the "validly" possible in the actual. It follows that Royce cannot
justify a "barely possible" experience which is not actual yet real. But he
invokes this notion to assure his Absolute freedom, and, consequently,
the freedom of the finite individual.* If the Absolute is free, we may
attack the argument for its existence by urging that it may be a "barely
possible knower": it will be sufficient to account for error, but not actual.
But suppose that the notion of possibility used to prove the Absolute's
existence is correct. This notion rules out a "barely possible knower,"
and the argument for the freedom of the Absolute will hinge on an unjus-
tified and contradictory notion of possibility. If the Absolute is free, we
may not be able to show that it exists; if it exists, we may not be able to
show that it is free.

---

* The lack of freedom of the Absolute does not *here* imply a lack of freedom for
the individual, but it is difficult to see how Royce would preserve individual freedom
were the Absolute "determined."

3

MORAL AND RELIGIOUS PHILOSOPHY
*1877–1897**

In the middle seventies Royce developed an interest in broadly reflective issues, but these interests were initially not philosophical. Rather, the literature of the German Romantics and the *Sturm und Drang* period of German intellectual history fascinated him. To be sure, he was widely read in the moral speculations of the post-Kantians, but if his notebooks and early essays are any indication, his concerns were those of Goethe's *Faust* and *Werther* and what we might might describe as "the existential quandary" which defines the work of Goethe, Kleist, and Novalis. When Royce turned to epistemology and metaphysics, he found these men and the post-Kantians inadequate thinkers, and made his way to Kant. But the German Romantics inspired him throughout his career, and the post-Kantians always provided hints of the form which a solution to Kantian problems would take.

When he wrote the first studies which take up philosophical aspects of moral and religious questions, there was a clear sense of priorities. The Romantic turn of phrase captured Royce and the moral rhetoric of the German idealists yielded fragments of doctrine, but his concern was always a technical puzzle and never simply exhortation. As a pragmatist, he related questions of value and knowledge, and in his work of the seven-

* In this chapter I speak of Royce's moral philosophy or ethics when I analyze what we would call today a mixture of metaethics and normative ethics. Because his ethics had intimate connections to religious problems, I have entitled the chapter "Moral *and* Religious Philosophy" without specifying throughout its religious aspects; these are obvious and were at the time almost synonymous with the ethical.

ties and eighties ethics and epistemology developed side by side. The structure of his early essays is consequently complex. They are motivated by a substantial moral issue, a spiritual dilemma, or the passional interests of youth; they then search for a moral philosophy which will provide a context for understanding this *Weltschmerz;* and end by seeking the epistemological ground for the ethical rationale Royce puts forward. The result is that this moral and religious philosophy concludes only with hypotheses and postulates: the work remains as "ungrounded" as Royce's epistemology of the period. Of course, the publication of *The Religious Aspect of Philosophy* changed this situation, but even in this book Royce chose a distinctive method of presentation. He "declined" to make a "strictly logical order" and instead set forth his religious and moral philosophy in the first half of the book, following it with the vindication for his thought in his argument for absolute idealism. "Our interest is, first of all," he says, "with the ideal [ethics] in its relation to human life." The order of exposition in *The Religious Aspect of Philosophy* is "not the order of the truth itself," but he can justify this reversal as "a useful concession" to human weakness and to our practical needs.[1]

Because I have been interested in the claims of logic, I have not followed Royce's order of exposition, and we must backtrack to examine those ethical questions which were the first philosophical questions to attract his attention and which his proof of absolute idealism resolved; we shall go on to outline the new problems of moral and religious philosophy which his idealism generated. As he writes in *The Spirit of Modern Philosophy*, only after we consider the theoretical have we the right "to draw what advantage we can for our spiritual interests from the truths that theory has taught us."[2]

Royce's starting point in developing his ethics is different from that often taken today but has much to recommend it. He assumes that we must make a cognitive distinction between right and wrong and that it is pretense to deny this distinction. In the 1877 Hopkins Lecture on "The Return to Kant" he stipulates that the "Critical Method" in ethics accepts "as a fact given beyond the possibility of dispute . . . the presence

of a power among us of a Moral Sentiment."[3] It is wrong, he writes elsewhere, to roast a man alive on a gridiron; wrong to dynamite a peaceful
man's dwelling to display dislike; wrong to beat a dog for the sake of
hearing him howl. "These are simple instances of moral distinctions.
Everyone competent to speak upon moral questions will make them."
Royce sometimes asserts that we possess a moral sense enabling us to
make these distinctions, but his essential claim is that we are aware of
the *denotation* of phrases like 'moral sense' and 'morally right'; for
example, the moral sense is that which allows us to apprehend what is
right or wrong, and we are perfectly able to point out what *is* right or
wrong. The problem of "ethical analysis" is to unpack the meaning or
connotation of these terms: we must analyze the nature of the moral
sense, of the morally right, or—to emphasize Royce's specific concern—
the moral consciousness.[4] The purpose of this analysis is to determine
the basis of moral distinctions. Recognition of them does not appear to
commit one to act on them; it seems possible to assert something like
"That may be the right thing to do, but I really don't care to do it;
there's nothing in it for me." In dissecting the notion of the moral consciousness, Royce hopes to show why an understanding of the dictates
of morality is a reason for obeying them. He must show that our conception of the moral has a supreme value and that we can obtain this value;
as we shall see, the exponent of prudential conduct is his chief enemy.

    In working out how we know right from wrong, Royce was led
to a study of epistemology—of how we know anything at all—and an
answer was not forthcoming until 1885. Consequently, his early ethics
was incomplete. We make moral distinctions to be sure, and Royce
asserts that right action contributes to harmonious living and to the interest human beings take in experience.[5] But if moral conduct is binding, the
"voluntary progress" which it brings must be ultimately worth seeking,
and Royce can give no iron-clad argument that it is. If we attained
harmony, we might find it "tedious and intolerable." But if he is dubious
of the ultimate value of what we shall take to be the aim of conduct, he
is more disturbed about our achieving the goal. If it is not achievable,
why ought it to constrain the lives of human beings? It would be a

foolish and irrational end, and on a common sense level we know that
both nature and man himself conspire to thwart man's best efforts.
History is a recounting of man's inability to make moral progress of
any note, and Royce sees no reason for being confident that good will
ever triumph over evil:

> According to our present notion of the universe, we stand alone,
> a few specks of life in the darkness of infinite space, in the midst
> of natural forces whose resources we shall never more than mea-
> gerly estimate, with an unknown future before us, in which what
> appalling accidents may happen, we can never even with faint show
> of accuracy foresee.[6]

Lacking an adequate epistemology, we cannot know that things
will come out all right in the end or that, if they do, we can pronounce
the result worthwhile; under these circumstances it is not easy to justify
the moral persuasion. Sometimes Royce is content to deliver paeans to a
free man's worship:

> if the triumph of the good is uncertain, if voluntary progress is
> always a venturing into a mysterious future, there is no reason why
> we should on that account work less vigorously, or make our aims
> less lofty. It is a cowardly soul that needs the certainty of success
> before it will work. It is a craven who despairs and does nothing
> because what he can do may turn out a failure. Whatever future
> growth eliminates from human nature, it is to be hoped that one
> trace of the era of universal warfare will survive, namely, the
> courage that can face possible, even probable destruction with the
> delight of a hero in resisting and planning and working so long as
> he can raise his arm.[7]

In less optimistic moments he could not rest with eloquence, and devoted
much time to examining the bases of a pessimism which rejected the
doctrines he felt so important. His investigation concentrated on Schopenhauer, and in setting out his objections to him, Royce developed
hypothetical answers to the ethical problems paralleling his work in
epistemology. Schopenhauer's metaphysics, "God knows, was a rotten
enough tub for a wise man to go down to the sea in,"[8] but the German's

pessimism contained insights which the American could work out more rigorously.

Schopenhauer, Royce asserts, finds the essence of life in the active or desiring principle of consciousness—the will. Life is made up of a continual flight from one object of desire to another: we are constantly in a state of longing; without this consciousness of desire, this unrest, there is no life. But Schopenhauer defines pleasure as satisfied desire, and if a desire has not arisen, there is no satisfaction, no pleasure. Pleasure is at best a neutral state for to desire an object is to lack, to want it, but not to have it; if we obtain it, we are "even": the pleasurable state is one in which we have cancelled the desire. The only positive element in consciousness is the longing, the process by which we gain the object of desire. The highest worth of life is zero—the satisfaction of all desires. We would attain the highest pleasure—the goal of life—were we free from desire. But freedom from desire occurs only in death.[9] Schopenhauer's pessimism rests on this analysis of consciousness:

> But if attainment of the absolute end means death, then in life the end cannot be attained. Life can, therefore, never have absolute worth. Whatever is a goal with nothing beyond cannot be life, but must be death. Whatever life has no final goal within its reach, must be an eternal failure.[10]

Insofar as Royce accepts this result, he sees the situation as more desperate. On Schopenhauer's view the best life is one in which we satisfy the desires we have, in which we always strive successfully. But this kind of life is rare. Under ordinary circumstances we do not achieve all of our goals and other people always thwart some of our aspirations.[11] Moreover, there is another demension to this normal state in which our aims conflict with those of our fellows with loss to ourselves. For Schopenhauer's pessimism the fact that others exist means that even the most successful individual will strive in vain to equal in his own pleasure "the immense riches of life embodied in these hosts of humanity." No self can possess the knowledge and power that exists in all of life. Even if nothing else opposes his desires, this consciousness of his own worthlessness in contrast to all around him must rob an individual of any self-satisfaction. Happiness is possible only if one is unconscious of how much life there is around him.[12] For Schopenhauer the goal of life has a "neutral" worth at best. But human beings can rarely come off "even," and can never do so while alive; in these circumstances there is little reason for the goal to win men's commitment.

Impressed as he is by these conceptions, Royce cannot accept pessimism, and the persuasive arguments he uses against it lead to a solution to the problems of ethics. He first urges that we cannot define life's goal in terms of *individual* satisfaction:

> The one goal is the rendering as full and as definite as possible all the conscious life that at any moment comes within the circle of our influence. Devotion, then, to universal conscious life, is the goal of conscious life itself; or the goal is the self-reference or self-surrender of each conscious moment to the great whole of life, in so far as that whole is within reach.

He also rejects the view that we calculate the goal's worth by a pleasure and pain arithmetic. It is impossible to carry out this summation, and, more importantly, human beings have to make their own appraisal of the value of life.[13]

When Royce worked at these problems in the late seventies and early eighties he could not demonstrate the truth of his position, but the idea is clear: more deeply considered, the end of life is perfect union and harmony with the whole of conscious life. It is unimportant that unfulfilled desire may predominate in an individual's life since we need not define the goal of existence in terms of fulfilled desire. Neither need we believe that the goal we have postulated is unobtainable, as is Schopenhauer's. The union of each being with the whole is achieved, Royce contends, if only in moments. Whatever impresses on each of us his own insignificance and "the grandeur of the great ocean of conscious activity" accomplishes this end. Self-sacrifice, work for an impersonal end, or even the contemplation of active life may exemplify it. Since we postulate our goal by "independent volition," we may also choose the extent to which occasional success will compensate for failures to reach it. We ask not for a tally on a set of experiences, but for a verdict on the value of experience. Royce can offer no proof that his goal is justifiable or that we can attain it. "Every man," he says, "has to deal with these queries quite by himself, even as with his own eyes he must see colors. It is our province merely to suggest the ultimate questions."[14]

Royce's dissatisfaction with pessimism hinges on Schopenhauer's indictment of life regarded as *individual life*. The German correctly maintains that "all life for Self is worthless." But he has not shown that we must construe values in terms of the individual or that some other valuational process must fail. Pessimism cannot touch Royce's argument for "Holy Living": "living not for Self, but for quelling, the putting down of Self, and for the building up of peaceful, harmonious, but entirely unselfish life."[15] This contrast between an end connected with individual life and one connected with all life provides Royce with an insight useful for a tentative solution to his problems. His epistemological studies had given a "postulational" basis for knowledge. Assuming moral distinctions as he does, he can analyze the moral consciousness in a way congruent with his epistemology.

What do I mean by myself? Royce claims that I am one being existent above and through all the changes of consciousness, the subject of my thoughts and experiences; but this being, he adds, is never *given* in experience. I directly experience only my present consciousness. I posit my own past and future, that which *must be* to fill out my conception of myself. But consider what we accept as the basis of prudential conduct. We approve conduct on this basis of "worldly wisdom" if we treat the expected consequences of an act with respect to their intrinsic desirableness to the individual in question. A prudent individual calculates both the long and short range consequences to himself of proposed actions. He decides not on the basis of the immediate enjoyments which some act may promise but weighs these against more far-reaching consequences. As Royce puts it, the prudent man avoids deciding on "the illusion of perspective in time"; prudence demands that if we know consequences at all, we estimate them with equal scrutiny however remote they may be. But the self of the prudent man is never given, and he acknowledges (or postulates) its reality as well as the reality of other selves. I do not know how or why I should postulate my own past and future as real when they are not given, although I do; and I do postulate my neighbor as real like myself. My preference for myself is based on a feeling called the selfish interest. But this interest is emotional; it is not based on my postulation of what is not given as real. To allow my interest in myself to determine my conduct is parallel to the imprudent man's allowing short range consequences to govern him.[16] The canon of prudential conduct is that

> . . . my conduct in these cases is approved if I treat all the consequences as if they were present, disregarding the prejudice created by my momentary interest, and then choose such consequences as are in this view intrinsically more desirable. My conduct is not approved, if I give myself over to the illusion of time-perspective, or choose a conceived consequence, not for its intrinsic desirableness, but because I am the slave of my momentary interest. Approved action consists in weighing all future consequences according to their conceived value, not according to the value that my passion gives them.[17]

Carrying out this principle, I should treat the future experiences of my neighbors in a similar fashion:

> I have not the same selfish interest [in my neighbors], but I do postulate them as equally real and unreal with my own conceived future. My existence as an enduring entity is not more immediately given than is the existence of my neighbor as an enduring entity. The same activity that postulates by expectation my future, postulates his future as well. The consequences of my act for me, are not more real than they are for him. If then, I am to order my conduct according to all future experience regarded as equally an object of striving, I must include my neighbor's future with my own and order my conduct accordingly.[18]

The essence of conduct which prudential activity illustrates is the putting of insight before desire, conceiving all experience as equally worthy of consideration when making a decision. Once we admit this step we realize that our analysis of consciousness does not yield *Me* as an entity distinct from all the world; we expect all future consciousness equally. We also acknowledge that moral distinctions exist concerning the intrinsic desirability of various experiences; and we have analyzed these considerations in cases which define the actions of a prudential man; and Royce concludes that consistency alone has brought us to the following postulate: we ought to act so that the end of our conduct is the good of the whole world of future experience as we conceive the world at the moment of action; in our conduct we ought to regard all future consciousness equally because all is alike not given but only expected, and all is alike real when it comes.[19]

This is Royce's early answer to the basic problem of ethics: his analysis of moral consciousness, of what it is to behave morally, explicates something of the ground of moral distinctions. He stresses, however, that he cannot demonstrate his solution, but can only state it:

> the rule of conduct is: Act as thou wouldst wish to have acted were all the consequences of thy act for all the world of being here and now given as a fact of thine own present consciousness. Or again: Choose thy deeds so that their outcome shall seem the best possible outcome when all the results are viewed at once as a whole in their intrinsic good or evil. Thus conduct is made absolutely consistent.[20]

From a logical perspective he can argue that his examination of moral notions proceeds on the claim of consistency. *Conduct* is action at one present moment for conceived future moments; consistent conduct shows a concern for *all* conceived future moments, and absolutely consistent conduct is the only conduct that meets moral approval: it looks to the worth of all expected consequences. In terms of this insight each moment of life is judged with regard to the whole of consciousness conceived as one being or, better, as one moment of being.*

* *Fugitive Essays*, ed. J. Lowenberg (1920; reprinted in New York, 1968), p. 217. Although Royce is not explicit in his indebtedness to Kant, I think that indebtedness is clear. We judge acts, Royce says, "according to their purpose, not according to their actual outcome" (p. 216). When he took up the moral insight in *The Religious Aspect of Philosophy* (Boston, 1885) (hereafter *RAP*), he again declared that "only the good intention is truly moral" (p. 219). The entire approach which linked ethical problems to those of knowledge is one he appears explicitly to have

Royce's ethical work has reached a stage parallel to his episte-mology, and he has a moral theory dependent on postulation. He may have succeeded in showing that Schopenhauer cannot defend pessimism on the basis of prudence and selfishness. He has not shown, however, that his own view of the "Holy Life" has ultimate worth, or is ultimately attain-able, and at this point he thinks the choice of a goal "defies logical demonstration."[21] Still, he argues that his view is an explication of the moral consciousness and urges persuasively that it deserves man's commitment.

The argument for the Absolute in *The Religious Aspect of Philoso-phy* proves that the ethical goal—the unity of all life in one moment—is achieved. Although Royce does not spell out the Absolute's moral quality in his theoretical chapters, it is easy to see why he assumes that this "Infinite Consciousness" has ultimate worth. Moreover, in the "prac-tical" part of the book, he does prove his position. We can assert that the world of absolute thought must be the *summum bonum*. If we examine the various ultimate ends men have proposed, a dialectical argument leads us to a commitment to the unity of conscious life. A full understand-ing of what the moral consciousness is warrants accepting its imperatives as premises of action.

Royce poses this problem in terms of "the warfare of moral Ideals." We may at once ask how we justify any ideal against any other, but the question which he addresses is how we justify an *ideal* at all. We must commit ourselves to an ideal, independently of the way the world is. What happens to these ideals?

Either nature favors them, and then they survive in the struggle for life, or they are unequal to the tasks of the real world, and then

---

derived from Kant. The 1877 lectures develop this motif, and Royce later explains that Kant's fundamental questions—What do I know? and What ought I to do?— "are of religious interest no less than of philosophic interest. They ask how the high-est thought of man stands related to his highest needs, and what in things answers to our best ideals" (*RAP*, p. 4). This is Royce's approach also: the pragmatic and Kantian strains are tied.

their supporters go mad, or die. But in the first case they are merely such theories as could have been much better reached by a process, not of guessing at truth, but of studying nature's laws. In the second case, the result is enough for common sense people. The moral theory that is destined to die out for want of supporters can hardly triumph over more useful opinions. If we want a moral theory, we must therefore consider what kind of action, what rule of life, wins in the battle of existence, and tends most to outlive its rivals. That rule is the one destined to become universal.[22]

A moral ideal which cannot survive can hardly be of ultimate worth. Consequently, we cannot choose an ideal on the basis of caprice; we must base it on something enduring which commands general assent. But now we are committed to the position that our ideal is dependent on the way the world is—it has some existential root. If this is so, we do not differ from those who say that might is right, that worldly success determines the criterion of goodness, or that what exists ought to exist. The ethical problem is not just that philosophers and moralists have suggested alternative ideals among which we cannot decide, but that it is not clear how we can justify any ideal at all.[23]

Royce traces the argument between ethical idealists and realists through the history of philosophy from Greek and Christian ethics to the theories of the eighteenth and nineteenth century, and always finds this paradox. If we ground our ideal in what is, we face the question of why it ought to be; if we stress that it is freely chosen, we may be accused of caprice.[24] The result is an initial skepticism about ethics, but in it is the answer to his concerns. [25] In this instance Roycean skepticism expresses the indifference we feel when we contemplate two opposing ideals; but in our indifference we *share* both of them momentarily, i.e., for the moment we realize them equally. The two conflicting wills which the opposed ideas represent become *our* will:

> Had we the will to choose the one end alone, we should unhesitatingly choose it, and should not see enough of the opposing will to be skeptics. Had we only the will that chooses the opposing end, we should feel equally indifferent to the first. Had we neither will at all in mind, did we realize neither one of the opposing ends, we should

be feeling no hesitation between them. Our doubt arises from the fact that momentarily and provisionally we are in the attitude of assuming both. Our indifference is not the indifference of ignorance, but of knowledge; not of failure to understand either end, but of readiness to realize both ends.[26]

For Royce moral skepticism is the result of an act: we act to realize opposing aims simultaneously.

When he speaks of opposing aims or ends, he notes that they are expressions of will, and to understand someone's will implies in some sense the performance of the act willed. This is a theme later to become all important, but Royce uses it now to make only a limited point. For example, to understand someone's *choosing* to walk is to initiate steps oneself; the conception of an act is physiologically connected with the fainter excitation of just the same nerve tracks as would be more intensely excited in the performance of the act.[27] All ideas about an individual's will in some measure "imitate" the will about which they are. We could not be skeptical about a single end—a choice, an act of will—viewed in isolation, for even to consider it would be to will it and thus accept it. We can only be skeptical—undecided—when various ends conflict, and in these cases our skepticism is actually the will to harmonize conflicting ends:

> What represents a Will but a Will? Who would know what it is to have an end unless he actually had ends himself? Who can realize a given aim save by repeating it in himself? . . . But . . . in so far forth as he reproduces this will alone, he cannot refrain from accepting the end. In so far forth as he reproduces this will, it is his will. And the end is his end. Therefore our skepticism itself was a hesitation, resulting from the realization of several opposing ends, and from a simultaneous reproduction of the wills that aimed at them.[28]

The skeptical end is to harmonize the conflicting ends in the world of life. Its aim, the moral insight, would be "absolute benevolence," harmony and unity of conduct.

But let us attempt to deny this end. On the one hand, the denial returns us to skepticism in which case we reassert what we have denied;

on the other, we put some other end in the place of skepticism. In this
case we will face our old arguments and, torn between the accusation of
caprice and of "might makes right" doctrines, we will be driven to
skepticism.[29] The dialectical argument for the existence of error assures
us that absolute thought exists; a similar dialectical argument demonstrates that the ultimate moral end is a state of consciousness which the
Absolute expresses.[30] We have found a moral doctrine "in the very heart
of our skepticism itself."[31] Royce notes in another place that here, as
elsewhere in philosophy, we reach the truth not by discountenancing the
doubt but by accepting, experiencing, and absorbing it until, as an element of thought, it becomes an element of truth. This Hegelian procedure
accompanies another, for Royce remarks that his depiction of the warfare
of ideals which led to the moral insight "pursued the definition of our
ideal through the imperfect forms of individualism."[32] The analysis
shows that moral activity consists in the attempt to reconcile all conflicting aims. The canon of conduct which we formerly justified on grounds
of consistency gets a logical derivation of its ultimate value. The ethical
precept becomes:

> Act as a being would act who included thy will and thy neighbor's
> will in the unity of one life, and who had therefore to suffer the
> consequences of the aims of both that will follow from the act of
> either.[33]

We would reach this goal if all conflicting wills "realized" one
another. Not abandoning its own aim, each would also embrace the aims
of the others. All the world of individuals would act as one being, having
a single universal will.[34] We may never reach this end, but it is an organization of life which would result if finite beings were fragments of one
larger self. Its consciousness would unify our fragmentary wills just as
we possess a unity of consciousness as individuals. But Royce has proved
that such a self exists. To be sure, the ultimate goal of Royce's ethics is
defined by a universal will, whereas the Absolute of the technical pages
of *The Religious Aspect of Philosophy* is absolute thought. Nonetheless,
this latter Absolute has a voluntaristic aspect, and it is obvious that Royce
means this Absolute to define that state of consciousness which has ulti-

mate value in his ethics. Indeed, after he proves the existence of absolute thought in *The Religious Aspect of Philosophy*, Royce returns to ethical problems, and demonstrates that absolute thought is all good.

Suppose the infinite thought desires some perfection that it does not possess; it is either right or wrong in supposing this perfection desirable. But the truth or falsity of a judgment about this desire exists as known truth or falsity for a higher thought which includes the thought that desires and which "has" (i.e., knows) what is desirable; this higher thought compares the desired object with the conception of the thought that desires the object. "The world then, as a whole, is and must be absolutely good, since the infinite thought must know what is desirable, and knowing it, must have present to itself the true objects of desire."[35] We have guaranteed that the goal of life is a unity of will; and the argument for the existence of the absolute identified with this unity simultaneously proves that the unity possesses all good.

Royce also explains why our experience might appear to justify the claims of pessimism. He defines goodness not as innocence but as the overcoming of evil; goodness is a whole which consists of experienced evil together with the condemning or conquering of this evil: evil is a necessary element in finite experience, but can never triumph. Just as in one moment of consciousness I may experience "the victory of the moral insight over the bad will" as the overcoming of a selfish impulse, so finite evil is conquered in the absolute's moment of infinite goodness. Finite triumphs over evil are specimens of the eternal realization of goodness, and although we do not witness the overwhelming of all evil in finite life, the existence of the Absolute guarantees that this must occur. An evil man is free to sin, but his wickedness forms part of a total good will, just as the evil impulse of a good man contributes to his goodness through the defeat of that impulse.[36]

The Religious Aspect of Philosophy resolved outstanding problems in Royce's ethics as it had in his metaphysics and epistemology, but it also generated a different concern. Royce took pessimism seriously, and the practical intent of his early work is to sanction some positive orientation to life in the face of the travail of which Schopenhauer made so much. The Absolute gives Royce a rigorous argument for what he could before justify only rhetorically, but in what I might call "an inverse form" the problem still remains: if the world is morally perfect, the best of possible worlds, why is there so much evil? James's condemnation of the "block universe" is a condemnation of the Absolute's moral universe, which both guarantees an answer to James's ethical concerns and justifies the wickedness he saw around him. I do not think we can deny that Royce saw something in this critique; he had previously been too sensitive to these questions to become a shallow optimist; the change in tone after 1885 indicates that he was not completely happy with his moral philosophy. As we have seen, the last part of *The Religious Aspect of Philosophy* takes up the existence of finite evil and attempts to show that the triumph of goodness entails the temporal existence of evil. Until the end of his life Royce wrestled with the tensions involved in this commitment, and this part of his philosophy shows more obvious changes through the first decade of the twentieth century than any other. Whenever he wrote on ethics up until 1900, however, he concentrated on establishing a more comfortable position connecting finite evil to absolute good; and in this task he did not go much beyond the conclusions of *The Religious Aspect of Philosophy.*

The *Spirit of Modern Philosophy* states that the existence of finite evil and the total perfection of the Absolute are opposing members of the *antinomy* of the spiritual world.[37] But although our world is Leibnizian—the best of all possible ones—Royce deprecates the popularity of optimism, urging that we not "rejoice . . . too easily" at the solution the Absolute appears to provide.[38] Once again, evil is a necessary prerequisite to the attainment of absolute goodness and certainly to whatever goodness we attain in human life. Royce argues for his position by using Hegel's view that only the tempted can be holy. If an impulse tempts me and if I resist it, hate it, and overcome it, in that moment I make it a part of my larger moral goodness: holiness presupposes temptation. Royce calls this "the paradox of all will":

> There are elements in a good world which, individually regarded, ought not to be there, which are in themselves hateful, regrettable, the just object of wrath. Yet they become part of the world of the good will just in so far as they are in fact hated, condemned, subdued, overcome. The good will is not innocent. It does not ignore evil; it possesses and still conquers evil.[39]

When a sinner triumphs, we know that he is a fragment of a good will—the Absolute—which is in part good because in the course of time it will vanquish this sinner himself. The Absolute is a self which overwhelms all (partial) sinful selves just as I may overcome an individual sinful impulse. God's hatred and condemnation of the sinner's life make God holy. And Royce clarifies the importance of moral effort in a perfect world. Whatever we are, we are a part of God's perfection. The question is: are we a scorned, despised part that God conquers, or are we beloved of Him? The importance of ethical striving lies in the assurance that we serve God positively and not "as vessels of his wrath."[40]

To these arguments Royce adds a conclusion which is never spelled out in *The Religious Aspect of Philosophy*,[41] but which expresses his dissatisfaction with his position. Despite the Absolute, finite human life will be a veil of tears. In addition to moral evils which we may control, there are the natural evils of fortune, chance, and time. From our point of view, Royce says, there is "no remotely discoverable justification for this caprice," and the existence of the Absolute offers little consolation and may even seem a fraud. But in a strange and touching fashion he tries to console us. If the Absolute were foreign to us, *then* his perfection would be indifference and cruelty; his goodness would be our despair, our remote and dismal helplessness. But he is "our own selves in unity," "our own fulfillment," "our own very flesh." Our defeats are his: of us he must say "O ye who despair, I grieve with you. Yes, it is I who grieve in you. Your sorrow is mine. No pang of your finitude but is mine too.

I suffer it all, for all things are mine; I bear it and *yet* I triumph." It is this thought of a suffering God—our own true self who actually and in our own true flesh bears the sins of the world and who still finds his peace and so ours—that is the answer to pessimism.[42]

Royce returned to ethics at various times throughout the nineties, but unlike his more technical work which developed significantly, he added no new dimension to his moral philosophy.[43] Evil is still a "logically necessary and eternal constituent of the divine life." Our solace is that as a consequence of absolute idealism, our sufferings *are* those of the divine.[44] Two further implications are worth considering. While they are not of any systematic or overriding importance, they add final touches to his position. As he has argued, the study of ethics is in no way noncognitive but a study "of science and of reason." He has also shown that the good is to be sought: knowledge of what is good is a reason for doing it. Royce puts these ideas together when he asserts that sinful choice involves "a certain deliberate ignorance"; it implies an "intellectual defect."[45] He does not elaborate on this Socratic position, but it is illustrative of those doctrines which prompted Charles Peirce to call Royce "an American Plato."[46]

In another passage Royce suggests why there is no conflict between an everlasting imperfect temporal world and the perfection of the Absolute. We must realize that the moral goal is never temporally achievable. As finite beings we never reach that universal harmony which is the ultimate end. To be sure, each moral triumph is such, and as time passes we progress: we gain victories over evil which are identical to the Absolute's and which were not present in our past. Yet the significance of the moral ideal is that we *cannot* conceive it temporally won, and our struggle for it is always remote. This notion may hold little satisfaction, but in "The Absolute and the Individual" Royce develops it with the aid of a daring metaphor. Any convergent infinite series, he states, approaches an unattainable limit. When its limit is an irrational number, we know the limit as the goal of the series which we approach asymtotically, proceeding from term to term. We may also declare that the aim of the moral consciousness is the unattainable limit of this kind of infinite series. But from the eternal point of view this limit is attained, and this should be no more surprising than that the mathematical consciousness defines a quantity in two ways: first as an infinite series which has no end; and second as the quantity which we view as the limit.[47]

4

THE WORLD OF DESCRIPTION
AND PHILOSOPHICAL PSYCHOLOGY

The dialectical argument for absolute idealism is a characteristic aspect of Royce's philosophy and was his trademark not only from 1885 to 1897 but also through 1913. But after the publication of *The Religious Aspect of Philosophy*, he also tried to show how the "real world" of the Absolute is related to the everyday world of external things, and how we can account for the latter on idealistic grounds. Unlike many of his post-Kantian predecessors, he had a high regard for the achievement of science, and considered a philosophy inadequate if it did not devote sufficient attention to the successes of the scientific world view. Finally, he believed that his own idealistic position rested on certain hypotheses in one area of science itself—the science of psychology. In fact, during the nineties Royce's interest in psychology best exemplified his concern to make his idealism congruent with science. When he found psychology important to this task, he carried out psychological experiments himself; toward the end of the century he delivered two major addresses on his empirical findings to the American Psychological Association, of which he later became president.[1] Royce's research is not crucial to his speculation, contains little of philosophic interest, and is incomplete. Yet it reveals a careful, cautious mind at work, a mind respectful of the laboratory. In this chapter we will examine his initial philosophizing about the natural world, the "World of Description," and how it prompted him to study psychology.

In 1889 Royce published two papers in *The Unitarian Review* entitled "Is There a Philosophy of Evolution?" Both were part of a long

address read before the Yale Philosophy Club, called "The Fundamental
Problem of Recent Philosophy."[2] The "fundamental problem" was to
relate the seventeenth-century mechanistic view of physical science to
the evolutionary conceptions of the nineteenth. Royce identified the
seventeenth-century position with the idea that universal laws and physical causation are ultimate explanatory principles:

> the conception to which the Seventeenth Century leads us is the
> conception of a world where an infinite number of facts are bound
> together as cases of simple principles, in such wise that if the prin-
> ciples are once discovered, through patient induction or skilful in-
> genuity, the most unsuspected connections between remote facts of
> nature may be expected to result, and the most minute data of ex-
> perience may become explicable.[3]

This is the world we think of when we consider the work of the natural
scientist.

The nineteenth century had produced a world view antithetical to
the Newtonian universe. Those ideas Royce labels evolutionary all imply
that the *history* of an event is an explanation of it. Darwin's theory as it
was construed best expresses this genetic conception: one explains the
origin of the species *homo sapiens* by relating the historical sequence
which leads finally to the descent of man. But Royce maintains

> . . . the world where history is the most significant of intellectual
> concerns is simply not to be reconciled with a world where there is
> no history, and where the world-formula has already expressed
> from eternity to eternity the transient facts of the flying moment.[4]

Insofar as we explain the world historically, it is not one of "rigid natural law." An explanation of an event in terms of its place in a history
is not identical to an explanation of the event as an instance of universal
law. Moreover, the historical element exists to the extent that we do not
understand the world of mechanism. Royce suggests that we examine our
historical understanding of the earth's crust:

> For us, who cannot explain the stratification of the world's crust as
> we explain the motions of the plants, the earth's crust appears as

a history. But it is for us a history, merely because we do not understand the mechanical facts that here express themselves. If we understood the earth's stratification as we understand the eclipses, the historical element would vanish into the realm of the merely picturesque, precisely as the story of the eclipses forms no part of the facts set forth in a text-book of mathematical astronomy. The oncoming and the flying of the shadow are indeed interesting phenomena; and for the physical astronomer, whose facts are once more not yet mechanically explicable, the series of events in an eclipse may, as series, be significant. But for the mathematical astronomer all the motions of the planets are alike expressions of a universal formula. The historical interest of the events is lost in their mathematical explanation. Just so with the crust of the earth. Were its formation something mechanically explicable in all respects, there would be no inductive and picturesque history of the earth's crust: there would be only mathematical explanation of why the earth's crust is as it is.[5]

If the results of the physical sciences give us an adequate account of the world, evolutionary studies are an illusion of our partial view; if these studies represent knowledge and not just ignorance, the world must be different from that which we would be led to believe from the physical sciences. Should evolutionary doctrines be true, the "real world" will not be a place of mechanical laws and the flux of atoms; it will be a world "of struggle and conflict, of the triumph of the good, or of the abolition of evil, of the moral importance of the world, of the transition from lower to higher conditions. . . ."[6] It will be a world of *ideals*.

Why does Royce see these implications in the truth of evolutionary doctrines? An evolutionary process is historical, and to appreciate it, he claims, we must forsake that kind of temporality which confines mechanistic explanation. Genetic explanation "takes in at a glance" a series of moments; it treats them as a whole. This temporal whole will have *meaning* or *significance,* and this dimension of time transcends that encapsulated in the moment to moment sequence which characterizes changes in the physical world. An evolutionary sequence may be a series of events which *qua* series is physical—a set of causally related conditions occurring in space and time; but to accept this series as an historical explanation is to emphasize unity, meaning, or significance in a way that a causal explanation will not.[7] When a temporal series functions this way as an explanation, when it affirms meaning or significance, our explanation takes on a moral dimension; it will be evaluative.

Royce elaborates these presuppositions in a different context when he turns to the conflict of the mechanical and historical views in psychology.[8] He claims that a natural science of psychology—essentially behaviorism—cannot account for the significance which my mental life has for me. In a "mechanical" explanation of mental life, the series of mental states involved will be *determined*, an earlier "configuration" passing over into a later one through a series of intermediate states. We will have explained mental life when we stipulate the law which indicates how the earlier condition leads to the later one. This explanation, however, cannot account for the character of the whole which might constitute, for example, the process of reasoning, but only its character as a sum of successive states. Let us take an illustration. A phonograph records and reproduces an intelligible series of sounds. Reverse the motion of the phonograph and the series of sounds becomes unintelligible. The reversed phonograph gives you all the sounds perfectly but loses their significance. Physically described, Royce claims, the two processes differ only by the substitution of a minus for a plus sign in the formula by which we describe the revolution of the phonographic cylinder. But "from the point of view of the intelligibility of the series as a whole, the alteration is much deeper." Analogously, imagine a physical description of a human consciousness. If we should reverse this description, the result would differ only by the substitution of minus for a plus. Nonetheless, as a conscious mind, there will not merely be "inverted significance":

> . . . mental life, considered as a consciously significant process, is *not* a reversible sequence; and the laws, whatever they are, that give it conscious significance, when read forwards, are not laws expressible in physical terms. It is precisely for this reason that the laws of the Association of Ideas must always remain inadequate expressions of the nature of mental life.[9]

The significance of mental life is *not* a function of the law-governed sequences of its states. The world of our mental states has a *history* from moment to moment, and we cannot reduce this history to sequence. If this dimension of mind, i.e., its consciousness, is real, then the world has *meaning;* it is a place in which moral ideals and the goals of conscious striving play a part.

Royce did nothing more in these articles to clarify the situation. On the one hand, he argued that it was dogmatic to defend either view; on the other, he was sure they were antithetically opposed. Evolution had to assume the presence of history, progress *toward* ideals; physical science had to assume causation to the exclusion of the historical; somehow we must be able to reconcile the two opposing positions rationally:[10]

> the doctrine of Evolution is the schoolmaster which teaches us to face at last the real question of the universe. This question is the issue between causation and the ideals. . . . in this way I have come here merely to state a problem. . . .[11]

Whatever Royce's hesitation in expounding a partial solution to the Yale philosophers, he proposed one in 1892 with the publication of *The Spirit of Modern Philosophy;* as we might expect, the solution was consistent with Royce's idealism: consciousness—the historical and evolutionary—was given primacy of place. Royce's mentor once again was Kant. In two ways he saw his solution as a Kantian one. First, he drew an analogy between his dilemma and Kant's doctrine of the phenomenal and noumenal realms. Examine the antithesis between the empirical science of psychology and our view of the significance of our conscious mental states:

> Here in the realm of consciousness one finds, as one reflects, a problem precisely similar to Kant's famous problem concerning the double existence of the Self. "I am," said, in effect, Kant, "at once *phenomenon* and *noumenon.* As phenomenon, I am subject to law, lost in the time-series, a mere succession of determinate conditions. As noumenon, I have moral significance, and, moreover, I transcend time; yes, I am without time." This problematic relation between the two selves Kant advanced as an hypothesis of a purely

ethical nature. Our own present consideration forces the double nature of the self upon us as a matter of theoretical presupposition. *Unless psychology is to remain a chaos, this double nature of self-consciousness must be not merely recognized, but comprehended.*[12]

If this Kantian position forms a background to the formulations defended in *The Spirit of Modern Philosophy*, there is another of equal significance. Royce now believed that the crucial aspect of the first *Critique* was that the deduction of the categories involved Kant in the doctrine of the transcendental self:

> the greatest thinker of this constructive period, Kant, recognized *his* Absolute only in the practical sense. Yet in essence he was the greatest constructive idealist of them all; and, to my mind, in Kant, and especially in the doctrine of the transcendental self, which finds expression in his great "deduction of the Categories," there lies the beginning of a doctrine which will become more and more nearly equal to the solution of our great human issue.[13]

Royce broke fully with his earlier interpretation of Kant formulated in the 1878 dissertation; the dissertation, he wrote, was based on a serious, indeed an entire, misinterpretation of Kant.[14] Royce the student saw only the pragmatic dimension of the *Critique*. Now he urged that in explicating the fundamental categories of the phenomenal world Kant was nearly driven to absolute idealism. Kant, Royce asserts, holds that all knowledge depends on my unity with "my deeper Self"; Kant errs chiefly in what he omits and, Royce adds in a reversal of his former evaluation, "in his assumption of those useless things in themselves." The great failure of German idealism after Kant is that it is unable "to construct the visible world upon any *a priori* rational scheme. . . ." The problem the post-Kantians have left unanswered is the comprehension of the world of experience in terms of fundamental idealistic tenets.[15] Ultimately we will see that the world of science is an "aspect" of the world of the absolute self, what Royce takes to be identical to the moral, historical world. He will reconcile the conflict between mechanism and evolution by carrying out Kant's intent, by deriving the forms of experience *and* the categories of physical nature from the premises of idealism. Assimilating the forms

to categories, Royce maintains this is the momentous problem of "the
deduction of the categories": he must show why the world of one self
appears to us as a world of externally existing objects; he must "reduce"
the world of space and time to a world of consciousness in which existence is only temporal.

In *The Spirit of Modern Philosophy* he began a life-long attempt
at this reduction by distinguishing between the "World of Description"
and the "World of Appreciation." He first locates a "provisional criterion
of objectivity" in that what is objective we can all experience; as finite
beings this amounts to "the outer order," the permanent and universal
elements of experience. "The test of objectivity," Royce declares, "is the
apparent similarity of our human experiences when two or more of us
are in given circumstances. This similarity . . . is critically examined by
comparing, as far as possible, the accounts that we can give to one another of the *relations* amongst the objects of our experience." "In other
words," he adds in language reminiscent of his doctoral dissertation,
"the test of objectivity is, so far, permanence and community of ideas."
The mark of this permanence and community of ideas is the sameness of
the descriptions we can give to each other of the connections among the
parts of our private experience: the essential characteristic of the real or
objective world is that all of us verify our experiences of it, and this
seems tantamount to saying that the real world is the world of externality,
of independently existing objects, for what we mutually verify is just
what we call external.[17] Royce designates it the World of Description.

Our describable experience possesses two attributes. First, the
experience will be reproducible: the act of description is a voluntary reproduction of the experiences described. What Royce seems to mean by
this definition is that if we describe something, we are able to conceive
and state explicitly the exact conditions under which we apply the description. Second, those aspects of an experience which permit us to
describe it must themselves fall under general types or what Royce calls
Forms or Categories of Experience: the forms involving ideas of space
or time; the categories involving numerical difference, comparisons of
likeness and difference, and so on.[18]

What status have these forms and categories, and why do *these* forms and categories exist? In broaching these questions, Royce gives the first of many specific answers to his problem of "the deduction of the categories." In *The Spirit of Modern Philosophy* the discussion is fragmentary and obscure. The categories express characteristics whose meaning is captured in the postulates, or a priori principles, or axioms of physical science, for example, "the axiom of causation." But we also "discover" these axioms which experience somehow "exemplifies." Royce is dallying with some notion of a Kantian synthetic a priori, but the notion is never spelled out. The reason we have the categories we do is just that they—and apparently only they—allow us to organize our experience so that we can communicate with our neighbors. That is, this "deduction of the categories" is vaguely pragmatic.[19] Royce was able to do much better than this in a few years, but before we take up his further ideas there is more to examine in *The Spirit of Modern Philosophy*.

Within its framework he offers what has become a common view of explanation. In the World of Description there are "groups" or "wholes" of facts and phenomenal elements whose forms we note in appropriate circumstances. These forms permit us to define other complex groups of phenomena as "having the same structure," as "being built up according to the same rule," or as "exemplifying the same law." We *explain* some aspect of a group of facts by bringing it under the law in question. When we explain a fact, we say that the law in question requires its presence, or makes it necessary. Royce's explication is disjointed but its thrust is clear:

> since the whole fact *abcd* resembles ABCD, or *pqrs*, not in its details as such (i.e., in its contents), but in their structural relations—i.e., in the general type or build of each of these whole facts—therefore the same rule or law which defines D by its relations to the other phenomena, A, B, C, of its own group, and which defines *s* by its relations to the other phenomena, *p*, *q*, and *r*, of the group *pqrs*, can be realized or exemplified when you pass to an *abc* group, only if there is present a fourth phenomenon, *d*, which is such as to have the same structural relation to *abc* in the whole fact whereof *abc* and *d* are parts, as was present in case of the facts ABCD and *pqrs*.

If we let 'if WXY then Z' indicate a lawlike generalization, then in the World of Description we have the following paradigm for Roycean explanation:

(1)	if WXY, then Z	*(covering law)*	
(2)	abc	*(facts, boundary conditions)*	explanans
(3)	d	*(fact to be explained)*	explanandum

where (3) may be derived from (1) and (2) by the appropriate logical manipulations which we should today call universal instantiation (of (1)) and *modus ponens* (using the preceding result and (2)). For Royce explanation and description go hand in hand: "to report whole facts is, to some extent, to explain their details." It is not one thing to describe facts and another to explain them; to the extent that you describe "wholes of facts," you explain the parts of these wholes.[20] To describe something is to bring it under a law, to relate it to a generalization.

So far, the objective, and, as Royce implies, the real, are the describable. How then are we to conceptualize what is not public and describable, the private and the fleeting, those aspects of our inner life which are in his sense *indescribable?* Royce calls this "world of feelings" the World of Appreciation. It is what makes a moment dear to us, the moment's value: those experiences which we might ordinarily call personal; we do not share them; others do not verify them. Of course, Royce's decision to label the World of Appreciation as "unreal" is only tentative. Appreciations would be real—objective—if they were sharable, i.e., verified, by all of us. Since we exist as finite beings, we share only the external and describable. But if human communication were of another sort, if all the moments of human lives were directly appreciable, i.e., felt by us together and at our pleasure, then the real world would have a different character from the World of Description. The real world would be a world "such as the organic Self in his wholeness might have present to him at a glance, or such as the community of a conceived group of spiritual mind-readers might share."[21]

The strategy is not difficult to anticipate. For Royce the real is the metaphysically real, and a likely candidate for this office are the entities of science—permanent, external objects. But for an idealist this approach can never be final, and although Royce never urges that the World of Description is "unreal," he attempts to prove that it is a finite aspect of the World of Appreciation; and we may construe these discussions as partial and general solutions to what Royce took in a wide sense to be the deduction of the categories. With this commitment in mind, he advances three arguments to persuade us that the World of Description cannot be ultimate. The first is based on the science of his day and asserts that scientific hypotheses become incoherent when they try to account for the universe as a whole; the second is a philosophical argument designed to show that the World of Description logically presupposes the World of Appreciation; the third is based on the teleological emphasis in his epistemology.

The Nebular Hypothesis, Royce writes, is the one plausible hypothesis concerning the nature and origins of the universe:

> Contraction, under the influence of gravity, most probably furnished the source of . . . heat in case of each of the great stellar masses. Contraction, read backwards, and interpreted in the light of the well-known and now pretty widely confirmed nebular hypothesis, indicates that each star must once have been far larger than it now is, and that the energy now radiated as heat must once have been stored up as the energy of position of widely diffused matter, whose particles gravitated towards one another, and whose state is probably indicated to us by such vast masses as certain of the nebulae show us. Condensation, the conversion of the energy of position into heat, radiation of the heat, the continued contraction of stellar masses: such is the process that we now probably see indicated before us.

As each celestial body contracts, it cools off, radiating heat. At one time this planet must have solidified; before that it was cooling as a liquid; and prior to that as a gas. At some time in the future, the process will "run down," and the universe grow cold and die.[22]

Is this conception coherent? The only argument which makes the idea plausible is that advanced by W. K. Clifford. Let us grant, Clifford says, that the present "laws" of geometry and mechanics have been applicable during all of past time. We can conceive of the universe at some earlier time as having consisted of ultimate molecules, all separate from one another and approaching one another. They would meet and form a great number of small hot bodies, and the process of aggregation which has brought us to the present and will lead to death will have begun. Looking back as far as we like, we should find the particles a given distance apart; and we could always conceive of their being further apart, that is, of there being a more remote time in the past.[23] But now, Royce contends, let us "pass to the limit" and learn what our hypothesis implies. At an infinite past time the particles of matter must have been infinitely distant from one another; moreover, every state, for example the present one, demands *all* the previous ones as physically necessary antecedents. We could not be in the present state unless the antecedent state of infinite remoteness actually preceded. But now we have contradicted ourselves. If I say

> . . . there are, in a certain state of the world, two particles of matter, *p* and *q*, and the distance between these two particles is an infinite distance, I contradict myself. For the line *pq* which joins these particles must by hypothesis end in one direction at *p* and in the other direction at *q*—in other words must be finite. And yet our present hypothesis as to the real world demands of us the assertion that such a contradictory state of things must have been real in order that the present state of the world should have come to pass.[24]

We are not dealing with a process which is unlimited however far we *choose* to follow it. Rather, unless an infinite distance is real, we cannot reach the limited distances. If this scientific process reflects the origin and nature of the universe, i.e., the metaphysically real, the infinite distance exists, and to state this view is to express its incoherence.

If his argument is correct, Royce has simply shown that Clifford's suggestion is insufficient. But Royce believes that this suggestion is the only one which explicates the philosophic significance of the Nebular Hypothesis, and that the Nebular Hypothesis exemplifies the best science can offer in the way of cosmology. Consequently, the world of science cannot be the "ultimately real world" but only "a seeming world whose anomalous character is due to our private and human point of view."

The scientific universe is "a fragmentary aspect" of the real. As he was to say at the turn of the century, the source of the World of Description lies in a "perspective effect."[25] Typified by the Nebular Hypothesis, the World of Description embodies a conception that we cannot generalize without contradiction. In all probability, Royce says, this conception is "of an essentially human character or else of no world-wide objectivity. It may have truth about it, but this truth will in part be due to our own limited point of view, to our particular station in the universe. This notion will be, so to speak, a *mortal* conception of things, not a conception of a really eternal truth."[26]

Royce is too thorough a thinker to allow his criticism of the World of Description to rest on a fault of contemporary science. He also presents a cogent philosophical argument. We conceive other human beings to be "real," but in what sense? We might exhaustively describe one another in scientific terms, that is, as biological or physiochemical entities; but these descriptions would not express the only sense or even the most important sense in which we regard our fellows as real.[27] My own inner life and those of others are not describable; they belong to the World of Appreciation. Yet, they are just that aspect of human beings which we wish to call real. We presuppose their reality even should we argue that the World of Description constitutes the real: when we describe, we do so *for* other beings like ourselves whose "reality" we admit cannot be captured through description. The implicit premise of our talk about objectivity is the belief that we do "truly communicate" with our neighbors. The objectivity of the World of Description consists in its sharability, in the fact that others experience it. But if this is so, its reality presupposes the "nonsharable" reality of these others:

> And still all along, even in trying so resolutely to confine the objective consciousness to the consciousness of whatever is describable, were we not meanwhile recognizing and appealing to this objective other consciousness of our fellow? Yes, we were; for we were speaking of what truth we could describe, and so share with the beings who possess this other consciousness. What we pretended to share, however, with them, was some abstraction or other, which in their experience we hoped that they could *also* realize.

Their experience as such we never hoped to share. That was private, inner, incommunicable.[28]

The criterion of the objective or real is our ability to verify experience in common, i.e., to have shared experience. We have heretofore taken the external objects which we describe as characteristic of what is real or objective. But description presupposes that we attribute an *appreciative* reality to others. If appreciation is real, however, it cannot in actuality be private, momentary, and fleeting, although it is from our perspective. We can make this state of affairs intelligible only if we assume that the World of Description does not characterize the real; and we must also suppose that our seemingly isolated and momentary appreciative consciousnesses do share in the organic life of one self in which everyone experiences the consciousness of everyone else. Appreciation is the reality of the infinite whereas description is the reality of what is finite and could not exist without its higher corollary:

> I *mean* my friend's inner life when I am fond of him. And yet my friend's inner life is not one of my finite experiences at all; nor can it ever become so, however much I peer about for his mind in all my own world of space and of time; nor can I describe how it must seem to all beholders, as I describe the things of nature. What do I mean by him, then? Anything definite? Yes, a most definite, although not a physical fact. I mean a fact in the same conscious spiritual realm with me, a fact whose relation to me, as true object of my thought, only the inclusive Self, in whose thought for whose reflection both my friend and I exist, —only he can know, and knowing can constitute.[29]

Royce concludes this discussion in *The Spirit of Modern Philosophy* by referring to his exposition in *The Religious Aspect of Philosophy*, to what I have called a third argument. Real objects are not the cause of my thoughts. A thinker assumes that his thoughts first agree with their object, where 'agree' means something like 'intend'. As we have seen, causation presupposes this agreement and cannot explain it. That is, we can never formulate our theory of knowledge by means of the categories of the World of Description (here causality). We must understand the connection between thought and object in terms of purpose, a teleological notion which Royce says is "logically appreciable." The relation of causation exists *among* certain objects of thought but is not adequate to express the intentional relation of idea and referent; once again description presupposes appreciation.[30]

History and evolution are teleological—they embody purpose, meaning, and significance—and particularly with his last two arguments Royce has an answer to the problems of his 1889 paper. The evolutionary and historical are ultimate and represent the appreciative reality which the World of Description presupposes. He accepts with equanimity the Darwinian hypothesis which threatened so many other religious thinkers. More than other contemporary scientific advances, the theory of evolution is explicitly genetic, and Royce uses it as a primary example of the real status of science:

> I know many who regret the tendency in our day to apply the doctrine of the transformation of species to humanity, who fear the apparently materialistic results of the discovery that the human mind has grown. For my part there lies in all this discovery of our day the deeply important presupposition that the transition from animal to man is in fact really an evolution, that is, a real history, a process having significance. If this is in truth the real interpretation of nature, then the romantic philosophy has not dreamed in vain, and the outer order of nature will embody once more the life of a divine Self.[31]

With the work of *The Religious Aspect of Philosophy* and *The Spirit of Modern Philosophy* assumed, Royce offers a new and different argument for absolute idealism. Although this argument is persuasive and speculative, as opposed to logical, it merits attention. The World of Description cannot explain the reality which we attribute to our fellows. We contend that they have an "appreciative reality" the World of Description never explicates but always requires. Moreover, a man's phenomenal movements, objects of possible experience for all observers, stand for, and phenomenally accompany, his inner life. They are manifestations of a finite appreciative life. We must then regard his limbs, his nerves, his brain, his circulatory and nutritive processes, and so on, as signifying an inner life. In short, Royce declares:

> you cannot separate your phenomenal fellows from the order of phenomenal nature. The continuity between man and nature, known to us first as the absolute inseparability of the expressive movements of our fellows from the nature-processes in which these movements appear to be imbedded, and of which they are phenomenally a part, has now become, in the light of our whole experience of natural phenomena, an all-embracing continuity, extending to cerebral and to general physiological processes, and to the ancestry and evolution of the human race, so that the highest in expressive human nature is now phenomenally linked by the most intimate ties to the simplest of physical processes. If, then, one's fellow is real, the whole of the phenomenal nature from which his phenomenal presence is continuous must be real in the same general fashion.[32]

We believe that our fellows are real in an appreciative sense, although our understanding is a postulate based on our belief in the efficacy of communication. By the argument from continuity we can state that the system of finite experience, the world of nature, is as real as our socially communicative fellows; it manifests its existence just as they do— through the phenomena which appear in space and time. Of course, we have an imperfect idea of the quality of nature's "appreciative reality," bereft of the help of "social communication." And Royce admits that this hypothesis, resting as it does on an argument from continuity, is speculative and not conclusive, but he insists that it is not analogic:

> Certain of the phenomena of nature do stand for real inner experience, viz., the expressive movements of men. It is impossible to separate these latter phenomena, however, from the rest of the natural world, whose phenomenal unity the doctrine of Evolution is now daily making more manifest. Hence—so we reasoned—the rest of phenomenal nature must be regarded as standing for systems of finite experience, whose inner unity has to be defined in the way that human experience illustrates. And it is thus, not by analogy, but by the very process whereby nature comes to be defined as real at all, that natural facts get conceived as like other finite experience.[33]

This move leads Royce to further cosmological ruminations concerning the universe. Other idealists, for example, Peirce, analogized men's habits to the laws of the universe which we might construe as the habits of some greater being. Royce dissociates himself from this reflection which had some currency in late nineteenth-century thought;[34] he also proceeds to use a similar idea in his own speculations. Habits mean regularities in phenomenal behavior, and the less variable the habit, the fainter human consciousness grows. A conscious being behaves habitually, but we associate consciousness itself with an irregularity in conduct:

> Not routine, then, as such, but irregularity, gives the physically interpretable sign of mind. Habit is always present, in the actions of the obviously conscious being; but, whenever he shows interpretable signs of consciousness, habit is always undergoing alterations.[35]

Despite his disavowal of the Peircean analogy between habits and laws of nature, Royce notes it to make another point. There appears to be greater regularity in nature than we are able to observe in human conduct. Nature's laws—habits, if you will—are of greater duration than men's habits. It might seem that since phenomenal irregularity is characteristic of the physical processes which indicate mind, the phenomenal regularity of nature indicates the presence of the "unconscious," whatever that may mean. But the laws of nature display great regularities only if we ignore large differences in time: if we made our time span great enough, we should observe irregularities in natural behavior just as we do in human behavior:

> Even if ultimate laws exist, then, and involve absolutely ideal regularities, which hold for all phenomena, organic and inorganic, it still follows that the observable and relatively rhythmic regularities of inorganic nature must be as truly cases of constantly altered "habits," continually adjusted to numerous conditions in the environment, as are the seemingly so irregular expressive acts of our socially expressive fellows. The difference lies in the enormously different times required to make manifest the alterations of phenom-

enal conduct in question. . . . A planet or a solar system alters the routine of its rhythmic processes in ways that it may take millions of years to make manifest. But in both cases the essentials of adjustment are present, viz., variations in the rhythm of characteristic movements occurring in correspondence to changing situations.[36]

The point is one about time. Human experience is subject to a limitation which Royce designates "the limitation of our Apperceptive Span": what we call the present has a brief but by no means infinitesimal length; changes occurring too quickly or too slowly either escape us altogether or, like the slower changes in nature, are noticed indirectly. A change in our routine which is so slow as to escape our own apperceptive span is still a fact in the phenomenal world, capable of being recorded and verified. *"Why may not just such facts be represented by experience which accompanies our own, and which is just as real as ours, but which is characterized by another apperceptive span?"*[37] Our apperceptive span seems arbitrary; and there is no reason why a particular series of instants should form one moment of our consciousness. If we grant this fact, it may be that there are other experiencers who have greater or lesser apperceptive spans.

We can imagine a series of experiencers, the content of whose experience is similar but whose consciousnesses differ in some graded fashion in terms of differences in apperceptive spans. For one of these experiencers the relation of new and old would represent for another swift and confused contents, or changeless contents. Conceivably, one consciousness might communicate its presence to the others by observable manifestations, and each might become indirectly aware of the presence and inner life of its neighbors. The significance of this inner life, however, would become "appreciatively meaningful" only insofar as the apperceptive span of one agreed with the other. Socially definite communication could occur between experiencers of "substantially the same apperceptive span."[38]

Having distinguished description and appreciation, Royce brings them up again in relation to psychology. Psychology is in an anomalous position among the sciences, since it purports to make individual consciousness the object of observation; that is, it supposes to describe the World of Appreciation. How is this science possible? It rests on the belief that

> . . . there actually exists in the world of truth an intimate correlation between what self-consciousness reflectively discovers in the inner life of the individual, and what the common consciousness of mankind detects somewhere in the describable processes of the physical world. Were there no such correlation discoverable, there would be no psychology possible. . . .[39]

Psychology is conceivable only if the World of Appreciation, the metaphysically real, has "actual ties" to changing physical states. Apart from an "embodiment" or "manifestation" of the inner life in a psychophysical process, the science would not exist. Royce also believed that we could discover the correlation in question by the study of defective nervous functions in the case of disease, by the comparison of nervous functions in man and animals, and by experimentation on man's nervous functions.[40] Royce himself was sidetracked before he made any progress with this program; but in the mid-nineties he did launch a theoretical study of the World of Description and its connection to psychology.

It is not difficult to see why this psychological problem took on enormous importance for him. The link between my individual consciousness and the public behavior which "expresses" it is parallel to the link between the world of the absolute self and the world of objects which expresses *it*. A study of psychology promised a deduction of the categories *writ small*, an explanation of the relation of the Worlds of Appreciation and Description which Royce was determined to achieve. Fifteen years would pass before he articulated this relation adequately, and when he did, he had long since forsaken psychology for another tool—logic and the foundations of mathematics. But in the nineties he thought psychology might solve the problem.[41]

We define the "true" or metaphysical self by a moral ideal which makes someone a unique individual and unifies a mass of empirical data. But why is a *given* mass of data chosen for unification? To answer this question we must examine the finite self.[42] Ordinary self-conciousness appears "as a relatively stable group of unlocalized sensory contents of feeling, and as the apparent controller of the train of associated ideas, impulses, and acts of attention or choice." These aspects are related: the "associative potency" of the ruling feelings and interests is responsible for the sense of inner self-control. Moreover, the self seems to its possessor larger than any present group of facts or functions. I regard my present self as the representative of a self which has been present in my past and will be present in my future. More importantly, the characters, attributes, and functions of the self extend beyond anything that is presented in my isolated inner experiences, however far they are extended; the self is related to the selves of others:

> When one is vain, one's self-consciousness involves the notion that one's self really exists, in some way or other, for the thoughts and estimates of others, and is at least worthy, if not the possessor, of their praise or of their envy. When one feels guilty, one does not and cannot abstract from the conceived presence of one's self in and for the experience of a real or ideal judge of one's guilt. In all such cases the self of self-consciousness thus appears as something that it would not and could not be were there not others in the world to behold, or to estimate it, to be led or other wise influenced by it, or to appeal to it. It is now from such points of view that the self of self-consciousness comes, in the end, to get form as a being who takes himself to have a social position, and office, a profession—in brief, a vast group of functions without which the self would appear itself to be, relatively speaking, a mere cipher, while these functions are at once regarded as organically joined to the self, and centered in it, and nevertheless, are unintelligible unless one goes beyond one's private consciousness, and takes account of the ideas and estimates of other people.[43]

A man becomes self-conscious only in connection with the growth of his social consciousness, i.e., his awareness of others, his knowledge of other minds. The two forms, ego and alter, are not ooparablc; they are interdependent. I am conscious of myself only in relation to some real or ideal persons, and apart from my consciousness of my fellows I have only derived states and habits and self-consciousness. Neither conception—the individual ego and the social alter—has any clarity apart from the other.*

Consider, he writes, the supposed natural and primal conflict between egoism and altruism. Many people assume that individuals are instinctively *self*ish, and that they must be persuaded to act altruistically. But the contrast is mistaken. The tyrant wills the lives and limited good fortune of his subjects, for without powerful, numerous, and even devoted subjects, he would be no tyrant; the master wills his slave's preservation, even in willing to preserve his own mastery; and the thief wills that the hoarding of valuable property should be advantageous enough to others to make them want to provide him with his livelihood. In short, there is "bad altruism"—a base wishing of social relations which involve the preservation and relative private advantage of others beside the self. All forms of egoism—vanity, pride, love of power, the greed of mastery, covetousness, oppression—suppose this kind of altruism. I can never will to be merely egoistic; my aims have to be social, just so far as I clearly define them. "The ethical problem is not," Royce says, "shall I aim to preserve social relations? but: What social relations shall I aim to preserve?"[45]

Royce often merely states and illustrates his contention that self and social consciousness are reciprocal. But when he urges that social consciousness *precedes* self-consciousness as given individuals mature, he offers an extended discussion as well as a "simple analytic proof." We shall consider each in turn.

How does the finite self develop? What is the process which distinguishes it and the social consciousness? To answer these questions Royce worked in experimental psychology. Influenced by the doctrines of James Mark Baldwin, he investigated the psychology of imitation

---

* *Studies of Good and Evil* (New York, 1898), p. 221. Royce pursued this idea, once adopted, with the remorseless consistency which made him famous. In *The Conception of God* he urges that the Absolute is self-conscious only because there is a "social contrast" among its separate yet unified aspects, for example, Thought, Experience, and Will (pp. 296–302).

and the related area of invention. Like Royce, Baldwin too was interested in imitation; and while Royce indicated that their research was independent although consistent, he also stated that Baldwin's work had affected him.[46] With a generosity rare in the history of scholarship, Royce declared that any priority dispute between him and Baldwin was a "trivial question."[47] The two men became friends and Baldwin extracted parts of a personal letter from Royce on imitation and published them in his *Social and Ethical Interpretation* (New York, 1897); in turn, Royce wrote laudatory reviews of Baldwin's work.[48] It is unnecessary to sort out their exact influence on one another, so similar are their views on imitation. What is significant is the place Royce gave to imitation in his analysis of self-consciousness and the use he made of it.

Early in 1893 he delivered a series of addresses under the unlikely title "Topics in Psychology of Interest to Teachers." In them he outlined the psychological aspects of his philosophy. The lectures are so complete that many of the doctrines advanced in them go far beyond anything he had published at the time; some of the positions he worked out only surface again during the first decade of the twentieth century. We shall survey the most significant ideas advanced in these talks, and return to an elaboration of the points developed in the nineties.

One of the main themes the lectures pursue is the link between two types of knowledge, immediate and derived. The two correspond to what we know in the worlds of appreciation and description respectively and always "go hand in hand." Whenever we obtain derived knowledge, he says, we do so on the basis of the immediate data of sense; whenever we are feeling, we are also thinking. Although the distinction is valuable, "I would not have you imagine that in our own consciousness there is the separation."[49] The 1895 statement on idealism delivered in California reintroduced a voluntaristic element into Royce's thought, but in 1893 this voluntarism was pragmatic. I think we can associate the two kinds of knowledge with cognition (description), on the one hand, and volition (appreciation), on the other. Royce urges the union of the processes. In fact, he puts forward a pragmatic analysis of the meaning of ideas: they are plans of action enabling us to respond

successfully to our environment and indistinguishable from the actions
they entail; the verification of ideas links the two. He was committed to
"the absolutely inseparable character of the intellectual and voluntary
life of man."[50]

There is another feature of Royce's thought which is striking
because it differs from what he says in print. He goes on to distinguish
two subtypes of derived knowledge, and although these two subtypes also
go hand in hand, they are "by no means the same." The two types are
reflective and descriptive: when we reflect on our own meaning and
activity, we have derived knowledge of the first kind; when we learn in
a way which implies that we must rely on "the nature of the outer truth,"
we have derived knowledge of the second kind; both of them are means
of passing from immediate to mediate knowledge:

> Whenever you answer the question *What do I mean?* you get re-
> flective knowledge. Whenever you answer the question: *What is the
> structure of these facts before me?* you get descriptive knowledge.
> Both kinds are articulate. Both are derived. Both are mediated.[51]

Royce developed his idea further in a paper read a few months later
to the Philosophical Congress at the Chicago World's Fair in August
1893. In a way that we shall examine more fully, descriptive knowledge
occurs when we *imitate* "the structure of outer things"—of our fellows
or of objects[52]—and in the World's Fair address Royce calls the two subtypes of derived knowledge *imitative* and *reflective*. He asserts that there
is tension between them. Human thinking is an effort which intelligent
beings make to imitate the form and structure of the truth existing
around them, but when I reflect I retire into my inner world; with a
"certain relative independence" I try to make sense of the world without
embodying "what an external authority suggests." Reflective knowledge
attempts to give our *own* ideas "a certain inner clearness, self-consistency,
assurance, self-possession—in a word . . . [to obtain] genuine self-
consciousness":

> When I reflect thus on my meaning, what I hold before me, then,
> is the identity of this meaning through a series of actual or possible
> changes of immediate experience. . . . if by reflection we . . . know

the identity of our meaning at various moments of our experience, the question of course arises, how can we know this identity, when the contents of immediate experience are themselves always changing? And it is an old idea in philosophy that this identity of meaning is to be somehow explained by saying . . . my meaning remains identical, because I, the thinking Subject, remain one, and because now, thus remaining one, I am able to recognize the identity of my own conscious act in many successive moments. To reflect on the identity of my meaning in various thoughts, is mediately to observe myself as one in act in the midst of the shifting floods of immediacy. This I do whenever I reflect. In reflecting on my meaning, I therefore presuppose and assume, as it were, the discovery of myself. It is then the Self, the Ego, the identical Knower of meaning, that forms the true object of reflective knowledge.[53]

It is difficult to ascertain the relation of these doctrines in Royce's mind. Reflection is surely to join the metaphysical to the imitative empirical self; that is, it appears to link the appreciative world of the individual to the descriptive world about him. But before Royce developed the notion, reflective knowledge ceased to have any significance *per se;* from the middle nineties he proceeded simply to contrast the two worlds of appreciation and description: there is nonmediated (appreciative) and mediated (descriptive) knowledge, *period.* Although there is little evidence, I think it is clear why "reflective knowledge" disappears. Even in the World's Fair address he states that "in every individual case" derived knowledge is imitative in character;[54] and the pragmatism of the 1893 lectures is not conducive to the preservation of a strictly mental realm. It is natural that he would assimilate reflective to descriptive or "imitative" knowledge.

As we have already seen, the growth of self-consciousness is not something that occurs in isolation; it depends on the social alter. Reflection would become a kind of imitation, a way of behaving toward external objects.*

---

* In his 1903 *Outlines of Psychology* (New York, 1903) the distinction between what I would call two kinds of imitation briefly reappears. Here our ideas are plans of action which have an "essentially imitative character"; all our "higher conceptions" involve conscious imitations of things. But Royce states that "The fact that all our

In a large undated manuscript which he appears to have written in the late nineties, Royce asserts that "Nobody can be clear in his mind without showing his clearness somehow in his bearing"; and indicates that he has assimilated reflection to imitation. When we think

> we are aware of a voluntary intent to set over against the facts about which we think something that serves to imitate them in a more or less abstract fashion. That is[,] thinking means in its inner aspect a voluntary process of depicting or representing, or reconstructing objects. . . . when we think we observe precisely *as in any knowing process* the likenesses and the differences amongst various facts. And we also make use of past experience. The only difference between thinking and any other kind of knowing lies in the voluntary process whereby we fill up the field of knowledge with more or less artificial and ideal objects that are to serve as the counterparts, the images, the intentional representation of the facts of our experience. . . . the characteristic of our ideas when we think is that they are conscious imitations of the general characters, of the forms, types, meanings, values, and relations of objects. And we possess such conscious general ideas, in other words we think, whenever we know how to use words, to describe objects, and to treat objects as conventional usage requires us to treat them. Human science, the highest expression of our thinking process is simply an effort to imitate the world in more or less symbolic terms.[55]

Thinking—or what I believe Royce formerly would have called reflection—is now some form of "imitation," just as our descriptive knowledge is a form of imitation.

---

general ideas have been formed under social conditions, and that the ways in which we describe, portray, and characterize things have been throughout determined by motives of communication, *by a disposition to imitate the behaviour of our fellows, and by a disposition to compare our own mental attitudes with theirs,* this fact sufficiently explains why *the social contrasts and comparisons in question have tended to make us and keep us conscious not only of our own objects, but of our own modes of rational behaviour in their presence.*" As awkward and unclear as this sentence is, it does distinguish between outright imitation of others (description?) and the comparison of ideas (reflection?) (p. 291; first set of italics mine; second set in original). See also *The Spirit of Modern Philosophy* (Boston, 1892), pp. 409–410, 430–432; and *The World and the Individual,* 2 vols. (New York, 1899; 1901) (hereafter *WI* 1 and *WI* 2 respectively), vol. 2 pp. 256–259.

Whatever the precise nature of reflection, this outline of its place in Royce's thought will clarify our study of his later work. In the nineties, however, he "reduced" reflection to imitation and explored this latter notion. A child imitates when he struts about as a soldier or runs on all fours like a dog. In these cases the child is aware of a model and finds his own body able to repeat movements of the model. But imitation also includes those intelligent functions which tend to the voluntary production of external objects "resembling" other objects, i.e. models. Drawing, painting, building, and the like are "imitative functions" of this sort. But imitation is not a process in which we reproduce one set of data by means of another set like the first; it is a process in which we get two sets of data whose contrasts are as instructive as their purposed resemblances: we get an interpretation of the model in our imitation. Imitation is an activity whose main motive is to *interpret* my perceptions by means of my deeds. A parody is an imitation, but its interest lies more in its contrast to that of which it is a parody than in its similarities. This kind of imitation will neglect everything about the model except chosen aspects of it, and we will reproduce even these aspects in an exaggerated way. Royce suggests that we define the "resemblance" of imitation and model by saying that an imitation means or intends its model: imitation may be a teleological conception and not one rooted in any idea of physical similarity.[56]

What distinguishes imitation from other motor processes—for example, looking, listening, and grasping? Royce pinpoints the distinction in his definition:

> my interpretation of what I am usually said to perceive outside of my organism, in the external world, is . . . conditioned upon my setting over against my perceptions a series of motor processes, or of perceived results of motor processes, which in its wholeness contrasts with the other series in the one principal fact that the motor processes, the imitative deeds or their results, appear to me relatively controllable, plastic, reproducible at will, while otherwise the two series are largely similar.[57]

Imitation is an act that interprets an uncontrollable perceptive series by setting against it a series that appears to be similar—at least *means* the

first series—but has its most important contrast in its controllability:
the model may be similar to my imitation but is beyond my power, independent of my movements.

In arguing that the resemblance between model and imitation may
consist only in the latter meaning the former, and that the important
contrast between the two is control, Royce considers the elements of
imitation that interest him most:

> an imitation appears as an adjustment that leads to the emphasizing
> or interpreting of a train of relatively external experiences, by vir-
> tue of the fact that the mental accompaniment of this adjustment is
> a train of relatively inner experiences . . . while the similarity of
> the train of internal experiences to the train of external experiences
> serves, in the midst of the mutual contrasts of the two trains, to
> make livelier the consciousness of each series, when viewed side by
> side with the other.[58]

The consciousness of the imitator is as truly a consciousness of his
adjustment as it is a consciousness of his model. Imitation is "the one
source of our whole series of conscious distinctions between subject
and object . . ."; the contrast between model and imitation is the first
appearance in consciousness of the differentiation between internal and
external experience.[59] Through imitation the individual separates himself—his appreciative world—from the World of Description and in so
doing develops his own self-consciousness.

Royce does not doubt that instinct begins the social life of the child
and that the child has some intrinsic interest in other persons which leads
him to respond to them. In some way, then, self-consciousness—which
we will see develop out of this interest—is also instinctual. Nevertheless,
the child is no atomistic consciousness, implicitly arguing from analogy
to the existence of other minds. The process is one dependent on imitation. An infant has an imperfect sense of self-consciousness, if he has
any at all. As he imitates, the activities imitated become comprehensible.
The models imitated come to possess intelligible and intelligent aspects,
and these are new ideas which the imitator did not previously have. The
child refers these ideas to the perceived organism of the people imitated

and rarely, or not at all, to what we call himself. The new ideas come to him embodying the meaning, the intelligible value, the purport of the acts he imitates. The new ideas are thought of at the outset as the ideas of others. The imitation *means* the model in two senses: it intends the model and furnishes ideas which allow the child to understand the model; for the child the model *is* what the child associates with the imitation. The problem of other minds takes a strange twist. Although we need not suppose a full-fledged distinction between the private and public worlds, the child at least perceives models as facts imposed upon him. He attributes to the models any idea which comes from imitating them. A person comes to mean those ideas associated with the imitation of the person: a gardener is someone who gardens, and the child attributes to his models the new experiences surrounding his imitation. Only *after* he has a conception of people external to him will his own self-consciousness develop:[60]

> I am convinced that each one of us believed in the existence of other minds before he became conscious of his own mind as such. And for all our life I hold this to be true, namely, that we do not get at the existence of the minds of our fellows by an induction from our own individual case, nearly as much as we make use of precisely the reverse line of reasoning. I do not often say to myself when thinking of my fellows: 'Yonder people behave as I do, hence they must be alive as I am.' The normal social consciousness runs rather thus: 'When I imitate these people, when I get under the influence of their suggestions, listen receptively to their words, follow their gestures, conform to customs, accept their authority,—well, then I constantly get new ideas, and these new ideas are as such the revelations of yonder minds. But now, as this result proves, I am capable of getting these ideas. Hence I am as much a real person, as truly a thinker, as they are.' In this way it is that I explicitly attain my self-consciousness.[61]

In addition to this explication Royce offers a "simple analytic proof" of his position. Suppose we were to try to think away all the knowledge we have accepted from other people. First, he claims, all the knowledge embodied in language would vanish: "In other words, as pure and naked private Ego, you will be speechless. Language, as you first learned it, was never for your consciousness, your independent invention."[62] Although Royce indicates that "wordless thought" exists, our abstract and mature thinking is linguistic, and he identifies self-consciousness with thinking about ourselves. Without language, then, there is no self-consciousness, and language is certainly a social acquisition. Self-consciousness is a *product* of social interaction:

> The question, of course, is not now of the certainty, but of the origin for me, of the thought 'I exist.' I insist: this thought I do, indeed, verify by my own inner reflection, but it first took its origin for me in social intercourse with my fellows. Had they never taught me that I exist, I should never have come to take note of the now so obvious fact. . . . my conscious idea of myself is derived, is secondary, for instance, to language, to which all my thinking is so deeply indebted, and is thus, oddly enough, a product of social intercourse. Who I am, I have first learned from others before I can observe it for myself.[63]

Whatever the relation between self and other, Royce connects this doctrine to his analysis of the World of Appreciation. An individual depends on others for his beliefs about the external world; no one experiences everything that constitutes the reality of the world. We rely on the reports and experiences of others. Royce, however, maintains that others play a role in determining what we mean by externality.[64] The World of Description is the common and public world, containing the experience that we as well as others can verify. If this is so, the social consciousness is a necessary condition for the existence of the World of Description—the external world: external facts exist for other conscious beings besides ourselves. No individual—for example a child—gets his belief in the World of Description until he develops a social consciousness. By an external thing we *mean* an object of experience which is, or may be, a common object for as many observers as you please; it will be common to the extent that they can verify it—that is, describe it in standard ways:[65]

> Apart from the social consciousness, if left to my private ex-
> perience, I should indeed come to know what Mill called the "per-
> manent possibilities of experience." I should expect them to be
> repeated in definite ways in response to definite acts of mine. That
> fire burns, that stone walls resist, that objects seen can under cer-
> tain circumstances be grasped; all this I could and, if sufficiently
> intelligent, should learn in isolation. But, so I maintain, these "per-
> manent possibilities of experience" . . . would lack an important
> note of my present external world, since I should not conceive
> them as social objects, objects existent for other persons besides
> myself. And it is the social consciousness that defines a most im-
> portant attribute of externality.[66]

Royce's elaboration of the logical priority of appreciation to
description and his relating of the latter to finite self and social consciousness never seem in themselves compelling. At least they are not so
compelling as the dialectical argument of *The Religious Aspect of Philosophy;* even less so is his speculation on the cosmological structure of the
universe. And I do not feel that Royce takes them to be compelling.
Over and over he indicates their connection to his proof of the Absolute—a question he never broaches directly in these "psychological"
essays. But if we grant his argument for the Absolute, his discussions
take on a different status. They become plausible and astute hypotheses
concerning the phenomenal realm; if absolute idealism is true and our
common sense beliefs about the world are still justifiable, then his
explanations of the nature of the finite self and externality are not
strange or untoward. They are arguments to make his position reasonable
insofar as our understanding normally limits itself to the finite. Assume
that we do really communicate with our fellows and do gain some comprehension of the natural world. We still know that the World of Description cannot be the ultimately real. How can we explain it in a manner
consistent with absolute idealism? First, we define the objective or real
in terms of what we may all experience. As finite beings the real will
be what is external to us, for what we will mutually verify as common
experiences will be what we conceive to be independently existing objects.

Externality is characteristic of what is real for a plurality of beings; if there is no plurality of selves there is no externality. But we know that a single absolute self is the metaphysically real and that finite selves are correctly conceived as "fragments" of it; hence describability and externality cannot embody the nature of things; what is ultimately real must be the appreciations of the absolute self. These appreciations will fulfill our definition of the real and objective since they will be sharable. This argument forms the background to Royce's ruminations about his two worlds, and in this light the doctrine is a rational construal of the status of the World of Description given the truth of absolute idealism.

The attempt to relate the World of Appreciation and the World of Description is the most important problem linking Royce's thought at this time to his work after the turn of the century. A concern for this "deduction" is implicit in all of his philosophizing, and is made explicit at strategic points. Of special interest is an 1894 article, "The External World and the Social Consciousness," which differs from the specific treatment of the deduction in *The Spirit of Modern Philosophy*. The article is worth examining for it is an account of the growth of the individual psyche and the origins of externality.

The child that has begun to possess a "social consciousness" is for the first time in the presence of supersensual reality; he has models *beyond* him and finds himself and his models imitating other objects—friends, playthings, animals, and the like. For a time he may think that his perceptions of an object are numerically identical with those of others, but social communication sooner or later involves differences of opinion, conflict of testimony, and evidence of variety in the experience of others. The child learns that his experiences of an object are not the same as those of others, although the experiences are assumed to be of the same object. What the child sees he comes to regard as the object for him; what I see, as the object for me. But through our ability to verify one another's experiences we still find that we are "imitating in common," and thus Royce explains the origins of representative theories of knowledge. We reconcile the subjectiveness of our perceptions and the commonality of our imitations by postulating a *tertium quid*, the

external object as it is for itself. It is directly present neither to me nor
to others, but it is our object insofar as we try "to imitate its structure
as we try to imitate each others thoughts"; an object is external to both
of us as we are external to each other.[67] Royce's mode of expression
should not distract us. To imitate each other's thoughts evidently means
that we imitate one another so that others are able to apply to us adjectives like 'intelligent', 'kind', and 'principled'. In these cases our imitations
are of behavior definitive of mind, of thinking beings: we "imitate"
our fellows' thoughts. Even so, we admit that another's consciousness is
beyond us. We do not experience it as the individual does. Similarly,
we must assume that imitating an *object's* structure is akin to describing
it: these imitations—a kind of activity—are ways of classifying that
enable us to verify our descriptions and those of others. To describe
something as five inches long is to be prepared to act in a certain fashion
and, if the description is correct, to enable others to verify it. Royce calls
this "imitating the structure" of a thing. But just as we are external to
one another, so the object is external to us.

Our world is dualistic: its social aspect consists of minds whose
thoughts we try to share when we communicate by gestures or the
devices of language; its physical aspect consists of entities which are
also "imitable" but which do not themselves imitate. All we know of
these objects is what we can mutually verify, even less than we know
of our fellows. What objects are in themselves, we can never discover:

> the object, as it is in itself, is indeed unknowable, for it—the object
> in itself—declines to tell us what its inner life is. If it would speak
> for itself, we should know something more about it, but it remains
> the stubbornly silent partner. Hence, we can only speak in common
> about it. Where we permanently agree, we suppose that we are
> touching the reality, not as it is for you or for me, but for us. And
> it is only as existent for us, who are by hypothesis external to one
> another, that the object shows any persuasive and verifiable indica-
> tion of existing externally to both and to all of us. Thus, the 'things-
> in-themselves' appear to us, on this level, as unknowable. . . .[68]

We know from a rigorous proof that all of the phenomenal world
"reflects" the absolute self; we also have arguments which make this

plausible to us in our finite capacities. Hence, the World of Description, of *Dinge an sich*, "is simply the way in which the world of appreciation, the world of the true and spiritual Self, *must needs appear when viewed by a finite being whose consciousness experiences in the forms of our space and of our time.* . . . Here is the permanent truth of Kant's doctrine."[69]

Psychology would carry Royce this far. The elaboration of the origins of dualism is a defense of Kant's formulations at the finite level of consciousness; it is a "mere restatement in rational fullness of the true spirit of the Kantian deduction."[70] But this "deduction" is incomplete, for Royce does not analyze the precise status of the forms and categories or show how the forms and categories we have grow out of our social consciousness; he has only demonstrated that the World of Description is the finite guise of the World of Appreciation. In the nineties he believed he could go no further: the exact relation of the World of Description to the World of Appreciation was inexplicable from the "human point of view." But from the perspective of the Absolute:

> we should see what now is dark to us, namely, why and how the world of appreciation, when viewed under the conditions of our finite experience, has thus to seem a world of matter in motion. As it is, however, we already know that the world of matter in motion is simply an external aspect of the true and appreciable world. That is, in substance, the whole of our philosophical insight into the matter.[71]

During the first decade of the century Royce changed this position. His central concern was to obtain a "full deduction," to probe the connection between the World of Description and the World of Appreciation. His *magnum opus, The World and the Individual,* published in two volumes in 1899 and 1901, initiated his quest to solve this problem.

5

THE WORLD AND THE INDIVIDUAL

The World and the Individual consists of the Gifford Lectures Royce delivered in Scotland at the turn of the century. In them he organized the thoughts he had been working on through the nineties and elaborated a system of philosophy. While writing the addresses, he thought them the effort of his life, a holy task for the sake of serious thinking on religion.[1] For the first time he used a newly won knowledge of mathematics to develop his ideas. I will not survey both volumes of *The World and the Individual* in this chapter, nor will I discuss the mathematical studies until later. I have also put off an accounting of his moral philosophy. In this chapter, with the aid of his Ingersoll Lecture of 1899, *The Conception of Immortality*,[2] and the 1903 *Outlines of Psychology*,[3] I shall sketch the metaphysics and epistemology of *The World and the Individual*, although even here I am deferring a study of his pragmatism.

The two volumes are Royce's most ingenious and sustained attempt to relate the worlds of description and appreciation; yet the work is one of the most difficult to read sympathetically. Royce's language is often archaic even for his time, and he fills *The World and the Individual* with theological phrases and conceptions which sound odd today. Moreover, the lectures run to nearly a thousand printed pages, excluding an important supplementary essay, and the discussion is often diffuse, wordy, and obscure. But it is a study which we must understand, and deserves an introduction.

Where we might speak of a statement about present facts or of belief, Royce often talks of ideas. His favorite expression in *The World and the Individual* is "an idea seeking its Other"—its object. This is a

99

less dubious notion than it might seem if we realize that it means we make statements about supposed factual relations, or have beliefs about the world; and that we verify the truth of our statements, and confirm our beliefs. For Royce an idea never "finds" its other because the verifications to which we subject our beliefs can be inexhaustible; as empiricists have said, our empirical knowledge is probable only and some possible experience may disconfirm our deepest claims. Of greatest interest is Royce's use of this conception to construct a pragmatic notion of the Absolute.

The ethical problems which his position generated nearly forced voluntarism on him, and in *The Conception of God* he gave a place to the will. In *The World and the Individual,* he formulates this doctrine more carefully: he joins his own ideas concerning the World of Description and some Jamesean principles to the emphases of *The Conception of God* to advocate a more subtle voluntarism. He previously urged that the will was a distinguishable yet inseparable "aspect" of the Absolute; he now asserts that the separation of willing and being has no meaning in the Absolute. This denial of traditional dualisms makes Royce not merely a voluntarist but a pragmatist. The usual distinctions take on value in our finite world, but they are imperfect abstractions, however useful they may be.[4] Our ideas, he declares, have a volitional aspect; they express plans of action. Insofar as ideas express purpose, they reflect our appreciative consciousness; they are associated with our activity, with doing. The world of objects—the World of Description—we consider external to our activity; it is the world of independent being which we attempt to know, cognitional as opposed to volitional.[5] In outlining the relation of ideas to object, Royce, of course, will argue that objects are ideal, but in *The World and the Individual* this argument takes a new turn. Pragmatists have refused to distinguish between volition and cognition, and Royce sees his position as expressing just this point: he will demonstrate that the World of Description, characterized as a world of being, is nothing more than the Absolute's World of Appreciation. In it, knowing and willing are one. We are not given any further "deduction of the categories," but a distinctive pragmatism welds together finite and infinite.

The pragmatic-Kantian insight is *prima facie* innocuous: we participate in the construction of the world. Royce perceives this participation as attention, an exercise of our wills. Thus knowing involves activity, but also a realization that there is something foreign to our activity. Consider again the manner in which empiricists have urged we verify our empirical knowledge. For Royce this is an attempt to reduce the world to ideas, for in each verification the object is experienced, i.e., we might claim that a portion of it occurs in our consciousness, occurs as idea. But verifications never "exhaust" the object, as the many failures of phenomenalist reductionism indicate. The *object* of knowledge remains beyond our grasp, beyond our activities which define our consciousness of the object. But if we knew it completely, it would not be beyond our will. To know an object perfectly is only to act appropriately in relation to it; indeed there is no "it," there is simply—if this interpretation is at all coherent—"pure activity" which is simultaneously "pure being." In these circumstances we would make no distinction between the object—existing externally—and our ideas, our plans of action.

Hopefully this overview will make Royce's position clear. But it is more important to consider how he develops it himself.

Royce begins *The World and the Individual* with a quotation which captures the problem he sets himself:

> I am one of those who hold that when you ask the question: What is an Idea? and: How can Ideas stand in any true relation to Reality? you attack the world-knot in the way that promises most for the untying of its meshes.[6]

What *is* an idea? Royce's analysis represents a return to his work of the early 1880s but is also indebted to James. Royce contends that an idea is not a state of mind which "images" external facts; cognition is never passive reception; it has an active volitional quality. The distinction between the cognitional and volitional is impossible to make; our ideas involve a consciousness of how we propose to behave to the things of which we have ideas. Although this interpretation is, I think, consistent with Royce's intentions, at times his position appears less clear. He sometimes implies that we may regard the excitations of our sense organs by the world as distinct from the experiences we have when we react to our impressions. If we form beliefs and judgments, however, we cannot distinguish what we "receive" from what we will "do" with it.[7] But even here he speaks of the intellectual and volitional aspects of consciousness, the latter adding to the receptive quality of the former.[8] Essentially, Royce lacks a vocabulary to make his points, and often depends on ideas of which he is suspicious. Finally, he admits an "abstract" distinction between cognition and volition in our finite world so that he can develop his arguments with greater rhetorical force. In *The Outlines of Psychology* he states his view at length, and if we are to understand his thought it is helpful to examine that discussion.

There he spells out the union of the intellectual and volitional processes: "thought," he says, "is either action or nothing."[9] But to appreciate this union we must explore consciousness. Consciousness is a stream of whatever is before the mind, and it is impossible to sort out all that is there. Suppose one is listening to a symphony; of what does one's consciousness consist?

> the notes or the chords may, in their series as they pass, appear as sharply separable contents. But these stand out, or float, upon a stream of mental life which includes one's estimate of the time sequence of the music as a whole, one's pleasure in hearing the music, one's train of associated memories, one's general sense of the current bodily comfort and discomfort, and much more of the sort, which no man can analyse into any collection of separate or even separable states. In consequence, we are never able, by any device at our disposal, to tell with certainty the whole of what is, or just was, present to any one moment of our conscious life.[10]

What is present in any conscious moment is dependent on our interests and purposes. Consciousness is "an inner interpretation of our own attitude toward the world"; it is an expression of our will.[11] Royce's meaning is not as strange as it sounds, and is analogous to the Kantian ideas he expresses in his dissertation. A state of consciousness does not exist if no one is conscious of it: to talk of the stream of consciousness implies that consciousness is conscious of it, and consciousness partially determines the content of the stream by its selective attention.[12] Mind is active: the preference for or interest in something helps to create what is before us, and this attentive preference is a form of willing.[13]

Consider the function of habits. Human beings behave so that they respond to stimuli in accordance with the responses they have made to similar past stimuli. Once human beings have established habits, their attention will be guided to states of consciousness associated with those accompanying habitual activity.[14] We are conscious of a *"brief abstract and epitome of our previous experience."* Indeed, people must be taught *how* to perceive, and will perceive no more than what they have been prepared to see.[15] We find that our interests and purposes partially determine the content of consciousness, and it becomes trivially true that any analysis of thinking—of "having ideas"—involves action, will. As we noted, selective attention itself is a voluntary act, and the interest it embodies includes a tendency to external expression.[16] A perception of an object is "a fragment of a possible consciousness involving a whole system of feeling and of conduct in the presence of such an object."[17] Thought must consist of a series of mental processes that will produce characteristic motor reactions. To have ideas about objects is to have plans of action, or responses, which one *would* carry out in the presence of the object about which one has ideas. The only test of one's understanding an idea is one's ability to express oneself in fitting acts: the idea is a disposition to action.[18]

James's impact on this discussion is obvious, but Royce did not take his pragmatism from his older colleague. The voluntarism of the younger man had long been apparent, and this analysis of ideas is also the offshoot of his work on imitation. Ideas are Jamesean plans of action which involve *"conscious imitation of things"*: we have exact ideas only so far as we know how objects can be *"imitatively reconstructed,"* that is, how we ought to act to use objects for the purposes we have. Our ideas will be *shared* because we may compare our imitations with those of our fellows.[19] My ideas are true or false not merely because I verify them but because others verify them in the World of Description, because we "imitate in common." Imitation is the process whereby "an idea seeks its Other." If imitation proceeds to its limit, Royce says, then "I shall face being. I shall not only imitate my object as another, and correspond to it from without: I shall become one with it, and so internally possess it."[20]

In *The World and the Individual* Royce states that an idea is "any state of consciousness" viewed as the partial expression or embodiment of a single conscious purpose; to have an idea one must be prepared to act in order to accomplish a goal in relation to the object of an idea.[21] But we also know that to have an idea is simultaneously to construct the object out of the stream of consciousness: in attending our wills *make* the world what it is. Our ideas are ways of acting toward that which we are helping to create. But our wills only *help* to create the external world; an idea only *partially* embodies a purpose; objects remain to some extent foreign to us and to our purposes. Here is the reason for the distinction between cognition and volition. Because an object is never given, we conceive of it as distinct from our dispositions to act in relation to it. We know it as external to our activity. The dichotomy between the object and our ideas (i.e., plans of action) about it parallels that between thinking and willing. When Royce distinguishes between the two he is making a point about a single phenomenon which the human point of view divides.[22] The distinction is useful if we are to understand our finite form of knowing, and Royce reiterates it when he formulates his notion of the internal and external meaning of ideas.

The internal meaning of an idea is that aspect of its purpose which a present idea immediately embodies.[23] The internal meaning is the most elementary aspect of the plan of action; so far as possible, we construe it as the immediate and spontaneous effort to create order out of the flux of consciousness, and do not associate it with the execution of the plan, the formulation of the tests which will verify the truth of an idea and the process of verification itself.[24] Consider an idea or state of consciousness at any instant. The essential quality of its internal meaning is not the sensations or images associated with it, but its expression of some purpose of ours.[25] This discussion becomes clearer if we recall Royce's early analysis of judgments as acts of will. Adhering to a self-defeating skepticism in the late seventies, he urged that a judgment was a momentary identification of subject and predicate made for a given purpose. Each judgment created its own agreement between subject and predicate and was indubitable—although different from any other judgment. I suspect that Royce's internal meaning of ideas amounts to the same thing. His favorite example is a melody which you sing to yourself. Singing the melody or silently listening to it constitutes a musical idea, and at least partially fulfills and embodies your purpose at the same time—your purpose of imagining the melody. Having the (internal) idea and fulfilling an instantaneous purpose are identical. The idea is its own fulfillment, and in terms of Royce's dissertation a certain element of knowledge. But now he contrasts this internal meaning with a "relatively external meaning"—the object or referent of the idea.*

By using 'relatively' or 'apparently' before his phrase 'external meaning of an idea', Royce warns of what is to come. But he needs the abstraction of the external meaning to make plausible his view of the acquisition of knowledge. The referent or object of an idea makes the idea true or false. Suppose the melody I imagine is a theme Beethoven composed. Then my melody embodies my purpose the instant I imagine it, but it is an idea that *means* its proper object—a Beethoven theme. The external meaning of an idea is that toward which we direct our plan of action. Royce also makes his distinction in the language of his earlier views. The internal meanings are the immediate "imitations" of a being (the external meaning) which appears separate from them.[26] Just as our purposes determined to what our imitations were to correspond and how they were to correspond, so the idea picks out its external meaning and decides the manner of correspondence.

---

* I have often simply used 'idea' for Royce's 'internal meaning of an idea' and 'object' or 'referent' for his 'external meaning of an idea'. He often writes this way himself.

We ascertain an idea's truth by comparing it to the object that "the idea itself means, selects, views with attentive expectation, [or] determines as its own object." My assertion about Caesar is not wrong simply because it does not refer to Napoleon; nor is it incorrect to assert that space has three dimensions because time has only one.[27] To understand how an idea refers to an object, we must invoke intention. We also need that notion, Royce adds, if we are to grasp the *manner* in which an idea will correspond to its referent. Correspondence does not mean similarity in any literal sense. A photograph may look like a man, but an algebraic equation does not resemble a geometric figure; yet both ideas may correspond to their respective objects. Correspondence depends on the possession "of some system of ideally definable characters that is common to both of them [idea and object], that is, for the purposes of our thought, the same in both of them, and that is such as to meet the systematic purpose for which the particular correspondence is established." We can explain the correspondence between idea and referent only in terms of purpose—the idea is true if it corresponds to its referent in the way the idea intends. He summarizes his position in a passage using a striking metaphor:

> Ideas are like tools. They are there for an end. They are true, as the tools are good, precisely by reason of their adjustment to this end. To ask me which of two ideas is the more nearly true, is like asking me which of two tools is the better tool. The question is a sensible one if the purpose in mind is specific, but not otherwise. One razor can be superior to another. But let a man ask, Is a razor a better or worse tool than a hammer? Is a steam-engine a better mechanism than a loom? Such questions are obviously vain, just because they suggest that there is some one purely abstract test of the value of any or all tools, or some one tool that, if you had it, would be good apart from any specific use. Yet there are philosophers who ask, and even suppose themselves to answer, questions about the truth of ideas that are just as vain as this.[28]

Royce has indicated two ways in which teleological concerns enter into any analysis of ideas and referents:

> if it [an idea] means to be true, it intends a sort of correspondence with an object. What correspondence it intends is determined, as

we saw, solely by the purpose which the idea embodies, i.e., by the internal meaning of the idea. Furthermore, the idea intends to attain this correspondence to some particular object,—not to any object you please, not to whatever happens to correspond to the ideal construction in question, but to a determined object. The determination of what object is meant, is, therefore, certainly again due, in one aspect, to the internal meaning of the idea. Nobody else can determine for me what object I mean by my idea.

As was the case in *The Religious Aspect of Philosophy*, he faces "the central dilemma" of epistemology. Despite what he has said, our ideas cannot entirely determine the correspondence of their referent to them. If that occurred, "truth would be mere tautology, error would be excluded in advance, and it would be useless even to talk of an object external in any sense to the idea."[29]

What follows is inevitable: the dialectical argument, now in pragmatic form; and it is helpful to put this conception in a wider context. In imitating we acquire knowledge of the world of external objects, the World of Description; just so—with the pragmatic quality of the position made explicit—our ideas (plans of action) enable us to deal with a world of objects. The internal meanings of true ideas will "correspond" with their external meanings. But Royce also argues that the World of Description logically presupposes the World of Appreciation, the world of the self. He now shows that we understand the external meaning of ideas through their internal meanings, the purposive quality expressed by the World of Appreciation: the world of objects is a realm of fulfilled purpose where willing and being are one.

Although the formulation is different, Royce's intent is the same—to reduce the World of Description to the World of Appreciation. And the structure of the argument does not change although the setting in which it occurs allows him to make an advance in describing the metaphysical structure of the world. The only novelty is the historical framework into which the argument is put. Volume one of *The World and the Individual* investigates four historical conceptions of being. Realism—a doctrine never held in its purity by any first-rate thinkers[30]—defines the real as independently existing objects. It represents the view of those who are mistakenly satisfied with the World of Description;

and Royce finds it deficient for reasons that are apparent in his work.
The diametric opposite of Realism is Mysticism—the view that what is
real immediately fulfills the purpose of ideas—and Royce displays great
sympathy for it. But in concentrating on appreciation to the exclusion of
description, mysticism cannot account for finite activity; it cannot give
any explanation of the domain of natural science. There is adequate
discussion of Royce's notion of these philosophies and his argument
against them, and I will not elaborate on them further. His "Third Conception of Being" is of greater significance, and I shall consider it in
the next chapter. This view, which he calls Critical Rationalism, asserts
that the real is what possible experience verifies, and he passes over the
"Fourth Conception of Being"—his conception—only after analyzing the
limitations of "possible experience." The fourth conception is important
here.

If an idea selects its referent and determines the correspondence of
idea and referent, how, Royce has asked, are error and nontautologous
knowledge conceivable? The answer guarantees the truth of his position:
they are conceivable only if the referent fully embodies the purpose which
the idea imperfectly and partially fulfills and if both idea and object
are part of a conscious whole. The dialectical argument assures this,
although the result is not absolute thought. The external meaning of an
idea is the "fully determinate" purpose of the "fragmentary" internal
meaning:

> the finally determinate form of the object of any finite idea is that
> form which *the idea itself would assume whenever it became in-
> dividuated, or in other words, became a completely determined
> idea, an idea or will fulfilled by a wholly adequate empirical con-
> tent, for which no other content need be substituted or, from the
> point of view of the satisfied idea, could be substituted. . . .* were
> not only some, but all possible, instances that could illustrate your
> idea, or that could give it embodiment, now present, even at this
> very instant, and to your clear consciousness, what would you ex-
> perience? I answer, first, *the complete fulfilment of your internal
> meaning,* the final satisfaction of the will embodied in the idea; but
> secondly, also, *that absolute determination of the embodiment of*

> *your ideas as this embodiment would then be present,—that abso-*
> *lute determination of your purpose, which would constitute an in-*
> *dividual realization of the idea.*[31]

Objects are ideas of the Absolute, that appreciative realm where ideas possess complete internal meanings only, and realize true purposes just as our (finite) internal meanings realize instantaneous purposes:[32]

> just what the internal meaning already imperfectly but consciously
> is, namely, purpose relatively fulfilled, just that, and nothing else,
> the apparently external meaning when truly comprehended also
> proves to be, namely the entire expression of the very Will that is
> fragmentarily embodied in the life of the flying conscious idea,—
> the fulfilment of the very aim that is hinted in the instant. Or, in
> other words, we are to assert that, in the case mentioned, the artist
> who composed, the beloved who sang the melody, are in verity
> present, as truly implied aspects of meaning and as fulfilling a pur-
> pose, in the completely developed internal meaning of the very idea
> [of the melody] that now, in its finitude, seems to view them merely
> as absent.[33]

Imagining a melody fulfills my instantaneous purpose to imagine the melody; likewise the moment of the Divine expresses and realizes an infinite purpose which from our perspective is the world of objects which our ideas seek to know. The proof of Royce's position is the same one he had used for fifteen years, but its detailed formulation describes more clearly the "conscious whole" of which we are a part.

When Royce introduced will in *The Conception of God,* he empha-sized it to indicate how finite selves can be free. As individuals, a unique quality characterizes finite selves, and this quality *ipso facto* is not subject to causal determination. But volition defines uniqueness and individu-ality: finite selves are the product of the Absolute's exclusive interest—another phrase for its selective attention or willing. In *The World and the Individual* the volitional plays a wider role, and individuality loses its moral connotation. The objects to which ideas refer are individuals, for they are creations of the Absolute's selective attention. Moreover, there is another criterion of individuality: these creations of ultimate

attention will be fully determinate. We would not be able to attribute to
them further content, verifiable as possible experience. Our imperfect
notion of individuality is based on our decisions to regard something as
"like no other," and

> . . . this disposition of our finite will, this tendency to a selection
> of our objects as unique, is precisely the character which our
> Fourth Conception regards as also belonging to that Absolute Will
> which faces the final meaning and fulfilment of the world. For the
> world as a whole is, from our point of view, an individual fact, not
> merely by virtue of the completeness of the contents of the Absolute
> Experience, but by reason of the definiteness of the selection of that
> object which shall be permitted to fulfil the final meaning. No sig-
> nificant purpose, no element of meaning that finite ideas demand
> as necessary for their own fulfilment, could indeed be, according to
> our thesis, wholly ignored from the absolute point of view. But, on
> the other hand, the very perfection of the fulfilment would logically
> require of the divine will the sort of determination of purpose of
> which we too are conscious when we deal with the objects of the
> exclusive affection.[34]

It is never clear how these two criteria are related, and they may have
been one for Royce, but with the dual notion of individuality he isolates
the way the Absolute itself is individual.

Objects or ideas of the Absolute do not exist as independent collections of finite ideas. They are parts of the system of ideas constituting
the Absolute. When a finite idea seeks its object, it ultimately seeks the
completed purpose which is the Absolute. But a system of fulfilled purposes is definitive of a life, and Royce calls his Absolute an individual
life, a union of more or less fragmentary individual lives. It is a whole
in which all ideas are satisfied, just as in a less complete way its ideas—
our objects—are systematic wholes.[35] We regard these objects as a limit
which our ideas seek. We test them by a never-ending process of verification through experience, and our ideas become "more determinate": we
become more sure that they are true and that they adequately describe
their object. If we could reach the "limit of determination" so that no further experience were possible, we would stand in the presence of the real:

the real is the series of actual and possible verifications, plus what is immediately beyond this series of efforts to bring "our own internal meaning to a complete determination."[36]

On Royce's view no finite idea is entirely false or entirely true; the purposes which these ideas embody are fulfilled insofar as our purposes are those of the Absolute, and insofar as our will is its will. In his discussion of what he calls "the Theoretical Ought" Royce turns to the way this occurs in our learning about the world. As rational beings, we do not conjure up whatever ideas strike our fancy. We recognize facts which are relatively external to our wills, to whatever ideas we have. A fact is *"that which I ought to recognise* as determining or limiting what I am here consciously to do or attempt." We acknowledge facts because we better fulfill our rational purposes if we do; our plans succeed and we verify ideas. But no instant gives this world of facts: it is defined by our consciousness that only certain future behavior will allows us rightly to express our wills. Royce calls this consciousness the Theoretical Ought: the consciousness that acknowledging what is foreign to us really serves present purposes. Consider the antithesis between will and wish exemplified by our wish to cross a bridge ignorant of its imminent collapse, and our will *not* to after being informed of the bridge's state. Our real purpose is to remain alive, but ignorance prevents us from immediately recognizing this purpose. For Royce our finitude causes our ignorance and the world appears to constrain us. But the realm of fact is only our purposes completely determined; we experience our will to be compelled by the facts.[37] Our finite purposes are the fragmentary expression of the world purpose, and acknowledgment of the Theoretical Ought is partial recognition of this fact. When we describe the world, we classify and explain the interrelations of objects so that our ideas about them will be true. That activity which Royce calls "imitation" defines this Theoretical Ought further; imitation defines what we acknowledge if our purposes will be served, what our embodied purposes are:[38]

> The true problem about the objective validity of my classifications [in the World of Description] is then the problem of the Ought . . . here considered with reference to the question, What ought to be

regarded as different or distinct, and what as equivalent, and in what respect? This is a teleological problem. It is to be solved, if at all, upon the ground of a consideration of the relation of this moment's passing purpose to the whole world-purpose of which it is a hint and a fragment. God distinguishes what it pleases him to distinguish. The logical as well as the moral problem is, Does my will accord with God's will?[39]

Royce still does not tell us why the World of Appreciation appears as a world of independently existing objects when we attempt to classify and distinguish its contents. As I shall explain later, he does offer a mathematical account of the relationship of the two worlds, but it is not apparent why, as fragments of a universal purpose, we perceive the world as one of external things. We only know that this world is an aspect of the World of Appreciation, and Royce's arguments on this point are those of his former work.

The World of Description is bound up with our belief in our fellows; we define it as what is known or as knowable to various men. There is nothing new in this position, although Royce illustrates it in a convincing way:

> Suppose that I told you that I was well acquainted with the existence and the properties of a material object which I had now and here before me. Suppose that I assured you that I could see, touch, weigh, and otherwise test the reality of this material object, but that I was quite sure that neither you nor any other man could conceivably see it or touch it, or otherwise get the least experience of its presence. Suppose, as a fact, that nobody else ever did verify my report; but that I continued to insist upon the reality, observable for me, of my material object. What would you say of that object of mine? The answer is plain. You would say that my object might indeed be real, but was real solely as a physical phenomenon, to wit, as a collection of states in my mind, in other words, as a certain fixed hallucination of mine.[40]

The mental world of the illustration above—normally the world of the individual self—is the World of Appreciation, and our belief in it is "logically prior" to our belief in the World of Description.[41] In effect, we have previously assumed other minds in order to justify this latter belief but we now have a more complete argument for their existence. From a psychological standpoint our self-consciousness is the product of social contrasts, while our consciousness of others even *precedes* self-consciousness.[42] From a philosophical standpoint we are faced with ideas which we cannot explain as our ideas. We suppose that they indicate the presence of other minds; other minds are constructs which explain what would otherwise be inexplicable:

> Our fellows are known to be real, and to have their own inner life, because they are for each of us the endless treasury of *more ideas*. They answer our questions; they tell us news; they make comments; they pass judgments; they express novel combinations of feelings; they relate to us stories; they argue with us, and take counsel with us.[43]

In metaphysical terms, since my fellows supplement my ideas, they supplement my fragmentary purposes. But just what helps to complete my finite purposes is truly real and has an appreciative reality.

There are three further conceptions which we must develop to finish this outline of *The World and the Individual*, and in deference to their ethical dimension and to Royce's Kantianism, I will discuss them under the headings of God, Freedom, and Immortality.

Our temporal form of experience is volitional. Our experience of change, of passing from a certain state toward a desired fulfillment or in search of fulfillment, is central to time. We are never content in the present so long as we view it as temporal, as an event in a series; this present has its meaning as a transition from its predecessors toward its successors. Because our experience of time is an experience of longing, pursuit, restlessness, its central facet is practical activity which Royce identifies with volition. Temporal experience, he says, is "the form of the Will as such."[44]

There are two senses in which we experience the consciousness of change which constitutes temporality. On the one hand, each event in a series has a direction: the succession passes from each event to its suc-

cessor. Events are in the past, present, or future. On the other hand, we
may view a series of events *at once*. We recognize the unity of the series
as well as distinguishing the order within it. Again a musical example is
helpful:[45]

> Whoever listens appreciatively to a melody, or to a sequence of
> chords of music, or even to a mere rhythm of drum-taps, or to the
> words of a speaker, has a twofold consciousness as to the way in
> which the facts to which he listens are *present* to him. (1) *Each*
> tone, or chord, or drum-tap, or spoken word, is *present*, as *this*
> member of its series, in so far as it *follows* some sounds and *pre-
> cedes* others, so that when, or in so far as, in *this* sense, it is present,
> the preceding notes of the melody or taps of the rhythm are *no
> longer* or are past, while the succeeding notes are *not yet* or are
> future. In *this* sense of the term *present*, the present excludes past
> and future from its own temporal place in the sequence. (2) But
> now the appreciative listener also grasps *at once* (or, as *totum
> simul*, to use the phrase of St. Thomas) the whole of a brief but
> still considerable sequence of tones or of taps or of words. In this
> second sense he may be said to find *present* to him the whole
> sequence.[46]

The extent to which we grasp a time sequence at once is, of course,
limited and depends upon our interest, temperament, and training—but
above all on the time span of human consciousness. Royce points out that
this span is a function of attention, of our elementary voluntary activity,
and this allows him to present an explication of eternity:

> a consciousness whose span embraces the *whole of time* is precisely
> what I mean by the term *Eternal Consciousness*. And what is pres-
> ent *at once* to such a consciousness, viz., the whole of what happens
> in time, taken together with all the distinctions of past and of future
> that hold *within* the series of temporal events,—this whole, I say
> constitutes *Eternity*.[47]

We grasp at once a brief sequence of temporal events and hold them in
consciousness without losing sight of the fact that they *are* a sequence;
similarly the Absolute grasps all of time at once, as a *totum simul*. The
world is present to it as one idea, yet *all* the time elements are present

with "perfect clearness" without losing their variety. For God the past, present, and future are viewed at once, yet they are distinct.[48]

The Absolute expresses a single Internal Meaning, but an Internal Meaning which seeks no object but is its own object. Its expression of purpose simultaneously defines being, and while temporal succession for us is an expression of will, the temporal experience of the Absolute expresses *both* being and will.[49]

This analysis provides Royce with an answer to those who argue that his God denies freedom. For his God is not pre-existent to man, a Being who foresees the future. This conception presupposes that a world in time is real beyond God and that temporal events occur *after* his foreknowing. But Royce's God "foreknows" only to the extent that He is expressed in finite beings, i.e., God's "foreknowledge" is no more than the foreknowledge that each of us may possess:

> God, viewed in his wholeness, does not *now* foreknow anything if by *now* you mean merely *today* or *at this moment*. For whoever *now* looks forward to the future merely as *not yet*, is a finite being, temporally determined, and not yet come to his own fulfilment in God. Divine knowledge of what to us is future is no mere foreknowledge. It is eternal knowledge.[50]

To this conception Royce adds his argument for the freedom of finite individuals. Causality is a notion belonging to the World of Description, and applies only to types of behavior, to objects so far as they are put into general classes. Everything about me expressible in general terms or capable of observation, we can and must explain causally—as due to ancestry, training, circumstances, environment, or dependence upon nature.[51] But as individuals we are unique—products of the Absolute's exclusive interest. Although we are not complete individuals, in our uniqueness we possess characteristics which no other possesses. To the extent that our deeds express an individual ideal or way of life, our lives are causally undetermined. Just that aspect of our future will be free and belong to us alone; even God temporally knows it only when our unique individuality *furnishes* this aspect as facts in time.[52] As a unique creature, my will is my own expression.[53]

This concept of God and His relation to man solves two ethical problems. On the negative side Royce denies God's foreknowledge. Because God is not "in time," he does not foresee or predict. On the positive side Royce asserts that the selective attention which defines the Absolute guarantees human freedom. Insofar as we are unique fragments of God's will we are not subject to causal determination. We resolve these dilemmas from a dual perspective:

> The knowledge that exists in time is the knowledge that finite selves possess, in so far as they are finite. And no such foreknowledge can predict the special feature of individual deeds precisely in so far as they are unique. Foreknowledge in time is possible only of the general, and of the causally predetermined, and not of the unique and the free. Hence neither God nor man can perfectly foreknow, at any temporal moment, what a free-will agent is yet to do. On the other hand, the Absolute *possesses a perfect knowledge at one glance of the whole of the temporal order, present, past, and future.* This knowledge is ill-called foreknowledge. It is eternal knowledge. And as there is an eternal knowledge of all individuality, and of all freedom, free acts are known as occurring like the chords in the musical succession, precisely when and how they actually occur.[54]

Royce's conception of God also allows him to develop a notion of immortality, although it is not a traditional one. The Absolute is *the* one complete life; Royce associates it with the real self; and he expresses this idea in *The World and the Individual* by saying that God is a person:

> A Person is a conscious being, whose life, temporally viewed, seeks its completion through deeds, while this same life, eternally viewed, consciously attains its perfection by means of the present knowledge of the whole of its temporal strivings. Now from our point of view, God is a Person. Temporally viewed, his life is that of the entire realm of consciousness in so far as, in its temporal efforts towards perfection, this consciousness of the universe passes from instant to instant of the temporal order, from act to act, from experience to experience, from stage to stage. Eternally viewed, however, God's life is the finite whole that includes this endless temporal process, and that consciously surveys it as one life, God's own life.[55]

The personality of God is identical to the conception of the Absolute as fulfilled purpose, as a single idea. Within this "person" we exist as partial persons. Just as phenomenal behavior is a sign of our personality, an appreciative reality, so too the physical world is an expression of the spiritual character of a larger personality. We cannot speculate on this since we have no knowledge of the "purposes" of large spatio-temporal segments of the universe, but Royce does expand on the cosmology he put forward in the nineties. As he argued before, we face a world of lives, conscious selves—subsystems of the Absolute—with whom we cannot communicate because their mental processes go on at different time-rates from ours and because we cannot adjust to a "live appreciation of their inward fluency."[56]

The novelty is his view of man's place in these subsystems. We have called them *selves,* and according to Royce they are precisely that: a meaning or purpose embodied in a conscious life present as a relative whole.[57] We could assert that the internal meaning of an idea represents a self—since it too expresses purpose, however imperfectly—but it is more illuminating to begin with human selves. We have a type of individual aware of the world but always more or less unclear of its will and plans of action. Because they are finite, these selves find a place *within* the life of a larger and more inclusive self. We hypothesize that the consciousness we illustrate arises out of a consciousness whose "temporal span" is different from our own. We again give evolution an interpretation consistent with idealism: a new individual—expressing the self-hood of a single man, or a finite individual representative of the self-hood of the race—is simply a new kind of embodied purpose. It will indicate a "new type of interest in the world, in God, and in finding the way to self-expression."[58] And Royce concludes that inasmuch as the origin of humanity consists in the differentiation of our experience from that with a different time span, the death of individuals and the extinction of the race consist in other changes of time span. Death is not a relapse into unconscious Nature, but a change in time span in the life involved.[59] In God—in terms of the whole of time—each of us possesses a different consciousness than "this our present flickering form of mortal consciousness."[60] As a fragmentary but greater part of the eternal world, my larger individuality is continuous with that which dies. Even this self-hood becomes one with the "Divine Selfhood." Although the consciousness that I know is transformed in God, it is never annihilated.[61] But as a finite being I never understand how my life continues in that of another, and in this sense, although in this sense alone, death is possible and will always be a mystery. And so Royce asserts at the end of *The Conception of Immortality*:

> I know not in the least, I pretend not to guess, by what processes this individuality of our human life is further expressed. . . . I know only that our various meanings . . . consciously come to what we individually, and God in whom alone we are individuals, shall together regard as the attainment of our unique place, and of our true relationships both to other individuals and to the all inclusive Individual, God himself.[62]

Because there is no specific evidence, I am hesitant to assert that Hegel and the other post-Kantians "influenced" Royce in the sense that Kant did, i.e., in the sense that Royce consciously and explicitly sought to solve the problems the first *Critique* generated. Nonetheless, Royce's Absolute is similar to that which the German idealists constructed. At the very least, I think Royce absorbed from them strategies concerning *how* to solve Kantian problems. Although he moved away from these formulations, his Absolute is close to his notion of Hegel's concrete universal. This was identical to an infinite individual, that is, Royce argues, a completely self-determined individual.[63] Hegel's Absolute Being is also a unity of theoretical and practical consciousness.[64] Most importantly, Royce asserts that finite human beings are "fragments" or "parts" of his Absolute. For Hegel, similarly—or so Royce claims—the world of facts does not exemplify the ideas which refer to it; these facts are combined into one whole which is the absolute *Idee*. This universal is *concrete* for it does not exist apart from the facts comprising it, and they are only facts so far as they are its parts.[65]

6

ABSOLUTE PRAGMATISM
1899–1913

After the publication of *The Religious Aspect of Philosophy* Royce suppressed the pragmatism of his youthful writings, and this facet of his thought only fully reappeared in the Gifford Lectures. Thereafter, he explicitly noted the relation of pragmatism to idealism and the connection of both to "Kantianism."[1] I agree with this appraisal, but whatever judgment we make, the evaluation is true if we examine Royce's philosophy. *The World and the Individual* contained an explication of the more familiar pragmatic position and led Royce to develop what he called *absolute* pragmatism. Finally, he approached the distinction between James's views and his own by grappling with the problem of possible experience which has been important for more recent American pragmatists.

In the first volume of *The World and the Individual* Royce devotes careful analysis to "the Third Conception of Being" which he feels is a partially adequate account of the real.[2] This philosophy defines reality as what "under conditions . . . would become knowable and known."[3] The real is what we do experience, will experience, and would experience, given that certain conditions are met. External objects exist as objects of possible experience; they are independent of private individuality but not of "the constitution of our experience."[4] Although many of its adherents might ignore or not recognize their inheritance, Royce traces this ontology back to Kant.[5] He does not mention James, but I am sure that Jamesean pragmatism is one of the targets of Royce's arguments. This

119

becomes apparent when he criticizes the position, which he also calls Critical Rationalism, "in one of its most recent forms."[6]

Exponents of this view believe that the real is what, "if present, would satisfy or tend to satisfy our conscious needs and meanings." The stress on "conscious needs and meanings" is evidence that Royce has James in mind. But Royce also casts his description in neutral language: "To be is precisely to fulfil or to give warrant to ideas by making possible the experience that the ideas define."[7] For an idea to be true is for that idea to lead to experiences that verify the expectations which accepting the idea entails. If I sincerely say 'The cat is on the mat', I believe that if I walk into the living room, I will see the cat on the mat. If the cat is on the mat, then I can verify this fact by walking into the room and having my expectations warranted. The Third Conception of Being defines what is real as the possible experiences which make my ideas true or false or, as Royce puts it, valid or invalid. To say that something is real, for example, the cat on the mat, is to say that if we behave in certain ways, under certain circumstances certain consequences will eventuate, for example, that I will see the cat. The real world is no thing in itself; but we also cannot construe it in terms of capricious, momentary, actual experiences; the real is beyond any particular experience, and we must characterize it in terms of well-defined possible experiences:

> You will, under given conditions, see certain sights, hear certain words, touch certain tangible objects—in brief, get the presence of certain empirical facts. This is all that you can find involved in very many of your statements about the Being of social and of physical realities. Having defined such ideas of possible experience, you then test them. If the result conforms to the expectation, you are so far content. You have then communed with Being.[8]

Some of the thinkers who espouse this view are scientists or may be narrow empiricists in their philosophy. But Royce notes that many condemn only "theoretical construction" in religion and are satisfied with "a reasonable and chastened moral faith." They believe that we must treat objects *"as if they were* finally real"; the "as if" or "as it were" becomes an ultimate category. Consequently, we no longer *prove*

that God exists but argue only that *"It is as if he were."* The Critical
Rationalist may still warrant "An impersonal conception of a Righteous
Order of the Universe."[9]

Whatever the religious proclivities of the Critical Rationalist,
Royce quickly points up a tenet of the doctrine which calls for further
discussion:

> there are countless possible experiences that you never test, and
> that you still view as belonging to the realm of physical and of so-
> cial validity. In fact, just when you express your own contentment
> with your tests, you transcend what you have actually succeeded in
> getting present to your experience. . . . The prices and credits of
> the commercial world involve far more numerous types of valid
> possible experience than any prudent merchant cares to test; for, if
> these facts are valid as they are conceived, their very Being in-
> cludes possibilities of unwise investment and of bankruptcy, which
> the prudent business man recognizes only to avoid. In fact, since
> our whole voluntary life is selective, we all the time recognize pos-
> sibilities of experience only to shun the testing of them.[10]

The Critical Rationalists' world of possible experience has a twofold
character. We verify its reality by testing our ideas about it from moment
to moment. But our belief in it recognizes that it possesses far more
"validity"—possible experience verifiable under proper conditions—than
we can test in our private capacity. Because of these peculiarities, the
Third Conception faces two problems which Royce often examines in
the ensuing years. The first concerns how the Critical Rationalist uses the
experiences of others which he never experiences. The reality of the
world consists of the experiences which confirm our ideas, but we see
this reality as independent of the experiences of any one of us. If we are
Critical Rationalists, we must find a way of using the experience of
others. This presents a *prima facie* problem because we have defined the
real in terms of possible experience, and are "given" no experience but
our own.

Royce also hits on a second significant problem. In addition to
using the sum of experiences of all human knowers, the Critical Rationalist must account for "possible experience" which no human being ex-

periences. What is the status of the cat on the mat when no one is experiencing it? In his own way Royce is analyzing a crucial philosophical problem. The empiricist tradition in Great Britain from Berkeley and Hume to Mill, and to Russell and Ayer, has struggled to construct an account of the world from a phenomenalistic basis. Royce's statement of the question and his answer are a contribution to a similar dialogue in the history of American philosophy. Peirce's attempts to deal with "unactualized possibilities" are well known; less so, perhaps, are those of the Harvard tradition after James and Royce—that of C. I. Lewis, Nelson Goodman, and Willard Quine—which has investigated the problems of modality and possibility.[11] We can interpret the dispute between James and Royce, between pragmatism and Absolute Pragmatism, pluralistic idealism and absolute idealism, as a debate about the notion of possible experience.

In *The World and the Individual* Royce examines both the issues connected with possible experience: the use to be made of the actual experiences of all human beings and the status of possible experience. We shall examine the latter first.

The Critical Rationalist must hold that some possible experience is *valid;* it will be different from the "fantastically" possible, or what is possible under absurd conditions. If I were to go into the living room, I can conceive that I might see pink elephants; if my home were a psychedelic zoo, I might find pink elephants in my living room. But these possibilities have a different status from "the determinately possible"— "that which would be observed or verified under exactly stateable, even if physically inaccessible conditions." We recognize the latter as "really valid and objective physical characters."[12] The Critical Rationalist must relate "valid" possible experience to actual experience in a way that the fantastically and absurdly possible is not related. Nonetheless, both the validly possible and what Royce calls the barely possible are unactualized kinds of experience, and Critical Rationalists have treated them similarly, if they have treated them at all. Royce contends that these philosophers construe all possibilities as "barely possible"; and although he does not define the "barely possible" further, his point is that the Critical Ration-

alists do not distinguish valid from fantastic or absurd possibilities. But
this view cannot be correct, for we conceive the valid possibilities to be
"real" in much the same way as actual experience is real; and it is clear
that Royce's analysis of the connection of valid possibility to the actual
is at work. Unlike Critical Rationalism, an adequate philosophy must
distinguish between the barely and validly possible, and must link the
latter to the actual. But at this point Royce's argument is destructive; he
has not yet advanced a solution:

> What our Third Conception so far fails to explain to us is precisely
> the difference between the reality that is to be attributed to the valid
> truths that we do not get concretely verified in our own experience,
> and the reality observed by us when we do verify ideas. In brief,
> *what is a valid or a determinately possible experience at the mo-*
> *ment when it is supposed to be only possible?* What is a valid truth
> at the moment when nobody verifies its validity?[13]

Royce's answer should come as no surprise. He had solved it in
"The Possibility of Error," and never wavered in his belief that *that*
argument settled the issue. The "valid" possible experiences *are* actual—
they are parts of the experience of the Absolute, as our actual experiences
are parts of this complete experience—while the barely possible are non-
existent. Although the Fourth Conception of Being sets forth this position, Royce's critique of Critical Rationalism only concludes that the
Third Conception is indefensible. But we can indicate its relation to absolute idealism.

We construe our ideas as fulfillments of purpose. Yet we know that
their fulfillment is incomplete, and if an idea is true, it is correct to say
that "certain further experience of the fulfillment of the idea is possible."
The real object which these possible experiences define is incompletely
defined; from Royce's perspective this means that the Critical Rationalist
never isolates any object as an individual object: its fully determinate
nature is ahead of us in possible experience, of what would happen if we
were to do thus-and-such. But since Critical Rationalists assume that
"valid" possibilities and "fantastic" ones have the same status, these
philosophers cannot state why just the *valid* possibilities define an object.

If all possible experience has the same status, they cannot characterize any object as "fully determinate."[14] Not only does Critical Rationalism neglect to analyze possibility, but it also fails to account for the individuality of our world of objects. The deficiencies in the Third Conception of Being lead us to an idea of the real which embodies more than our finite ideas ever give and which defines individuality in its uniqueness.

If Royce was first to see that the issue between him and James hinged on their doctrines of possible experience, James was not far behind. When he discusses the difference between monism and pluralism in his *Pragmatism,* he urges that "The whole clash of rationalistic and empirical religion is thus over the validity of possibility."[15] Just how he could resolve this clash in his favor, James was unsure. Long an admirer of Royce's dialectic, the older man had freed himself from a commitment to his younger colleague's idealism. But in James's work there is an idealistic strain which reveals itself in his conception of possible experience.

He describes his radical empiricism as a doctrine which allows into its constructions those and only those elements which some experiencer directly experiences. Truth does not consist in a relation between our experiences and something trans-experiential. So far, James is an "idealist." He even urges that the *Identitätsphilosophie* of post-Kantian idealism is akin to radical empiricism. He offers "a new *Identitätsphilosophie* in pluralistic form"; his pure experiences are "so many little absolutes."[16] But if James were this much an idealist, he could not subscribe to a monistic variety of the position. When Royce raised the question of possible experience, James was sure of what answer he could not accept, but it was difficult for him to meet Royce on logical grounds. The closest James came to confronting his colleague with a formidable argument occurred a few months before publication of volume one of *The World and the Individual* and the attack on Critical Rationalism.

James wrote to Royce that the idealistic principle demands only that where there is no knowing, there is no fact, i.e., no experience, and that so far as we find experience we find knowing. When Royce speaks of "valid" possible experience, he ignores this idealistic principle: he ac-

cepts experience which is assumed unknown. Then he concludes that because we accept this experience, it cannot be unknown and must be
known by the Absolute. All that we need to commit ourselves to is that
"if a thing can't be shown to be a fact [i.e., experience] for any finite
consciousness, it is no fact at all." Royce should not consider "valid"
possible experience; for the idealist it is an unintelligible realm:

> Behind the first knowing actually found, Royce says that you need
> a second knowing to account for the fact [i.e., experience] that it is
> found. But whose is this second knowing? It is that of us critics
> who discuss the first. We then are the second knower, not the Ab-
> solute; and so long as nobody discusses us and knows us as such
> knowers, there is no higher knower in the field. If, later, we proceed
> to talk about the "fact" of our second knowing, then we should be
> third knowers, and so on ad infinitum, but no Absolute Knower
> would ever logically be required.

James comes close to confronting the problem in a sophisticated
form. The question is one of "translating" our talk of possible experience
into ontologically less mischievous language. James hints that we should
not speak of new, non-actual entities at all, but say something new about
old actual entities. We should attempt to define the possible in terms of
relations among the actual; we take the difficult step of constructing the
world in terms of actual "sense data." In what respect, James asks, can
you call an actual egg a "possible chicken"?

> "Possible chicken" is only one way of naming "actual egg," by a
> mind that considers present and future things together. If there be
> no such mind, then there is no status for the possibility as such.
> We have no business to say, with Professor Royce, that since for us
> discussing critics the possibility is objectively there, the Absolute
> Mind must be there to support it. What is there in the universe it-
> self apart from us, is the egg—nothing more—and later, the
> chicken; distinct facts which may perfectly well be realized in suc-
> cessive steps, each one of which may be a fresh surprise to the
> learner.[17]

Unfortunately, as many have pointed out, James was not a
philosopher who worked out insights. This suggestion that we construct the possible from the actual remained just that—a suggestion.

More frequently than not, James avoided the work that an argument with Royce would have entailed. His interest in epistemological debate *per se* waned, and he defended his ideas on broader, more popular grounds. To the extent that he broached the problem of possible experience, he was content to flirt with panpsychism: the "valid" possibilities never experienced by some organism—human or animal—could perhaps be said to be self-conscious.[18]

Whatever argument James might have made to connect actual to possible experience, he would not have silenced Royce. In *The World and the Individual* and in the years after its publication, Royce frequently attacked pragmatism's or Critical Rationalism's notion of truth so far as it was stated in terms of *actual* experience. Let us, Royce says in effect, forget about the problems of possible experience. Suppose pragmatism defines truth in terms of actual human experiences. The other fault in Jamesean pragmatism is its inability, Royce claims, to give this kind of definition.[19]

Royce's first argument along these lines is one that others made; it criticizes James for stressing the individual aspects in his analysis. Royce presents this account in his popular *Philosophy of Loyalty* and in the book singles out James as well as relating him to Kant and the idealistic tradition.

Royce concedes the extent of his agreement with James. The assertion of truth is a deed, "a practical attitude, an active acknowledgement. . . . the effort to verify this acknowledgement by one's own personal experience and the attempt to find truth in the form of practical congruity between our assertions and our attained empirical results, is an effort which in our individual lives inevitably accompanies and sustains our every undertaking in the cause of truth seeking." Royce declares that "all search for truth is a practical activity, with an ethical purpose . . . a purely theoretical truth, such as should guide no significant active process, is a barren absurdity." An idea is true if it is practically and genuinely successful; but can we define 'success' in terms of what is successful *for an individual?* Suppose a man is indebted in a secret fashion to someone dead, and suppose he testifies about the estate of the deceased. We don't need to ask what this man's moral duty is, but simply "what it is that he rationally means to do in case he really intends to tell the truth. . . ." The man is not trying to predict the consequences which he expects to result from his testimony; nor will the truth of his statement be equivalent to the expediency or success of the consequences—either to himself or others—that may follow the statement; nor is the statement's truth defined by his belief in the statement or its congruence with his present memories.*

When we assert that something is true, we mean something different from all of the above, and Royce states his criticism in a provocative form. If 'true' means 'expedient', then it is redundant to ask 'That's expedient but is it true?' But this question is *not* redundant; to designate a belief as expedient is to give "just a scrap of your personal biography."[20] The view that we can define 'truth' in these terms defines what "we all alike regard as the attitude of one who chooses *not* to tell the truth." The contrast between James's doctrine and an adequate theory "is not between intellectualism and pragmatism. It is the contrast between two well-known attitudes of will—the will that is loyal to truth as an universal ideal—and the will that is concerned with its own passing caprices."[21]

However crudely and dramatically James sometimes stated his theory, this criticism, as Royce himself realized, was equally crude.[22] James could be more ingenious in espousing his position, and Royce used his most formidable analysis against this defense. Not surprisingly it relied on a dialectical argument.

A sympathetic account of James stresses that true statements are not merely verified by an individual; they are statements that others will or would verify; and we believe some statements are true because we assume that although they are not verifiable now, they will be so "in the long run." This formulation raises many of the problems in-

---

* Note that these are all themes Royce himself expressed in the late seventies and early eighties, and rejected by 1885.

volved in the Critical Rationalists' account of possible experience, but Royce takes a different turn. He previously emphasized that we did not verify some "possible experience", although we might have. Now he concentrates on another issue: what is the status of those truths, or rather those statements, which are theoretically unverifiable, which it is logically impossible for a human knower to verify, given our present conception of a human knower? James says that we accept the verifications of others. Does the totality of the experiences of many men then exist? If so, how, on pragmatic grounds, can we claim *that* statement true? James says a statement may be true because we assume it verifiable in the long run. Will "the long run" then verify a statement? If so, how, on pragmatic grounds, are we able to claim *that* statement true? Royce contends that if pragmatism is a correct doctrine, these statements must be true, but that on Jamesean grounds we can never warrant their truth.[23]

Examine the following assertion: 'The testing of ideas by the course of experience as pragmatism presupposes actually takes place'. Suppose it is true; if pragmatism is an adequate position the statement should be verified or verifiable. Yet it is logically impossible for any individual or group of individuals to verify the statement or for it to be verifiable for human individuals or groups of them. Royce assumes that it is improper to call an experience verifiable if it is *inconceivable* that anyone would verify it. We are not dealing with unactualized possibilities that someone could verify, like the cat in the living room, but with possible experience that no human knower could have. No man experiences the experience of anyone but himself; he cannot verify the experiences of *others;* nor can he now verify that he has verified something in the past or will do so in the future:

> Any statement like the above may be regarded with scepticism, since it is, for human beings, unverifiable. Nobody experiences, in his own person or at any time, the identity of the ideas, meanings, expectations, of yesterday and today, of himself and of another person. . . . One may, in each special case, doubt, therefore, whether the idea formed yesterday is the same in meaning as the idea tested

today, whether two men mean the same by the hypotheses which they are trying to verify together, and so on.[24]

Our unverifiable statement above must be true if pragmatism is true. We can be pragmatists only "by constantly presupposing certain assertions about experience, about the order of the interrelations, the significance, and the unity of empirical facts, to be true, although their truth is never verified and could not be verified, in James's sense of an empirical test, at any moment of our experience."[25] Royce concludes that Jamesean pragmatism accounts for how human beings *seek* truth, but it demands other truths for which it cannot account; that is, it fails as a conception of truth—a conception which only a more rigorous pragmatism can define:

> Whoever does verify the fact that the experience of many men exists, if such a verifier there be, is a super-human being, an union of the empirical lives of many men in the complex of a single experience. And if our credit of the assertion that many men exist is convertible into cash at all, that cash is not laid up where the moth and rust of our private human experience doth from moment to moment corrupt the very data that we see; but is laid up in a realm where our experiences, past, present, future, are the object of a conspectus that is not merely temporal and transient.[26]

In short, Royce accepts James's pragmatism to the extent he does because he sees its outcome as absolute idealism.

In light of these remarks Royce espoused what he called "Absolute Pragmatism." In effect, the debate with James took Royce back to an argument he had settled with himself twenty-five years before: although he changed the emphasis, his Absolute Pragmatism is not much more than the idealism of *The Religious Aspect of Philosophy*. In one sense the entire dispute was a retrogression; in terms that he had gone beyond, he is forced to reconsider his old viewpoint, and the result is curious. The logical and mathematical aspects of *The World and the Individual* which we shall consider in the next chapter were leading him into a new and different path, but because he was constrained to defend himself against James, much of Royce's pub-

lished work during the first decade of the century gives little indication that a transformation in his thought is occurring. There are hints
about his logical studies, but Absolute Pragmatism follows a well-
worn trail.

Even if James explains how men seek knowledge, in Royce's
view that explanation is epistemologically insufficient. It explains our
activity as truth-seekers only if there is a unity of experience which
it cannot explain. A correct theory of truth must elucidate *both* our
activity *and* the framework which this activity presupposes. Royce
first analyzes those truths which cannot be analyzed in pragmatic
terms:

> We never find unity present to our human experience in more than
> a fragmentary shape. We get hints of higher unity. But only the
> fragmentary unity is won at any moment of our lives. We therefore
> form ideas—very fallible ideas—of some unity of experience, an
> unity such as our idea of any science or any art or any united peo-
> ple or of any community or of any other cause, any other union of
> many human experiences in one, defines. Now, if our ideas are in
> any case indeed true, then such an unity is as a fact successfully
> experienced upon some higher level than ours, and is experienced
> in some conspectus of life which wins what we need . . . which ful-
> fils our rational will, and which has in its wholeness what we seek.[27]

Although we never experience this unity, we interpret this not as a
"defect in the truth, but as a defect in our present state of knowledge,
a limitation due to our present type of individuality."[28] Concepts such
as the objectively real world are our constructions, determined by our
desire to conform to an absolute standard, but they always go beyond
what we could verify.

Suppose we are wrong, that our constructions err:

> Then there is still real that state of facts, whatever it is, which, if
> just now known to us, would show us this falsity of our various
> special ideas. Now, only an experience, a consciousness of some
> system of contents, could show the falsity of any idea. Hence this
> real state of facts, this constitution of the genuine universe, what-

ever it is, must again be a reality precisely in so far as it is also a conspectus of facts of experience. . . . For I am in error only in case my present ideas about the true facts of the whole world of experience are out of concord with the very meaning that I myself actively try to assign to these ideas. My ideas are in any detail false, only if the very experience to which I mean to appeal, con- tains in its conspectus contents which I just now imperfectly con- ceive. In any case, then, the truth is possessed by precisely that whole of experience which I never get, but to which my colleague also inevitably appeals when he talks of the "long run," or of the experiences of humanity in general.[29]

The possibility of error still ensures the existence of the Absolute.

As we should expect, however, there is a different emphasis. Our ideas are plans of action, modes of responding to the world. We have also seen that it is contradictory to deny some statements. Some forms of thinking, that is, are reasserted in denial; and since cognition and volition are one, Royce contends that certain forms of *willing* are absolute:

what does one discover when he finds out such absolute truths? . . . what one discovers is distinctly what I must call a voluntaristic *truth*,—a truth about the creative will that thinks the truth. One discovers, namely, that our constructive processes, viewed just as activities, possess a certain absolute nature and conform to their own self-determined but for that very reason, absolute laws. . . . what one may call the pure form of willing is an absolute form, a form which sustains itself in the very effort to violate its own laws. We thus find out absolute truth, but it is absolute truth about the nature of the creative will in terms of which we conceive all truths.[30]

There is nothing new in much of this analysis, but, as we shall see, Royce is able to bring his logical investigations into his discussion. At this point he believed that the truths of mathematics are those that are reasserted in their denial. For example, consider the denial of '$pv \sim p$', and you are led to its assertion. We find in logic truths whose denial presupposes their assertion, and are therefore necessary to all thinking. Ultimately, we can get support for Absolute Pragmatism from mathematics.

Whatever the peculiarities of Royce's logical truths, for some years after 1900 he appears to have made a conventional distinction between them and empirical truths. His analysis of empirical truths in science also seems conventional, or was before long to become so in the canonization of the hypothetical-deductive method. Following Peirce, Royce defined two aspects of the inductive method, both of which presumed that we can draw a "fair sample" from given data. We begin with a hypothesis—a putatively true generalization—and take a "fair sample" of the indefinite number of consequences of this hypothesis; second, we test these consequences by observation. "This outcome of observation, repeatedly confirmed by samples fairly chosen . . . leads to the *probable* assertion . . . that one is dealing with a genuine law of nature." Although we possess absolute truths, the scientific method ensures that "your hypothesis may become very highly probable. But induction never renders it altogether certain."[31] The logical and empirical seem comfortably distinct.

But, Royce contends, "the progress of science largely depends upon still another factor"—upon the choice of what he calls "leading ideas"—and we must examine yet another pragmatic dimension of his thought.[32] A leading idea in the natural sciences is a hypothesis, but it is different from the hypotheses we test by observation and experience. Rather, a leading idea is a hypothesis that scientists use as a "guide"—it is too general to be tested by the means at any scientist's disposal, although it does determine the direction of his researches. Making clear the connection between his own work and that of Kant, Royce urges that leading ideas are regulative principles.

Like Absolute Pragmatism, leading ideas have a long history in his studies. His dissertation makes the cleavage between analytic and synthetic truths dependent on our purposes, and defines the basic principles of science as both arbitrary and irrefutable.[33] In *The Spirit of Modern Philosophy* the "axioms" of natural science come close to being synthetic a priori. That volume also argues that mathematical truths are empirical truths of a simple kind, defending the position of John Stuart Mill.[34] Twice Royce cites a biblical example to illustrate concept formation: when a viper stung Paul, the barbarians did not allow this to falsify their hypothesis that men die when bitten; they rather denied that Paul was a man.[35] In embryo "Men die when vipers sting them" is a leading idea: it is not a conceptual truth, yet experience will not falsify it. During the middle nineties he argued that the "law of contradiction" is a truth of this type. It is "neither a purely immediate truth, nor a purely immediate certainty"—as it appears to be in the later work we have discussed. Rather, the law is tied to Royce's "reflective knowledge": it is won "only by Reflection upon what we do when we think." As a "regulative and heuristic principle of method," its truth and certainty are "highly mediated results of the meaning and process of judgment."[36] About the same time Royce declared that these "fundamental ideas" encapsulate the conditions under which our *social* consciousness originated.[37] I am not sure how these notions fit into Royce's earlier philosophy, but they suggest his tenuous commitment to classic empiricist doctrines of the conceptual-empirical connection. After the turn of the century he often used the phrase 'leading idea' to mean 'organizing principle' and wrote essays which leading ideas govern or which explicate the 'leading ideas' of some other thinker.[38] Toward the end of his career he was to give a fuller account of them.

In his introduction to Henri Poincaré's *The Foundations of Science* (1913) Royce draws on Poincaré's formulation of the same notion.[39] Leading ideas are valuable "*despite,* or even *because,* of the fact that evidence can *neither* confirm *nor* refute them." They are devices of the understanding which unify discrete and confused facts or principles about the structure of the world. Royce's treatment of Euclid's parallel line postulate reveals their mediating role. Royce had long since digested the discovery of non-Euclidean geometry, and the postulate is no candidate for one of his absolute logical truths: it is simply a leading idea.[40] But unlike the Kantian regulative principles (and perhaps the categories), we may alter leading ideas like Euclid's axiom. They are subject to "suggestions" of experience. We can conceive other interpretations of experience, that is, other leading ideas, and those that we use are merely the most convenient. Leading ideas possess a dual nature. They are "pragmatic," although not to the extent of being subjective or arbitrary; simultaneously, experience (ambiguously) "imposes" them on us. Royce expresses their status in terms of his own work in a cautious way:

> while experience is always the guide, the attitude of the investigator towards experience is determined by interests which have to be partially due to what I should call that 'internal meaning,' that human interest in rational theoretical construction which inspires the scientific inquiry; . . . the theoretical constructions which prevail . . . are neither unbiased reports of the actual constitution of an external reality, nor yet arbitrary constructions of fancy.[41]

Royce uses one example that indicates the continuing importance in pragmatic thought of a search for a Kantian "third thing" between the factual and the conceptual. C. I. Lewis's idea of the pragmatic a priori is founded in this bit of Royce's work, and Willard Quine's wrestling with the same problem has its roots in a similar approach to philosophical puzzles.[42]

Consider the principle of the nature of disease which the German scientist Virchow enunciated in the nineteenth century. "We have learned to recognize," says Virchow, "that diseases are not autonomous organisms, that they are no entities that have entered into the body, that they are no parasites which take root in the body, but that they merely show us the course of vital processes under altered conditions." Logically regarded this is not a hypothesis which observation tests. When he propounded it in 1847, Virchow had not yet formulated the empirical principle of cellular pathology for which he became famous; he also saw the science of pathology as in its infancy and the causation of disease as unknown. Finally, it is difficult to see what would refute the disease principle if we considered it false. Should we recognize bacteria or their products or accompaniments as causing disease or affecting its course, Virchow could claim that these causes constituted the "altered conditions" under which "the course of the vital processes" occurs. Even if the Devil caused disease, the principle would remain "unrefuted and empirically irrefutable." The principle merely states that whatever affects the organism—fire or air or bullet or poison or devil—that entity is not the disease but constitutes the changed conditions of the organism.[43] If the disease principle is stated with generality,

> . . . it amounts simply to saying that if a disease involves a change in an organism, and if this change is subject to law at all, then the nature of the organism and the reaction of the organism to whatever it is which causes the disease must be understood in case the disease is to be understood.[44]

Virchow's notion of disease is a resolution to search for the connection between disease and the behavior of the organism, to find the relation of the pathological and normal states. Without a leading idea of this kind, the significant empirical findings could never have resulted, and scientists would never have observed the facts in respect to the hypotheses they do test. The value of leading ideas like the disease principle lies in the experimentation which they lead men to undertake and also in the ideas they discourage. They organize science, keep it in touch with the researchers' culture, and assure its service to humanity.[45]

7

MATHEMATICS AND METAPHYSICS
1899–1904

In examining the relation of mathematics and logic to Royce's metaphysics, we take up the most abstruse and difficult problems he broached. Royce himself thought such an examination necessary. He saw the essential goal of his profession as answering questions about what he more than once termed "the philosophy of life," but the philosopher must initially provide a theoretical ground for practical speculation—that is "the only order for the student of philosophy."[1] He had always been interested in mathematics, and in addition to his first published book, the logic primer,[2] mathematical examples of metaphysical points occur frequently in his early writings. From the nineties onward this interest became more systematic, and in 1898 he attended Peirce's Cambridge lectures on logic, an event which Royce felt changed his thinking.[3] As his son has written, Royce "did a great deal of long and laborious work" on logic during the first decade of the next century.[4] One of his characteristic pastimes was the frequent sea voyage, whose goal was to give him uninterrupted time for logical studies. In 1903 he exhorted the public that logic was essential for the future of philosophy; but the justification for this research lay in its power to save "some vital interest of humanity." Technical undertakings themselves, he concluded, "bake no bread."[5] Logic, he wrote a colleague ten years later, was not an end in itself but a means of stating exact relations; it was necessary to avoid a "desolating pragmatistic psychologizing."[6]

The target of Royce's logical work at the turn of the century was F. H. Bradley. His review of *Appearance and Reality* was highly complementary,[7] and he made ample use of Bradleyan ideas in *The Conception of God*.[8] But he dissented from Bradley's contention that the Absolute transcended self-consciousness, and briefly argued against this position in *The Conception of God*.[9] He saved his most significant argument, however, for Bradley's belief that we cannot understand the way finite creatures are *aufgehoben* in the Absolute. In the "Supplementary Essay" to *The World and the Individual*, he assaulted Bradley with his recently gained mathematical knowledge. The essay has a close relation to "the most fundamental theses" of his first volume, and is "one of the most serious and important things that ever I shall be able to write, or that ever I have written."[10]

In *Appearance and Reality* Bradley states that it is "wholly impossible" for human beings to render "any explicit and detailed reconciliation of the One and the Many, or any positive theory of how Individuals find their place in the Absolute."[11] His *magnum opus* rests on a dissection of what occurs in considering an object, o, in the world and the relation R linking o to the world. To R, as itself an object, there exists R^*, R's own relation to the world. We are never able to say that o is R-related to the world without becoming involved in an infinite regress, for R^* has its R^{**}, R^{**} its R^{***}, and so on. As Bradley puts it, "endless fission" "breaks out." Royce agrees with this statement of the problem, and both Bradley and Royce agree *that* the unification of finite experience in the Absolute takes place; but Bradley continues that *how* it is effected is insoluble for us. We should have to approach this puzzle via an endless succession of relations; we should have to enumerate an "actual infinite," and an "actual infinite multitude" is a self-contradiction for Bradley.[12]

The Absolute is comprised of the internal meanings of our ideas—actual experiences—and the validly possible experiences which make our world "determinate." The totality of these experiences is infinite: Royce implies that the Absolute is "infinitely self-conscious." Each time we might suppose we had "collected" every experience, we would have to recall that there is an experience of all of them, and so on infinitely. But Royce believed that we can understand the structure of this infinite set and that there is nothing contradictory about it. The regress generated gives him the chance to display his new philosophy of mathematics and, so he thought at the time, to refute Bradley's skepticism.[13]

The crux of Royce's reply in "The One, the Many, and the Infinite" is his definition of a particular system. In it (1) to every element M^r there corresponds a unique element called M^r's image or successor that, taken in its order, is the *next* element, (2) every image is distinct, and (3) at least one element M, although imaged by another, is itself the image of no other element. The natural numbers exemplify this type of order: they form an infinite series beginning with zero in which each term is followed by a next. Most importantly, the system is capable of definition "as a single internal purpose, in advance of the discovery that such purpose involves an endless series of constituents. . . ." Illustrating this claim, Royce asks his readers to ponder the attempt to draw in England a perfect map of England. This resolve would involve us in drawing an endless number of maps: when we come to that part of the map which is to represent the portion of England where we are mapping, we would have to draw another map, and so on indefinitely. We could never carry out our attempt, but our purpose could be seen as a single plan. "We should see," he explains, "why the one purpose, if it could be carried out would involve the endless series of maps."[14]

Royce introduces the phrase 'internally Self-Representative' to describe this kind of system, but his point is initially unclear since it is not until later in the text that what the phrase means becomes unambiguous. An internally Self-Representative system is one which can be represented by a part or "portion" of itself, produced by leaving out elements of the whole; this kind of system is said to be infinite. Citing the work of Richard Dedekind, Royce holds that we can prove infinite systems to exist if we consider the totality S of all things that can be objects of my thought. Let s_o be some thought, an element of S, and let s_o', also an element, be the thought "That s_o can be the object of my thought." Obviously for any thought s_n, there can be a corresponding thought s_n', and hence the set of thoughts S′ containing $s_0′$, . . . , $s_n′$, . . . corresponds in a one-to-one fashion with the elements of S. But S′ is a "constituent portion" of S, i.e., every element of S′ is by definition an element of S, but at least one element of S, s, is not an element of S′. Hence "my own realm of thoughts" is infinite.[15]

Dedekind's formulation is more acceptable if we realize that various "portions" of the natural numbers, say the powers of 3, represent all the natural numbers:

$$0 \quad 1 \quad 2 \quad 3 \quad . . . .$$
$$1 \quad 3 \quad 9 \quad 27 \quad . . . .$$

But Dedekind's emphasis on thought plays a role in the rebuttal of Bradley, for Royce asserts that he can answer the main question: *how* the one and the many are reconciled in the Absolute is supposedly clear. We construe the "actual infinite" which Bradley holds to be self-contradictory as an internally Self-Representative system. Just as a single plan defines the production of an infinitude of elements, so the Absolute embodies the Many. Royce concludes that we cannot avoid "conceiving the realm of Being as infinite in precisely the positive sense [of the internally Self-Representative system], now so fully illustrated. The Universe, as Subject-Object, contains a complete and perfect image or view of itself. Hence it is, in structure, at once One, as a single system, and also an endless *Kette* [i.e., series]."[16]

The consequences of his construction for his own philosophy are as significant to Royce as his dispute with Bradley. He adds to the above conclusion: "Its form [the universe's] is that of a Self." Accepting Dedekind's result, Royce urges that we must understand the internally Self-Representative system in question as a completely self-conscious self. Let s be any given thought; and let us reflect fully on s. We at once define an infinite system: s, s′ (s is a thought), s′′ (s′ is a thought), s′′′ . . . . We form an internally Self-Representative system whose structure "is precisely parallel to the structure of an ideal Self." The "formal order" of first, second, and in general of *next*, "is an image of the life of sustained, or, in the last analysis of complete Reflection. Therefore, this order is the natural expression of any recurrent process of thinking, and above all, is due to the essential nature of the Self when viewed as a totality."[17] We can claim that the connection between each finite creature and the Absolute is structurally identical to that of various "portions" of the natural numbers and the system itself. Each of us as "completed plans of life" and each of the Absolute's individuals—our objects— are like the infinite number of the partial but endless "fragments" of this system—the powers of 3, the odd numbers, the primes, and so on indefinitely.[18]

Royce's attack has a wider scope than the "Supplementary Essay" immediately conveys. The first volume of *The World and the Individual* describes the relations of finite individuals to the Absolute as they are in reality, in the World of Appreciation. In his system, all that is is a function of the Absolute's purposes to know itself, and all finite selves are ideas of the Absolute. In addition to querying Bradley's skepticism, "The One, the Many, and the Infinite" provides a way for "mathematicizing" Royce's metaphysics. An internally Self-Representative system with the structure of the Absolute contains an infinite number of infinite subseries which are capable of representing the whole, and we may conceive human selves as these subseries of the Absolute.

The lectures which comprise the first volume of *The World and the Individual* were delivered in early 1899 and went to the publisher in October of that year, but although Royce gave the second set of lectures in January of 1900, he did not get them into print until October of 1901. The two-year delay resulted from even more striking mathematical discoveries than those Royce capitalized on in his dispute with Bradley; they necessitated "a reform" in the second series Royce presented in Scotland.[19] In this less known book Royce turns from the World of Appreciation to the World of Description, the world in which our finitude constrains us to live. It is the world of facts, a world of likenesses and differences which we discriminate and classify. Although we know that this world cannot express the inmost nature of things, it retains enough significance for Royce to announce that he will present a "new deduction" of the categories: he will again investigate why the Absolute Self appears as a world of external objects.

Likeness and difference are correlative concepts: when we classify two objects as alike, they are *ipso facto* in some way different; if we classify them as different, they are because of that fact itself also alike. Love and hate are different emotions but they are both emotions. Finally, the likenesses and differences we heed are not thrust on us "without our consent or connivance." They are objects of our "attentive interest"; in attending we note of likenesses and differences, and we could largely disregard or ignore that to which we attend. All "the correlated likenesses and differences which appear before us in the observed facts are such as the direction of our attentive interest in some measure favors. The world of facts is thus not merely *given* . . . it is at any moment *regarded*. . . ."[20]

We can also define how we determine likenesses and differences. We engage in the process of *discrimination*, and in comparing two objects by discriminating, we signify that something is *between* the two. Royce based his notion of "betweenness" on the work of the mathematician Alfred Bray Kempe, of whom we shall hear later. Making use of a broad notion of "between," Kempe argued that within limits the properties of any complete system of logical classes are identical to the properties of a geometrical system of points. Royce disclaims any investigation and perusal of Kempe's monographs or the betweenness relation, but uses this relation to analyze his concept of discrimination.

Let there be, says Royce, a collection of objects which are discriminable. But let it also be possible that we do not in fact discriminate two of them, i.e., let it be possible for us to regard the two as equivalent, their differences not counting for a given purpose. Then, following Kempe, he writes:

> let an object *m* of the system in question be so related to *a* and to *b* that *if* you, either by inattention, neglect, or deliberate choice, disregard their difference, so that in any way they blend or become equivalent, *m* thereupon of necessity blends with both or becomes equivalent to both. In this case we shall say that, in the generalized

sense, m is such a member of the system in question as to lie *between* a and b. The mathematical way of symbolizing this relation would be briefer. It would take the form of merely saying: "m is such that, if $a=b$, then $m=a=b$. And *if* this is the case, m is regarded as *between* a and b."[21]

As Royce expounds this procedure, it represents the logical structure of discrimination. We need not go into its correctness, but because of what follows, we do need to make some remarks about it. Discrimination subsumes at least *three* elements, a, b, and something else that helps us keep them apart, or illustrates or determines their difference. The relationship is *not* dual but what "one may technically name a *triadic* relation." We know pairs of facts "*through a single possible act of discrimination and comparison.*" Alleging that when we discriminate we place an object m between a and b, Royce states that we have the beginnings of series which can proceed indefinitely. We discriminate between a and m by placing m_1 between them, and between m and b by placing m_2 between them. Thus: a . . . m_1 . . . m . . . m_2 . . . b. Theoretically this operation can continue *ad infinitum,* although it will cease quickly because of our physical limitations or the satisfaction of our interests, or both. Nevertheless, we have generated the first terms of a dense series, a series in which there is no next term, in which between any two there is a third.

This explication of betweenness has a direct application. Royce maintains that in the World of Description "*all understanding of facts in terms of general laws*" hinges on discrimination. The "working postulate of our process of comprehending things" is that between any two is a third, and the process is that upon which "all scientific description of given facts depends." The better I conceive and verify a series of discriminations a . . . m_1 . . . m . . . m_2 . . . b, the better I define stages of "a single process of ideal construction" which expresses how one can pass from a to b, how, in mathematical terms, one can "transform" a into b. We may view discrimination as the means by which, say, the stages connecting two states of a body are the stages transforming the former state to the latter. But since likeness and difference are correlative, a and b are alike in some way throughout the transformation. The like features are "the invariant characters of this system of transformations." The whole of our empirical knowledge is made up of these various transformational systems; we discriminate systems of facts from one another and link them by intermediate systems as we linked a and b. In discovering these invariant characters, Royce believes that we have ascertained the laws governing the systems of facts in question. Moving a body from one part of space to another leaves the shape of the body unchanged, and the discovery of that fact is the discovery of the spatial property defined as the "axiom" or "law" of "free mobility." Another example of law is that all physical and chemical changes leave the mass of matter unaltered: the transformations that a gravitating system of bodies undergoes are ones which leave invariant the system of relationships that the law defines.

It is unclear why Royce takes this as another attempt at his "deduction": there is no argument to show that his analysis has any relation to the Absolute. What Royce *has* ventured is an explication of concepts of the World of Description. Although he limits his examination to the "most fundamental" of the categories, likeness and difference and a basic relational category, betweenness, he is able to reach what he calls the category of "ordered series"; and he notes the complexities that any full inquiry would bring and the way in which he can introduce other categories. He also emphasizes that the concept of series provides the basis for ordered systems of relations and laws. On the basis of an analysis of elementary concepts we can outline the structure of the World of Description, the world in which we finite individuals live.[22] In whatever way we understand this "deduction," it has interesting connections to his earlier work. In the nineties he produced one deduction which was pragmatic, another that was psychological. Here we have a synthesis which is both pragmatic and psychological but whose main feature is that it delineates the mathematical structure of the human consciousness.

We can perhaps explain the "deductive" nature of the enterprise if we specify the bond between the World of Description and the World of Appreciation. The mathematical relation Royce conceived to exist between them is one of the crucial elements to be extracted from *The World and the Individual.* Although he does not tie this question to his deduction as he should have, even at the time he calls special attention to the problem.[23]

The dense series characteristic of discrimination in the World of Description is, for Royce, "less perfect" than the series characteristic of the World of Appreciation.[24] The series of ordinals exemplifies the mathematical nature of the "order" of the World of Appreciation. Such a series is called "well ordered" and each term in the series has a *next.* It is the ordinality of the number series which is its "most important and fundamental character." In the World of Appreciation, the real world, as opposed to the World of Description, "The intellect has been studying itself, and, as the abstract and merely formal expression of the orderly aspect of its own ideally conceived complete Self, and of any ideal system that it is to view as its own deed, the intellect finds precisely the Number System,—not, indeed, primarily the cardinal numbers, but the ordinal numbers."[25] The "order" of the number system is the "original type of all order in heaven and upon earth." The World of Description which discrimination reveals has no such order, but discrimination occurs in a series of well-ordered acts of an individual. But no individual can order all the theoretically possible discriminations: between any two we can find a third. The World of Description has the characteristic of "endless fission" which Bradley pointed out, and it is only in the Absolute that the discriminations are, as it were, "gathered up" into a well-ordered totality. In the World of Appreciation objects would not be discriminated in pairs; they would be "logically given, all at a stroke," an expression "of a single self-representative Purpose."[26] Were the world comprehended as a self-representative system, Royce asserts, "for one who grasped the facts in the order of that system, the recurrent process of the interpolation of intermediate terms in a series already recognized would no longer express the final truth."*

---

* One footnote to this is that Royce denies the infinite divisibility of time. It is a conception due to "that tendency of our own discriminating attention to an endless interpolation of intermediary stages." But, he adds: "We have, however, seen reasons,

Even in the World of Description discrimination "tends to acquire
the unity of a single volitional act" and "may always be viewed as having
one general direction, that leads *from* A to B, *through* the intermediary
stages."[27] In *The Outlines of Psychology* Royce writes that we learn of
the differences in things as these differences appear in succession; we
"interpret the simultaneous [the objects of the World of Description] *in
terms of the successive* [the structure of our appreciative conscious-
ness]." Our ideas are imitative processes; they involve a succession of
discriminative acts between any two of which we could place a third and
through which we reconstruct our view of objects. What this means precisely is difficult to say, but Royce is indicating that our own activity
attempts to reduce the World of Description to the World of Appreciation. We survey the "results of our deeds" "as if from above, as the
traveller who has reached a height looks back with appreciation on the
country through which he has wandered."[28]

The facts of the World of Appreciation are well ordered; every
fact will have a next-following fact, but as finite individuals discriminate
the world, they do not seize the facts in the order in which the Absolute
particularizes them. "In the last analysis," Royce insists, "the Absolute
Will must be viewed as expressed in a well-ordered and discrete series of
facts, which from our point of view may indeed appear . . . capable of
discrimination *ad infinitum.*" We must interpret the World of Description, he says elsewhere, via the World of Appreciation. The order characterizing the World of Description is of a "derived type."[29]

When Peirce reviewed *The World and the Individual* for *The
Nation,* he wrote Royce that Royce's view of logic was "antagonistic to

which, applied to time, would lead us to declare that an absolute insight would view
the temporal order as a discrete series of facts ordered as any succession of facts expressing one purpose would be ordered, viz., like the whole numbers. On the other
hand, we have no reason to suppose that our human consciousness distinctly observes
intervals of time that in brevity anywhere nearly approach to the final truth about
the temporal order. Within what is for us the least observable happening, a large
insight may indeed discriminate multitudes of events" (*WI* 2, p. 137).

all that is possible for progressive science" and entreated him to study logic. But *why* did Peirce think the logic "most execrable?"[30] In the unpublished portions of his reviews, he revealed the grounds for his displeasure. The map metaphor is inadequate; it requires a deep emendation; as an analogy, it lacks "several of the essential characters of the class of signs to which ideas belong." Royce must apply all "the new conceptions of multitude and continuity, and not merely that of the endless series," and he must apply them in more than a "single narrow way."[31] We do not know if Peirce was more detailed in his deprecation or if he communicated it directly to Royce, but there is a simple and unassailable objection to Royce's presentation consistent with Peirce's protests.

In his contrast of description and appreciation, Royce's strategy is unmistakable. As Gabriel Marcel put it, Royce argues that "there are two worlds, which undoubtedly correspond to one another and penetrate one another for a higher mind, but which philosophical analysis must distinguish and even provisionally oppose to one another."[32] But Royce never gives the "reduction" of the structure of one world to the other. There is a reason for this: the undertaking could not succeed. Although we can achieve a one-to-one correspondence between the members of the series of natural numbers and a dense series, namely, the rational numbers, Georg Cantor had shown that we *cannot* preserve order. There is no way for Royce to reduce the logical structure of the World of Description to the World of Appreciation. At best from a dense series we can *pick out* a subseries which is isomorphic to ω, the series of natural numbers.[33]

From one perspective Royce recognized his difficulties. In an undated fragment written about the turn of the century, he speaks of this problem as an antinomy. On the one hand the "Infinite Reason (whatever that may be, for we know not, but only assume it as true, it is above us and incomprehensible)" must realize the "Ideal Totalität." On the other, in the phenomenal world, activity proceeds on the basis of endless division. Royce concludes that there must be a synthesis in which "the incomprehensibility of the absolute reason vanishes by the use of my 'Possibility of

Error' principle. Can this be done?"[34] In a lengthy "Note" dated January 1901 he makes the point again: we must explain the relation of idea to object in terms of a self-representative system. But we can always find a third idea between any idea—a partial expression of purpose—and its object—its fulfilled purpose; this third idea is a result of reflection; it is the "reflective consciousness that i [the idea] is aiming at what I [the object] expresses or that, in aiming beyond itself, i is still aiming only at the expression in full of itself. Call this consciousness [the third idea] a mediating consciousness . . . a reflective Mediator." A system like this is "inclusive" of the self-representative system, and it is not clear, Royce ends, how he can put the two together.[35]

At the end of the second volume of *The World and the Individual*, he writes:

> we should see clearly that, although the world of the Absolute In-
> dividual is, from our point of view, an individual selection from an
> infinitely wealthy realm of unactualized possibilities, its internal
> structure, in order that it should be self-representative at all, must
> invoke the sort of formal complexity here suggested, and must
> therefore make inevitable that interpenetration of the lives of count-
> less and various Selves. . . .[36]

Lucidity is not a hallmark of this passage and others like it, but Royce seems to recognize that we cannot transform the mathematical structure of the World of Description ("our point of view") into that of the World of Appreciation: the Absolute "selects" from this "infinitely wealthy realm." If this is the case, then the World of Description may satisfacto- rily correspond to the World of Appreciation. A citation from the end of volume one suggests that this takes place:

> That the world is what it determinately is, means, from our point of
> view, that its being excludes an infinitely complex system of "barely
> possible" other contents, which, just because they are excluded
> from Reality, are conceived by a thought such that not all of its
> "barely possible" ideal objects could conceivably be actualized at
> once . . . the Real is exclusive as well as inclusive. On the side of its
> thought the Absolute does conceive a barely possible infinity, other
> than the real infinity,—a possible world, whose characters, as uni-

versal characters, are present to the Absolute, and are known by virtue of the fact that the Absolute also thinks. But these possibilities are excluded by reason of their conflict with the Absolute Will.*

But Royce does not say how this "exclusion" is to occur.

Against the presumption that he sees these shortcomings is that he thinks he has refuted Bradley. The latter asserts that solutions of *how* the Absolute comprehends the one and the many appeal to the self-contradictory notion of the "actual infinite." Royce's "Supplementary Essay" shows that on one formulation this infinite need not be self-contradictory, but this does not overturn Bradley's claim. The invocation of a satisfactory infinite collection is not enough; it does not intimate how we can apply this conception to the World of Description. Royce has restated Bradley's riddle in a mathematically more sophisticated form: *how* are we to reconcile the finite world, marked by a dense series, with the Absolute, marked by a well-ordered series? In short, *The World and the Individual* takes up the challenge of *Appearance and Reality* but does not meet it.

In addition to this enigma two other mathematical perplexities are unresolved in Royce's metaphysics. They are not ones that Royce himself seemed aware of at the time, but since they were to become important later, it is worthwhile to isolate them. The first concerns the mathematical relation of finite individuals to the Absolute; the second, the mathematical structure of the Absolute itself.

I have argued that the Absolute of the first volume of *The World and the Individual* bears similarities to Hegel's concrete universal. And Royce's writing is filled with statements that finite creatures are parts, fragments, of the Absolute.[37] The relation of an individual to the Absolute is intuitively like that of my hand to my body. But how do we translate this notion into mathematical language if the Absolute is an infinite

---

* *WI* 1, pp. 567–569. I assume that these bare possibilities are those which assure the freedom of the Absolute. But Royce never reveals the connection between this aspect of his ethics and his metaphysics. The puzzle appears often in his work, but he never discusses it.

collection? There is a simple mathematical way of indicating the part-whole relation, the relation of inclusion between classes. For example, the class of birds includes the class of ravens. If we let R stand for the class of ravens and B of birds, we may symbolize this fact by writing R ⊂ B; similarly, when Royce translates metaphysical concepts into mathematical ones. I think we can claim that F ⊂ A, where F is a finite individual and A is the absolute. But his theory is more complex and confusing than this. We must distinguish the class inclusion relation, which we have used to define the part-whole notion, from an element's relation to the class of which it is a member. Ravens are *members* of the class of ravens, but no individual raven is a *part* of the class of ravens, and the class of ravens itself is not a *member* of the class of birds. If we let 'ϵ' stand for 'is a member of' and let r be any given raven, then r ϵ R and r ϵ B, but neither r ⊂ R nor R ϵ B. I have no desire to take up the contemporary technicalities involved in making this elementary point, but we must consider one further idea. Suppose we have a class with one member (the unit class) ; we still distinguish the element from the class and do not say that the element is included in, i.e., is a part of—or "equals"—its class. Suppose we return to the Roycean formulation, F ⊂ A, with these distinctions in mind. Although a finite individual is a part of the Absolute, he cannot be an individual, an element; rather, we must be able to construe the finite individual as himself a class. Royce makes exactly this move, although it sometimes involves ignoring the difference between an individual and its unit class.

As we have seen in *The Conception of God*, the Absolute is an individual which unites thought and experience and yet simultaneously keeps them apart. The Absolute Consciousness *both exemplifies and totally fulfills* the Absolute Idea.[38] In other words Royce blurs the distinction between the unit class and its member. In *The Conception of Immortality* he writes that an individual is an essentially unique being so that this individual *constitutes the type of individual* which it is. *The World and the Individual* makes the same point: "What is real is not only a content of experience, and not only the embodiment of a type, but it is an individual content of experience, and the unique embodiment of a type."[39]

Here is Hegel's concrete universal: form and content are one; or in our
terms the unit class is indistinguishable from its single member. If we
assume this to be true of all Roycean individuals, F ⊂ A is true because
qua individual a partial self is similar to a unit class; F can be *part* of A.

Whatever this idea has to recommend it, the result is that Royce
fails to distinguish between unit classes and their elements in a way that
has consequences for his future work. He also changes his ideas in later
material, and for both of these reasons it has been well to examine the
issue. But we must explore a further puzzle.

In the "Supplementary Essay" Royce contends that his conception
of the Absolute as a self-representative system is not due to Hegel and
the other post-Kantians, although their accounts imply a theory like
Royce's. His complaint is that Hegel's contempt for mathematics prevents
him from giving any definition of the infinite which must characterize
the Absolute.[40] And we can interpret Royce's analysis as a "mathematical equivalent" of the Hegelian universal. The individuals of Royce's
self-representative system do not "exemplify" the concept of the series;
rather, taken in their order, they *realize* the concept. That is, we may
look at the system as a unity of many in one where we cannot distinguish
its conception from its concrete embodiment. Our definition explicates
a type, Royce says; yet only one individual whole—the members of the
series taken in their entirety—embodies this type in the form of immediate experience: "immediacy and idea completely fuse, so that what is
here conceived is also given."[41]

The mathematical notion of unit sets reflects the way individuals
are "parts" of the Absolute. I am not sure of—and Royce does not spell
out—the connection between this idea *and* the mathematical notion of
the Absolute as concrete universal. But Royce's understanding of this
latter notion is paradoxical. The structure of the absolute self represents
perfectly reflective self-consciousness: a finite individual is not "wholly
conscious" of his own consciousness. To be completely self-conscious
"would be to be aware of the completion of an infinite series of presented
facts." That is, the Absolute must be self-conscious of its own self-
consciousness; it must verify what it is that it is presently verifying.[42] In

the Absolute all the infinite contents of self-consciousness are "supposed immediately given"; they are "seen, experienced, presented . . . all at once."[43]

We may express the fact that an infinite series is generated in its order of succession by its defining principles, but for the Absolute this infinite series is *actually present*. In *The World and the Individual* Royce never clarifies how we could express this formulation mathematically, but it is mentioned elsewhere as the class of all classes.[44] If my previous analyses are correct Royce's choice of "the class of all classes" to represent the Absolute is understandable. Each finite individual is a class, but also part of a greater but similar whole—in short, a class composed of every class; and this infinite class appears to have an infinitely reflective structure. Unfortunately we cannot construe this conception coherently: Cantor had proven that it was contradictory; indeed it involves Cantor's paradox.[45]

At the time Royce wrote, Cantor had not published his 1899 discovery of the paradox which bears his name, and when Royce later discovered his error, he asserted that Russell pointed out the difficulty.[46] And, to be sure, Russell's *Principles of Mathematics* takes up related issues. The curious fact is that Royce was aware of Russell's work in *The Principles*.* As late as 1904 Royce spoke of the Absolute as the class of all classes; yet in August of 1903, just six weeks after *The Principles of Mathematics* was published in the United States, he wrote a long article on the logical problems the book expounds. Royce shows a clear and sophisticated comprehension of the matters he discusses: he recognizes the distinction between inclusion and membership, and explicates *Russell's* paradox which has since become so famous. Regrettably, Royce did not pursue his study of *The Principles* to the end, and neglected—

---

* Royce had a great respect for Russell and knew the latter's writings. Disappointed in 1913 after he could not convince Russell to accept a permanent Harvard appointment, Royce wrote Ralph Barton Perry that Russell was "a great man" who had "seen deeply into the dark (*Letters of Josiah Royce*, ed. John Clendenning [Chicago, 1970], pp. 569, 591–592).

at least in this article—to master Russell's discussion of the relation of
the paradox to infinite sets and to Cantor:

> Of the relation of our author's discussion to the fascinating prob-
> lem upon which he lays such stress,—the problem regarding the
> series of Cantor's cardinal numbers, and regarding the logical ex-
> istence of the "class of all objects," I have here had no time to go.
> I recognize that this leaves my account very fragmentary.[47]

Royce's logical work is fragmentary indeed. Cantor has shown
that any reduction of the mathematics of description to that of appreciation cannot succeed. Royce's mathematical conception of the Absolute
involves a logical paradox. And his conception of the way finite parts
fitted into the infinite whole trades on an ambiguity in his understanding
of the unit set. It is unfair to abandon him with these three problems, but
if we are not to get too far ahead, we must interrupt the narrative to
review the development of Royce's "practical" thought in this period.

8

MORAL AND RELIGIOUS PHILOSOPHY
1900–1912

After 1900 Royce devoted much time to the unresolved problems of *The World and the Individual,* mathematical in nature. Simultaneously he returned to questions of moral philosophy which he had not reexamined since *The Religious Aspect of Philosophy.* As he developed what was to become famous as the "philosophy of loyalty," his researches in this area had at least heuristic value for the solution to the logical puzzles he still confronted. But in his eyes moral and religious philosophy remained an "application"—although the supremely important one—of his more abstruse work.

For any student of Royce this problem of interpreting his technical and practical philosophy as a coherent whole is vexing and worthy of comment at this point. If we are to understand the problem, we must first look at its sociological facet. In 1900 philosophy in America was relevant to more than a tiny segment of the academic community; the philosopher had an almost ministerial duty to a wider audience of laymen, and we can treat much of Royce's lecturing as the successful behavior of anyone in his position. *The Philosophy of Loyalty* was not meant to be an "elaborately technical philosophical research"; he wrote the book "not merely and not mainly for philosophers." Rather, it was an appeal to any reader fond of ideals. In *The Sources of Religious Insight,* the last work of the period we are considering, Royce addressed "a general audience of thoughtful people" and limited the technical exposition of his work because of his audience.[2] As the Chicago *Record-Herald* congratulated him, "Professor Royce has, with Professor James, the rare gift of translating the thinking of the scholar into the language of the plain people."[3] However one views the value of this social role, its existence presents serious difficulties which Royce himself discusses:

> Popular philosophizing . . . is never favorable to the finer estimate of technical distinctions between one doctrine and another. For practical applications, meanwhile, the public may be thankful to the philosopher; but they never repay him for such services by trying to understand his theories. Why should they? Nobody cares what is in such cases applied. The public interest is only in the apparent patness of the application.[4]

Since Royce's death the problem has acquired a different complexion. Many expositors forget the technical. They make part serve for whole and take little notice of his most serious thought; those not interested in him assert that he is not a serious thinker. Both views ignore a significant dimension of Royce's writing and violate his oft-stated intention: the technical, he says, grounds the practical, and the philosopher's primary commitment is explicating the former, although only the latter justifies his enterprise. The villain in the piece is *The Philosophy of Loyalty*; whatever the worth of the book, it symbolizes all that he is about. But Royce no more deserves the title "philosopher of loyalty" than he does "founder of the logical tradition at Cambridge." We must examine how the evidence confirms this epigram.

In *The World and the Individual* and earlier works Royce points out that the empirical self is a mass of sensations, a grouping of experiences which we differentiate from the rest of the world through imitation. The "true self" of finite experience is an ideal, something never given, a plan of life which reflects one's goals and unifies the empirical self. No set of aims, however, gets a complete definition and embodiment in our present lives, and for this reason it is ideal, fulfilled only in God. Royce also sees the execution of our life plans—however faulty—proceeding on the basis of social contrasts:

> we still retain our individuality, and our distinction from one another, just in so far as our life-plans, by the very necessity of their

social basis, are mutually contrasting life-plans, each one of which
can reach its own fulfilment only by recognizing other life-plans
as different from its own.[5]

The finite self has two linked but different aspects; it temporally appears
as a product, a result, a determined creature of destiny; and were it not
to appear this way, we could not specify it as a self at all; yet in order
to justify its existence as a self and its individuality and freedom, we
also regard it as a unique aspect of the divine.[6] In *The World and the
Individual* Royce does not discuss the tension between this divine character (the inner appreciative quality of a life lived according to ideals)
and finite dependence on the external (social) order. Adherence to a
plan of life gives the finite self a moral quality, but this remains only an
ideal. Royce is left with another instance of the general problem of
relating the World of Appreciation (here the inner being of finite selves)
to the World of Description (the world of social contrasts).

In the nineties "Reflective Knowledge" functioned as a bridge
between the two worlds, and beginning with volume two of *The World
and the Individual* Royce introduces a mediating element into his moral
thinking. Imitation is the name he gives to the activity which provides
human beings with knowledge of the World of Description: it is "a construction of something that lies, in a technical sense, *between* the acts of
my model, and what were formerly my acts." Here imitation does not
describe how we gain scientific knowledge, but how the self develops as a
moral creature. In imitating we discover what our life plan is, and the
process contrasts with action indicative of the "self-representative life"—
of doing again and again what one's already known plan of life demands.
Finally, imitation is the principal source of "novel forms of self-expression." Imitation never repeats the act of a model; it has an originality
about it, and gives the individual a new consciousness of the unity of his
life.[7] Although Royce has no way of showing *how* the appreciative characteristics of the finite self are expressed in the World of Description, he
is saying *that* finite selves do display novelty and originality in organizing their life plans when they imitate; and in this novelty and originality finite individuals come closest to expressing the uniqueness and
freedom which characterize them in the Absolute. When Royce speaks

of the imitation which gives scientific knowledge, he distinguishes it from the World of Appreciation; when imitation defines our moral growth, the distinction between description and appreciation is not so clear. In short, "non-scientific" imitation begins to link the empirical and metaphysical selves.

Royce spent the first years of the century understanding and reinterpreting these doctrines in relation to Kempe's mathematical work. By 1906, however, he had again taken up moral problems, and in a series of lectures given at the University of Illinois, he presented the results of his labor.

The framework in which he presented his theory is reminiscent of the view he had sketched twenty-five years earlier. We distinguish conduct as right or wrong, Royce asserts, and the goal of "the general doctrine of values" is to formulate the basis of this distinction.[8] Although he is not as explicit as he had been in the eighties, he identifies an evaluation with an act of will. We must regard all these acts *qua* facts in the world as having the same kind of value. In a hypothetical debate with a head-hunter over the goodness of taking his life, Royce urges that so far as they both have a "rational consciousness" of human values, he and the head-hunter recognize each other's valuation as facts, each equally deserving in any determination of values:

> Herewith, however, I state a sort of first principle of ethics,—a crude principle I admit, but a principle. All sincere valuations of things, by whomsoever made, are themselves facts having value. Whoever wills anything,—that will has its own value. Whoever wants to know the values of things must take account of all values that any will sets upon things. Here is already a starting point for an objective doctrine of values. . . . In principle, I am simply insisting on the truth that whoever wills anything in this world defines thereby a value, a something that is declared to be worth doing. I am drawing a conclusion, so far that what, in an impersonal sense, is objectively worth doing, depends as much and of course as little upon his private valuation as upon mine. Now just this sort of truth is the sort of truth that we recognize whenever we deal with men dispassionately, justly, fairly.[9]

Royce's second principle concerns the possibility of harmonizing wills. Suppose we conceive some plan in which we might have to change around the lives of two moral opponents but in which we would enable each of them to carry out his "essential will." This situation *"possesses more objective value"* than the former situation: a situation in which two wills cooperate is *ipso facto* better than one in which they conflict. Consider again Royce's debate with the head-hunter. We might be able to alter the conduct of the latter's tribe in the direction of the customs prevalent "in a well-regulated company of civilized gentlemen." The head-hunter might remain Royce's enemy, but might obtain the prestige he achieves through head-hunting by victory in philosophical debate or quest for political office. The head-hunter would be satisfied, and Royce would retain his head. This second principle—the intrinsic goodness of harmonizing conflicting wills—is in part obvious because it has successful instances. Believing as do many in his culture that historical change is progress, Royce argues that history offers us examples of the increased harmony of human wills. The evolution from savagery to civilization has been morally good. The civilized man has sophisticated ways of adjusting his nature to the facts of the social world; in 1906 everyone's purposes are carried out with less conflict than was necessary while men remained upon the savage level; war has given way to commerce and men gain prestige through peace rather than killing.[10]

Whatever the force of this Victorian vision, Royce admits that he must detail how men proceed to harmonize their conflicting wills. His two principles are essential for understanding how he conceives this process.[11] Consider how we might apply them to achieve harmony within ourselves. We would admit all of our valuations—present and future—as equally worthy of regard; we would attempt to devise a plan to bring them all into harmony: that plan of living would be *ipso facto* the best way to live—considering the individual alone. This formulation is consistent with Royce's earlier thought. To it he adds that the ideal—the plan of life—defines the finite self as a moral creature. As in *The Conception of God* and *The World and the Individual*, the true self is a dynamic structure, a conscious life lived according to a plan. But in

the Urbana Lectures Royce goes further and invites us to examine
what individuals achieve the greatest harmony and what "life styles"
bring about the greatest social harmony. We will investigate the types
of personal ideals, the distinctive sorts of self-hood.

Royce's procedure follows the evolutionary—perhaps Hegelian—
theorizing which leads him to argue that history demonstrates the growth
of harmony. *The Religious Aspect of Philosophy* "pursued the definition
of our ideal through the imperfect forms of individualism"; we now
analyze four personality types arranged in an evolutionary order: each
one represents in turn a "higher" and chronologically more recent kind
of self; and each one in turn is, in what we may call "its logical development," superior in its attempt to achieve self-harmony.[12]

Imitation is as important to Royce's scheme as is this version
of social Darwinism. The lives of moral agents—and in particular of
Royce's four personality types—are a "union of independence and social
plasticity." Nothing, he says, can be right for me unless *I* will it, but,
simultaneously, I do not determine my own purposes without consulting
the social order; the self learns to will through imitation. I differentiate
my former self from my model and my new behavior expresses my individuality. Royce considers this behavior *between* my prior behavior and
that of the model who provides the social context on which my notion
of self depends:

> it remains always the case that the decision of an individual about
> his own life plan can never *merely* depend upon the imitation of
> other people or upon the following of a social tradition. For every
> individual has a task that is in some respects unique, has instincts
> that nobody else possesses in just the same way, has a social train-
> ing that nobody else repeats, and consequently comes to himself
> only by making decisions that nobody else can ever make. Hence
> duty is indeed individual. There is some duty for you that is not
> only duty in so far as you yourself see it to be such, but that is
> actually duty for nobody else, because as a fact nobody else either
> wants to do it or can do it. Yet even this unique duty, this unique
> choice of our own will and our own way comes to the consciousness
> of each of us by virtue of our social education, our learning of moral

values which depends upon a very great plasticity and imitativeness which all of us normally possess.[13]

The first in logico-chronological order of Royce's four personality types is the heroic or stately self whose deeds compel a community's admiration. Whenever the stately self becomes prominent as an ideal type, a culture will emphasize socially serviceable righteousness. Although this type embodies worthwhile elements, Royce contends that it cannot represent an ethical ideal. The success of the hero is contingent on good fortune, strength, and the praise of the world; yet if we are to define moral goodness in terms of the self, this goodness must be something which would survive ill fortune, weakness, and worldly contempt. Consequently, the stately self cannot serve as a guide for the achievement of universal harmony: it is an ideal dependent on conditions which we intuitively feel are extraneous to exemplary moral behavior.[14]

Passing to the saintly or self-denying self, Royce argues that we value this ideal because of its sacrifices and renunciations. It emphasizes that the perfect life is one in which we abandon or destroy our "worldly" self and seek a peace of resignation. This ideal appears to evolve out of the realization that the ethically valuable is superior to fortune, and leads to the view that the self should achieve renunciation. Although Royce is mindful of his insight, he sees it as partial.[15] From our notion that moral goodness transcends circumstance we could conclude that the ideal self is defiant; the ideal self learns from the wreck of fortune that we must put ideal value on our "unconquerable soul." This titanic or defiant soul is Royce's third personality type, but he will not accept it as ultimate.[16] The stately self weds virtue to social triumph; it is inadequate since it makes social position and not merely the social order essential to moral worth. The saintly self is faulty in urging that social triumph cannot have any place in virtue. And the titanic self is faulty in asserting that the social order itself is unnecessary for the ethical ideal. In concluding, Royce declares that we must surpass the saintly self because it seeks excellence only in the renunciation of social position; similarly, the titanic self fails because it assumes self-assertion in the absence of a social order. Royce finds the ideal in the fourth personality type—the loyal self. It synthesizes the insights of the three which are evolutionarily and logically prior. It is just to our dependence on the social environment without sacrificing our need for individual expression.[17] In this context Royce wrote and lectured on his famous philosophy of loyalty, detailing the importance of his fourth personality type.

The loyal individual has a willing, practical, and thoroughgoing devotion to a cause. The devotion of a patriot to his country, a martyr to his religion, and a robber to his band, are examples of loyalty, but Royce stresses that loyalty is exemplified in more common situations— the father's love for his family, the businessman's allegiance to his firm.[18] In fact, Royce packs into his definition of 'cause' all he needs to make the loyal personality an adequate ideal. To the loyal person the cause is objective, i.e., it serves more than the individual's self-interests. The cause will not be impersonal; the interests beyond one's own must be those of other people; that is, the interests will be social. Lastly, one will not be loyal to a cause regarded only as a collection of the interests of separate individuals; the cause will involve a social unity:

> you can be loyal only to a tie that binds you and others into some sort of unity, and loyal to individuals only through the tie. The cause to which loyalty devotes itself has always this union of the personal and the seemingly super-individual about it. It binds many individuals into one service.[19]

"Where there is an object of loyalty," Royce writes, "there is . . . [a] union of various selves into one life."[20]

The loyal person achieves harmony by ordering his desires as loyalty to a cause demands; the cause preserves the social aspect of morality without sacrificing the individual's expression of choice. Once again, imitation is the means enabling the loyal individual to achieve independence in a social context. And we do not merely *imitate:* the loyal person "interprets these plans [of his models] with reference to his own personal interests."[21] Royce hints in *The Philosophy of Loyalty* that loyalty achieved through imitation or "interpretation" mediates between the worlds of description and appreciation. How can we fulfill ourselves—express our own appreciative consciousness—in the external world? Our "divided being," he declares, "demands reconciliation with itself"; it has "one long struggle for unity." Its inner and outer realms are naturally at war, and only loyalty reconciles them.[22]

The Philosophy of Loyalty develops Royce's principle of "loyalty to loyalty" as the criterion for determining choices among conflicting causes. We should act to increase loyalty in the world and to prevent its destruction. Although any loyalty is good, we have evidence of the war of causes, and the principle of "loyalty to loyalty" yields a decision procedure to resolve these issues.[23] But Royce admits that we must limit our judgments on the loyalty of others; we best apply his "general guilding maxim for conduct" to conflicts of personal loyalties, and even here it offers a general guide, and cannot prescribe specific courses of action.[24] He also introduces loyalty to loyalty to explain how an individual may guide his choice "insofar as he considers not merely his own supreme good, but that of mankind." Here Royce returns to his concern of the Urbana Lectures. We have examined the loyal personality not only because it achieves individual harmony, but also because it best contributes to that cooperation of all wills which is of ultimate value. When he urges that "loyalty to loyalty" secures "the greatest possible increase of loyalty amongst men," and the "supreme good" of mankind,[25] he addresses himself both to a more or less technical problem and to the practical one which is the focus of *The Philosophy of Loyalty*. The individual who is "loyal to loyalty" is acting to bring about that universe which the ultimate harmony of wills would define.

While Royce's earlier work puts a high priority on showing that the harmonization of wills is the highest good, this question does not preoccupy his later work. After his analysis of the moral consciousness he assumes this conclusion, and there is no argument from skepticism, as there had been in *The Religious Aspect of Philosophy*. In that book, however, a second question disturbs him; and in 1908 he treats it as he had in 1885.

Is the ultimate good attainable? Does it have "reality"? What must be true about the universe if loyalty is a genuine good and not an illusion? Royce answers that if loyalty has "any basis of truth," human lives can be linked in some spiritual unity; causes will have a real "existence" outside of private selves:

> loyalty, as we have seen, is a service of causes that, from the human point of view, appear superpersonal. Loyalty holds these unities to be good. If loyalty is right, the real goodness of these causes is never completely manifested to any one man, or to any mere collection of men. Such goodness, then, if completely experienced at all, must be experienced upon some higher level of consciousness than any one human being ever reaches. If loyalty is right, social causes, social organizations, friendships, families, countries, yes, humanity, as you see, must have the sort of unity of consciousness which individual human persons fragmentarily get, but must have this unity upon a higher level than that of our ordinary human individuality.[26]

As in *The Religious Aspect of Philosophy*, the argument from "the possibility of error" assures us of this fact.[27] Loyalty has a metaphysical and a practical character: it conceives the moral aspects of life in a superhuman way and views social organizations as personal unities of consciousness. There exists in these unities an actual experience of that good which we partially apprehend in our loyalty. These tenets are typical Roycean doctrines, but in *The Philosophy of Loyalty* he draws together the theoretical and the practical.

His thesis is that whoever speaks of truth presupposes a spiritually unified world whose consciousness is higher than that of individual minds. The world of truth is a world similar to that in which the loyal believe when they believe their cause is real. This world of truth also has a goodness about it like that which the loyal attribute to their causes. "Truth seeking and loyalty," he concludes, "are therefore essentially the same process of life merely viewed in two different aspects." The loyal individual serves a cause he takes to be true. The truth-seeker—and Royce often has in mind the scientist exploring the natural world—is serving a cause which unifies life upon some higher level of being than the present human level; the scientist's work implies the union of his experiences with those of the scientific community. The activity of the scientist is moral, and he is loyal.[28] This view of truth, Royce maintains, "meets at once an ethical and a logical need."[29]

This is a vague statement of the relation of the "technical" and "practical" aspects of his work, and of the way in which the scientist's World of Description is really a World of Appreciation. Nor is the notion of imitation developed to suggest that Royce has worked out these problems. *The Philosophy of Loyalty*'s main task is to show that the self is an ethical concept—the unification of our instincts, passions, and interests around a central set of purposes; that in its highest form this unification involves loyalty; and that loyalty permits the individual to express his individuality and simultaneously to contribute to his social order.[30]

These ethical concerns are consistent with the metaphysics of *The World and the Individual,* and it is important to detail in what respect this is so if only because the next few years were to bring alterations in both. Royce states in the "Preface" to *The Philosophy of Loyalty* that he has no changes to report in his "fundamental metaphysical theses"[31] since the publication of *The World and the Individual.* We shall see that his mathematical work through 1908 accomplishes nothing but a reformulation of Kempe's notions and a refinement of the categories of the World of Description. Royce does not appear to have resolved the puzzles concerning the logical paradoxes; and he was not to answer the question about the relation between the two worlds until later; but if he was not aware that these were questions when he wrote volume two of *The World and the Individual, The Philosophy of Loyalty* indicates that they had become problems by 1908. Our science forsakes us, he writes, "precisely as to the *details* of the system of facts whereby our life is linked to the eternal." With Bradley he concludes that "we can know *that* we are thus linked. *How* we are linked, our sciences do not make manifest to us."[32] It is not surprising that Royce's concept of the connection individuals have to causes does not go beyond anything he says in *The World and the Individual.*

He uses the word 'cause' in two distinct senses. In the usual sense, it is the union of individual lives into one supra-personal life. Our social organizations are "actual personal unities of consciousness,"[33] a "union of various individuals in one."[34] Alternatively, he views the cause as an ideal which *creates* a social group when individuals are loyal to the ideal. He implies that the cause exists independently of the loyal group. Truth seeking is this kind of cause. The truth-seekers form a unit whose ideal is a certain unity of experience. This unity transcends their own experience and is realized by a higher experience.[35] We can justify this ambiguous use if we recall that Royce's Absolute is a concrete universal. As an ideal separate from the individuals seeking it, the cause is an "abstract universal," and its "extension" is the individuals who define themselves in its terms. As finite creatures we view our causes as something external to us. In the Absolute, however, we no longer make this distinction since individuals are "fragments" of a consciousness which is one with all of them. Royce speaks of this kind of concrete universal when he defines the cause as a social union of individuals. In these cases he is describing the cause as it is in reality, in the world of the Absolute. But we can put the matter in a more perspicacious way. The ideal we seek as a union of the lives of many individuals is an external meaning of an idea, an idea in the mind of the Absolute; the internal meanings of that idea are our finite purposes to realize the ideal, our practical commitment to a cause. The metaphysics of *The World and the Individual* governs the ethics of *The Philosophy of Loyalty*.

In his earlier work Royce did not make a distinction between moral and religious doctrine, but in *The Philosophy of Loyalty* there is a demarcation between the two. The task of ethics is to define the moral life and to show why it is the best life. This Royce accomplishes after he delineates the loyal personality and examines how it provides for the harmonization of human wills. But when he goes on to show the existence of the spiritual unities loyalty presupposes, he points out that he is doing something more. In 1908, to describe the relation of loyalty to the real universe was to formulate "a religion, to help out one's ethics":

> Purely practical considerations, then, a study of our human needs, and ideal of the business of life—these inevitably lead us into a region which is more than merely a realm of moral activities. This region is either one of delusion or else one of spiritual realities

of a level higher than is that of our present individual human experience.[36]

We must construe this "region of spiritual realities" as constituting the religious nature of existence.

With this in mind Royce refines his "inadequate" definition of loyalty. Loyalty is not only a guide to life but also a revelation of our connection to an everlasting and embracing spiritual unity. Rightly conceived, loyalty is the will to manifest the eternal—the conscious and superhuman unity of being—in the life of finite persons.[37] Religion makes loyalty comprehensible by appealing to the emotions and to the imagination. It interprets the "world-life" in a symbolic way.[38] In this context we again approach the problem of evil to which Royce returned throughout the nineties. Now the problem gets a redefinition in religious language—in terms of salvation, or the achievement of our goal of harmony. Alluded to in an aside in *The Philosophy of Loyalty*,[39] the notion provides the framework for *The Sources of Religious Insight*.

The definitions Royce gives to the words in his title capture the aim of *The Sources of Religious Insight*. Insight is knowledge that makes us aware of the unity of many facts in one whole. The concern of such *religious* knowledge is the salvation of man, for Royce specifies man's need to be saved as the fundamental characteristic of religion: it is interested "in freeing mankind from some vast and universal burden, of imperfection, of unreasonableness, of evil, of misery, of fate, of unworthiness, or of sin." This idea is contingent on two simpler ones. First, that human life has some ultimate end; and, second, that man *"as he naturally is"* is in danger of missing this end and making his life a senseless failure.[40]

The Sources of Religious Insight investigates our knowledge of man's struggle to achieve his highest goal when it appears that this struggle will not be successful, and Royce makes it clear that it is the evil in the world which makes the situation so grim. What is puzzling about the way he sets the book up are his statements that our salvation is imperiled. His analysis of the ultimate value in life is not surprising:

> We need to give life sense, to know and to control our own selves, to end the natural chaos, to bring order and light into our deeds, to

make the warfare of natural passion subordinate to the peace and
the power of the spirit. This is our need. To live thus is our ideal.
And because this need is pressing and this ideal is far off from the
natural man, we need salvation.[41]

* * *

We are naturally creatures of wavering and conflicting motives,
passions, desires. The supreme aim of life is to triumph over this
natural chaos, to set some one plan of life above all the others, to
give unity to our desires, to organize our activities, to win, not
indeed, the passionless peace of nirvana, but the strength of spirit
which is above the narrowness of each one of our separate passions.
We need to conceive of such a triumphant and unified life, and
successfully to live it. That is our goal: Self-possession, unity,
peace, and spiritual power through and yet beyond all the turmoil
of life—the victory that overcometh in the world.[42]

We know from the dialectical argument that this goal is reached
and that mankind is saved. Since Royce repeats the argument in *The
Sources of Religious Insight,* there would seem to be no question about
the goal's achievement. Since 1885 Royce's problem had been to reconcile the necessity of the triumph of harmony with the world's evil. In
urging that we must "hope" for assurance of salvation,[43] he implies that
we no longer can rely on the Absolute. His premise that "damnation"
for the species is a possibility recasts the context in which he examines
the problem of evil; it does so, however, only by pretending that we are
in doubt about the most basic truth.

Another element of *The Sources of Religious Insight* also merits
comment. One reason Royce had for writing the book was to answer
William James's *Varieties of Religious Experience.* We may interpret
James as arguing that we justify religious doctrines because they explain
otherwise inexplicable personal needs and feelings. For Royce this view
made religion nonrational, and watered down doctrine to vague emotions whose foundation was individual intuition. In part, *The Source of
Religious Insight* attempts to salvage a religion based on reason and metaphysical truth. Of course, James feels that the alternative to his approach
is the "abstract" theorizing he associates with Royce, and the "abstrac-

tion" James has in mind is Royce's Absolute. The block universe of Royce's divine, James holds, is not adequate for capturing our religious experience. When Royce delivered the 1911 Bross Lectures, published as *The Sources of Religious Insight,* he posed another alternative:

> Must one chose between inarticulate faith and barren abstractions? Must one face the alternative: Either intuition without reasoning, or else relatively fruitless analysis without intuition? Perhaps there is a third possibility. Perhaps one may use one's process of abstraction as a sort of preparation for certain articulate and noble intuitions that cannot be approached, by our human sort of consciousness, through any other way. Perhaps analysis is not the whole process which determines demonstrations. Perhaps synthesis—the viewing of many facts or principles or relations in some sort of unity and wholeness—perhaps a synoptic survey of various articulate truths, can lead us to novel insights. In that case inarticulate intuitions and barren abstraction are not the only instruments between which we must choose. For in that case there will be another sort of aid, a more explicit sort of intuition, a more considerate view of our life and its meaning, which we may adopt, and which may lead us to novel results.[44]

By the time Royce wrote this, he had gone far in redefining the mathematical bases of his thought. He had gone so far that he may have rejected the dichotomy between description and appreciation which had been so fundamental. In *The Source of Religious Insight* he merely claims that there is knowledge other than the experience of the data of sense or feeling and the analysis of abstract ideas. It is impossible to know what Royce had in mind or how much further he was prepared to go. Since he will not discourse on logic, he says, he cannot indicate what we can accomplish through this source of insight.[45] The considerations at the center of his system are technical and complex issues which he cannot talk about in a popular lecture series; but as we should expect, he mentions that they rest on the "revision and transformation of the Kantian theory of knowledge."[46]

These two themes—the existence of the Absolute and Royce's alternative to James's dichotomy—come together in the discussion of reason.

Reason is a source of religious insight because it shows us that the goal of life is attained in a higher unity. The argument from the possibility of error demonstrates that "a superhuman type of life is a real fact in the world."[47] Of course, this type of life is that in which our ultimate values are realized, and the argument is a paradigm example of religious insight. Royce's position differs little from the previous ones with which we are acquainted. The novelty is that this "wider insight" is described as *"an all-seeing comprehension of facts as they are."*[48] It exemplifies the third kind of knowledge which Royce offered as an alternative to James's division between the "nonrational" and "abstract." Although this *tertium quid* is important, Royce does not discuss its difference from the "appreciative Absolute" of his earlier works. In *The Sources of Religious Insight* the significant conclusion is that the "new" Absolute justifies the religious interest. Our need for salvation *must* be met, although as I have indicated before, I do not see how we can be in danger of damnation: our salvation is certainly not contingent on a Harvard professor's proving God's existence.

Whatever these complications, we must examine the book's other themes—really extensions of *The Philosophy of Loyalty*. Royce asserts that there is a distinction and even a conflict between the claims of morality and religion. Morality is concerned with defining man's highest ideal and proclaiming the best means to attain it. That is, morality directs us to life in the pursuit of duty. The religious motive is connected with our desire to know that we can attain our ideal:

> It [religion] appeals for help, or waits patiently for the Lord, or rejoices in the presence of salvation. It therefore may assume any one of many different attitudes toward the problem of duty. It may seek salvation through deeds, or again it may not, in the minds of some men, appeal to the active nature in any vigorous way whatever. Some religious moods are passive, contemplative, receptive, adoring rather that strenuous. It is therefore quite consistent with the existence of a religious interest to feel suspicious of the dutiful restlessness of many ardent souls.[49]

Knowing that we are to be saved, could we not renege on the good fight? Is there a morality, essentially religious, that reconciles our need for salvation with the moral need for action? Is there "a consciousness which equally demands of those whom it inspires, spiritual attainment and strenuousness, serenity and activity, resignation and vigour, life in the spirit and ceaseless enterprise in service?"

The answer is yes—the religion of loyalty. On the one hand, loyal individuals are resolute and have wills of their own; they have social motives and their faithfulness is a recognition of what in their eyes is an important calling. On the other hand, the cause is a unity which links many lives in one. It is superhuman in the same sense in which the "wider insight" presupposed by the necessity of error is superhuman.[50]

But what do we do with the evil of the world, which Royce admits to be dreadful and persistent? How do we reconcile our knowledge of the triumph of good with the eternal existence of pain and suffering? Royce puts the question in more pointed terms, for he declares that without real and present evil, religion is trivial: we are in need of redemption only if "evil is deeply rooted in the very nature of reality"; yet if it is so rooted, religion would appear to be a failure.[51] He approaches this problem by stating that our deepest ills can become sources of religious insight: they can bring us knowledge of spiritual truth. Although his meaning is unclear, it is obvious what is going on. Some evils, he says, we "assimilate" or "idealize." This at least means that we are able to live with them and perhaps triumph over them; he also suggests that we "take them up into the plan of our lives, give them meaning, set them in their place in the whole."[52] When this occurs, these evils enable us to understand in however imperfect a fashion how our "world-embracing insight" can take up into its life evils too terrible for us to bear. These may have places as stages and phases of expression in the larger life to which we belong. The function of lesser evils may be to give us hints—sources of religious insight—into the way the wider insight incorporates greater evils. Royce speaks of the religious mission of *sorrow*: when we use the evils in our lives to forge the morally good, our sorrow and the overcoming of evil awaken us to what the spiritual realm may be.[53] Once again good triumphs in the world only if temporal existence is riven with evil: goodness is not simply the absence of strife or suffering; it is the triumph over strife and suffering.[54]

Loyalty exists as a morality and a religion because there are evils to war against, moral goods to win. There could be no loyalty in a world where the loyal met no adversities that belonged to and entered their inner lives.[55] We define loyalty in a context where man faces evil—the trials and tribulations of human existence—and devotes himself to overcoming it. If we recall that the loyal personality type is our ideal, it is plausible for Royce to say that "the most rational type of life" demands the existence of adversity.[56] Our religion of loyalty becomes a major fount of religious insight.

The point in sorting out the sources of spiritual knowledge is to ground our faith in the triumph of goodness when the finite world contains ineradicable evil. But this context makes the book for me the most unsatisfying of Royce's works. He makes damnation intelligible by intimating that the salvation *of the species* is in doubt. Royce's argument is justifiable on a personal level: a given man might need assurance that loyal effort can result in his salvation; that his failures are eventually made good; and that he is not one of those evil-doers who is vanquished in the infinite. But after Royce proves the Absolute's existence, he assumes that the achievement of mankind is positive. If we are to doubt mankind's salvation, the Absolute's existence will give us little comfort: we may construe the species as an evil which is overwhelmed in God. Although the interpretation is labored and requires a more precise definition of salvation than Royce gives, this may be the nub of his discussion. Perhaps both the individual and the species are damned; but because the Absolute exists, it is reasonable to hope that both are positive elements in experience and that we can justify moral effort.

If we realize that it is *logically* necessary that the world is perfect *and* that evil exists, Royce's position still involves an awful tension: he has to explain why a perfect world *must* contain evil. Although he treats the problem in a new and distinct setting which carries him away from his earlier concerns, I do not feel he has made any advance over his nineteenth-century solutions; I am not convinced that we have in part justified some finite evils by saying they may help us to understand the inexplicable and unutterable horrors of existence. Is a perfect world one in which the function of evils we can bear is to explain those we cannot bear? With James, I find Royce's perspective grotesque.

In the last chapter of *The Sources of Religious Insight* he briefly surveys how "the church"—in some way he associates it with Christianity—acts as *"the crowning source of religious insight."* The church, he asserts,

> . . . is to be to us a source of insight. This means that we must enter into some sort of communion with the faithful if we are to enjoy the fruits of their insight. And, apart from one's own life of loyal service itself, the principal means of grace—that is, the principal means of attaining instruction in the spirit of loyalty, encouragement in its toils, solace in its sorrows, and power to endure and to triumph—the principal means of grace, I say, which is open to any man lies in such communion with the faithful and with the unity of the spirit which they express in their lives.[57]

Royce's survey is superficial. The limitations of his lectures forbade him to consider the church in any detail;[58] more importantly, he was planning what would be his last major study, *The Problem of Christianity*, while delivering the Bross Lectures; for this reason they ignore Christianity.[59] He would later attempt "an application of some of the principles that underlie the present lectures to the special problems which Christianity offers to the student of religion."[60] We must turn to *The Problem of Christianity* for an examination of the connection between Royce's religion of loyalty and Christianity. But first it is imperative to investigate the foundations of this thought. As Royce states, *The Problem of Christianity* is an *application* of doctrines *underlying The Sources of Religious Insight*. We have seen even in this chapter that his work takes novel twists after the publication of *The World and the Individual*. Indeed, we have gotten ahead of our story: after writing *The World and the Individual* Royce continued his study of mathematics, and altered the basis of his thinking. By the time he wrote *The Sources of Religious Insight*, he had begun to translate these logical innovations into metaphysical language. Before we can understand their blossoming, in *The Problem of Christianity*, we must explore Royce's work on his logical system Σ.

9

FOUNDATIONS OF MATHEMATICS, 1
The Nineteenth-Century Background

Plato is reported to have said "God ever geometrizes,"[1] and philosophers from Plato to the present have used mathematical and particularly geometrical notions to clarify their thought. Metaphysics, Peirce wrote in his review of Royce's *Conception of God*, has always aped geometry.[2] The reason for this is easy to fathom: mathematics—and traditionally Euclidean geometry—is a paradigm of that exact and rigorous thought whose conclusions seem undeniable; and this precision and intelligibility is what many philosophers seek. Kant was mindful of this heritage; only continental philosophers since Hegel have deviated from it, and are, so far, outside the tradition. The prominent role that mathematics plays in Royce's thinking is further evidence of the centrality of Kant, rather than the post-Kantians, to his development. The problems which troubled Kantians who paid attention to nineteenth-century discoveries in mathematics also engaged Royce.

The history of nineteenth-century mathematics is one of a relaxation of the idea that the discipline is in any way related to the world—that mathematicians must "intuit" the correctness of proofs. Although mathematicians were not trying to achieve abstract conceptions, there is a growing emphasis on formalization in their work. If we are to understand Royce's concerns, we need to explore two strands of this development and its relation to philosophy. One is the increasing formalization of geometry. The other is Boole's contribution to logic; his work is essential in tying together algebra and geometry. This connection is crucial to the solutions Royce propounds to the philosophical puzzles generated by the crisis in the foundations of mathematics.

Let us imagine that we are looking with one eye at a given figure and that a ray of light—in the future I shall simply say line—proceeds from each point on the figure to the eye; this collection of converging lines is a projection. Let us also imagine a glass screen intersecting the projection at various intervals; the collection of points where the lines of projection intersect the screen may be called sections, and we can visualize the figures that would appear on various sections. For example, if the figure is a rectangle and we designate the eye by O, one section on the screen will be the following, where the section is in a plane parallel to the rectangle (Figure 1):

FIGURE 1

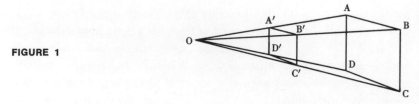

We can generate another example if we imagine the eye viewing a square from a position off to the side (Figure 2). Whereas A'B'C'D' is similar to ABCD, D'E'F'G' is obviously not a square as is DEFG. The kind of section obtained in Figure 2 is different from that of Figure 1.

This simple phenomenon suggests interesting questions to an enterprising geometer. Shouldn't sections of a figure viewed from different positions have some properties in common, since they all derive from the same figure? And shouldn't different sections viewed from the same position also have common properties? In other words, we can look for geometrical properties common to all sections of the same projection and to sections of different projections. This was historically the task of projective geometry.

If we begin this investigation we see that length, angle, area, and parallelism may be altered from section to section; two sections of the same or different projections need not be congruent or similar; the study of properties common to various sections is not within the province of

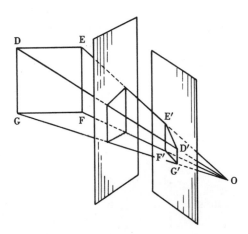

FIGURE 2

Euclidean geometry. The kinds of properties invariant under projection and section—"projective transformations"—deal with the collinearity of points, that is, the properties of points lying on the same line. Take a section of a line divided by four points as in Figure 3. Corre-

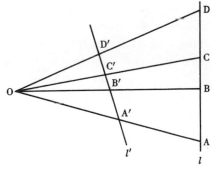

FIGURE 3

sponding segments (e.g., A'B' and AB) are not equal; but neither are corresponding ratios (e.g., $\frac{A'C'}{B'C'}$ and $\frac{AC}{DC}$). What is equal is the ratio of ratios—or the cross ratio as it is called: $\frac{AC}{CB} \div \frac{AD}{DB} = \frac{A'C'}{C'B'} \div \frac{A'D'}{D'B'}$. Any line intersecting OA, OB, OC, and OD will contain segments possessing the same cross ratio as the original segments. This ratio is a "projective invariant"; if we form a projection of these four lines and take a section of this projection, the section will contain four intersecting lines whose cross ratio equals that of the original figure. In Figure 4 we have made a projection of OABCD (formed by the lines OA, OB, OC, and OD of Figure 3) from O". In this section O'A'B'C'D', the cross ratios of O'A', O'B', O'C', O'D' and OA, OB, OC, and OD are the same.

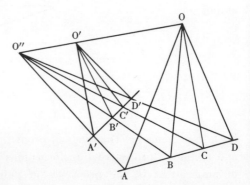

Euclidean geometry deals with the equality of lengths, angles, and areas; projective geometry deals with collinearity. What is the relation between the two? Morris Kline writes: "A comparison of these two classes of properties suggests that projective properties are simpler than those treated in Euclidean geometry. One might say that projective geometry deals with the very formation of the geometrical figures . . . studied in Euclid. In other words projective geometry is indeed logically prior to Euclidean geometry and . . . the latter can be built up as a special case."[3]

We shall explore later exactly what this means, but it is now possible to give a diagrammatic account. Consider the projection of a rectangle and a section in a plane parallel to the rectangle. The section is a rectangle similar to the original; we have an example in Figure 1. Now let O move off to the left. The lines of the projection come closer to being parallel. If O becomes "the point at infinity," they are parallel and the two rectangles become congruent (Figure 5). We study the relations characterizing Euclidean geometry from the standpoint of projective

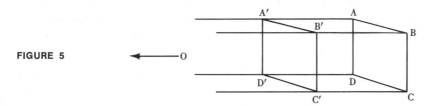

FIGURE 5

geometry by examining projection and section *for special projections.* Euclidean geometry considers geometric properties invariant under specified projections: it is a special case of projective geometry when we stipulate the "whereabouts" of O.[4]

By a similar choice of projections we can obtain the *non-Euclidean* geometries as special cases of projective geometry. The difference between Euclidean and non-Euclidean geometry arises from the differences between the definition of magnitudes like the distance between two points. All these geometries are *metrical* and to derive any of them from projective geometry all we need do is make an additional postulate stipulating (in my simplified example above) the location of O. These geometries are structurally identical, and for every theorem about an invariant property in one geometry, there is a "dual" theorem about a corresponding property in each of the others. If we consider the metrical geometries as abstract calculi they make no contradictory assertions about physical space, the external world; rather they exhibit in different notations an identical pattern of relations. If we give any of these geometries a precise physical interpretation—as I have been doing in a simplified way with projective geometry—only a variety of experimental tests will determine whether any of them is true of the world.

The process of projection and section is an example of a mathematical transformation, and projective geometry studies invariants under this transformation.[5] We set up machinery whereby each element of one assemblage (our projection of a figure) corresponds to an element of a second (our section), and each element of the second to an element of the first;[6] and we learn what properties (e.g., the cross ratio) remain invariant under these transformations.

It is possible to state what we have done in formal language. Given any system S of elements, let us establish a one-to-one correspondence— call it T for transformation—between the elements of S and the elements of another system S'. We say that T transforms S into S' or write $T(S) = S'$. Suppose two transformations, T_1 and T_2, are applied successively to a system S, such that $T_1(S) = S'$ and $T_2(S') = S''$. The transformation which transforms S directly into S'' is called the resultant or product of T_1 and T_2. We can represent it by the symbol T_2T_1, following from the relation $S'' = T_2(S') = T_2(T_1(S)) = T_2T_1(S)$. If T transforms S into S', we call the transformation which transforms S' into S the inverse of T, and denote it by T^{-1}; that is, from the relation $T(S) = S'$ follows the relation $T^{-1}(S') = S$. The product of a transformation by its inverse leaves every element unchanged. This transformation is called the identical transformation or simply the identity, and is symbolized by 1. Thus, $TT^{-1} = T^{-1}T = 1$ and $1T = T1 = T$.[7]

Suppose we have a set of transformations in which the inverse transformation of every transformation of the set is in the set, and in which the resultant of every two transformations of the set is also in the set. We have defined two important characteristics of a *group* of transformations. It is possible to define any geometry by a group of transformations by way of "a fundamental principle" which in the late nineteenth century became a "classic in geometry." Let G be any group of transformations. The body of definitions and the theorems which express properties unchanged under the transformations of G (but not unchanged under the transformation of any other group containing G) is called the geometry associated with or defined by G.[8] The properties which a geometry explores are those which are invariant under a set of transformations: the invariant properties and permitted transformations determine each other. We may take either the invariant properties or the set of transformations to characterize the geometry. For example, we say that ordinary Euclidean geometry studies the property of magnitude between segments, angles, and so on; or, we say that it studies those properties left invariant under translation and rotation.

This conception of geometry is a powerful advance. It makes apparent the connection between the "arithmetic" branches of mathematics and geometry, and the formal nature of the latter—for it is only on an interpretation of the elements of a group as points, lines, and so on that a geometry has its customary meaning as a (physical) geometry. Moreover, this conception enables us to order various geometries logically in terms of their generality. Since this is a point of importance, let us examine it for a while.

We may consider metric geometries as projective systems for which we have stipulated a distance function, i.e., specified the location of O. In logical terms we have added a postulate. The additional postulate "reduces the number of independent parameters on which the transformations of the system depend, and yields a narrower system."[9] It turns out that there are other transformations more general than projection and section whose invariants we can study. The "widest" system is topology, and its relation to projective geometry is like the relation of projective geometry to metric geometry: if we consider the question logically, we add postulates to topology to get the narrower system of projective geometry.[10] The classificatory theory is such that the fewer postulates we have to satisfy, the less restricted the resulting geometry. We may think of a basic set of postulates to which we add other postulates; with each addition we establish a more narrow geometry.[11]

We must stress that the relation between, for example, projective geometry and Euclidean geometry (a metric geometry) is not one of logical deducibility: that is, we cannot derive Euclidean geometry from projective geometry. This point is significant, since geometers often mistook the relationship for logical deducibility, and Royce makes the same kind of error in a similar context. The actual relationship should be plain: every postulate of projective geometry is a postulate of Euclidean geometry, but there are postulates of the latter which are not postulates of the former. If we add postulates to a "projective space," it will become a "Euclidean space"; and a Euclidean space becomes a projective space on the elimination of these postulates. David Hilbert's axioms illustrate this idea. We formulate projective geometry with a class of postulates which take the point as the only undefined primitive. These are called the postulates of connection; they, along with postulates of order which introduce the relation of "betweenness," are sufficient to yield affine geometry—a geometry more general than the metric geometries but less general than projective geometry. If we add to these postulates those of congruence *and* more specific postulates which characterize parallelism, we arrive at Euclidean geometry.[12]

Arthur Cayley, a product of Trinity, Cambridge, first attempted to demonstrate the relation of metrical geometry—he was interested in Euclidean geometry—to projective geometry. For him this involved establishing the notion of distance on the basis of projective principles:

> As a definition, we say that the two points of a circle are equidistant from the center. Now imagine two points P, P'; and take the point P' ' such that P and P' ' are a circle having P' for its center; take in like manner the point P' ' ' such that P', P' ' ' are a circle having P' ' for its center; and so on. . . . We have a series of points . . . [P, P', P' ', P' ' '] at equal intervals of distance. . . . It is clear that according to the definition, if P, P', P' ' be any three points taken in order then
> $$\text{Dist}(P,P') + \text{Dist}(P',P'\,') = \text{Dist}(P,P'\,')$$
> which agrees with the ordinary notion of distance.

We pick as a "point pair" on a line the points in which a circle intersects the line; the center of the circle will be equidistant from the points. If we proceed as described above, we obtain equal intervals on the line and can introduce coordinates to denote their points.[13] Cayley calls the original point pair the "absolute." Upon its specification we can generate Euclidean out of projective geometry just as above we generated Euclidean from projective geometry by specifying projections from the "point at infinity." The point pair here—the absolute—is a degenerate conic, and in 1871 Felix Klein showed that we can obtain the metrical geometries—Euclidean and non-Euclidean—by Cayley's method: by a suitable choice of the conic, the absolute, we can define different distance functions, and this is all we need to yield the metric geometries.[14]

A year later, in 1872, Klein used these results to proclaim his famous *Erlanger Programm* and to assert his conviction that each geometry is defined by those properties left invariant under a series of transformations. The *Erlanger Programm* became the paradigm for geometrical thinking for the next fifty years. It embodies just that idea we have considered: the goal is to classify all geometries in terms of those properties left invariant under transformation and to establish a hierarchy of geometries, from the most general to the least general.[15]

It is often argued that this notion resolved the disorder which the advent of the non-Euclidean geometries created; at least the ferment in geometry is said to have refuted Kant's argument that Euclidean geometry has a special form of necessity. But although the work of Cayley and Klein was an advance in mathematical thinking, it is an oversimplification to view this work as the death knell of Kantianism. Kant's view had a powerful hold on geometricians; the discovery of the non-Euclidean geometries led *not* to the overthrow of this view, but to various attempts to patch up the Kantian position and make it congruent with the new discoveries. The standard argument was that although mathematicians had proved the consistency of non-Euclidean geometries, Euclidean geometry itself was more "useful" because space was, in fact, Euclidean; it had been shown that we could apply the other geometries *in* Euclidean space with a change in the definition of distance: they were consistent because Euclid was.[16] This was the view of Cayley and Klein, who regarded questions concerning the various metric geometries as questions of distance and not of space; Euclidean space was given primacy of place.[17]

The most fascinating study of the hold of Kant and Euclid on nineteenth-century thinking is Bertrand Russell's *Essay on the Foundations of Geometry*. It contains a sophisticated and logically impeccable criticism of Cayley and Klein, but its philosophical perspective is worth examining itself. Russell later wrote that the book seemed "somewhat foolish" and that relativity theory "swept away everything at all resembling this point of view."[18] But in 1897, when Russell wrote his book, he was a Kantian: for him the mind had to possess some "form of externality" in order to experience space. Although Russell argues that the a priori properties of this form of externality are not the postulates of

Euclid, he *does* find these a priori properties in projective geometry. He claims that we must determine empirically which of the additional postulates that generate the metric geometries will be true of the world; and he is fairly sure that the Euclidean one is correct.[19] What is remarkable is that Russell anchors geometry to "a form of externality." To be sure, projective geometry—at that time considered the most general geometry —and not Euclidean is the geometry which our spatial intuitions presuppose. Nonetheless, in 1897 Russell was not a formalist, and like his predecessors justified formal geometric reasoning as a technical aid. Geometry was the science of space, and the new discoveries were compatible with Kant's ideas.[20]

Russell's later criticism of the *Essay* maintains that some of its "details" are "valid," and it is crucial for our view of the work of Cayley and Klein to examine a few of these details. Cayley accomplishes his 1859 "reduction" of metric to projective geometry by discussing distance in terms of the cross ratio, and this conception is based on the metric conception of distance which it is designed to eliminate.[21] Using ideas of the geometer Karl G. C. von Staudt, however, Klein does give a definition of the cross ratio in projective concepts. In part because of this achievement, Cayley and even Klein assume—wrongly as we have seen—that it is possible to *deduce* the metric geometries from projective geometry:[22] they misconceive the relation existing between the geometries. Russell pointed out the error in 1897, a considerable feat when we realize that it is an error made even today.[23]

Both Cayley and Klein regard the definition of distance—the specification of the absolute—as arbitrary and as requiring no additional postulates. But Russell demonstrates that this view is incorrect. For Cayley or Klein to obtain a specific metric geometry just *that* conic which will yield the requisite distance relation must be stipulated, and this cannot be done using projective principles alone. As Russell writes, in projective geometry collineation—the property of points lying on the same line—is the only method of distinguishing points from one another; and every pair of collinear points shares all its projective properties with all other pairs of points on the line. Unfortunately, we can derive the projective definition of the cross ratio only when we have sets of *four* points. "The projective definition of distance must accordingly be a definition in terms of four points, not of two."[24] Cayley regards two of these points—his absolute—as independently determined in order to derive his analogue of metrical distance in projective geometry. The choice of the absolute fixes the distance relation which the cross ratio describes, and this choice is not arbitrary: different choices give different distance functions. Russell correctly argues that if we introduce the notion of distance to specify our absolute, or postulate that we can specify it, we obtain a metric distance, but not on projective principles; if we maintain our projective principles, we cannot get our metric distance.[25]

Although the idea that geometry is related to our intuitive notion of space exercised a powerful hold on Cayley, Klein, and Russell, the *Erlanger Programm* did much to contribute to future conceptions of geometry's formal nature. Klein's view of geometry is also compatible with any attempt to link geometry to algebra, a link which might encourage formal conceptions. But the most important figure investigating these issues was George Boole. Boole's "algebra of logic" attracted little attention from mathematicians during the nineteenth century,[26] but thinkers like Royce were quick to see in it an expression of a philosophical tie between geometry and algebra. Our interest in Boole, therefore, is in understanding those of his views which philosophers took up and joined to the Cayley-Klein-Russell view of geometry.

Boole's intent was to investigate and formulate the fundamental laws of the mind which allow us to reason; he wanted to give them expression in a symbolical language, calculus, or algebra. His work reflects the idea that we can base our mathematics in some intuitive interpretation, however formal some aspects of the discipline may look. Boole accepted this idea, and the title of his well-known book makes this explicit: *An Investigation of the Laws of Thought on which are founded the Mathematical Theories of Logic and Probabilities.* His algebra is abstract and empty in that we are to look on it as devoid of content; he wishes to show that we can use it to solve problems about the properties of number, on one interpretation; about geometrical properties on another; about dynamics on a third; and so on. In one sense we are dealing with an abstract system of postulates. But Boole believed that the system had some "ultimate interpretation" in its reflection of rational thought processes.[27]

From a contemporary perspective, Boole's work does not distinguish his "uninterpreted" system and its various interpretations, and following the explication of William and Martha Kneale, I begin my analysis with an interpretation of Boole's system as an algebra of classes. We let x and y denote classes and use the symbol $=$ between two class symbols to indicate that the classes have the same members. We can represent the intersection or overlap of two classes—the class consisting of all those things belonging to both x and y—by xy. This convention may have been suggested by the way we string adjectives together to specify some class like that of large, red, soft balls. To take another example, we may denote the class of good men by xy if x is the class of good things and y that of men. This way of speaking permits Boole to blur the distinction between classes and the members of the class. In fact, he sometimes calls his letters "elective symbols," meaning that they are symbols which elect (i.e., select) *certain things* for attention. Thus by xy he sometimes simply means good men. Since Royce learned his logic from Boole and Booleans,[28] it is not surprising that he is vague about the distinction between inclusion and membership.

In addition to using letters to denote ordinary classes Boole uses the special symbols 1 and 0 to denote respectively the universal class, of which everything we are considering is a member, and the null class, of which nothing is a member. It is then obvious that $1x = x$ — the class of things common to x and 1 is equal to x. Similarly, $0x = 0$; and we find that $xx = x$, which Boole feels is the distinctive feature of his calculus. Although the full development of the algebra is more complex than indicated here, with the aid of what amounts to eight postulates Boole introduces a mechanical and abstract method for obtaining the reasoning recognized in Aristotelian logic.

There is another interpretation of his calculus which deserves mention. Suppose we add to our eight postulates a ninth: either x $=1$ or x $= 0$. We then derive a different interpretation of the calculus than the algebra of classes: "we have here all that is needed for an interpretation of Boole's system in terms of the truth-values of propositions with the symbols 1 and 0 standing for truth and falsity." x $= 0$ is taken to mean that x is false; x and y will be true if xy $= 1$, and false if xy $= 0$; and so on.

Boole does not note the difference between his system of eight postulates which admits of an interpretation in terms of classes, and that system with an additional postulate which does not; the distinction, however, is essential, and inattention to it can have disastrous results. The relation is much like that between projective and metric geometry. Our second system is *narrower* than the first; although we may interpret the first as an algebra of classes, we cannot give this interpretation to the second. It is true, however, that anything that can be proved in the second system about the truth value of propositions without the additional postulate will have an analogue in the algebra of classes. Every postulate of the latter—abstractly considered—is also a postulate of the "propositional" interpretation.[29]

10

FOUNDATIONS OF MATHEMATICS, 2

The Erlanger Logic, 1905–1910

C. I. Lewis is the only philosopher, and the only logician of note, to take Royce's logic seriously; now it rarely commands even passing historical notice. Lewis believed that the roots of Royce's idealism "are to be found in his logical theory," but Lewis never examined them and in fact gives the impression that logic was cut off from the rest of Royce's thinking.[1] Although it is difficult enough to master the technical considerations, my main interest in the logic is the philosophic framework within which Royce works it out; and if we are to construe this matrix properly, we must survey the speculative climate in which Royce and his contemporaries wrote.

Royce had long been interested in the relation of mathematics to philosophy. Teaching in California in early 1880, he wrote an astounding letter to William James which bears citation. Royce proclaims that he had extended his mathematical study to understand thinking. But the primary philosophical problem is to define an adequate conception of space:

> the space problem, who shall master it? What is needed is I think this:—Someone must master the whole science of Geometry in its latest forms as well as in its long history. Then this same man must have complete control over physiological psychology. Then he must master all the uses that have been made of space-science as an aid to other sciences either directly or not directly dependent on it, and so come to see the true connection of geometry and logic. . . .

Then he must have control of the philosophic literature about space from Zeno of Elea to Kant and the present day. On the basis of all this he must write a special treatise, say on the "Properties of Space," which shall develop the principles of a new philosophic science, a synthesis of all the previous material, an elaborate account of what is empirical and what is not empirical in our knowledge and application of space-properties. Give me ten years and nothing to hinder, and I will undertake that work myself. But I have neither the time nor the material.[2]

History does not record how James responded to this credo of the twenty-four-year-old Royce. Five years later, however, in *The Religious Aspect of Philosophy*, he declares in a similar way that the Absolute comprehends all experience as an algebraic equation expresses all the values of its variables; for us the achievements of mathematics and science are a shadow of the perfection of the infinite thought. And concluding in this manner, he asserts, "There must be then in fact a universal formula."[3] In *The Spirit of Modern Philosophy* he elaborates on what this "formula" is like:

> Higher beings than we may have other forms of descriptive science, based upon a consciousness, say, of some other form of space and time, e.g., of a "non-Euclidean" space of three dimensions, or of a space of four or more dimensions, and of a time that includes the truth of ours and still makes clear how the world-process somehow returns into itself. . . . our vague infinities of space and time, never finished, never explorable as wholes are very poor embodiments of [t]his truth.[4]

Royce was not the only one interested in this sort of speculation. In Boole's unpublished papers he mentions a higher, more comprehensive logic than his algebra which we cannot reduce to a calculus at all. This higher logic is, he says, "the Philosophy of *all* thought which is expressible in signs, whatever the object of that thought."[5] In looking for the basis of logic in the constitution of the human intellect, Boole may have been searching for something from which we could "derive" both geometry *and* algebra: from a more ethereal algebra reflecting all thinking we will be able to deduce all of our reasoning concerning space (the province of geometry) and time (the province of algebra). Russell's essay on geometry shows the same concerns. The explication of the errors of Cayley and Klein is not simply an exercise in formal virtuosity. Russell was disturbed that their "reduction" of metric to projective geometry would be a profound argument for idealism—of the view that we could regard "externality" as deducible from a priori notions which themselves are independent of externality. Any Kantian would eschew this conclusion and Russell has mathematical grounds for doing so. "In spite of its immense technical importance, and in spite of the complete logical freedom of projective Geometry from metrical ideas," Russell maintains, what Cayley and Klein had achieved is *"purely* technical, and is not philosophically valid"; it is "philosophically irrevelant"; physical space is "irreducibly metrical"; it can be derived from nothing more basic. Kant believed that the postulates of Euclidean geometry were necessary a priori judgments about a space for which we had fundamental intuitions; and so Russell believed that projective geometry involved necessary a priori judgments about "a form of externality" for which we had an equally fundamental intuition.[6]

There were, consequently, important stakes in the disputes over these abstruse mathematical and geometrical matters, and after the turn of the century Royce was quick to see the possibilities for philosophic advance. Although his position was different, he was operating in the same context of argument as Russell's *Essay.* Suppose Royce could show that we could deduce spatial presuppositions, let us say the postulates of Euclidean geometry, from the postulates of logic which did not involve any notion of distance. He could then argue that the latter postulates were presuppositions of externality. From Royce's Kantian frame of reference this fact would have momentous significance: he could obtain his long sought-after deduction of the categories, a deduction of the concepts inherent in our talk of an external world, from concepts untainted by externality. He might show, that is, how the World of Description was generated from the World of Appreciation, how to reconcile his dense series with the series of natural numbers. We might find in the intellect —the world of algebra or logic—the conditions of the possibility of spatial experience.

In its broadest terms Royce's project has much in common with Boole's speculative epistemology and is an analogue in logic to Klein's *Erlanger Programm*. There are hints to this effect throughout Royce's work; in a long "Note" detailing his interest in these problems he wrote that the *Erlanger Programm* was "the source" of his new theorizing.[7] He will construct a system ostensibly abstract but actually rooted in the structure of the absolute intellect and the fundamental forms of thinking. Like Klein he wanted to obtain from this system a hierarchy of the "order systems" sufficient for man's knowledge of the world. Like Cayley he thought that we could derive the less general from the more general and that ultimately externality presupposes mind; and like Cayley's idea—as we shall see—Royce's was also logically erroneous.

With this overview in mind we can return to a more detailed narration. To do this we must go back to 1849, and the birth of Alfred Bray Kempe. Kempe was educated at St. Paul's School and Trinity College, Cambridge, where he received a B.A. in 1872 with distinction in mathematics as twenty-second wrangler. Like many young men with a mathematical bent, Kempe could not pursue his interests professionally and turned instead to the law. In 1873 he was admitted to the bar and began a highly successful career as an ecclesiastical lawyer: he was knighted in 1912, and when he died in 1922 was Chancellor of six Dioceses including that of London. But Kempe kept up his mathematical work, contributing articles to the professional journals and serving as President of the London Mathematical Society for two years. In 1881 he was elected a Fellow of the Royal Society supported by "a group of the foremost mathematicians"—including Arthur Cayley and James Joseph Sylvester.[8]

Kempe's significance here is not his work in the law or mathematics but his influence on two American philosophers—Charles Peirce and Josiah Royce. Peirce had the highest respect for Kempe's essays and thought his work "profound and masterly." In 1909—the middle of an intensely creative period in the history of logic—Peirce wrote that

Kempe was the greatest living logician;[9] this is no small compliment when one considers that this meant that Peirce himself felt outranked by the Englishman. Royce's praise was equally unstinting through the first decade of the century; he felt Kempe's essays were the most promising logical advances "that we have made for generations"[10] and so praised the articles that Bertrand Russell was induced to study them.[11]

Kempe was interested in the relation of geometry to logic. As early as 1877 he worked on the connection with Sylvester, a man so close to Cayley that they have been called the invariant twins.[12] Sylvester believed that the inner (mental) world of each individual man—the mathematician's world of observation—stands in the same relation to the external world as does an object to the shadows projected from it: to Sylvester the mental order was "more real" than the physical, and the foundation for the former was mathematics.[13] In 1877 he went to Johns Hopkins, where he taught until 1884.[14] Whether Royce or Peirce, who were both at Hopkins in this period, picked up anything of Sylvester's speculative ideas on mathematics is unclear; but in London Alfred Bray Kempe had. The culmination of his research was a treatise, "A Memoir on the Theory of Mathematical Form," published in *The Philosophical Transactions of the Royal Society* of London.[15] Four years later, in 1890, he produced another version of his findings in the *Proceedings of the London Mathematical Society*.[16] And at the end of the same year he published a general and nontechnical discussion of his work in *Nature*.[17] We have already seen that by 1900 Royce had drawn informally on Kempe's studies for the second volume of *The World and the Individual*. Thereafter Royce studied them with a passion, and although there are differences of technical detail, his logic was simply an extension of Kempe's, and so we must scrutinize the latter's treaties.

The two major papers formulate the connection among logic, geometry, and his "base system." A set of elements and five postulates define the base system, of which Kempe writes:

> In the present paper . . . I first consider and fully discuss the properties of a special system of entities here called the *base system*, the form of which is fully determined by laws which define the mode

of distribution of certain like and unlike triads of its component entities—i.e., laws that specify which triads are like and which unlike. I then show that this system is precisely that which is under consideration by the logician, when discussing classes and their mutual relations. I further show that certain entities of the base system, selected in accordance with a simple law, compose a system which is precisely that which is under consideration by the geometrician when discussing the points and their mutual relations.[18]

If Kempe is correct, we can derive both logic and geometry from a more general system. Both the methods and results fascinated Royce, but the precise formulation did not satisfy him, and he worked out Kempe's achievements in a logically more rigorous and metaphysically more perspicacious form.

The first four of Kempe's postulates depend on the base system's primative: a generalized notion of betweenness; he defines the fifth by negation—no entity is absent which can consistently be present.[19] However much the betweenness principle impressed Royce, it was important for him to set up the system on another basis, and the fifth postulate was inelegant and obscured some of Kempe's results. Royce spent nearly five years poring over Kempe's essays, and by 1905 he produced his masterwork in symbolic logic, "The Relations of the Principles of Logic to the Foundations of Geometry."[20] In it he reinterpreted Kempe's results in the system Σ.

Σ is supposedly a formal system whose "elements" are "simple and homogenous"; it also contains collections of these elements and collections of these collections, and so on. We can designate collections in Σ by writing $(x,y, \ldots)$ where x, y, and so on are elements of the collection. Royce uses Greek letters to designate collections; thus a, β, and λ designate collections. Although one of Royce's postulates enables him to achieve the results Kempe does with the betweenness principle, the six postulates of Σ depend on a primitive O-relation and on what Royce calls O-collections. To say that a collection is an O-collection we write $O(x,y, \ldots)$, and any collection not an O-collection is an E-collection. Collections may be adjoined to collections, and to designate that we have added an element to a collection, we write (a,x).[21]

We must pause for comment at such an early stage, because this curious terminology requires explication. It is, first, not clear why we should use parentheses around the Greek letters, for they already stand for a collection, e.g., (x,y,z). But there is a more important ambiguity here. a specifies a collection of elements, that is, a certain class of them, say [y,z]; to adjoin an element—say x—to a, we require the union of that element and a; but [y,z] U x is, as it stands, incoherent for we cannot join a class to an element in this way; the element x must itself be a class, and we must at least have [y,x] U [x'] where [x'] = df. x; this element is really *a unit class*, and given that our other "elements" are similar, we must write: [[y'], [z']] U [[x']]. All this comes to saying that Royce's elements are not uninterpreted variables, "simple and homogeneous," but unit sets. In an early version of his work he says just this: Σ is a system of objects "such that they are classes of a logical U. of D. [Universe of Discourse]."[22]

If we recall that Royce makes no distinction between a unit set and its element, this construal becomes plausible. We must also remember that the idea of the difference between an uninterpreted system and its "most general" interpretation is vague, and in at least three places Royce makes no distinction between the formal system and its interpretations. The elements of Σ, he writes, "possess the properties of a system of logical classes or of entities to which the usual algebra of logic applies." Because we can give an interpretation of the system in terms of the algebra, Σ "was so far identical with a totality of logical classes."[23] Finally, he shows that the postulates of Σ demand an infinite number of non-equivalent elements.[24] If the elements are "simple and homogeneous," it is unclear how we obtain this wealth and diversity. But, as Royce admits, Σ is not composed of "simple and homogeneous" elements; rather, they are to be so regarded "in the present discussion."[25]

It is dangerous to speculate about what someone "must have meant," but having ventured so far, I would like to make another educated guess. Royce's Σ is a version of Boole's higher, more comprehensive logic from which we may derive the forms of all our reasoning processes. The elements of Σ have the same structure as—in fact are—the

basic ideal constituents of the universe. They are Royce's internal meanings which synthesize form and content in a miniature concrete universal. Taken together, the elements of Σ form the class of all classes which
reflects the structure of—indeed, again is—the divine mind; their order
must be that of a self-representative system which is also capable of
generating a dense series. In developing Σ, Royce is delineating the consciousness of the Absolute and attempting to join the worlds of description and appreciation.

Let us write $O(x,y)$ to mean that (x,y) is an O-collection, definitionally equivalent to the O-collection $[\ [x']\ [y']\ ]$; and let us drop the
parentheses around collections designated by Greek letters: for example,
where Royce writes $O(a,x)$, let us write Oa,x, definitionally equivalent
to the O-collection $aU[x]$. If $O(x,y,\ldots)$, Royce calls $x,y,\ldots$ mutual
obverses of each other; the order in which they appear in the O-collection
is indifferent: $O(x,y,z)$, $O(y,z,x)$, $O(x,z,y)$, and so on are all the same.
If two elements, x and y, are equivalent, then any O-collection remains
an O-collection if we substitute one for another, and Royce writes $x = y$;
if the substitution makes the O-collection an E-collection, $x \neq y$. The
postulates of Σ are:

1. $(\alpha)\ (\beta)\ (O\ \alpha \supset O\alpha,\beta)$
2. $(x)\ (\alpha)\ (\beta)\ [(x\epsilon\beta \cdot O\beta \cdot Oa,x) \supset O\alpha]$
3. $(\exists x)\ (x\epsilon\Sigma)$
4. $(x)\ [(x\epsilon\Sigma) \supset (\exists y)\ ((y\epsilon\Sigma) \cdot (x \neq y))]$
5. $(x)\ (y)\ [(x \neq y) \supset (\exists z)(O(x,y,z) \cdot E(x,z) \cdot E(y,z))]$
6. $(\exists x)\ \{Oa, x \supset (\exists y)\ [Oa,y \cdot (z)\ ((z\epsilon\alpha) \supset O(x,y,z))]\}$

Royce demonstrates that all obverses of an element are equivalent and
that every element has an obverse, and he designates any obverse of x,
$\overline{x}$, as representative of the class of obverses of x. He also shows that all
one-element collections are E-collections and that no element is equivalent
to its own obverse. And Royce concludes that if $O\ (xy)$, then $x = \overline{y}$.[26]

To develop the algebras of classes and propositions Royce needs
the asymmetrical inclusion or implication relation which he writes $\prec$.
To obtain it he introduces F-collections: we generate F-collections from
any O-collection by dividing the members of the O-collection into two

sets by a stroke and replacing the elements on one side by their obverses. If $O(v,w,x,y,z)$, then we have $F(v/\overline{w},\overline{x},\overline{y},\overline{z})$, $F(\overline{v}/w,x,y,z)$, $F(v,w/\overline{x},\overline{y},\overline{z})$, $F(v,z/\overline{w},\overline{x},\overline{y})$, $F(\overline{w},\overline{y}/v,x,z)$, and so on.[27] The triadic F-collections are of utmost importance to Royce; they are asymmetrical and he introduces the special notation, $z \longrightarrow<\frac{x}{y} =$ df. $F(x,y/z) =$ df. $O(x,y,\overline{z})$ (or any equivalent O-collection). The triadic F-relation is identical with Kempe's betweenness relation, and in Royce's system the Kempean triad is a special case of the O-relation.[28] The triadic F-relation is the key to Royce's work. He demonstrates that if we pick out any arbitrary x (or y) in $F(x,y/z)$ as the zero element or origin, we get "z is included in y," where z and y are classes; "z implies y," where they are propositions; and "z precedes y," where they are points in one dimension. Accordingly Royce drops the subscript in $\longrightarrow<_x$ and writes, for example, $z\prec y$ for "z is included in y." As a consequence of this series of proofs he concludes that on different "interpretations" of Σ, we obtain various Boolean algebras; and he finishes by showing that on another interpretation, Σ provides a foundation for geometry: Oswald Veblen's system of postulates for geometry is a consequence of the postulates of Σ or results from restricting Σ's postulates themselves.[29]

If Royce had simply shown that we could use a symmetrical relation as the primitive of Σ, obtain various Boolean algebras on interpretations of Σ, and derive sets of geometrical postulates by restrictions to subsystems of Σ, he would have achieved enough.[30] But we must understand Royce's accomplishment in a more complex way. He makes no real distinction between a formal system and its interpretation; moreover, his work also has a metaphysical significance which must be pointed out. These two issues are related, but we shall take up the logical one first.

Suppose the elements of Σ are uninterpreted variables. Then we may get Boolean algebras on interpretations of the system. But to get the geometrical postulates involves us in another procedure. In respect to geometry, Royce writes:

> the lines that we are here first and mainly to consider are to be subjected to the entirely arbitrary restriction (foreign to the first principles of our system Σ, but quite capable of being satisfied by

> a due selection of its elements as their existence has now been established), that if any two non-equivalent entities of a line are given, *no other line*, in the set of lines that we are to consider shall at once contain both of these elements.

and:

> The principle of continuity is, for such a geometry, merely a principle of the selection of the elements, a principle which the system permits, but does not require to be carried out.[31]

But these restrictions and principles are not arbitrary; they are new postulates which have the effect of limiting the original postulates. We obtain the geometrical postulates not from Σ but from another system Σ *, which is like Σ in including Σ's postulates but unlike Σ in including additional ones. The situation is analogous to the one we surveyed in the last chapter. We cannot deduce geometry from Σ; rather, every postulate of Σ will be a postulate of Σ *, and we will obtain Σ * by adding postulates to those of Σ; the resulting system is a narrower, less general one, but one that is irreducible to Σ. As early as 1906 Theodore de Laguna pointed out a difficulty as important for the work of Royce and Kempe as Russell's strictures were for Cayley's "reduction" of metric geometry to projective. Just because Σ *is* more general than Σ *, de Laguna urged, Σ is subject to just as much a limitation as the lesser generality imposes on Σ *.[32]

If we suppose that Σ is not an uninterpreted system but, as I claimed, a peculiar system of unit classes, the same difficulties arise. In this case the various logics and geometries must be subsets of Σ. Royce writes that "One may view the points of space as a select set of logical elements, chosen, for instance, from a given universe of discourse," and that we may satisfy geometrical requirements "by a due selection" of Σ's elements.[33] Even if we neglect the problems in making a formal system indistinguishable from its "ultimate interpretation," we must still specify an additional postulate to give us the elements we need; we cannot derive our geometrical system from the postulates of Σ alone.

However we analyze Royce's work, and similarly that of Kempe, the critical flaw is that they accept Cayley's supposed derivation of metric from projective geometry. In our arbitrary selection principle, Kempe writes, "we are doing precisely the same thing as the geometrician who regards 'distance' as a relation between *two* points and not as one involving the geometrical 'absolute' as well as those two points."[34] Royce follows Kempe in using this appropriate analogy,[35] and consequently makes the error for which Russell chastised Cayley.

Although its correction necessitates a conceptual reorientation, the difficulty in the logic of Kempe and Royce is not one which requires an overhaul of their essays. And despite the fact that they lack any clear idea of a formal system, Russell also lacked one in 1897. We would not now regard what we do regard as confusion if intelligent men had not at one time been purveyors of confusion. The real problem for Royce lay in the philosophic implications he drew from his studies. For he was not concerned merely with the mathematical issues his work entailed; he thought "a revision of Kant & a new Critique . . . [were] in sight."[36] He believed "that all the serial and other ordinal relations known to logic and geometry, and all the operations known to both, so far as they are pure exact sciences, are ultimately reducible to assertions that certain entities do, while certain entities do not stand to one another in the perfectly symmetrical O-relation."[37] His aim was a broader and mathematically more sophisticated interpretation of what he had set out to do in the second volume of *The World and the Individual*. There he outlined the way we could derive the laws that encapsulate our empirical knowledge from a few fundamental concepts. Although making use of the betweenness relation in a general way, he did not attempt any development of his thesis, but in "The Relation of the Principles of Logic to the Foundations of Geometry" he believed he had established a *mathematical* deduction of the categories. By "arbitrarily" selecting subsets of Σ (or by giving the variables of Σ appropriate interpretations), we procure specialized "order systems" characterizing the procedures of all branches of knowledge.

In published and unpublished work from 1903 to 1905 Royce discusses these issues directly. [38] He asserts that two different sorts of concepts—levels and series—characterize thinking. Roughly speaking, our spatial concepts which the relation "coexistent with" expresses are prototypical of the levels; objects coexist with one another in space, and this relation is symmetrical and transitive. Prototypical of the series are our temporal concepts; to say "a is the successor of b" is to state the central temporal relation, and this relation is asymmetrical and transitive. Then, Royce claims:

> it would appear that the world of what is sometimes called pure experience presents to you rather series of various sorts than those levels of existence which constitute the world of physical facts as the latter coexist in space. And your belief that the facts do coexist in space would appear to be due to certain needs of your own intelligence,—needs which guide your interpretation of the realm of phenomena. And so far the concept of the level, to say the least, would appear to be forced upon you, in this respect at all events, because of your character as the intelligent interpreter of your experience.

We see that the symmetrical relation "coexistent with" is a "complex" of two asymmetrical temporal relations. To say "a coexists with b" means "a may be made, in my experience to follow b or to precede b, indifferently." But this complex is symmetrical. It is unnecessary to follow Royce to see how we "reduce" levels to series, but the connection to his logical work is plain. The primitive of Σ is the symmetrical O-relation. We construe conceptually secondary spatial notions in terms of this symmetrical relation, possessing an essential temporal aspect.[39]

Along with other working in logic, Royce believed that the discovery of non-Euclidean geometries falsified Kant's claim that a special intuition—like one of Euclidean space—had a peculiar kind of necessity.[40] Nevertheless, this setback to the post-Kantian ambition of unifying the sciences around a few categories was counterbalanced by advances in logic made concomitantly with the discovery of non-Euclidean geometries. Royce's use of Σ aimed to demonstrate that the axioms of geometry and logic could be "reduced to" or "derived from" some further set of postulates. We could then regard these postulates as "presuppositions" of all knowledge. In Royce's case, the "reduction" of the geometrical axioms to some ideal system of entities which need only exist in the mathematician's mind is singularly important. Royce would develop a system of postulates which are preconditions of our knowledge of objects; they are the logical ground of the possibility of spatial, i.e., external, experience. If his reasoning were correct, he would obtain a deduction of the categories consonant with idealism, a deduction reaffirming the primacy of mind and the derivation of matter from it.

He still had to face several problems. He had been adamant in insisting that his work in volume two of *The World and the Individual* applied only to the World of Description. The 1905 paper does not show in what respect the World of Description is an "aspect" of the World of Appreciation. And we have remarked on the insurmountable obstacles that blocked his approach, at least as Royce conceived it in terms of his two kinds of mathematical order. As we have also mentioned, he had formulated a contradictory notion of the Absolute. If these complications were unrecognized at the time, they did not remain so. Finally, there is a wider and more complex issue. Royce was proud that his idealism was a practical philosophy which he could relate to worldly concerns; he felt it incumbent upon him to "translate" technical doctrines into positions intelligible to less mathematically oriented followers and readers. He wrote to James jokingly that "his faithful disciples had certainly never understood him."[41] Consequently, many of his writings during the first decade of the century display a struggle to state his thought more adequately and more accessibly. Royce published nothing nearly so recondite as "The Relation of the Principles of Logic . . ." after 1905, but his less formal work both before and after it is a search for a further adumbration of his main theses and simple enunciations of his new convictions. He repeatedly underscores the critical nature of Kempe's work and iterates that a novel deduction of the categories is in the offing. In the light of these considerations *The Philosophy of Loyalty*, often looked upon as bridging the thought of *The World and the Individual* and *The Problem of Christianity*, assumes a minor place for anyone interested in more than a popular and oversimplified account of Royce's ideas.

In a study published before his logical paper, he states that "the union of mathematical and philosophical inquiries, in the future, will tend to become closer and closer." Their concern is "the theory of the categories" and their "somewhat distant goal," "the relatively complete rational analysis and tabulation of the fundamental categories of human thought."[42] He contends that this pursuit will succeed because of the reductions of one system of order to another that Kempe has accomplished. When he asserts that non-Euclidean geometries have rendered Kantian positions unjustifiable, he still proclaims the "enormous advance" due to Kant's doctrine of the categories. Again extolling the work of Kempe in 1906, Royce affirms that symbolic logic is of "fundamental importance" for the study of thinking.[43]

In these expositions he did no more than speculate on the philosophic millennium which a grasp of logic would bring. It is true that he did not publish many of his findings because, as his son reported, "his researches were never completed" and because his work ever led him back "to the starting equation." Having labored "off and on for years" on these notions, Royce was afraid "that if he did not get far enough in this subject, it would lie dormant for another hundred years. . . ."[44]

We should not underestimate the significance of this enterprise to Royce, or the energy with which he threw himself into it after exploring the limitations of psychology. He did not have a respite from his furious work until 1910. At the end of that year he evidently finished an outline of what he called the equivalent in the algebra of logic to the "harmonic construction." Unfortunately the "harmonic construction" first appeared in German as part of the *Encyclopaedia der Philosophischen Wissenschaften* entitled "Prinzipien der Logik"; the English translation was not in print until 1913. Royce's marginalia in the German edition evince his distress at the lack of such a translation, and he explicitly calls attention to the article's merit. The sketch of the idea of logic as the "Theory of Order," he notes, goes back to the *second* volume of *The World and the Individual* and not to the more famous first volume. The "Prinzipien der Logik" outlines his position more fully than any previous inquiry. "This paper," he concludes, "is thus a programme of a future possible

Logic; and *as* a programme has a place in a fairly extensive plan. The issues discussed have, in J. R.'s opinion, an importance that is greater than the length of the paper indicates."[45]

The first two sections of the "Principles of Logic" are a survey of recent developments in symbolic logic and methodology. The third section—"The Logical Genesis of the Types of Order"—is more speculative and is the most enigmatic of all the Roycean texts. But its brevity and complexity ought not to detract from its significance in the corpus of Royce's work. He suggests there the principles which "will enable us in the future to make an indubitable endless progress. . . ." "Of the fundamental philosophic importance of such problems [i.e., those treated in the section] no student of the Categories, no one who understands the significance of Kant's great undertaking, no one who takes Truth seriously, ought to be in doubt. The Theory of Order will be a fundamental science in the philosophy of the future."[46] We must turn to a study of this essay.

Royce believed that he had reduced logic and geometry to the entities and relations of Σ, but he also wanted to say something about Σ itself. For non-mathematicians he described his reasearches and those of Kempe by saying that we could view the sciences as characterized by the *"purely symmetrical relation of opposition,"*[47] i.e., Royce's O-relation. This relation, the "not-relation," is "one of the simplest and most fundamental relations known to the human mind"; it is one of "the most momentous of all relations for the organization not only of all the exact sciences, but to all the systematic study of human experience and of all our knowledge concerning the order of the world and our own conduct. . . ." "In brief," he remarks, "it is essential to the whole business of thinking that propositions and the judgments which affirm or deny them go in pairs of contradictories. . . ."[48] Conscious voluntary action is possible only to a being who understands the meaning of 'not': we are able to act voluntarily, only because we are also able to *refuse* to act.

Royce wished to go further than this. Our voluntary activity largely determines that there are objects of a particular sort to relate, that they are related, or that any given relation is present in the world. In this sense relations and classifications are arbitrary—they are "creations" or "constructions" of our own. But that there are relations at all among propositions, objects, and so on, is *necessary.* Without them *"no rational activity of any kind is possible."* Here Royce links his logic to Absolute Pragmatism. The not-relation exhibits a mode of activity which is a law of the "rational will." We reinstate it in any attempt to presuppose that this mode of activity does not exist.[49] Take the tautology '$p \equiv (\sim p \supset p)$'. This is implied by its denial and must be true. We deny it only at the penalty of "the self-destruction of the thought which [its denial] undertakes to violate. . . ."[50] But since denial is a form of willing, truth is that form of willing which reasserts itself in our attempt to do away with it:

> In brief, whatever actions are such, whatever types of action are such, whatever results of activity, whatever conceptual constructions are such, that the very act of getting rid of them, or of thinking them away, logically implies their presence, are known to us indeed both empirically and pragmatically (since we note their presence and learn of them through action) ; but they are also absolute. And any account which succeeds in telling what they are has absolute truth. Such truth is a "construction" or "creation," for activity determines its nature. It is "found," for we observe it when we act.[51]

Royce's central revision of Kempe's base system is the introduction of the O-relation as primitive in place of Kempe's betweenness relation; the reason for this substitution should be plain. The primitive of Σ not only defines the structure of the divine mind, but also reflects the "mode of willing" in terms of which Royce proves the existence of the Absolute. Since we develop all of the sciences out of Σ, they are founded "upon the consciousness of our own activity and some of its necessary characters"; all of our exact knowledge is the "will to act in an orderly fashion, the will to be rational."[52]

Having claimed ambiguously in his 1905 paper that the elements of Σ were "simple and homogeneous," Royce now argues that the elements of this "logically necessary system" are "modes of action." But the exposition still forces us to say that there is no clear conception of a formal system. After urging that the "modes of action" are the *elements* of Σ, he goes on in effect to show that we can give an *interpretation* of Σ in terms of a "calculus" of modes of action.[53] For the sake of simplicity let us proceed as if we were demonstrating that we may interpret Σ as this calculus of modes of action. This does no injustice to Royce's work so long as we bear in mind—aided by the phrase 'modes of action'—that we should associate Σ's elements with the finite internal meanings of ideas with which we construct the Absolute.

We express a mode of action in English by the infinitive or present participle of the verb; for example, 'to sing' and 'singing' are alternate ways of verbalizing a single mode of action. To every mode of action there corresponds a contradictory mode of action (e.g., not singing); pairs of modes of action have logical products (e.g., singing and dancing) and logical sums (e.g., singing or dancing); the implication relationship holds among them (e.g., singing and dancing implies singing). On the basis of these observations Royce concludes that the calculus of modes of action satisfies all the postulates of Σ which are necessary to get the Boolean algebras of classes and propositions.[54] Actually, this result is no different from that of 1905. But if we are able to give an interpretation of Σ in terms of the modes of action calculus, the calculus must possess other characteristics as well.

In 1910 Royce saw two new requirements. First he had to construct an adequate set of modes of action. We pointed out previously that the mathematization of the notion that the Absolute has actually present to it a completed infinite series involves a paradox in *The World and the Individual*. His first step solves this logical problem. He has another problem in relating his World of Appreciation to the World of Description: he cannot link the betweenness relation which characterizes the latter and is represented by a dense series to the well-ordered series which characterizes the former. Royce's second step is to show that we can apply the betweenness postulate of Σ to a well-ordered set of modes of action. He does not seem to have doubted his ability to derive the geometrical postulates from Σ; the system is rich enough for that. Rather, he is concerned to show that the modes of action calculus satisfies Σ in this respect. Or to put the matter in his terms, he wants to show that Σ *consists* of modes of action, and consequently that it makes sense to say that they satisfy the betweenness postulate. Even should this be the case, we will not have derived the geometrical postulates from Σ ($=$ the modes of action calculus): we would require the addition of other postulates. Royce's second step examines a difficulty in *The World and the Individual,* and not the one we have seen in the 1905 paper. Let us look at each of the two steps in detail.

In the "Supplementary Essay" Royce urges that the Absolute has the structure of a perfectly self-conscious self capable of fully reflecting on a given thought. Now he redefines in "The Principles of Logic" a similar structure of modes of action:

> it is perfectly possible to define a certain set, or "logical universe" of modes of action such that all the members of this set are "possible modes of action," *in case* there is some rational being who is capable of performing some one single possible act, and is also capable of noting, observing, recording, in some determinate way every mode of action of which he is actually capable, and which is a mode of action whose possibility is *required* (that is, made logically a necessary entity) by the *single* mode of action in terms of which this system of modes of action is defined. Such a special system of possible modes of action may be determined, in a precise way; by naming *some one* mode of action, which the rational being in question is supposed to be capable of conceiving, and of noting or recording in some reflective way any mode of action once viewed as possible.

This statement is consistent with Royce's Absolute Pragmatism and his emphasis on negation. The determination of some one mode of action (say willing, choosing, or reflecting) excludes the contradictory mode of action and is reasserted in its denial. The calculus of modes of action has a "logical reality" which we cannot question "without abandoning the very conception of rational activity itself." Any rational being capable of conceiving any mode of action at all must recognize it.[55]

Throughout this portion of "The Principles of Logic" the meaning of Royce's thought is clouded, but its thrust is clear. An Absolute defined by the totality of all possible modes of action—as it appears to be in *The World and the Individual*—is paradoxical. Royce recognizes this in the later paper:

> it would indeed be impossible to attempt to define with any exactness "the *totality* of all possible modes of action." Such an attempt would meet with the difficulties which the Theory of Assemblages has recently met with in its efforts to define certain extremely inclusive classes. Thus, just as "the class of all classes" has been shown by Mr. Russell to involve fairly obvious and elementary contradictions, and just as "the greatest possible cardinal number" in the Cantorian theory of cardinal numbers, and equally "the greatest possible ordinal number" have been shown to involve logical contradictions, so (and unquestionably) the concept of "the totality of all possible modes of action" involves a contradiction. There is in fact no such totality.

A choice is made *among* the possible modes of action in such a way as to maintain its infinite reflective structure.[56] Significantly, this choice helps to resolve the other difficulty in *The World and the Individual*. Royce defines the discrimination in the World of Description by a dense series. As Cantor had shown, however, the order of the natural numbers cannot be preserved if put into a one-one relationship with a dense series. But Royce can say that the Absolute picks out a set of discriminations (modes of actions) from the possible discriminations which could occur.

But if the discriminations are well-ordered, how are they sufficient for an analysis of the World of Description, where the betweenness principle applies? Royce asserts that this set of modes of action is "of the form of the foregoing system Σ" which "*has an order which is determined entirely by the fundamental laws of logic, and by the one additional principle thus mentioned.*" The principle in question "is analogous to a principle which is fundamental in geometrical theory. This is the principle that, between any two points on a line, there is an intermediate point, so that the points on a line constitute, for geometrical theory, *at least a dense series.*"

The paragraph in which Royce describes how the calculus satisfies the "betweenness principle" is, like much of this article, worth quoting:

> what we may here call the Calculus of Modes of Action, while it makes use of all the laws of the Algebra of Logic, also permits us to make use of the principle here in question, and in fact, in case a system of modes of action, such as has just been indicated, is to be defined at all, *requires* us to make use of this principle. The principle in question may be dogmatically stated thus: "If there exist two distinct modes of action p and r, such that $p \prec r$, then there always exists a mode of action q such that $p \prec q \prec r$, while p and q are distinct modes of action and q and r are equally distinct." This principle could be otherwise stated thus "for any rational being who is able to reflect and to record his own modes of action, if there be given any two modes of action such that one of them implies the other, there always exists at least one determinate mode of action which is implied by the first of these modes of action and which implies the second, and which is yet distinct from both of them."

Ironically the further discussion has that flavor of mystery associated with Fermat's Last Theorem. Royce concludes that "this principle holds true of the modes of action which are open to any rational being to whom any mode of action is open." But the demonstration hinges on "considerations for which there is here no space. . . ."[57]

What has Royce accomplished in his own mind? Σ is necessary to all rational thought. We might say that a set of possible modes of action of a perfectly self-conscious being yields a consistent interpretation of Σ's variables; as such the modes of action are well-ordered. Hence, Royce states "any orderly succession of deeds in which we pass from one to the next has certain of the characteristics of the series of ordinal whole numbers. . . . there is indeed something about the nature of our activity, insofar as it is rational,—something which necessitates a *possible* next deed after any deed that has been actually accomplished." But the set of modes of action which satisfies the postulates of Σ also defines

> an order-system of entities inclusive not only of objects having the relation of the number system, but also of objects illustrating the

geometrical types of order, and thus apparently including all the order-systems upon which, at least at present, the theoretical natural sciences depend for the success of their deductions.*

The modes of action calculus is additionally rich enough to provide the types of order which Royce thinks typical of the World of Description. He had finally circumvented Bradley's dilemma. Moreover, if we are to take Royce's view of logic seriously, the modes of action really *are* the entities of Σ. This is the ultimate deduction of the categories: in a mathematically precise way we see *how* the constituents of the Divine Will come to be regarded as the World of Description.

If we are mindful of his preoccupations from *The World and the Individual* to "The Principles of Logic," it is easy to grasp why Royce thinks he has completed the "harmonic construction," why logic has become an *idée fixe* for him. But there remains the task of reformulating his attainment into metaphysical, epistemological, and religious forms. This is the primary result of *The Problem of Christianity*.

---

* *Royce's Logical Essays*, ed. D. S. Robinson (Dubuque, Iowa, 1951) (hereafter *RLE*), pp. 367–368, 377 (the original appears in italics). This compares with the following statement in *WI* 2: "we shall be led to see something regarding what enables us to view all acknowledged facts as linked in a single Ordered System, in which countless definable Series of real facts are interwoven; and hereby we shall be led to a more definite idea of what is meant by the acknowledgment of Law in the natural, in the social, and in the moral order of the world" (p. 70) (the original is almost entirely in italics).

11

THE ABSOLUTE AND THE COMMUNITY

We should read *The Problem of Christianity* conscious of the mathematical gains Royce had made. Even then, however, our anticipations will not be satisfied. Royce was convinced that he had achieved a spectacular deduction of the categories; since this work is at the center of his system, advances in this area should lead to advances—indeed now solutions—in more comprehensible regions. We might naturally expect that *The Problem of Christianity* will reveal the secret of the universe; the scales will drop from our eyes; and the glorious truth will emerge, mounted on invincible logic and clad in Pauline grace. Something less than this occurs. The connection between logic and Royce's less technical concerns is plain; but the details are not worked out and are often cryptic. There may be good reasons for this failure—not the least of which may have been Royce's declining health. But the architectonic design remains unfulfilled, and *The Problem of Christianity* does not succeed as an analogue of the "harmonic construction."

The ambiguity of the book is not surprising if we consider that Royce made two revisions in a system that had been abuilding for almost thirty years. His work in mathematics demanded changes, and his practical studies yielded new insights. Both revisions concerned the relation of finite to infinite: one the connection of the individual to the Absolute; the other the reconciliation of description and appreciation. The first volume of *The Problem of Christianity* applies these changes to Royce's religious thinking; the second works them out in their epistemological and metaphysical context. We shall examine the second volume first, beginning with the question of the two worlds.

211

The striking aspect of this volume is Royce's defense of a novel kind of knowledge—interpretation—and it is not paradoxical to say that his explication of interpretation solves the two worlds problem by denying it. The antithesis between description and appreciation is a decisive theme in Royce's work from the late 1880s. But his discussion of them is metaphysical—he is interested in the "grade of reality" which we can attach to each and in the relation between these grades. When he takes up epistemological questions, his position is that of an (absolute) pragmatist, and although the connection between description and appreciation *and* Absolute Pragmatism is treated obliquely, it is clear that the relation exists. As a pragmatist, Royce argues that we verify our ideas by engaging in activities which will lead to appropriate experiences if our ideas are true. In an article written about the same time as *The Problem of Christianity* he describes this enterprise as one in which we formulate hypotheses "prevailingly conceptual" and test them through direct experience, "perceptual knowledge," "knowledge by acquaintance." For the pragmatist knowledge brings percepts and concepts into an "active synthesis";[1] it depends upon "the marriage of the two processes."[2] Although he discusses description and appreciation in metaphysical contexts, he says that for certain purposes we can identify knowledge by acquaintance, perceptual knowledge, with appreciation; conceptual knowledge, with description.[3] In epistemology he also aims at bringing together two different realms of experience.

Although Royce's doctrine of interpretation elaborates this aim, it proceeds on a repudiation of perception and conception, i.e., a repudiation of the two worlds distinction. He urges in *The Problem of Christianity* that human beings are never possessed of either pure perception or pure conception; our knowledge is an imperfect union of the two. But after mentioning Absolute Pragmatism as an attempt to synthesize perception and conception, he asserts that pragmatism presupposes not some synthesis of perception and conception but interpretation.[4] He previously contended that Jamesean pragmatism entails a unity of experience in principle unverifiable in James's terms. Of course, Absolute Pragmatism accounts for this unity: the implication throughout Royce's work up to

The Problem of Christianity is that this unity has an appreciative reality, i.e., it is the absolute experience. But in *The Problem of Christianity* he claims that our belief in the experience which none of us can verify is an interpretation—the new form of knowledge.[5] In effect Royce argues that his previous formulations of Absolute Pragmatism were incorrect.[6] The new form of knowledge transforms the two worlds problem. Since it furnishes a basis for metaphysical idealism and becomes "the main business of philosophy,"[7] we must examine the idea closely.

Interpretation is that form of cognition involved in the knowledge of mind. When a man clarifies his own interests and meanings and acquires knowledge of his self, he is interpreting. Through interpretation we also learn of the social relations between man and man, our knowledge of other minds. The comparison of ideas, however, is the most elementary kind of interpretation, and a paradigmatic form of this knowledge. In order to compare our ideas of two objects—let us say two pieces of fruit—we must have in mind a third or mediating idea which specifies how our two objects are similar or different. It will tell us, for example, that one tastes sweeter than the other. The third idea interprets one of the original ideas to or in light of the other.[8] Whereas perception and conception are dyadic relations—of perceiver to immediate datum and conceiver to abstract universal—interpretation is triadic even in its elementary exemplification.[9]

We can best grasp interpretation if we consider it as sign translation. A sign is anything that determines an interpretation, but, hinting at the full doctrine we must explicate, Royce notes that a sign indicates the existence of mind. For example, a road sign expresses a mind, and calls for an interpretation by some other mind which acts as a mediator between the sign (or its maker) and someone who reads the sign. I can probably interpret this sign myself, in which case a mind interprets a sign for itself; but if we suppose the sign to be in a foreign language, I might require a third person to translate the sign's meaning for me. In these circumstances, someone interprets something to a third party. Royce uses 'interpretation' to denote both the triadic relation and the mediating term; and he often construes this term as the result of the interpretive process. These inelegancies, however, are usually semantic, and the meaning is contextually unequivocal. He also ambiguously calls what is interpreted an object (or idea), or mind; similarly he calls the interpretation, *qua* mediating term, a further object (or idea), or mind. But this ambiguity is consistent: the object or idea interpreted is expressive of mind, as is the interpretation—the further object or idea—addressed to the mind in need of interpretation. Finally, each interpretation (the mediating term) may provide a further interpretation, i.e., any given interpretation acts as a sign which a further interpreter (sign) may interpret for another. Ideally the social activity involved is endless.[10] Every interpretation mediates between mutually contrasting ideas, minds, and purposes.[11] Royce's goal is to argue that signs constitute our world, and that the "world process" is mental. This becomes clearer when he defines individual selves in terms of interpretation.

When a man reflects, Royce contends, he interprets himself to himself. Although in the usual sense of the word there is only one person, the relation is triadic. Suppose I remember a former promise. I am then interpreting this bit of my past self to my future self; the present self interprets signs (= my past self) to my future self; and I may say, "I am committed to do thus and so."[12] Since self-consciousness defines mind and self for Royce, he regards selves as sign series, series of interpretations: we achieve the unification of separate ideas and experiences through interpretation. "In brief," he writes, "my idea of myself is an interpretation of my past,—linked also with an interpretation of my hopes and intentions as to my future."[13] The interpretation which defines the individual self is an extended series of comparisons of ideas, and self-knowledge is also a paradigmatic form of interpretation.

Royce took much of his work on his new kind of knowing from Peirce's articles of the late 1860s on the same subject. Although he follows Peirce's exposition and is eager to express indebtedness,[14] we do Royce a disservice to explain his last work simply by citing the influence of another man. Royce himself claims that we can find the "germ" of his position in the possibility of error argument in *The Religious Aspect* *of Philosophy;*[15] and it seems clear that he retrospectively has in mind the necessary third and higher thought which includes my idea and its object. There are also many passages in his earlier work which search for some *tertium quid* between description and appreciation.[16] Two of these efforts bear recall. The first is the Reflective Knowledge which Royce explored in the nineties: it is our way of coming to self-consciousness by comparing our ideas. The second, which Royce at one point tied to Reflective Knowledge, is his notion of leading ideas: they are between the conceptual and the empirical or, to use the language of *The Problem of Christianity*, between conception and perception.*

The most important Roycean sources for interpretation are the logical studies which he undertook after the publication of the second volume of *The World and the Individual*. This work required an emendation of the two worlds doctrine; interpretation provided the proper emendation. In fact, from a close reading of volume two of *The World and the Individual* and subsequent articles we might suspect interpretation to be a form of the discrimination of *The World and the Individual*. We might then be led to disregard the remarks about the structure of the self in the "Supplementary Essay." For example, Royce states in *The Problem of Christianity* that it is "not the Self" among other con-

---

* Prior to *The Problem of Christianity* Royce made many attempts to clarify the distinction between the conceptual and the empirical, but that work contains his best efforts. He claims in effect that mathematical and logical truths are synthetic a priori: in these disciplines we obtain results by reflecting on our thought processes, i.e., the results are a priori. But we do not merely explicate the *meaning* of our logical premises; it is inappropriate to construe the conclusions of mathematics as implicit in the meaning of the premises with which we begin; the results are non-analytic or synthetic. Indeed, Royce ends this passage by claiming that deduction, the process we use to get our results, is a form of interpretation (*The Problem of Christianity*, intro. John E. Smith [Chicago, 1968], hereafter *PC*, pp. 309–310; see also *WI* 1, pp. 252–257). But this synthetic a priori doctrine is what we should expect if we grant that Royce felt he had achieved a mathematical deduction of the categories: because logic reflects the nature of our modes of experiencing, for Royce as for Kant, logic should yield truths necessary for all experience. Following this Kantian line, we may conclude that principles constitutive of human knowledge have a parallel in the leading ideas which Royce has already observed to be analogous to Kant's regulative principles.

cepts but the community of interpretation which will be the ruling category of his philosophy.[17] Moreover, in *The Philosophy of Loyalty* and other works discrimination and imitation become progressively richer notions. This belief is corroborated by Royce's stress from 1901 to 1913 on the triadic nature of discrimination and betweenness, and the similar stress on the triadicity of interpretation. The strongest pieces of evidence in this respect are two discussions in *The Problem of Christianity*. The first concerns one of the "most familiar instances" of the paradigm form of interpretation, the comparison of ideas. The instances are relations of similarity and difference,[18] and Royce's remarks on these relations parallel his examination of the likeness and difference characterizing discrimination in volume two of *The World and the Individual.** The second discussion is more compelling: Royce argues that our knowledge of the physical world—in *The World and the Individual* we achieved this knowledge through imitation and discrimination—is a form of interpretation.[19]

But it is a serious mistake to take interpretation and the "discrimination" of the World of Description as equivalent. Royce thinks that discrimination and betweenness will yield only imperfect knowledge. The mathematics characterizing them is the dense series; interpretation is a process in which every interpretation has a *next*. In *The World and the Individual* Royce limits this property to the World of Appreciation. Interpretation has aspects which he denies to the World of Description.

All of this speculation becomes more clear if we inquire into the formulation of these theses in Σ. Consider what Royce thought true of the modes of action which comprise Σ: they are a well-ordered set to which the betweenness principle applies. Interpretation is a triadic process in which one term mediates "between" the other two. The result of any interpretation will have a next interpretation. To be sure, it is not true that

---

* John Smith argues that Royce's identification of comparison and interpretation is misguided and perceptively points out that, unlike interpretation, comparison has no essential relation with a time order, i.e., with Royce's series of deeds in which each one has a next (see *PC*, pp. 28–30). Whatever the force of this criticism, Royce *means*, as we shall see, the comparison of *The Problem of Christianity* to have an order different from the comparison of the second volume of *The World and the Individual*.

each interpretation demands a *unique* next. Unlike the well-ordered series of natural numbers, any interpretation may have various *next* interpretations. The exact interconnection of the theses of "The Principles of Logic" and *The Problem of Christianity* is uncertain.* It is at least true, however, that interpretation synthesizes features of *both* the Worlds of Appreciation and Description just as Σ was "an order-system of entities inclusive not only of objects having the relations of the number system, but also of objects illustrating the geometrical types of order. . . ."[20]

To this complex of factors we must add a final one. In a series of addresses delivered at Berkeley in 1914 Royce devoted a long section of the first lecture to explaining the origins of his new theory of knowledge. He argued that when he advanced his philosophy of loyalty in 1907 and 1908, he had no idea that it presupposed the epistemological views of *The Problem of Christianity*. This is just what we should expect, for the bases of *The Philosophy of Loyalty* are the doctrines of *The World and the Individual*. If we can take Royce's reminiscences at face value, what appears to have occurred is that the novelties in *The Philosophy of Loyalty* led him to see his logical studies in a different way and to reappraise Peirce's work.[21] Advances in his practical thinking were instrumental in bringing about a reinterpretation of the foundations of this practical thinking. If this is true, we should predict a refinement of this practical thinking with an adequate formulation of its basis. This is what takes place, and if we are to understand how the loyalty of *The Philosophy of Loyalty* differs from the loyalty of *The Problem of Christianity*, we must examine the social dimensions of interpretation.

Royce always claimed that the argument from analogy could never solve the other minds question. He repeats this claim in *The Problem of Christianity*, and using interpretation formulates another solution to the problem which the two worlds distinction had not allowed.

What knowledge do we have of the existence of the minds of our

---

* It is not clear that Royce recognizes the "one and only one" aspect of the "next-ness" in the ordering of natural numbers; that is, he may think interpretation is identical to his "self-representative" process (see *RLE*, pp. 367–368, 377). If this is so, the mathematical and epistemological doctrines are more closely linked.

fellows? Although Royce does not elaborate, he rejects the claim that we can view our neighbor's mind as "an abstract and universal idea," and it is difficult to know what this could mean. Alternatively, we don't have immediate perception of another mind. This remark appears to be a critique of his earlier views. If we had this kind of perception, "my neighbor and I would so far simply melt together, like drops in the ocean or small pools in a greater pool"; there would be no question of there being other minds at all.[22] Rather, we know other minds because we have interpretative knowledge: ideas confront us which contrast with our ideas; their novelty and unexpectedness lead us to believe that they are not our ideas;[23] attempts to interpret them as our ideas fail. We interpret "these relatively alien ideas," Royce says, only by using the familiar hypotheses that they belong to the mind of someone else:

> Neither of my neighbor nor of myself have I any direct intuition. But of my own ideas I can hope to win the knowledge which the most successful comparisons exemplify. Of my neighbor's ideas I can never win, under human conditions, any interpretation but one which remains hypothetical, and which is never observed, under these human conditions, as face to face with its own object, or with the idea of the other neighbors to whom the interpretation is addressed.[24]

We treat certain behavioral manifestations as signs, that is, as expressive of mind; but the mind of which they are signs is not our own, and so we postulate other minds.

Royce's use of 'postulate' is worthy of comment. The word occurs most frequently in his work *before* the writing of *The Religious Aspect of Philosophy*, and *before* the proof of the Absolute which obviates the need for his "world of postulates." As we shall see, postulation is an intermediate procedure, but we ought to note that the postulational position of *The Problem of Christianity* is no retreat from absolute idealism. Even after *The Religious Aspect of Philosophy* he admitted that we could not "prove" the existence of other minds. The World of Description presupposes their appreciative existence; the argument for other minds depends on our belief that social communication is efficacious. Now he asserts that other minds are constructs. We need them to give coherence to experience, and our knowledge of them is structurally similar to the knowledge we have of ourselves, i.e., it is interpretive.[25]

If someone interprets a second to a third, Royce declares that a community of interpretation exists, and the term 'community' is crucial: it signifies that the mind interpreted and the mind to which the interpretation is addressed are brought into a unity and become in a sense one individual. We see that this is so if we grant that self-knowledge is interpretation, but many ostensibly different selves achieve a unity as well. The interpreter who possesses the mediating idea shares this unity, and is the most important member of the community. His task is "to create and to make conscious, and to carry out, their [the two others involved] united will, in so far as they both are to become and remain members of that community in which he does the work of the interpreter."[26] In lofty moments Royce calls the possessor of the mediating idea "The Spirit of the Community."[27]

The community of interpretation described above is one of the most primitive communities; even so, it has a future goal—the achievement of a satisfactory interpretation. Moreover, because every interpretation demands another and ideally has one, the community may share past interpretations. Royce does not take up in any detail the past of communities of interpretation like the above, but he delineates the characteristics of all communities when he discusses a notion of "community" of which our community of interpretation is an example. A true community, he says,

> is essentially a product of a time-process. A community has a past and will have a future. Its more or less conscious history, real or ideal, is a part of its very essence. A community requires for its existence a history and is greatly aided in its consciousness by a memory.[28]

Consider the real or supposed identity of the features of the past which each one of many men may regard as belonging to his own historically extended former self. This situation is a ground for saying that these men constitute a community with reference to their common past: each one interprets himself to the others by this third idea of a shared past. This community is one of memory; and Royce also discusses communities of expectation or hope, defined by the shared expectation of the same future events.[29] The essential aspect of these communities is their relation to time and history. Royce makes this plain when he spells out the three conditions on which the existence of communities depends. We must first have an individual self capable of extending his life to regard it as including past and future events perhaps far away in time and not personally remembered. This we all can do. Second, as is also true, there must be distinct selves capable of communication, that is, there must be a plurality of beings who interpret one another over time. Third, the extended past or future selves must share at least some events.*

The emphasis on the importance of time to the community leads us to reexamine the connection between interpretation and description. The two processes are similar, and the mediating interpreter "links" the mind interpreted to the mind to whom the interpretation is addressed. But the mathematical notion defining description is a dense series in which between any two terms we can find a third. Like description, interpretation is triadic, but each interpretation has a next; the next need not be unique, but we cannot place between any two interpretations a third. The interpretative order reflects the order in which human beings act in time: they carry out deeds, *one after another,* as expressions of their purposes, i.e., the interpretative order resembles that of the World of Appreciation. Interpretation combines the two kinds of order Royce separates in *The World and the Individual;* this synthesis is the way he resolves the cleavage between his two realms: they become one.

If we can make this connection between Royce's logic and his

---

* *PC*, pp. 253–256. Royce's statement is that there must be events which are identical for the selves involved. Our later discussion will shed light on the extent to which this means more than that they remember or hope for the same things. We should also note that the question of a definition of finite individuality almost disappears. It is touched upon only in these few pages, and it is no longer a central concern that we analyze individuality and preserve freedom.

metaphysics and epistemology, we must also consider a second connection which is equally significant, particularly for his ethics. Through 1908 Royce conceived the Absolute as a concrete universal. The relation of individuals to the Absolute is a relation of part to whole, and this idea is strengthened by his belief that we need not distinguish the unit class from its member. It is not clear whether in the 1910 work on Σ Royce distinguishes subsumption from membership, although I would venture to say that he does.[30] By 1913, however, there is no ambiguity: the elements which comprise a class are distinct from the class itself. In a long letter to Warner Fite written in 1913, Royce explicates this distinction. It is, he says, the most elementary logical problem involved in his theory of the community, but one that he has said nothing about in *The Problem of Christianity* "because my audience was popular." Royce concludes his letter by saying that his book deals with a special case of the class-member relation.[31] If we remember this, we will appreciate the impact of this second logical point on his philosophy.

All communities of interpretation have the structure of selves, and extended ones have an organic life of their own:

> we can compare a highly developed community, such as a state, either to the soul of a man or to a living animal. A community is not a mere collection of individuals. It is a sort of live unit, that has organs, as the body of an individual has organs. A community grows or decays, is healthy or diseased, is young or aged, much as any individual member of the community possesses such characters. Each of the two, the community or the individual member, is as much a live creature as is the other. Not only does the community live, it has a mind of its own—a mind whose psychology is not the same as the psychology of an individual human being.[32]

This "social mind" expresses itself in language, customs, and religions; individual human minds cannot produce these phenomena, nor can a group of people unless they are organized into a community. Communities themselves are organized in composite communities of "higher grades." A group of individuals may form a state; states are united into empires; and many have hypothesized about a future "world state."[33]

As we shall see in detail, Royce's true communities of interpretation are almost identical to the causes of the loyal, and the ultimate community is the universal church. Ideally, he says, the community of mankind would be as united "as one conscious self could conceivably become"; true membership raises us out of the self's narrowness to participation in a creative and conscious spiritual whole.[34] But the relation between man and community is not the old one of finite being to Absolute.

There are two "levels" of human existence: individuals exist and communities of them do. Man's natural existence is predicated on the distinction between these two levels, but his highest good involves a "loving union of the individual with a level of existence which is essentially above his own grade of being."[35] For a person to become a true member of a community, his natural self must be destroyed; the "merely natural relation" of the individual to the community will be transformed and the primal core of the social self will vanish.[36]

The "natural" self's connection to a community reflects Royce's logic. His earliest statements of Absolute Idealism conceive man's relation to the Absolute as that of part to whole, and even after *The World and the Individual* he assumes a similar relation of finite to infinite. With the publication of *The Problem of Christianity*, this problem receives a new solution. We cannot regard the connection of individuals to their "social," "natural" communities as that of part to whole; finite man is no part of some greater being, but a member of a class. But suppose the Divine transfigures this community; this gesture transforms man and raises him to a higher level. At this level we may view mankind as "one conscious spiritual whole of life."[37] Royce's religious philosophy investigates the transformation, but here we can examine its technical structure and point out that the unity will not be one in which parts compose a whole.

We postulate other minds because we cannot interpret the signs we assume they express as we interpret our ideas. The latter interpretation is that basic triadic form Royce calls comparison. While the structure of comparison and of the interpretation of signs as other minds is the same, with comparison I may achieve a "luminous self-possession." This gives

me an ideal of the success of interpretation which my interpretation of
my neighbor lacks:

> if I could succeed in interpreting you to another man as fully as, in
> my clearest moments, I interpret one of my ideas to another, my
> process of interpretation would simply reduce to a conscious com-
> parison of ideas. I should then attain, as I succeeded in my inter-
> pretation, a luminous vision of your ideas, of my own, and of the
> ideas of the one to whom I interpret you. This vision would look
> down, as it were, from above. In the light of it, we, the selves now
> sundered by the chasms of the social world, should indeed not in-
> terpenetrate. For our functions as the mind interpreted, the mind
> to whom the other is interpreted, and the interpreter, would remain
> as disinct as they now are. There would be no melting together, no
> blending, no mystic blur, and no lapse into mere intuition. But for
> me the vision of the successful interpretation would simply be the
> attainment of my own goal as interpreter. This attainment would as
> little confound our persons as it would divide our substance. We
> should remain, for me, many, even when viewed in this unity. Yet
> this vision, if I could win it, would constitute an event wherein
> your will to be interpreted would also be fulfilled. For if you are
> indeed ready to accept my service as interpreter, you even now
> possess this will to be interpreted. And if there exists the one to
> whom I can interpret you, that other also wills that you should be
> interpreted to him, and that I should be the interpreter.[38]

The goal of any interpretation is a unity only self-consciousness exemplifies on the level of finite individuals. For this reason Royce urges that
in a true community members would have identical pasts or futures. As
members of a community we extend our present selves to include past
and future deeds of our fellows. As human beings this extension takes the
form of "*acting as if we could survey* in some single unity of insight,
that wealth and variety and connection which, as a fact, we cannot make
present to our momentary view."[39] We cannot achieve unity in our ordinary self-hood.

Although the higher union of *The Problem of Christianity* is similar to the union of selves in the Absolute, even when transformed we do
not become fragments of a whole. It is true that the later conception is

structurally identical to the unity we find in self-consciousness, and the
self has always been Royce's model for the Absolute. Additionally, the
later goal is one in which the time process is spanned by one insight
which surveys the whole of time's meaning. But this view is not timeless
and does not occur in any one moment of time. These sentiments are
comparable to those of *The World and the Individual*. Nonetheless, we
may contrast the realm of the higher self in *The Problem of Christianity*
to that in *The World and the Individual*. In the 1913 book reality is not
the "welding" of ideas into a single idea, and the "Divine Idea" is a
favorite phrase he had used previously for the ultimately real.* Consider
also the relation of community to member in our lives as human beings
and in our transformed lives. This relation is different from anything
Royce earlier expressed either in regard to the World of Description or
to the World of Appreciation. In particular, after the natural individual
is transformed, his relation to the community is defined by interpretation, which differs from self-representation or discrimination. The metaphysics of *The Problem of Christianity* synthesizes aspects of *The World
and the Individual's* two realms. It is impossible to define these relations
with any more clarity, and perhaps they were ambiguous in Royce's
mind, but out of his mathematics comes a redefinition of his position.†

Royce's proof of this position proceeds as we should expect, but the
argument is truncated, and like much else in *The Problem of Christianity*
has new twists. Although there was to be no repetition of previous discussion, the principle at the heart of his doctrine was one that he had
"repeatedly defended" with "various dialectical explanations."[40] By the
real world Royce means whatever is the true interpretation of our prob-
lematic situation: that is, to determine what is real requires the comparison of two ideas, for example, between present experience and the goal

---

* *PC*, p. 337. To be sure, even in *The World and the Individual* Royce contends
that our ideas never "blend" in the Divine Idea, and in *The Problem of Christianity*
the Divine Idea he eschews is one in which all others are blended.
† The title of chapter ten of *The Problem of Christianity* (p. 251), "The Body and
its Members," displays these ambiguities. The members of a (human) body may be
its parts but the members of a body may also be elements of a class.

of experience, between ignorance and enlightenment, between appearance and reality. To understand what the contrast is and means, is to define what the real world is. But to contrast two ideas requires that we devise an interpretation; the correct interpretation of them is the real world. And now the dialectical argument makes its appearance. Suppose we say there is no solution—no true interpretation. If true, we could verify *that* hypothesis only by "an experience that in itself would constitute a full insight into the meaning of the real contrast, and so would in fact furnish a solution." A true solution must exist, the real world will include its interpreter, and this mediating idea will clarify the contrast between our antithetical pair and be viewed in unity with them.[41] If we deny this principle, we do so "only by presenting . . . some other interpretation as the true one. But thus," Royce asserts, "you simply reaffirm the principle that the world has an interpreter."[42]

Because some interpretation is definitive of the real, the appropriate community is also real; because this interpretation is true, Royce says that the community reaches its goal: the interpreter succeeds in mediating and reconciling the contrasting elements. Unless it is interrupted, interpretation demands an infinite series of interpretative acts; we know that the interpretation constituting the real world exists, i.e., it is not interrupted; hence, *this* interpretation expresses itself in an infinite series of individual interpretations. Because this interpretation which is constitutive of reality reaches its goal, the infinite series must itself be interpreted; or, as Royce declares, it is spanned by an insight which surveys the series' meaning.[43] We bring together description and appreciation in the world of interpretation.

Since interpretation is expressive of mind, and since there is one interpretation which constitutes the real world, the dialectical argument insures that what is, is a single ideal synopsis.* Royce describes it as a

---

* What we called the "postulate" of other minds here receives a more adequate warrant. We made the postulate because we believed that the behavior of our fellows were *signs*, that is, entities manifesting mind and requiring interpretation. But Royce has shown that the real world is an infinite series of interpretations: all the things that are, are signs, and this knowledge confirms our postulate of other minds.

self which compares the ideas of all the members of the community. It is therefore consistent for him to write that "a genuinely and loyally united community which lives a coherent life, is, in a perfectly literal sense, a person. . . . On the other hand, any human individual person in a perfectly literal sense, is a community."[44]

Royce's purpose in *The Problem of Christianity* was to delineate the character of the religion and to urge that it was worthy of modern man's commitment.[45] What we have discussed—basically the second volume of the work—provides the technical background for considering these issues. He had promised an analysis of Christian belief in *The Sources of Religious Insight*,[46] and one assumes he felt this analysis to be a culminating effort: with the groundwork laid, he could consider the significant practical problem. Having examined the connections between morality and religion, and indicated that a religion of loyalty could resolve the conflict between the two, he now deals with his religion of loyalty,[47] defining loyalty as the love of an individual for a community.[48] His new definition is a sign that loyalty no longer involves a cause which is a concrete universal, but a community with a different form.* But this technical matter is not our prime concern in Royce's application of his thinking to Christianity. The Christian community possesses the attributes of any developed community of interpretation, but our task must be to examine why Royce urges that the religious doctrine associated with Christianity expresses metaphysical truth.

The first volume of *The Problem of Christianity* contrasts with other theological writing appearing at the time. As in *The Sources of Religious Insight,* he attempts to give a rational basis for religious be-

---

* Royce's notion of the "lost cause" in *The Philosophy of Loyalty* is very likely one source of his conception that the members of a community must have a shared history ([New York, 1908], hereafter *PL*, pp. 276–288). All three books are related attempts to refine Royce's position as it develops after *The World and the Individual.* But whereas work in *The Philosophy of Loyalty* leads Royce into logical investigations, the latter results in the more subtle changes of the two other books.

liefs, and continues his deprecation of James's stress on the nonrational. At a time when "the quest for the historical Jesus" and descriptions of "the religion of Jesus" are in vogue, Royce relegates these aspects of Christianity to a minor place. He is not concerned with the details of the life of Christ and the historiographical questions about them except to say that they are peripheral to his interests and beyond his competence to answer. More significantly, he believes that the teachings of the master— the religion of Jesus—cannot be the focus of study. Royce's most telling argument is that the Christian church has always regarded the meaning of the suffering and death of Christ as critically important; although an account of the work and parables of Jesus is worthwhile, this kind of account will not encompass what is essential to Christianity. The central dilemma of the religion has been to understand the crucifixion. So, Royce contends, the basic Christian ideas are those that came to the mind of the ancient world in later attempts to explain the meaning of the Kingdom of Heaven. Pauline Christianity is, for Royce, "real" Christianity.[49]

In *The Problem of Christianity* he organizes his presentation around three explicit "leading ideas," and an implicit fourth one, the conception of grace.[50] We shall begin with an examination of the first, that membership in a spiritual community determines the salvation of man. All that he has said about communities of interpretation applies to this universal community to which all men belong "in ideal"; and only if one is a member can one achieve the goal of life, what religion calls salvation.[51] Although there are differences between them, loyalty to a cause is the ancestor of membership in a community. The members of a religious community love the community as if it were a person, and devote themselves to it, serve it, and live and die for it. This love and devotion express the philosophy of loyalty; Royce notes that a universal religious community is an ideal generated by our knowledge of and participation in many smaller quasi-religious communities—the family, one's clan, one's country.[52] But none of these is a whole of which the lives of the members are parts, i.e., it is no cause in the sense of *The Philosophy of Loyalty's* notion of cause. Rather, Royce emphasizes that love within a community has two objects; it occurs at two levels. For example, in the Christian community, the Christian's sincerity, trust in God, and submission to the will of the Lord are the services he renders the supreme ruler. But there is a second object of love—the neighbor who is (ideally at least) a fellow-member of the (universal) community. The Christian's primary task here is to make his neighbors members of this community, lovers of God. He may achieve this task by example, precept, kindliness, patience, and courage—the traditional moral virtues; but benevolence is only a means to an end, the universal Christian community, and the individual must ultimately leave to God the care for the true and final good of the neighbor whom he loves.[53]

To these teachings concerning the community, Royce claims, Paul adds another which has the utmost significance and constitutes the meaning of Christian love. We need something to reconcile the two levels and kinds of love in a way that was not necessary in *The Philosophy of Loyalty*. They are both directed at persons—the human beings who surround us and God the supreme ruler. Royce asserts that both they and their relation are mysterious. Paul's doctrine introduces a third entity—the body of Christ—which brings the two other mysterious beings together and makes of them a *community*. The "divinely exalted Christ" *is* this "particular corporate entity," the church—a one in many and a many in one. From the point of view of Royce's metaphysics the "love of Christ" is the third or mediating idea which creates the community and interprets God to finite individuals; Christ is the spirit of the community who reconciles the finite and the infinite.[54]

On this formulation we cannot identify the Absolute with God; or if we do, we cannot claim that the Absolute is the ultimate reality, and this latter thought seems to be the one Royce expounds. In the mediating Christ "the Community, the Individual, and the Absolute would be completely expressed, reconciled and distinguished." We can identify the community with its "spirit" or interpreter,[55] and God with the Absolute. *Qua* Absolute He would not be unified with the many; Christ as "spirit" would unite the many and the Absolute. The real world which is the ultimate interpretation would still be an ideal synopsis whose structure is that of self-consciousness.*

Paul's transformation of Christianity is his belief that Christ unites human beings to God by expressing and creating Christian love or loyalty. This is the meaning of Royce's first leading idea: the notion of a spiritual life which the work of Jesus defines. In this life loyalty expresses the union of God and man which the interpretation of Christ achieves. To explicate this notion we must investigate the second leading idea, the moral burden of the individual.

This defining element of Christianity highlights Royce's concern with evil and redemption. Human beings, he says, are by nature subject to a moral burden from which they cannot escape unaided; only "divine" intervention can save man from spiritual ruin.[56] Although we can express this characteristic of Christianity by analyzing original sin, Royce "translates" this doctrine into contemporary terms by construing as interpretation his earlier work on the imitation of the World of Description. He previously argued that imitation defined the way we develop ideas of the self and others. He now indicates that socialization is really the most primitive form of interpretation, comparison. We conceive socialization as my comparing my behavior with that of a real or ideal comrade: through comparison I observe or estimate myself by interpreting others.[57] But Royce contends that the more we are trained, and the more sophisticated social behavior we learn, the more we elevate and emphasize *self*-consciousness. The procedure which makes us social beings is one which "taints" the conscience of man. We are marked "with the original sin of self-will," "a clever hostility" to the very social order on which we depend. This sin belongs to the essence of *homo sapiens* as a social species—the "diseases" of self-consciousness are due to our nature.[58] As human beings—by that fact itself—we can never achieve salvation, the social harmony and union

---

* "If we consider the temporal world in its wholeness," he writes elsewhere, "it constitutes in itself an infinitely complex Sign [the infinite series of human interpretations?]. This sign is, as a whole, interpreted [by a mediating idea] to an experience [God? the Absolute?] which itself includes a synoptic survey of the whole of time" (*PC*, p. 346).

which Royce takes to be the ultimate good. The procedure used to attain
this end is self-defeating. This is the moral burden which attaches to the
human condition, and which human beings alone can never cast off.

In *The Philosophy of Loyalty* Royce claims that the way to our
highest good lies in loyal devotion to a variety of causes. Loyalty is possible where no mention is made of the Divine, and he devotes a chapter
to "Training for Loyalty." In *The Problem of Christianity* the only community to which we can be loyal is one that the Divine has touched.
Natural communities and social training can never give rise to loyalty.*
This doctrine makes for an ambiguity in *The Problem of Christianity*.
It is never clear if we can have a *community* at all without loyalty and
love. Royce sometimes implies that there are no communities without
them, but also speaks of "purely secular forms of loyalty"—seemingly a
contradiction in terms. He alternatively writes that without loyalty or the
divine spark we have primitive, lesser, or natural communities.[59] At any
rate, I shall make a distinction between natural communities and those
which loyalty—or love, as Royce often calls it—transforms.

Man's relation to any natural community imperfectly resolves the
conflict between him and it—the two levels remain distinct. But Paul
develops a concept whose truth dissolves our moral burden:

> There is a certain divinely instituted community. It is no mere
> collection of individuals, with laws and customs and quarrels. Nor
> is its unity merely that of a mighty but, to our own will, an alien
> power. Its indwelling spirit is concrete and living, but is also a
> loving spirit. It is the body of Christ. The risen Lord dwells in it,
> and is its life. It is as much a person as he was when he walked the
> earth. And he is as much the spirit of that community as he is a
> person.[60]

---

* See *PL*, pp. 249 ff. The difference seems to be that in *The Philosophy of Loyalty*
loyalty is a "human illusion" if we cannot conceive the world in religious terms (see
pp. 349 ff.), while in *The Problem of Christianity* there is no loyalty at all without
a religious consciousness. If this consciousness is necessary for the existence of any
community, however, it is a nice question whether interpretation presupposes the
divine spark. If it does, our natural self-consciousness develops through a form of
interpretation which cannot really be interpretation.

In this community and in this community alone, the natural self will die; a new life will possess man; he will exhibit a new type of self-consciousness. To be a member of this community is to be saved, and Royce says that only the miracle of love will suffice for salvation. Although there may be many redemptive communities arranged in increasing complexity and universality, they will all be religious.

The creation of a true community—the gift of loyalty to a community—is accomplished by Divine Grace.[61] Although it is not labeled as such, Royce is defining another leading idea which clarifies Christ's relation to the community and to the individual's moral burden. We know that the work of Christ is in technical terms the creation of a mediating idea—the community—between God and man. Jesus appears as individual and "spirit of the community" because through Him the community becomes the loyal entity it is. For Him as for anyone who serves as spirit of the community, says Royce,

> his origin will be inexplicable in terms of the processes which he himself originates. His power will come from another level than our own. And of the workings of this grace, when it has appeared we can chiefly say this: That such love is propagated by personal example, although how, we cannot explain.[62]

The creation of loyalty which the life of Christ expresses, and which conversions to Christianity illustrate, is an act of grace, an incomprehensible gift that begins our reconciliation with God. This is the clearest version of the Roycean doctrine of the trinity and an impressive analysis of Christianity in terms of his epistemology. The Holy Spirit in the guise of the work of Christ brings together God the Father (the Absolute) and God the Son (as finite man).[63]

The third leading idea is atonement. By grace a loyal community comes into existence, or an individual not yet a member of a redemptive community attains loyalty. A member of a religious community may, however, lose his relation to this community through disloyalty. As with an individual who is not yet loyal, no act of his own can restore the traitorous individual. The work of Christ—the supreme act of grace—atones for the sins of mankind, the sins of self-ishness; similarly, a loyal fellow, someone other than the disloyal member, must atone for him.[64] It is unclear why men are guilty for what is inevitably their nature or why other acts of atonement are necessary once the life of Christ has been lived, but if we put aside these questions, we may see the strategy behind the atonement doctrine.

Royce is not concerned with any one creed or any particular immoral activities. He states that when a person is self-aware of his actions and sets up a code, that person makes it possible to act in a way which would destroy what makes life morally worthwhile for him. The person can commit moral suicide. He could express this feeling by saying, "If I were to do that, I would never forgive myself."[65] Suppose some person to have done this kind of deed. This man will also have betrayed a true community, for in order to have an ideal, one must be loyal; our traitor is outside the saving community. His own acts will not enable him to be received into it again or to restore the community to what it was before his treachery.

Royce's solution to this religious dilemma is a complicated one, with many difficulties. In the passage of time some loyal member of the community will behave in a way that will atone for the disloyal act. His action will restore the community to its former state and the traitor to his former estate. The betrayal will create the conditions for an atonement which will be the source of more righteous communal life than would have been possible had the betrayal not occurred. The loyal member acts as the spirit of the community, and his deed mediates between the traitor and the broken community:

> this creative work shall include a deed, or various deeds, for which only just this treason furnishes the opportunity. Not treason in general, but just this individual treason shall give the occasion, and supply the condition of the creative deed which I am in ideal describing. Without just that treason, this new deed (so I am supposing) could not have been done at all. And hereupon the new deed, as I suppose, is so ingeniously devised, so concretely practical in the good which it accomplishes, that, when you look down upon the human world after the first creative deed has been done in it, you

say, first, "This deed was made possible by that treason; and, secondly, *The world, as transformed by this creative deed, is better than it would have been had all else remained the same, but had that deed of treason not been done at all.*"[66]

There are two complexes of problems in this account. The first requires only clarification; but the second is more puzzling and reflects Royce's last efforts to deal with the problem of evil in a perfect world. It is in one sense understandable why the traitor can never forgive himself. Even this may be dubious, however, if the atoning act makes the world better than it would have been otherwise. But Royce does not spell out why the traitor's act can never atone for his sin against the community. Royce simply asserts that no deed of the traitor's can revoke his betrayal. The reconciliation must come from another who "transforms the meaning of that very past which it [the reconciliation] cannot undo."[67] It is comprehensible that I, as traitor, will never reconcile myself to my act, but why should this prevent me from atoning for the past in the sense Royce specifies? The impossibility of self-reconciliation is the only reason he gives.[68] But this issue is not a serious one. No critical points hang on it, and Royce can maintain that the traitor is no longer in a state of grace, and therefore cannot serve as a creator of loyalty. Only one who possesses grace may achieve this goal, and that one will never be the betrayer.

There is a second and harder set of questions for which there seems to be no acceptable answer. Why is it true that disloyalty sets the stage for a situation in which atonement will make the world better than it otherwise would have been? Royce gives us no reason to assume that this should be the case, but if we understand his metaphysics, we can see why he supposes that treason plays this role. We know that the universal community "reaches its goal," that Christ reconciles mankind with God; implicit in the idea of this goal is progress *toward* it. The historical process *must be* one in which evil is overcome by good. The world is evolving morally, and with the passage of time acts of atonement will raise the moral quality of civilization. This is so despite the goal's infinite distance. We still do not know why an act of atonement presupposes one particular act of disloyalty, but the view is consistent with Royce's belief that evil is necessary to good.

The initial statement of this last leading idea occurs in the first volume of *The Problem of Christianity* before Royce offers the proof of his position. He calls the belief in atonement a "postulate."[69] After we are shown that the Pauline community reflects the structure of the universe, Royce still insists that we have no knowledge of when and how the reconciliation of disloyalty occurs. In the course of endless ages every problem has its solution, and every tragedy its atoning triumph, but we cannot know when problems are solved or how mankind atones for tragedies. The endless order of time in which salvation takes place "stands in contrast to its ideal goal"; and only the final interpretation of the contrast of this time order and its goal atones for all the evils of temporal existence:

> This pursuit of the goal, this bondage of the whole creation to the pursuit of that which it never reaches,—this naturally tragic estrangement of this world from its goal,—this constitutes the problem of the universe. . . . The salvation of the world occurs progressively, endlessly, in constant contest with evil, as a process that is never ended.[70]

> We do not declare, in our metaphysical doctrine, that the divine consciousness is timeless. We declare that the whole order of time, the process of the spirit, is interpreted, and so interpreted that, when viewed in the light of its goal, the whole world is reconciled to its own purposes. The endless tragedies of its sequence are not only interpreted step by step through deeds of charity and of atonement, but, as it were (I speak now wholly in a figure), 'in a moment, in the twinkling of an eye,' the whole of time, with all its tragedies, is, by the interpreter of the universe, reconciled to its own ideal. And in this final union of temporal sequence, of the goal that is never attained in time, and of the divine spirit through whom the world is reconciled to itself and to its own purpose, the real community, the true interpretation, the divine interpreter, the plan of salvation,—these are expressed.[71]

Royce admits that the reconciliation of divine perfection and the "infinite" tragedy of temporal existence is the problem of the universe. On the one hand, the same difficulties of *The Sources of Religious Insight,* and of most of Royce's work in ethics, remain. Why does a perfect world have an evil character? And why, if the ultimate reconciliation (interpretation) must occur, does it make sense to speak of man's *need* for salvation? On the other hand, there are some developments. In *The Sources of Religious Insight* we see only obscurely that *natural* man's salvation is in danger; in *The Problem of Christianity* Royce works out what the meaning of this natural state is and how men escape it. Of course, they still must be saved in *The Problem of Christianity* because the Christian vision is true, but the treatment is an advance if only it is a retreat: although he has mathematically resolved the problem Bradley had set at the turn of the century, Royce's later metaphysics represents a falling back to Bradley's conception. We are not told *how* the Spirit of the Community interprets the infinite series of interpretations to its goal. Royce admits that temporal beings cannot know when or how salvation occurs. In so doing, he acknowledges that the problem of evil is beyond our comprehension.

Royce concludes his work by returning to Peirce for support.[72] From this survey Royce does not want a demonstrative argument for his ideas; rather, he wants a dramatic illustration of his belief that the whole of time is a manifestation of a progressive world-order whose aim is beyond the temporal. The best example of a Peircean community is the scientific one. For Peirce this community attains truth in the infinite future, and in so doing constitutes the absolute mind. Although no scientific community possesses truth, the scientific endeavor is regarded as a progressive one. We have an example of men engaged in progressively interpreting an infinite series of signs; they presuppose a final interpretation and also believe that it lies beyond their grasp. In actuality, Royce maintains, the Pauline community behaves like this despite the moral disorder which veils our view of existence. He closes his work by drawing out this analogy. "We can look forward to no final form, either of Christianity or of any other special religion. But we can look forward to a time when the work and insight of religion can become as progressive as is now the work of science."[73]

Royce makes important revisions to his system in *The Problem of Christianity*, but the book's structure reflects a remarkable and powerful consistency in his thinking. In *The Religious Aspect of Philosophy* he set out first to describe the moral order, next to outline the world's ontological makeup, and then to show that the former expressed the latter. The plan of *The Problem of Christianity* is the same: we have ended by demonstrating that the Christian world-view is a true vision of the universe.

In 1914 the war in Europe motivated Royce to pour his energies into a harsh anti-German campaign. Although frustration, bitterness, and even a decline in intellectual achievement mark the years after 1913, his last addresses are an outgrowth of *The Problem of Christianity*. We know that history guarantees that the moral quality of human life will improve. Even after the beginning of World War I, Royce was optimistic on this issue: he held that from the eighteenth century onward the idea of a community of mankind had become more concrete and more related to the affairs of men. Natural science and technology had furnished the basis in terms of which the "Great Community"—a brotherhood of men —might become a reasonable goal. The time had arrived when moral progress could begin to resemble the progress of science. Although the "international crime" associated with the war had intruded on this vision, men's hope lay in keeping before them the ideal of what the great community might become despite this calamity.[74] Congruent with his position in *The Problem of Christianity*, Royce contended that great tragedies—in this case a betrayal of mankind—were great opportunities: the evil of the war could lend itself to an atonement and leave the world better off than it otherwise might have been. "The new griefs which to-day beset the civilized nations," he preaches, "call for new reflections and new inventions"; the future will invent and practice forms of international activity which might lead the way toward "the united life of the great community."[75]

The betrayer was the German war machine. The invasion of Belgium, German submarine policy in general, and the sinking of the *Lusitania* in particular were blows to his view of Germany. The Germans possessed the spirit of Cain, an enmity to mankind; they were the willful, deliberate enemies of the human race.[76] The opportunity for atonement and a glimpse of the millennium which the war fashioned was international insurance. Consistent with his more technical work, Royce elaborates this idea through interpretation.[77]

Whatever their specific causes, wars are a result of dyadic relations between men and nations: armed conflict involves one group of powers *against* another. All bilateral relations are fraught with social tension: pairs are what Royce calls "an essentially dangerous community."[78] The insurance relation is triadic: an insurer—the spirit of this community—interprets the risks of an "adventurer" or risk-taker to a beneficiary. The insurance community tends to demand some larger union in the social order.[79] Royce proposes that nations insure themselves against hazards like war. An impartial board would act as the spirit of this community, and he believes that this contribution to the dark problem of the World War will *"most tend to bring peace on earth and to aid us towards the community of mankind."*[80] The reparations the victors would demand can provide the resources to fund the "International Board of Insurance Trustees." While in peacetime no thinker could persuade the nations to make the sacrifice, the (Allied) victors might force the Germans to finance the proposal.[81] Betrayal itself contains within it a possible atonement. Out of the evil of the war—and out of it alone—might come the means to eliminate war and *"to make visible to us the holy city of the community of all mankind."*[82]

EPILOGUE

Royce died in 1916 when he was sixty, an age at which a philosopher may be at the height of his powers. His accomplishments are more striking if we consider that a rapid decline marked the last three years of his life. In the summer of 1910 he lost his closest friend with the death of William James. A few weeks later the son who had accompanied him to Cambridge in 1882 died of typhoid fever.[1] For someone as lonely and shy as Royce, these personal calamities had a telling effect. An added tragedy was his own sense of incompleteness and even failure. Many philosophic doctrines attracted American thinkers in the second decade of the century, but Royce rightfully felt that the tide of idealism was on the wane; and he had been unsuccessful in creating a viable school around him. In early 1912 he suffered a mild stroke, and although he made a remarkable recovery, producing *The Problem of Christianity* a year later, he never regained his health. Toward the end of 1913 he drew up plans to publish a series of logic articles in *The Journal of Philosophy;* he thought he would finish them within four months, but he wrote only one.[2] William Ernest Hocking believed that this inability to put together "his major work on logic" was another reason for Royce's early death.[3]

In fact, with the publication of *The Problem of Christianity* Royce's logical work took on a frenzied character. In 1905 he had shown to his satisfaction that we could generate Veblen's geometrical postulates from Σ; for reasons that seem unclear he later became discontented with his derivation of the postulates for projective geometry. The logic books which date from his last years are filled with unfinished and fragmentary attempts to redo what he thought he had done earlier. And frantic notes on the difficulties of these attempts accompany his work. In June and July of 1914 he took what appears to be the last of the voyages which provided leisure for his mathematical studies. The journey ended with "a discovery of the first importance" for his latest undertaking. But the next entries are devoted to the revisions of the last of the 1914 Berkeley Lectures, all originally intended to deal with interpretation.[4] With the outbreak of war in August he threw himself into new explications of the applications of his doctrines.[5]

In the other Berkeley Lectures delivered prior to the Sarajevo assassination he hinted at changes in his thinking more dramatic than even interpretation had yielded. He conducted an exploration of the concept of the probable, a predicate which lies *between* truth and falsity.[6] Probability was also at the basis of his ideas on international insurance,[7] but what philosophical formulations he had in mind—if any —are unknown to us.

His continuous preoccupation with World War I made him the leading anti-German ideologue. After *The Problem of Christianity* he developed no new ideas, and by 1916 verged on senility.[8] His death in September of that year ended the most important and productive era of philosophical speculation at Harvard. As President Lowell had written him toward the end of his career, "The University is built not of bricks but of men; and you have been one of the cornerstones. A dozen such men would alone make a great University."[9]

BIBLIOGRAPHIC NOTE AND
FOOTNOTE ANNEX

The best bibliography of Royce's published works is the "Annotated Bibliography of the Published Works of Josiah Royce" by Ignas Skrupskelis in *The Writings of Josiah Royce,* edited by John J. McDermott (Chicago, 1969), pp. 1167–1226. This bibliography lists bibliographies of secondary works and of the contents of the Royce manuscripts. In addition to the Royce, James, and Peirce papers at Harvard, I have used the papers of F. H. Bradley, Alfred Bray Kempe, and Theodore de Laguna. The Bradley papers are in Merton College, Oxford; the Kempe papers in the possession of his son, Reverend A. H. M. Kempe, Bedford Hotel, Southgate, Chichester, Sussex; the de Laguna papers in the possession of his wife and daughter, Grace and Frederika de Laguna, 221 N. Roberts Road, Byrn Mawr, Pennsylvania, 19010. While the Bradley and de Laguna papers were not useful for my study, Mrs. Grace de Laguna was most helpful in giving me a long and pleasant interview. Reverend Kempe provided invaluable assistance.

Most substantive "footnotes" are starred and appear in the text. Those that follow ought to be self-explanatory. Throughout these notes, the following abbreviations are used:

CG	*The Conception of God,* New York, 1897
CI	*The Conception of Immortality,* Boston, 1900
FE	*Fugitive Essays,* ed. J. Lowenberg, 1920, reprinted in New York, 1968
HGC	*The Hope of the Great Community,* New York, 1916
LJR	*The Letters of Josiah Royce,* ed. J. Clendenning, Chicago, 1970
LMI	*Lectures on Modern Idealism,* ed. J. Lowenberg, foreword by John E. Smith, New Haven, 1967

GP	*Outlines of Psychology*, New York, 1903
PC	*The Problem of Christianity*, intro. John E. Smith, Chicago, 1968
PIK	"On the Principles of the Interdependence of Knowledge," Ph.D. Dissertation, John Hopkins, 1878, Harvard University Archives
PL	*The Philosophy of Loyalty*, New York, 1908
RAP	*The Religious Aspect of Philosophy*, Boston, 1885
RLE	*Royce's Logical Essays*, ed. Daniel Robinson, Dubuque, 1951
RP	Royce Papers, Harvard University Archives
SGE	*Studies of Good and Evil*, New York, 1898
SMP	*The Spirit of Modern Philosophy*, Boston, 1892
SRI	*The Sources of Religious Insight*, New York, 1912
WAI	*War and Insurance*, New York, 1914
WI 1, WI 2	*The World and the Individual*, 2 vols., New York, 1899, 1901
WJ	*William James and Other Essays on the Philosophy of Life*, New York, 1911

INTRODUCTION

1. Murray G. Murphey defends this contention at length in his important article "Kant's Children: The Cambridge Pragmatists," *Transactions of the Charles S. Peirce Society*, 4 (1968).

1. EARLY PRAGMATISM, 1877–1884

1. *LJR*, pp. 59, 66.
2. *LJR*, pp. 121–123. For a more complete account of Royce's early life see *LJR*, pp. 45–116; Thomas F. Powell, *Josiah Royce* (New York, 1967), pp. 1–23; and John Clendenning's forthcoming biography.
3. *LJR*, pp. 59, 86.

4. *RAP*, p. xiii.

5. "Before and Since Kant," *Berkeley Quarterly*, 2 (1881), pp. 134, 145, 147. For Schopenhauer's influence see *PC*, p. 39.

6. "Before and Since Kant," pp. 145–149; "Kant's Relation to Modern Philosophic Progress," *Journal of Speculative Philosophy*, 15 (1881), p. 372.

7. *PIK*, p. 39. Royce presented the dissertation to the faculty at Johns Hopkins in April 1878. I have taken the citations from a xerox of a typewritten copy made in 1927 and deposited in the Harvard University Archives. I have taken the liberty of correcting some typographical errors in my quotations.

8. *PIK*, pp. 43–44.

9. *PIK*, pp. 65–66.

10. *PIK*, pp. 50–56.

11. *PIK*, pp. 58–61.

12. *PIK*, pp. 87–88.

13. *PIK*, pp. 63–65.

14. *PIK*, p. 4.

15. *PIK*, pp. 65–66.

16. *PIK*, pp. 78–81.

17. *PIK*, p. 82 (italics in original).

18. *PiK*, pp. 4, 94 (italics in original). Royce makes this point more dramatically four years later in "How Beliefs are Made": "The only absolute truth of which we mortals seem to have any clear notion would be found in a perfect agreement of all rational beings with one another; and this agreement would simply express the fact that we were all in perfect moral harmony." Reprinted in *FE*, p. 346. The title and date and place of original publication of published articles later collected are not normally cited in my footnotes; reference is simply made to the collection in question; it may be consulted for a complete citation.

19. *PIK*, pp. 110, 129–130, 135, 138, 145.

20. *RP*, p. 64. Found in Box 79.

21. Cited in Ralph Barton Perry, *The Thought and Character of William James*, vol. 1 (Boston, 1935), p. 789. Royce had also pondered Peirce's classic *Popular Science Monthly* articles (see p. 788).

22. "The Eternal and the Practical," *Philosophical Review*, 13 (1904), pp. 116–117. See also *PL*, pp. 325–326; and *WJ*, p. 43.

23. For the fullest statement of his doubts see "Kant's Relation," p. 374; for others, "On Purpose in Thought," 1880 (unpublished but later printed in *FE*), pp. 226, 248.

24. "Kant's Relation," pp. 373–374.

25. "Tests of Right and Wrong," 1880 (unpublished but later printed in *FE*), p. 199; see also *FE*, pp. 347–348.

26. "Tests of Right and Wrong," p. 201; see also "Kant's Relation," p. 377.

27. "Tests of Right and Wrong," pp. 203–204. By 1882 Royce goes further than this: "for what we produce, we are in some sense morally responsible; and thus . . . in discussing the nature of knowledge, we are trespassing on the borderland of ethics" (*FE*, p. 372).

28. "Kant's Relation," p. 378; see also George Dykhuizen's articles, "The Early Pragmatism of Josiah Royce," *Personalist*, 18 (1937), pp. 127–128; and "Royce's Early Philosophy of Religion," *Journal of Religion*, 15 (1935), pp. 317–318.

29. "On Purpose in Thought," pp. 249–253.

30. Cited in "Introduction," *FE*, pp. 32–34; see also "Kant's Relation," pp. 378–379.

31. "On Purpose in Thought," p. 256.

32. *RP*, Box C, "Lectures on 'The Return to Kant,'" pp. 66, 68, 167–168.

33. *PIK*, pp. 5, 150–151.

34. *FE*, pp. 112–113, 338; see also Dykhuizen, "Early Pragmatism," pp. 128–129.

35. See Dykhuizen, "Early Pragmatism," p. 133; and "Mind and Reality," *Mind*, O.S., 7 (1882), pp. 30–54.

36. "Mind and Reality," pp. 52–53.

37. *RP*, Box 79, "Reality and Consciousness" [draft of "Mind and Reality"], p. 6.

38. *RP*, Box E, Notebook, "J. Royce, Lecture on Rel. Phil., Philosophy Notes," n.p.; there is a hint of this tentativeness in *RAP*, p. 279.

39. *WI* 2, p. vii.

2. ABSOLUTE IDEALISM, 1885–1897

1. *RAP*, pp. 337 ff., 386 ff.
2. *RAP*, p. 390.
3. *RAP*, pp. ix, xiii, xvi–xvii (italics mine).
4. *SMP*, pp. vi–vii.
5. *SGE*, p. iii.

6. *RAP*, pp. 385, 389, 392 (italics in original).

7. *SMP*, p. 349.

8. *SMP*, p. 435.

9. *RAP*, pp. 359–363.

10. *RAP*, pp. 300–302.

11. *SMP*, pp. 350 351 (italics in original).

12. *RAP*, pp. 339 ff.; and *SMP*, pp. 350–363; pp. 354–360 of the latter book provide a different context for the argument.

13. *RAP*, pp. 346–347.

14. *RAP*, pp. 339–354; see also *SMP*, pp. 358–362.

15. *RAP*, p. 341.

16. *RAP*, p. 354; *SGE*, p. 156.

17. *RAP*, pp. 354–356.

18. *SGE*, p. 158 (italics in original).

19. *RAP*, p. 357; see also pp. 358–362.

20. *RAP*, p. 385.

21. *RAP*, pp. 370–376, 393–395.

22. *RAP*, pp. 390–392.

23. *RAP*, p. 397 (italics in original).

24. *SMP*, pp. 369–370.

25. *RAP*, p. 399.

26. *RAP*, p. 405.

27. *RAP*, pp. 419–420.

28. *RAP*, pp. 407–413, 415. I have tried to clarify the last part of this argument which appears in fragmentary form in *RAP*, pp. 409–410.

29. *RAP*, pp. 422–423.

30. *RAP*, p. 425.

31. *RAP*, pp. 426–430; *SMP*, pp. 375–376; *SGE*, pp. 165–166. I have made Royce's capitalization and hyphenization consistent.

32. "Introduction," *LJR*, pp. 22–23.

33. Quoted in *LJR*, p. 24.

34. William James, *Pragmatism and four essays from The Meaning of Truth*, ed. Ralph Barton Perry (New York, 1955), p. 260, n. 6.

35. *SMP*, pp. 368–380.

36. *SGE*, pp. 162–165.

37. Published as the first essay in *CG*, together with other addresses and Royce's supplementary essay, "The Absolute and the Individual," pp. 15–30.

38. *CG*, p. 43.

39. *SMP*, pp. 360–374.

40. *SGE*, p. 162.
41. James, Review of *RAP*, *Atlantic Monthly*, 55 (1885), p. 842.
42. *CG*, p. 135.
43. *RAP*, pp. 441, 454.
44. James, Review, p. 842.
45. *RAP*, pp. 468, 475–477; see also p. 448.
46. *CG*, pp. 49–50.
47. *LJR*, p. 326.
48. *CG*, p. 136 (italics in original).
49. *SGE*, p. 167.
50. *CG*, pp. 9–15, 44–48.
51. *CG*, pp. 182–192; for Royce's first analysis of attention and will see *FE*, pp. 348–357.
52. *CG*, pp. 269.
53. *LJR*, p. 326.
54. *CG*, pp. 247–258.
55. *CG*, pp. 258–266.
56. *CG*, p. 266.
57. *CG*, p. 294.
58. *CG*, p. 291 (italics in original).
59. *CG*, p. 295.
60. *CG*, pp. 295–296.
61. *CG*, pp. 36–38.
62. *CG*, pp. 198–199 (italics in original).
63. *CG*, pp. 193–199. The only other extended treatment of this problem with which I am acquainted is equally unhelpful; see *RP*, Box 67, Augustus Graham Lectures on Theism [1896], especially Lecture III, "The Moral World and the Revelation of God," pp. 40–46.
64. *CG*, pp. 200–203; see also pp. 211–316, 320.

3. MORAL AND RELIGIOUS PHILOSOPHY, 1877–1897

1. *RAP*, pp. 18–19.
2. *SMP*, pp. 435–436.
3. "Return to Kant," p. 165.
4. *FE*, pp. 197–198.
5. See the discussion in *FE*, pp. 96–132.
6. *FE*, pp. 130–131.

247*

7. *FE*, pp. 131–132.
8. *RAP*, p. 94.
9. *FE*, pp. 139–140.
10. *FE*, p. 180.
11. *FE*, p. 179.
12. *FE*, pp. 148–149.
13. *FE*, pp. 181, 183–185.
14. *FE*, pp. 184–186.
15. *FE*, pp. 152–153.
16. *FE*, pp. 210–213.
17. *FE*, p. 213.
18. *FE*, p. 213.
19. *FE*, pp. 210–215.
20. *FE*, pp. 215–216, 218.
21. *FE*, pp. 176–177.
22. *RAP*, p. 23.
23. *RAP*, pp. 58–60.
24. *RAP*, pp. 32–130.
25. *RAP*, p. 106; see also pp. 127–130.
26. *RAP*, pp. 133–134.
27. *RAP*, pp. 134–135.
28. *RAP*, pp. 137–138.
29. *RAP*, pp. 141–146.
30. *RAP*, p. 467.
31. *RAP*, p. 141.
32. *RAP*, pp. 170, 211.
33. *RAP*, p. 148 (italics in original).
34. *RAP*, p. 145. For the aspects of this doctrine due to Schopenhauer, see pp. 93–94.
35. *RAP*, p. 444.
36. *RAP*, pp. 451–456, 465.
37. *SMP*, p. 437.
38. *SMP*, pp. 440–441.
39. *SMP*, p. 459.
40. *SMP*, pp. 460–461.
41. See *RAP*, pp. 458–459.
42. *SMP*, pp. 470–471 (italics in original).
43. See *SGE*, *passim;* and *CG*, especially pp. 338–345.
44. *SGE*, p. 14.
45. *SGE*, pp. 120–121.

46. See Peirce's review of *RAP* in *The Collected Papers of Charles Sanders Peirce*, vols. 1–6, ed. Charles Hartshorne and Paul Weiss; vols. 7–8, ed. Arthur Burks (Cambridge, Mass., 1931–1935; 1958*)*, 8.39–8.54. The first three pages of this review, entitled "An American Plato: Review of Royce's Religious Aspect of Philosophy," may be found in the Peirce Papers in the Houghton Library at Harvard, MS 1369.

47. *CG*, pp. 345–348; see *RAP*, pp. 466–467, for another expression of the frustrations involved in human progress.

4. THE WORLD OF DESCRIPTION AND PHILOSOPHICAL PSYCHOLOGY

1. See "The Imitative Functions and Their Place in Human Nature," *Century Magazine*, 48 (1894), pp. 137–145; "Preliminary Report on Imitation," *Psychological Review*, 2 (1895), pp. 217–235; and "The Psychology of Invention," *Psychological Review*, 5 (1898), pp. 113–144. As head of the "Presentiments Committee" of the American Society for Psychical Research in the late eighties, Royce demonstrated his solid capacity as a thinker. For the best statement of his thought see "Hallucination of Memory and 'Telepathy,'" *Mind*, O.S., 123 (1888), pp. 244–248.

2. *Unitarian Review*, 32 (1889), pp. 1, 97.

3. *Ibid.*, p. 8.

4. *Ibid.*, p. 13 (italics in original).

5. *Ibid.*, pp. 17–18.

6. *Ibid.*, pp. 18–19.

7. For this point see *SMP*, pp. 424–426.

8. "Is There a Philosophy of Evolution?" pp. 22–29.

9. *Ibid.*, pp. 25–26 (italics in original).

10. *Ibid.*, p. 98.

11. *Ibid.*, pp. 106–107. *PIK*, pp. 64–65, and *RAP*, pp. 150–151, both anticipate this conflict.

12. "Is There a Philosophy of Evolution?" pp. 98–99 (first set of italics in original; second set mine).

13. *Ibid.*, p. 108 (italics in original).

14. *SMP*, p. 105.

15. *SMP*, pp. 273, 305; see also *SGE*, p. 140.

16. *SMP*, p. 405.

17. *SMP*, pp. 383–392 (italics in original). I have cited the relevant portion of the dissertation in Chapter 1.

18. *SMP*, pp. 387–391.

19. *SMP*, pp. 391, 397–404. This discussion concerns the categories, not the forms.

20. *SGE*, pp. 126–127.

21. *SMP*, pp. 393–397.

22. *SMP*, pp. 315–318.

23. *SMP*, pp. 318–319, 331.

24. *SMP*, p. 332.

25. *SMP*, pp. 334–335. For the "perspective effect" comment see *WI* 1, p. 420.

26. *SMP*, pp. 321–322 (italics in original).

27. *SMP*, pp. 407–408; see also *SGE*, pp. 223–227.

28. *SMP*, pp. 403, 406–407, 409 (italics in original).

29. *SMP*, pp. 407–408.

30. *SMP*, pp. 413–415.

31. *SMP*, p. 291.

32. *SGE*, p. 228.

33. *SGE*, p. 231.

34. *SGE*, p. 237.

35. *SGE*, pp. 238–239.

36. *SGE*, p. 241.

37. *SGE*, p. 243 (italics in original).

38. *SGE*, pp. 243–246.

39. "Can Psychology be Founded Upon the Study of Consciousness Alone, or is Physiology Needed for the Purpose?" *Addresses and Proceedings of the International Congress of Education of the World's Columbian Exposition* (New York, 1894), p. 691.

40. *Ibid.*, pp. 691–692.

41. "Is There a Philosophy of Evolution?" p. 104.

42. The relation between the "two selves" is not always clear, nor is it always made. For one discussion, see *CG*, pp. 266–292; I take up the question in Chapter 8.

43. *SGE*, pp. 173–174.

44. *SGE*, pp. 201–202.

45. *SGE*, pp. 201–203.

46. *SGE*, p. 182; "The External World and the Social Consciousness," *Philosophical Review*, 3 (1894), p. 531.

47. *RP*, Box 69, "Social Factors in the Development of the Individual Mind," 1898, Lecture 3, "The Beginnings of the Social Life of the Individual," pp. 4–5.

48. I have been able to locate only the fourth edition (1906) of this book of Baldwin's; the letter is printed there on pp. 569–570. For Royce's review of *Mental Development in the Child and the Race*, 2nd ed. (New York, 1895), see *Psychological Review*, 3 (1896), pp. 201–211.

49. *RP*, Box 65, Lecture 8, "The Psychological Theory of Self-Consciousness from the Teacher's Point of View," pp. 32–33.

50. *RP*, Box 63, Lecture 1, "What is a General Idea?" pp. 60–71; Lecture 2, "General Ideas and the Theory of Habits," pp. 22–26, 40–43.

51. *RP*, Box 65, Lecture 8, pp. 34–39.

52. *Ibid.*, p. 36; Box 63, Lecture 1, p. 62.

53. "The Two-Fold Nature of Knowledge: Imitative and Reflective, an Unpublished Manuscript of Josiah Royce," ed. Peter Fuss, *Journal of the History of Philosophy*, 4 (1966), pp. 327, 329–330.

54. *Ibid.*, p. 327.

55. *RP*, Box H [large undated, untitled fragment], pp. 33, 35, 38 (italics mine).

56. "Preliminary Report on Imitation," pp. 225–228.

57. *Ibid.*, p. 223.

58. *Ibid.*, pp. 226–227.

59. *Ibid.*, p. 230.

60. "The External World and the Social Consciousness," pp. 536–539; see also *SGE*, pp. 181–187.

61. "The External World and the Social Consciousness," p. 540.

62. *Ibid.*, pp. 533–534.

63. *Ibid.*, pp. 534–535. This "inner reflection" does not appear to be related to "Reflective Knowledge."

64. *Ibid.*, pp. 514–515.

65. *Ibid.*, pp. 516–519.

66. *Ibid.*, p. 529.

67. *Ibid.*, pp. 540–543.

68. *Ibid.*, p. 544.

69. *SMP*, p. 411.

70. "The External World and the Social Consciousness," pp. 543–544.

71. *SMP*, p. 417.

5. THE WORLD AND THE INDIVIDUAL

1. *LJR*, p. 378.
2. *CI*.
3. *OP*.
4. *WI* 1, pp. 282, 299, 385, 387.
5. *WI* 2, p. 26. See also *SMP*, p. 436, for this idea.
6. *WI* 1, pp. 16–17.
7. *WI* 1, pp. 20–22.
8. *WI* 1, p. 311.
9. *OP*, p. 351; cf. pp. 334, 365.
10. *OP*, pp. 84–85 (italics in original).
11. *OP*, pp. 164, 194, 196 (italics in original).
12. *OP*, pp. 108–109.
13. *OP*, pp. 367–369.
14. *OP*, pp. 197–208.
15. *OP*, pp. 222, 226, 236.
16. *OP*, pp. 367–368.
17. *OP*, p. 226 (italics in original).
18. *OP*, pp. 280, 286–290.
19. *OP*, pp. 291–293 (italics in original).
20. *WI* 1, p. 38.
21. *WI* 1, pp. 22–23, 152.
22. *WI* 1, pp. 33–37.
23. *WI* 1, p. 25.
24. *WI* 1, pp. 48–50.
25. *WI* 1, p. 31.
26. *WI* 1, pp. 23–29.
27. *WI* 1, pp. 317–318.
28. *WI* 1, pp. 300–306, 308–309.
29. *WI* 1, pp. 319–320.
30. *WI* 1, p. 70.
31. *WI* 1, pp. 337–338 (italics in original).
32. *WI* 1, pp. 324–331, 335, 390–391, 398–400.
33. *WI* 1, p. 36. For the melody theme see also *SMP*, pp. 456–457.
34. *WI* 1, pp. 459–460.
35. *WI* 1, pp. 340 341.
36. *WI* 1, pp. 37–43, 298–299.
37. *WI* 2, pp. 28–33 (italics in original); the example is taken from Vincent Buranelli, *Josiah Royce* (New York, n.d.), pp. 117–120.

38. *WI* 2, pp. 53–62.
39. *WI* 2, p. 52.
40. *WI* 2, p. 167.
41. *WI* 2, pp. 168, 173.
42. *WI* 2, pp. 259–265.
43. *WI* 2, pp. 171–172; see also pp. 257–258.
44. *WI* 2, pp. 122–126.
45. *WI* 2, pp. 114–121.
46. *CI*, pp. 84–85 (italics in original).
47. *CI*, p. 88 (italics in original).
48. *WI* 2, pp. 140–141, 143–144.
49. *WI* 1, pp. 424–427; 2, pp. 142–146.
50. *CI*, p. 90 (italics in original).
51. *WI* 2, pp. 325–327.
52. *WI* 2, p. 148.
53. *WI* 2, pp. 330–331.
54. *WI* 2, p. 374 (italics in original).
55. *WI* 2, pp. 418–419.
56. *WI* 2, pp. 225–226.
57. *WI* 2, pp. 268–269.
58. *WI* 2, pp. 303–309 (italics in original).
59. *WI* 2, p. 233.
60. *WI* 2, p. 435.
61. *WI* 2, pp. 442–443, 445.
62. *CI*, p. 80.
63. "Hegel's Terminology (in relation to the Hegelian Philosophy)," in James Mark Baldwin, ed., *Dictionary of Philosophy and Psychology* (New York, 1901), I, p. 464.
64. *LMI*, pp. 168–169.
65. *SMP*, pp. 224–226, 492–506.

6. ABSOLUTE PRAGMATISM, 1899–1913

1. *LMI*, pp. 235–238, 241, 257–258.
2. *WI* 1, pp. 251, 266.
3. *WI* 1, p. 196 (italics in original).
4. *WI* 1, pp. 221, 236.
5. *WI* 1, pp. 205, 234.

6. *WI* 1, p. 202. See also pp. 362–368 where Royce's argument against the third conception of being is identical to his later arguments directed against James; for the later arguments see below.

7. *WI* 1, p. 203.

8. *WI* 1, pp. 257–258.

9. *WI* 1, pp. 205–206 (italics in original).

10. *WI* 1, p. 258.

11. See Murray G. Murphey, *The Development of Peirce's Philosophy* (Cambridge, Mass., 1961), pp. 169–171, 394–397, 400–402; Lewis, *Mind and the World Order* (New York, 1929); *The Analysis of Knowledge and Valuation* (La Salle, 1946); Goodman, *Fact, Fiction, and Forecast*, 2nd ed. (Indianapolis, 1965); Quine, *From a Logical Point of View* (Cambridge, Mass., 1953).

12. *WI* 1, pp. 242–243.

13. *WI* 1, p. 260 (italics in original).

14. *WI* 1, pp. 356–360.

15. *The Writings of William James*, ed. John J. McDermott (New York, 1967), p. 465.

16. *Ibid.*, pp. 195, 231–232, 279, 309; but see also the cryptic remark in Perry, ed., *Pragmatism*, p. 264, n. 6.

17. Perry, *Thought and Character*, pp. 727–728. On this problem see Goodman, esp. pp. 31–58.

18. Perry, *Thought and Character*, pp. 394–395; McDermott, *Writings of William James*, p. 213.

19. In addition to the citations below, see *WI* 2, pp. 13–16; and *LMI*, pp. 238–240, 253–254, 258.

20. This discussion derives from *PL*, pp. 324–348 (italics in original).

21. *RLE*, p. 86 (italics in original).

22. *RLE*, pp. 81–85.

23. This argument occurs in *WI* 1, pp. 326–368, where it is used against Critical Rationalism, and James is not mentioned. An identical argument is used against James in *PL*, pp. 334–348, and in *RLE*, pp. 78–81, 116–118, and this leads me to suspect that Royce has James in mind in his earlier attack on Critical Rationalism.

24. *RLE*, pp. 116–117.

25. *RLE*, p. 116.

26. *PL*, pp. 336–337.

27. *PL*, pp. 341–342.

28. *RLE*, p. 88.

29. *PL*, pp. 342–343.

30. *RLE*, pp. 93–94; see also *WI* 1, pp. 221–222, 225–226 (italics in original).

31. *RLE*, pp. 260–262.

32. See Murray G. Murphey's discussion of this point in "Kant's Children," pp. 19 ff.

33. *PIK*, pp. 135, 145–146; see also *RP*, Box 80, "Some Illustrations of the Structure and Growth of Human Thought" [1880].

34. *SMP*, p. 386.

35. *FE*, pp. 238–240; *SMP*, p. 402.

36. *RP*, Box 81, "A Critical Study of Reality [beginning of a book on metaphysics, c. 1897]," pp. 102–103, 132, 152.

37. *RP*, Box 68, "On the Psychology of the Intellect," Lecture II, "The Social Basis of Intellectual Life" [dated: New Orleans, 1897?], pp. 11–12.

38. For the first case see *PC, passim,* but especially pp. 49–51; for the second case see (of particular importance) "Herbert Spencer and his Contribution to the Concept of Evolution," *International Quarterly,* 9 (1904), pp. 335–365; and also "Charles Sanders Peirce" (with Fergus Kernan), *Journal of Philosophy,* 13 (1916), pp. 702–706.

39. Reprinted in *RLE*, pp. 268–290. At some points in his discussion Royce merely states Poincaré's views, but he agrees with them to such an extent that I have used the entire introduction as a statement of Royce's position.

40. *RLE*, pp. 263, 274 (italics in original).

41. *RLE*, p. 279.

42. See *Mind and the World Order,* esp. pp. 101–102, 213, 228, 254–268; and *From a Logical Point of View, passim.*

43. *RLE*, pp. 263–265.

44. *RLE*, p. 281.

45. *RLE*, pp. 265–266.

7. MATHEMATICS AND METAPHYSICS, 1899–1904

1. *WI* 2, pp. 1, 4, 6.

2. *Primer of Logical Analysis for the Use of Composition Students* (San Francisco, 1881).

3. *LJR*, p. 422.

4. Daniel Robinson, *Royce and Hocking: American Idealists* (Boston, 1968), p. 149.

5. *RP*, Box 73, "Introductory Statement at the Philosophical Conference of October 19, 1903."

6. *LJR*, p. 556.

7. *Philosophical Review*, 3 (1894), pp. 216–217.

8. See *CG*. p. 141.

9. Especially pp. 298 and 302.

10. *LJR*, p. 392.

11. *WI* 1, p. 473.

12. *WI* 1, pp. 475, 472–482, 493. The same regress occurs in regard to R's relation to O.

13. Renouvier also seems to have played a part in forcing Royce to develop his ideas; see "The External World and the Social Consciousness," pp. 521–525.

14. *WI* 1, pp. 504–509.

15. *WI* 1, pp. 510–511. I assume that s_0 functions as O does in the series of natural numbers.

16. *WI* 1, p. 553.

17. *WI* 1, pp. 532–535, 538.

18. *WI* 2, pp. 449–452.

19. *WI* 2, p. v; *RP*, Notebooks on Logic, Box 2, Notebook Psychology Lectures ["Note," February 5, 1901], p. 49.

20. *WI* 2, pp. 449–452.

21. *WI* 2, pp. 77–79 (italics in original).

22. *WI* 2, pp. 80, 85–89, 91–96.

23. *WI* 2, p. x.

24. *WI* 2, p. 72.

25. *WI* 1, pp. 529, 538.

26. *WI* 2, pp. 81–83, 88, 104–107.

27. *WI* 2, pp. 93, 17. Royce qualifies this statement by saying that "we abstract from certain complications that we need not here consider. . . ." We shall stipulate later what these are.

28. *OP*, pp. 251–257 (italics in original).

29. *WI* 2, pp. 76, 106–107, 138, 156.

30. *Collected Papers of Charles Sanders Peirce*, 8.117, n. 10; 8.277.

31. *Ibid.*, 8.125; 8.131. See also 3.563–3.570.

32. *Royce's Metaphysics*, trans. Virginia and Gordon Ringer (Chicago, 1956), p. 95.

33. William and Martha Kneale, *The Development of Logic* (Oxford, 1962), p. 438.

34. *RP*, Notebooks on Logic, Box 6, Notebook [otherwise unlabeled]. The antinomy which this fragment discusses may, of course, only represent the one which Bradley poses to Royce and which Royce feels his "Supplementary Essay" solves. In this case it would probably date earlier.

35. *RP*, Notebooks on Logic, Box 2, Psychology Lectures ["Note," February 5, 1901], pp. 45–47.

36. *WI* 2, p. 448.

37. See, e.g., *CG*, pp. 295–307.

38. *CG*, p. 288; see also pp. 199, 266.

39. *CI*, p. 8; *WI*2, p. 431.

40. *WI* 1, pp. 526–527.

41. *WI* 1, pp. 585–587. And see footnotes 63, 64, and 65 of Chapter 5.

42. *WI* 2, p. 18.

43. *WI* 1, p. 583.

44. See *CG*, pp. 207–210; and "The Sciences of the Ideal," in [*International*] *Congress of Arts and Science, Universal Exposition, St. Louis, 1904,* vol. 1, ed. Howard J. Rodgers (Boston, 1905), pp. 164–165.

45. See Bertrand Russell's *The Principles of Mathematics,* 2nd ed. (New York, 1938), pp. 362 ff.

46. Kneale, *The Development of Logic,* pp. 652–653; *RLE,* p. 375.

47. *RP*, Box 73, "Mr. Bertrand Russell's Problem of 'The Contradiction'" [August 9, 1903], pp. 54–55. Kenneth Blackwell, archivist of the Russell Papers, has informed me that *The Principles* was published in Britain in May 1903; in the U.S., June 27.

8. MORAL AND RELIGIOUS PHILOSOPHY, 1900–1912

1. *PL*, pp. vii, xi.

2. *SRI*, pp. 3–4.

3. Cited from an advertisement for *WJ*, printed in the back of *HGC*.

4. "Introduction" to Anna Boynton Thompson's *The Unity of Fichte's Doctrine* (Boston, 1895), p. xiii.

5. *WI* 2, p. 289 (most of the original appears in italics).

6. *WI* 2, pp. 276–277, 286–293.
7. *WI* 2, pp. 310–314.
8. "Royce's Urbana Lectures: Lecture I" [and "Lecture II"], ed. Peter Fuss, *Journal of the History of Philosophy*, 5 (1967), pp. 64–65.
9. *Ibid.*, pp. 70–71.
10. *Ibid.*, pp. 72–74 (italics in original).
11. *Ibid.*, pp. 74–78.
12. *Ibid.*, pp. 78, 269–270, 274–276.
13. *Ibid.*, pp. 272–274.
14. *Ibid.*, pp. 272–273, 276–277, 281–283.
15. *Ibid.*, pp. 278–279, 282–283.
16. *Ibid.*, pp. 279–284.
17. *Ibid.*, pp. 285–286.
18. *PL*, pp. 16–17, 43.
19. *PL*, pp. 19–20.
20. *PL*, p. 52.
21. *PL*, p. 34.
22. *PL*, pp. 124–126.
23. *PL*, pp. 116–122.
24. *PL*, pp. 162–166, 179–196.
25. *PL*, p. 121.
26. *PL*, pp. 307–310.
27. *PL*, esp. pp. 340–348.
28. *PL*, pp. 313–315.
29. *PL*, p. 376.
30. *PL*, esp. pp. 167–179.
31. *PL*, p. ix.
32. *PL*, p. 390 (italics in original).
33. *PL*, p. 310.
34. *PL*, p. 227.
35. *PL*, pp. 311–312, 344.
36. *PL*, p. 355.
37. *PL*, pp. 356–357.
38. *PL*, pp. 377, 396.
39. *PL*, pp. 394–396.
40. *SRI*, pp. 5–6, 8–9, 12 (italics in original).
41. *SRI*, p. 31.
42. *SRI*, pp. 44–45.
43. *SRI*, esp. pp. 220–225.
44. *SRI*, pp. 89–90.

45. *SRI*, pp. 89–93.
46. *SRI*, pp. 123–124.
47. *SRI*, p. 102.
48. *SRI*, p. 114 (italics in original).
49. *SRI*, p. 170.
50. *SRI*, pp. 197–200.
51. *SRI*, pp. 219–227.
52. *SRI*, p. 235.
53. *SRI*, pp. 235–241.
54. *SRI*, pp. 250–251.
55. *SRI*, pp. 234, 252–253.
56. *SRI*, p. 238.
57. *SRI*, p. 291.
58. *SRI*, p. 278.
59. *LJR*, pp. 561–562.
60. *SRI*, p. 10.

9. FOUNDATIONS OF MATHEMATICS, 1: THE NINETEENTH-CENTURY BACKGROUND

1. Eric Temple Bell, *The Development of Mathematics*, 2nd ed. (New York, 1945), p. 190.
2. *Nation*, 65 (December 30, 1897), p. 524.
3. "Projective Geometry," in *The World of Mathematics*, ed. James R. Newman, 4 vols. (New York, 1956), pp. 638–639.
4. All of the above is heavily dependent on *ibid.*, pp. 625–640.
5. *Ibid.*, p. 640.
6. Julian Lowell Coolidge, *A History of Geometrical Methods* (Oxford, 1940), p. 268.
7. John Wesley Young, *Projective Geometry* (Chicago, 1930), pp. 105–107.
8. Young, *Projective Geometry*, p. 151; Cassius J. Keyser, "The Group Concept," in Newman, ed., *The World of Mathematics*, pp. 1538–1539.
9. Murphey, *Development*, p. 193.
10. Kline, "Projective Geometry," p. 640.
11. Bell, *Development*, p. 444.
12. Coolidge, *History*, pp. 85–87.

13. Quoted in Murray G. Murphey, "The Synechism of Charles Sanders Peirce," Ph.D. dissertation, Yale University, 1954, p. 129.

14. Bell, *Development,* pp. 350–353; Bertrand Russell, *An Essay on the Foundations of Geometry* (London, 1897; reprinted in New York, 1956, with an unpaged foreword by Morris Kline), p. 29.

15. Bell, *Development,* pp. 443–448.

16. *Ibid.,* pp. 331–332.

17. Russell, *Essay,* pp. 29–30.

18. *My Philosophical Development* (London, 1959), pp. 39–40.

19. Kline, "Introduction" to Russell's *Essay.*

20. Russell, *Essay,* esp. pp. 41–46.

21. Bell, *Development,* pp. 348–350.

22. Murphey, *Development,* p. 191.

23. Kline, "Projective Geometry," p. 639.

24. Murphey, "Synechism," p. 132.

25. Russell, *Essay,* pp. 30–38, 130–131.

26. Bell, *Development,* pp. 259–260.

27. Alexander Macfarlane, *Lectures on Ten British Mathematicians of the Nineteenth Century* (New York, 1916), pp. 56–57.

28. Royce, *Primer,* p. 4.

29. The above discussion is dependent on Kneale, *The Development of Logic,* pp. 404–415.

10. FOUNDATIONS OF MATHEMATICS, 2: THE ERLANGER LOGIC, 1905–1910

1. See "Review of RLE," *Philosophy and Phenomenological Research,* 12 (1951–1952), p. 431; "Types of Order and the System Σ," *Philosophical Review,* 25 (1916), pp. 407–419; and *A Survey of Symbolic Logic* (Berkeley, 1918), pp. 362–372. The new edition of the latter book (New York, 1960) drops the discussion of Royce.

2. *LJR,* p. 76.

3. *RAP,* pp. 461–463.

4. *SMP,* p. 421.

5. Quoted in Kneale, *The Development of Logic,* pp. 406–407 (italics in original).

6. Russell, *Essay,* pp. 36, 41, 54–63, 117, 134–135 (italics in original).

7. *WI* 1, pp. 212, 303–304; *WI* 2, pp. 95–100; *RP*, Notebooks on Logic, Box 2, Notebook "Psychology Lectures" ["Note," August 2, 1901], pp. 103–104.

8. "Obituary Notice," *Proceedings of the Royal Society*, A., Vol. 102 (1923), pp. i–x.

9. Quoted from Murphey, "Synechism," pp. 139–140.

10. "Sciences of the Ideal," p. 167.

11. See the Kempe, Royce, Russell, and Turner letters in the Kempe Papers, now in the possession of Rev. A. H. M. Kempe, The Bedford Hotel, Southgate, Chichester, Sussex.

12. Bell, *Men*, p. 378; Macfarlane, *Lectures*, pp. 115–116.

13. Macfarlane, *Lectures*, p. 113.

14. Bell, *Men*, pp. 394–403.

15. 177 (Part 1, 1886), pp. 1–70; see also Macfarlane, *Lectures*, p. 116.

16. "On the Relation between the Logical Theory of Classes and the Geometrical Theory of Points," 21 (1889-1890), pp. 147–182.

17. "The Subject Matter of Exact Thought," 43 (1890), pp. 156–162.

18. "On the Relation between . . . ," p. 147.

19. *Ibid.*, pp. 148–149.

20. Reprinted in *RLE*, pp. 379–441, to which all citations have been made; pp. 379–388 summarize the Kempean background to Royce's work.

21. *RLE*, pp. 388–389.

22. *RP*, vol. 73, Note 6 of "Notes on Logic, 1903" [*circa* August].

23. *RLE*, pp. 427–428.

24. *RLE*, pp. 393, 412.

25. *RLE*, pp. 388.

26. *RLE*, pp. 390–397; I have taken my formalization of the axioms from Lindley J. Burton and Hugues LeBlanc, Review of "The Relation of . . . ," *Journal of Symbolic Logic*, 17 (1952), p. 145.

27. *RLE*, pp. 398 ff.

28. Lewis, "Types of Order," p. 413.

29. *RLE*, pp. 415–438.

30. See Burton and LeBlanc, Review, p. 146.

31. *RLE*, pp. 434, 438; see also pp. 436–437 (italics in original).

32. Review of "The Relation of . . . ," *Journal of Philosophy, Psychology, and Scientific Methods*, 3 (1906), pp. 358–359.

33. *RLE,* pp. 381, 434.

34. "On the Relation between . . . ," p. 175 (italics in original).

35. *RLE,* pp. 384, 438.

36. *RP,* Notebooks on Logic, Box 6, Notebook [otherwise unlabeled], "Survey of the Problems to be discussed in the Yale Graduate Course" [*circa* 1909].

37. *RLE,* p. 388.

38. See "The Sciences of the Ideal"; "Symmetrical and Unsymmetrical Relations in the Exact Sciences," *RP,* vol. 72 [dated 1905]; and vol. 74, Columbia Lectures [1904], "Some Characteristics of the Thinking Process."

39. *RP,* vol. 74, Columbia Lectures, Lecture Five, pp. 13–54a.

40. "Kant's Doctrine of the Basis of Mathematics," *Journal of Philosophy, Psychology, and Scientific Methods,* 2 (1905), especially pp. 206–207.

41. Perry, *Thought and Character,* p. 819. I have translated this from the German.

42. "The Sciences of the Ideal," pp. 157, 160, 168.

43. "Kant's Doctrine," p. 207; "The Present State of the Question Regarding the First Principles of Theoretical Science," *Proceedings of the American Philosophical Society,* 45 (1906), p. 91.

44. *Royce and Hocking,* pp. 149, 154–155.

45. *Royce and Hocking,* pp. 153–155. Royce's son intimates that Royce's result was published but denies that it appears in *RLE.* I feel that the article in question is "The Principles of Logic," reprinted in *RLE,* pp. 310–378.

46. *RLE,* pp. 368, 378.

47. "The Sciences of the Ideal," pp. 164–165 (italics in original).

48. *RLE,* pp. 182, 184, 187–188.

49. *RLE,* pp. 363–365.

50. "Primitive Ways of Thinking with Special Reference to Negation and Classification," *The Open Court,* 27 (1913), p. 584.

51. *RLE,* p. 365 (italics in original).

52. *RLE,* pp. 354, 367.

53. *RLE,* pp. 373–375, 377.

54. *RLE,* pp. 373–375.

55. *RLE,* p. 375.

56. *RLE,* pp. 375–376.

57. *RLE,* pp. 373, 376, 376–377.

11. THE ABSOLUTE AND THE COMMUNITY

1. *RLE*, pp. 149–150.
2. *PC*, p. 279.
3. *RLE*, p. 156.
4. *PC*, pp. 278–279.
5. *PC*, pp. 327–329.
6. *RLE*, pp. 158–159.
7. *PC*, pp. 38, 274, 297.
8. *PC*, pp. 299–304.
9. *PC*, pp. 286–290.
10. *PC*, pp. 289–290, 340.
11. *PC*, pp. 344–346.
12. *PC*, pp. 286–288.
13. *PC*, p. 245.
14. *PC*, pp. 275–276.
15. *LJR*, p. 618.
16. In addition to the citations I have given in previous chapters, especially 4 and 8, the following have struck me as most provocative: *SMP*, p. 426; *SGE*, pp. 219–220; *CG*, p. 45; *CI*, pp. 9–10; *OP*, pp. 229, 236, 275, 295–296; *LMI*, pp. 251–252; *WJ*, pp. 40–42; "The Reality of the Temporal," *The International Journal of Ethics*, 20 (1909–1910), pp. 263–267; "Some Psychological Problems Emphasized by Pragmatism," *Popular Science Monthly*, 83 (1913), pp. 409–410.
17. *PC*, p. 344.
18. *PC*, pp. 299–302.
19. *PC*, pp. 327–332.
20. *RLE*, 377 (italics in original).
21. *RP*, vol. 84, Berkeley Lectures on Loyalty, Lecture I, "Illustrations of the Philosophy of Loyalty," pp. 5–14.
22. *RLE*, p. 163.
23. *PC*, p. 360.
24. *PC*, p. 313.
25. *RLE*, p. 167.
26. *WAI*, p. 52 (italics in original).
27. *WAI*, p. 54.
28. *PC*, p. 243.
29. *PC*, pp. 247–249.
30. See *RLE*, pp. 352–354. The reason this is such a perplexing

problem is that as early as 1903, as we know, Royce was quite sophisticated in making the distinction in regard to *some* classes.

31. *LJR*, pp. 604–609.
32. *PC*, p. 80.
33. *PC*, pp. 80–81.
34. *PC*, p. 195.
35. *PC*, p. 218.
36. *PC*, p. 194.
37. *PC*, p. 218.
38. *PC*, pp. 313–315.
39. *PC*, p. 267 (italics in original).
40. *PC*, p. 357.
41. *PC*, pp. 337–339.
42. *PC*, p. 361; see also p. 349.
43. *PC*, pp. 339–342.
44. *LJR*, pp. 645–646.
45. *PC*, p. 64.
46. *SRI*, p. 10.
47. *PC* restates these ideas; see pp. 42, 187.
48. *PC*, p. 41.
49. *PC*, pp. 45, 67, 70.
50. This contrasts with the presentation in *WJ*, pp. 131–135.
51. *PC*, pp. 72–73, 85.
52. *PC*, pp. 82–84.
53. *PC*, pp. 89–91.
54. *PC*, pp. 92–95.
55. *PC*, p. 319.
56. *PC*, p. 100.
57. *PC*, pp. 106–109.
58. *PC*, p. 118.
59. *PC*, pp. 83–85, 113, 124–129.
60. *PC*, p. 118.
61. *PC*, e.g., pp. 128–129, 238.
62. *PC*, p. 131.
63. See *PC*, p. 137.
64. *PC*, pp. 50, 73.
65. *PC*, pp. 154–155.
66. *PC*, p. 180 (italics in original).
67. *PC*, pp. 180–181.

68. *PC*, p. 163.
69. *PC*, pp. 63, 186, 207–208.
70. *PC*, p. 382.
71. *PC*, p. 383; see also p. 387.
72. *PC*, pp. 388 ff.
73. *PC*, p. 405.
74. *HGC*, pp. 39–42.
75. *WAI*, p. 1; *HGC*, p. 59.
76. *HGC*, pp. 9–11. For his doubts about the morality of the other participants see *HGC*, pp. 30–33.
77. *HGC*, pp. 71–92; *WAI, passim.*
78. *WAI*, pp. 30–39 (italics in original).
79. *WAI*, pp. 55–63.
80. *WAI*, pp. 63–65; *HGC*, pp. 84–90 (italics in original).
81. *WAI*, pp. 79–81.
82. *HGC*, p. 76; *WAI*, p. 80 (italics in original).

EPILOGUE

1. *LJR*, p. 36.
2. *LJR*, pp. 609–611.
3. "On Royce's Empiricism," *Journal of Philosophy*, 53 (1956), p. 57.
4. *RP*, Notebooks on Logic, Box 3, Notebook [otherwise unlabeled], "Notes at Sea," 17 and 18 May 1912; Box 4, Notebook [otherwise unlabeled]; Box 5, Notebook [otherwise unlabeled], "In Mass Bay Crossing to the Light Ship," 5 July 1914, pp. 25–27, 92.
5. See *WAI*, pp. iii–v.
6. *RP*, vol. 84, Berkeley Lectures, 1914, Lecture III, pp. 33 ff.; see also *RLE*, pp. 35–62.
7. See *WAI*, p. x.
8. See Horace Kallen's estimate in "Remarks on Royce's Philosophy," *Journal of Philosophy*, 53 (1956), pp. 132–133.
9. *LJR*, p. 553.

INDEX

Absolute
  as cognitional and volitional, 61–62, 100–101
  as consciousness 23, 41
  as God, 40–41, 44–48, 228–229, 231
  as hypothesis, 22–24, 29, 39
  as person, 116–117
  relation to community, 215–217, 221–226, 228–229
  as system, 110, 117–118, 140–141
  as theoretical and practical, 118, 164–165
  as thought and experience, 42, 46
  as thought, experience, and will, 42–44
  See also appreciation; description; self-representation
"Absolute and the Individual, The," 42–48, 86n
Absolute Pragmatism. *See* pragmatism (Absolute)
appreciation
  defined, 75, 78–79
  relation to description, 73, 78–80, 83–84, 89, 94–98, 99–101, 107, 112–113, 144–146, 148–149, 157–158, 162–163, 165, 169, 191–192, 196, 201, 211–213, 216–217, 220
  World of, 89, 94–98, 107, 109, 112–113, 149
  see also Absolute; community; description

atonement, 231–235
attention, 44–48, 103, 109, 116

Baldwin, J. M., 86–87, 250, 252
Berkeley, George, 22, 28–31, 38, 122
betweenness, 142–144, 157, 194, 197, 205, 207–208, 216–217, 240
Boole, George, 175, 185–187, 190–192, 195, 205
Bradley, F. H., 5, 138–141, 165, 209, 235, 256

Cantor, Georg, 147, 152–153, 207
causality, 29–31, 74–76, 79–80, 132. *See also* description
cause, 162–163, 165–166, 221–222, 226, 227, 230–231. *See also* community, loyalty to loyalty, *Philosophy of Loyalty*
Cayley, Arthur, 182–185, 191–192, 198–199
Clifford, W. K., 76–78
community, 14–15, 72
  and causes of the loyal, 221–222, 226, 227, 230–231
  Christian, 225–236
  Great, 236
  of hope, 219–220
  insurance, 237, 240
  of interpretation, 216, 219–220, 221–224, 227–232
  of memory, 219–220
  and relation to individual, 221–224, 225, 229–237

A Parent's Guide to Bedwetting Control

A STEP-BY-STEP METHOD

Nathan H. Azrin, Ph.D.
and
Victoria A. Besalel, Ph.D.

SIMON AND SCHUSTER
NEW YORK

Copyright © 1979 by The Azrin Trust
All rights reserved
including the right of reproduction
in whole or in part in any form
Published by Simon and Schuster
A Division of Gulf & Western Corporation
Simon & Schuster Building
Rockefeller Center
1230 Avenue of the Americas
New York, New York 10020
Designed by Stanley S. Drate
Manufactured in the United States of America

1 2 3 4 5 6 7 8 9 10

Library of Congress Cataloging in Publication Data

Azrin, Nathan H, date.
    A parent's guide to bedwetting control.

    Includes bibliographical references and index.
    1. Enuresis. 2. Behavior therapy. 3. Toilet
training. 4. Parent and child. I. Besalel, Victoria,
joint author. II. Title.
RJ476.E6A97   649'.6   79-17008

ISBN 0-671-24804-9

Contents

Foreword

Why write a book about bedwetting? Doesn't everyone simply outgrow the problem? These are the same questions asked when the earlier book *Toilet Training in Less Than a Day* was written. Both books seemed to be dealing with a problem that didn't exist except for a very few children. But the reaction of parents to the earlier book on toilet training was substantial and indicated that the toilet-training problem was of great concern to parents, perhaps to most parents.

So, too, does bedwetting seem to be a problem of universal concern, but which is generally considered a rarity because it is seldom discussed and only in extreme cases to be considered serious enough to seek out professional assistance. Bedwetting is a "closet problem," by its very nature concealed from the awareness of all but members of the immediate family. Yet, survey studies reveal that millions of children have the bedwetting problem long after the age at which popular opinion considers it to be absent and often persisting into the teenage years. Consequently, this book has been written in the hope that it will help parents learn how to deal with the bedwetting problem, rather than to hope in vain that the child will suddenly outgrow it.

This book is a self-help book intended to provide information whereby the parents can do something about eliminating the bedwetting problem. The principal reason for eliminating bedwetting is, of course, the many benefits to the child, rather than just for the convenience of the parent. In this spirit of emphasizing the child's perspective, the training program is designed to involve the child as a partner in the program, rather than as the unwilling object of a training program imposed on him. Accordingly, the training program is a self-help program for the child, as well as of the parents. The child is given a thorough explanation of the rationale of the program. If the child is very young, his understanding is enhanced by a bedtime story (Chapter 10) describing the efforts of a fictitious bedwetter with whom he can identify. For the older child, we recommend that he read this book along with his parents. The self-help is intended to be a joint effort.

How likely is it that the parents and child will receive help from the program described in this self-help book? We hope that many, and even most, readers will be successful, but recognize that no training method for any problem is successful with everyone. Bedwetting is no exception, and even for those children for whom the training program is effective, individual differences always exist, with some children requiring a longer period than others. To provide the reader with informed expectations regarding the likelihood of success, we have taken pains to summarize the results obtained in the published studies using the present program. Similarly, we have taken care to describe the results of those studies in terms of the percentage reduction of bedwetting, rather than merely as cured or not cured, and to provide information about the duration of the benefit. The benefits were substantial, but no miracle should be expected, and some children may require considerably more time and effort than the "average child." And, unfortunately, some children may, of course, not benefit from the program depending in part on how well the training is done, but also in part because of the inevitable individual differences between children.

Although success cannot be guaranteed for any training program for any problem, as we have noted, considerable research has been carried out with the present program before writing this self-help book. This research has covered several years during which the procedures have been tested in several published studies with children and parents of very different backgrounds and age levels.

To simplify and improve the training program, changes have been made continually as problems have emerged. Controlled comparisons have been made in the studies with alternative methods of treating bedwetting in order to discover how much more effective the new program is. Professional trainers have been used in some of the studies to assure that the training program was being followed as intended. In other studies, the parent did all of the training after being instructed by the trainer. And, finally, we have tested the success of parents who, after reading about this program, trained their children with little or no outside assistance. All of these studies have attempted to develop a training method that would be effective for the largest percentage of children in the shortest time and with minimal inconvenience. The favorable results obtained in the studies showed that, even though no overnight cure of bedwetting could be guaranteed for all children, the training program was substantially effective with most of the children in a fairly short time when the training was performed correctly.

A noteworthy feature of this instructional method is that we tested its effectiveness by giving a copy of the procedures to several parents to learn how to train their children. Changes in the writing were made to correct passages that were reported as unclear. The preliminary results are that bedwetting stopped for about two-thirds of the children and was greatly reduced for the other third. These results indicate that this book can serve as the means of stopping bedwetting for most children, but that professional assistance may still be required for some.

Is the present method the final answer to the bedwetting problem? Definitely not. Research is actively being conducted by many investigators on new methods, and better ones should be available as their results become known. Meanwhile, the authors also will continue their studies on how to improve the treatment for bedwetting and, when sufficient progress is made, to revise and update this book. In this manner we hope to give parents a better understanding of the bedwetting problem and information on new training methods to alleviate it.

Gender-specific pronouns present a problem in referring to the child who is to be trained. To avoid the awkwardness of the he/she or him/her designations, the authors have used the male designations "he" and "him" —in large part because the majority of bedwetters are male. We hope that appropriate pronouns will emerge which are not gender-specific and this problem will not exist in the future.

The assistance of many individuals is sincerely acknowledged.

Robert S. Buffington drew the preliminary sketches on which the illustrations in this book were based.

Much of the writing of this book occurred while the senior author was a Fellow at the Center for Advanced Study in the Behavioral Sciences in Stanford, California. Many individuals assisted and participated in the development and testing of the new training program over a period of many years; these include T. Sneed, L. Denno, R. Foxx, D. Millard, and P. Thienes.

Much of the writing of this book occurred while the senior author was a Fellow at the Center for Advanced Study in the Behavioral Sciences in Stanford, California.

1 | How Much of a Problem Is Bedwetting?

How Common Is Bedwetting?

Bedwetting is a very common problem; just how common depends on the age of the child. During the first year of life, all children wet their bed and we accept this as a normal development. So, in a sense, bedwetting is universal. However, when the child learns to toilet himself during the day at the age of two or three years, we feel that he has developed control over his bladder and should be able to stay dry at night. Most children do, in fact, stop wetting their beds by the age of three or four years. Yet, many children do not. Many studies have been done to determine when children stop wetting their bed. The results are surprising in revealing just how many children continue bedwetting long after they have learned to stay dry during the day.

For children three years of age, over one-third are wetting their bed.

For the four-year-old, the percentage of bedwetters has decreased greatly to about one out of four, still a large fraction.

For the five- and six-year-old children, who are just enrolling in school for the first time, about one in seven are still wetting their bed. Two or three years have passed since the children had achieved bladder control during the day. Yet, in a school class of thirty children, about three or four are still having a problem.

At eight or nine years of age, long after infancy, one in about every fifteen children is still bedwetting, which means two children in an average-sized class of fourth and fifth graders.

As adolescence approaches at the ages of twelve to fourteen, one would expect that bedwetting would be a dim memory of the process of growing up. But still, about one in every twenty-five children has not "outgrown" the problem.

And at full maturity, seventeen or eighteen years of age, one in every fifty persons still has the problem. Studies of army draftees have discovered that about 2 percent of the soldiers wet their bed at night.

Some of the studies and books that have revealed these statistics are listed in the References section at the back of the book. References are also given to the other facts about bedwetting to be described later for the reader who desires to read more about this topic or to read the original reports. The general pattern that emerges from the studies on bedwetting at different ages is that it does not suddenly disappear for all children at the age of two years, or three years, or four years. Rather, a progressive but gradual decrease occurs between infancy and adulthood in the proportion of persons who have the problem.

About twice as many boys are bedwetters as girls.

Boys versus Girls

Girls do not wet their bed as often as boys do. Bedwetting is about twice as common among boys as among girls. This difference is true at each age level. There is no explanation for this difference, although the reason may be physical. Another possibility is that boys are often treated differently than girls and parents may be less insistent with them about bedwetting as with so many other problems. Yet, in every country for which surveys have been published, boys are at least 50 percent more likely to be wetting their bed and usually twice as likely.

Bedwetting Is a Secret

Because bedwetting is commonly considered to be a problem of infancy, it is usually kept secret when it persists after infancy. Children are ashamed to let other children know. Parents often take pride when their child stops bedwetting at an early age and will conceal the problem if their child continues. Other types of growing-up problems such as thumb-sucking or wetting one's pants during the day are highly visible. Everyone can tell whether a child wears diapers during the day, or wets his pants, or sucks his thumb. But bedwetting occurs at night and no one need know except the child and the parent. Consequently, bedwetting is a private problem and for that reason is undoubtedly much more common than the survey results indicate, since parent and child alike are often embarrassed to admit it.

The truest information about bedwetting should come from studies which actually count the number of wet beds. But such studies are possible only in institutions such as hospitals, orphanages, institutions for problem children, training institutions for retarded children, summer camps, and other places where large numbers of children sleep overnight. Indeed, observations of this direct nature have been made in a few instances and reveal that bedwetting is far more extensive than the embarrassed questionnaire reports indicated. Direct observations of young children in an Israeli kibbutz reported by M. Kaffman in 1972 revealed that up to five years of age about 30 percent of the children were still bedwetting. In another set of direct observations in 1970 in an institution of 321 deaf children, five to nineteen years of age, Baller and Giangreco found that over 40 percent of the children were wetting their bed every night. In a classic study by the Mowrers in 1938, half of the twenty-four children, four to twelve years of age, in their Children's Community Center in New Haven, Connecticut, were bedwetters. If one were to judge from the questionnaire reports, bedwetting should be absent among fully mature adults. Yet, as was mentioned previously, about one out of every fifty military recruits was found to be bedwetting. Because it is so embarrassing to admit bedwetting, the myth exists that very few children have the problem when in fact it is very common. If your child is wetting the bed, whatever the child's age, you can be assured that many, many children of the same age also have the problem. And possibly, just as you and your children may have done, they and their parents are keeping it a secret.

How Many Persons Are Bedwetters?

Let us consider that bedwetting is a normal part of growing up during the first two years and that it is only a problem when a child is three years old or older. How many persons are bedwetting after three years of age? We have made a calculation based on the number of children at each age level as revealed by the Census Bureau reports, and by the results of the studies for each age group. The answer is about five million persons in the United States. This estimate, based on the questionnaire reports which we saw, may be an understatement. The true number may be closer to ten million persons who are bedwetters.

What Inconveniences Are Caused by Bedwetting?

Since bedwetting occurs in the dark of night, one might conclude that no inconvenience would result. But, the reactions of parents and children demonstrate that the problem is very real. The various reasons for wishing to solve the bedwetting problem are probably best stated by listing typical statements made by the parents of these children.

HIS BROTHERS TEASE

My boy is eight years old and has never had a dry night. His two brothers, who are five and seven years old, are never wet and whenever they have a quarrel they call him "pee-baby" and tease him so much that he doesn't want to play with them.

IT SMELLS

If I don't do anything about it, her room smells like a toilet in some of the train stations I've been in. So, I change her sheets as quickly as I can each day and spray the room with a sweet-smelling fragrance to hide the smell.

NO CAMP

He is dying to go to camp each summer. All of his friends are away then. But he is too scared to go because of what will happen when he wets his bed there. I don't blame him.

SHE HATES HER CRIB

I know I should get her a regular bed and not keep her in the crib. She's seven years old. But I don't want to spend a lot of money on a good bed that she is going to dirty up every night. I'll wait until she stops.

CAN'T SPEND OVERNIGHT WITH FRIENDS

His friends are always inviting each other for sleep-overs at each other's house, especially on weekends and vacations. Whenever he is invited he makes up excuses. And, of course, he'd never dare to invite anybody else over to sleep with him.

HE WON'T OUTGROW IT—FOURTEEN YEARS OLD

Every year since he was four years old I think that he'll outgrow it soon, and I needn't worry. But here he is looking like a grown-up man and still the same.

NO LONG TRIPS OR VISITING

My husband and I try to keep regular contact with our parents who live a day's drive away. Sarah wet the bed in my parents' house the last time we visited when Sarah was five years old. Since then we haven't taken Sarah after all the apologies I had to make. We just don't go on long trips very often anymore. She's too young to leave behind.

NO SLEEPING BAGS

He's twelve years old and wants a sleeping bag just like his friends to go camping with them. But how would you dry out a soggy sleeping bag? And how could he hide it from his friends?

THAT RUBBER SHEET

The last time my daughter had her girlfriend over to the house, the girlfriend sat on the bed and felt the rubber sheet crinkling under her. My daughter was so ashamed that now she won't invite any friends over.

CHANGING BED SHEETS

I change the bed sheets once a week for all of the beds except Julie's. For eleven years now, I have had to change her sheets and make up her bed and wash her pajamas every single day. Thank God for washing machines and dryers. But, what a waste of money, and all that trouble every day.

NO DRINKS FOR DEBBIE

It's an unwritten rule around our house now. No soda or milk or drinks or ice cream for Debbie after supper or before bedtime. At first she objected, but now she'll refuse even when a friend offers it to her.

I CAN'T HELP IT, MOMMY

I was told not to punish my child for bedwetting and that she would outgrow it if I just ignored the problem and didn't make her upset about it. My disappointment must show through though, because whenever she sees me check the bed, or change the sheets, she tells me it's not her fault.

Children who bed-wet are ashamed to go to camp.

SPANKINGS DIDN'T HELP

My mother said she handled the problem with all her children by spanking them and taking away privileges. I didn't like the idea but after six years I tried it in desperation. My son became so terrified of me, I stopped after two months and decided to live with it.

The seriousness of the problem of bedwetting goes far beyond the distress of embarrassment or inconvenience for the child. The annoyance to the parent can reach the point where the parent vents his or her frustration with harsh punishment of the child. Since bedwetting is so serious a problem for the child, we can understand why so much attention has been directed to discovering a cure both by parents as well as by professional persons, including the present authors. In the following chapter, we shall examine the effectiveness of some of these proposed remedies, including medical, psychological, and family remedies, with special attention to a newly developed educational method. We shall see that some methods of effective treatment are now available and that the bedwetting children and their parents no longer must suffer the consequences of this problem without hope.

2 | Methods of Treating Bedwetting— Common Practice and Professional Treatments

What Are the Chances That My Child Will Outgrow It?

Many different types of treatment are currently being used to treat bedwetting, the simplest method being to do nothing more than common practice. We can ask what the chances will be that our child will stop bedwetting within the next year if we do nothing more than common practice. The answer to this question has been provided by examining the results of the surveys which showed how common bedwetting is at different ages.

If your child is three or four years old, there is a 25 percent chance that bedwetting will stop during the next year.

If your child is five to nine years old, there is only a 20 percent chance that he will stop bedwetting during the next year.

If your child is ten to fourteen years old, the chances are only 15 percent that bedwetting will stop during the next year.

These calculations can be stated differently.

If your child is bedwetting at three or four years of age, the chances are 75 percent that bedwetting will still be a problem a year from now.

And if your child is bedwetting at thirteen or fourteen years of age, the chances are 85 percent that a year from now his bedwetting will still be with you.

What if you wait longer than a year? What are the chances of a spontaneous cure during the next two years? or three years? five years? ten years?

If your child is bedwetting at six years of age, the chances are 66 percent that he will still be bedwetting two years from now, 54 percent that he'll be bedwetting three years from now, and 37 percent that he'll still be bedwetting five years from now. Even ten years from now there is a 16 percent chance that the sixteen-year-old child will still be wetting his bed.

Children will eventually outgrow bedwetting under common and ordinary practices, but the chances of that happening soon are not very high.

What Are Some of the Common Methods of Treating Bedwetting?

We have just seen that the chances of stopping bedwetting within one year are less than 25 percent under common family practices. What are these commonly used practices which have been so ineffective?

The most common procedure seems to be to restrict the fluid intake. The child is not allowed to have any drinks before bedtime in the reasonable expectation that if there is less fluid in the bladder, the child will be less likely to urinate at night.

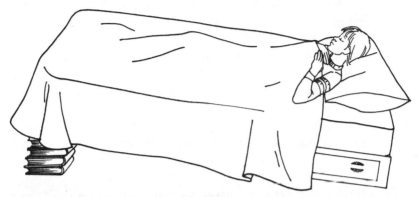

Unusual remedies have been used for bedwetting, including raising the level of the foot of the bed.

Another common procedure is to awaken the child regularly throughout the night and to require the child to toilet at those times. Parents often attempt a schedule of toileting their child every two hours or even every hour, but usually abandon the effort after one or two nights because of the sleeplessness that results for them as well as the child.

Punishment is used by many parents, especially as other efforts fail. Punishment takes the form of scolding, spanking, belittling comparisons, and shaming. The child himself usually feels that he is being punished for an action over which he has no control.

Some of the less common family treatments are:

Requiring the child to sleep only on his back
Conversely, requiring the child to sleep on his stomach
Raising the head of the bed
Conversely, raising the foot of the bed
Sleeping on a very hard surface or on the floor

Conversely, sleeping in a very soft, cushiony bed
Sleeping with very warm covers to prevent cold-induced urination
Conversely, sleeping with no covers
Sleeping in the same bed or room as others
Conversely, sleeping alone in a separate room
Emphasizing meats in the child's diet
Conversely, eliminating all the meats from the diet
Requiring the child deliberately to urinate in bed while the parent watched

Some parents report that bedwetting stopped when they used one of the methods described above, but the chances are that coincidence was responsible for their belief. The situation is somewhat similar to having a common cold. Bedwetting, like the common cold, eventually disappears for almost everyone even if one does nothing for it. If the bedwetting, or the cold, happens to stop after a new treatment was started for a child, the parents understandably, but mistakenly, conclude that the treatment cured the bedwetting or the cold. No scientific tests of the above family remedies have been conducted, so we cannot say that any of them have been proved to be valueless. We can say, however, that as a group these family remedies seem to have little value since we saw that bedwetting shows only a slight decrease from year to year even though one or another of these remedies has been used by almost all parents of children who wet their beds.

Indeed, several of the home remedies prescribe the opposite of other home remedies, such as sleeping with covers versus sleeping with no covers, or sleeping alone versus sleeping with others. Similarly, we have seen that some parents believe in punishment for bedwetting as a remedy, whereas another school of thought believes that punishment perpetuates the problem. The most common home remedy is to restrict fluids, but in this case experimental evidence exists demonstrating that an increase of fluids is beneficial because of the resulting increased ability of the bladder to retain urine. We must conclude that experimental evidence is needed before we can trust any home remedy, however reasonable that remedy may seem.

Professional Treatments

The bedwetting problem has not been ignored by professional persons and scientists. As early as the sixteenth century, the medical profession had recognized it as a problem and various treatments were considered, especially medicines and special diets. Scientific tests of treatments have occurred only very recently, however. We will describe briefly the four major types of treatment now being used by the medical and psychological professions.

MEDICAL TREATMENT OF BEDWETTING

What percentage of bedwetting cases are caused by a medical problem? Medical examination of bedwetters has shown that about 1 or 2 percent of the children who wet their bed have medical problems that could account for the bedwetting. If a medical cause is suspected, then there should be a medical examination and treatment before attempting special training procedures. For almost all (98 percent) bedwetting children, however, no specific medical cause of the problem is likely to be discovered.

PSYCHOTHERAPY AS A TREATMENT FOR BEDWETTING

A common belief is that emotional problems and nervousness cause bedwetting. Psychotherapy is occasionally used for this reason to resolve existing emotional problems in the hope that the bedwetting will then stop. Unfortunately, the studies that have used psychotherapy for this purpose have not provided encouraging results. The psychotherapy usually extends over a period of many months and only a small percentage of the children are cured of bedwetting during that time. If a child has emotional problems, treatment should certainly be considered for those problems in their own right, but little help for bedwetting should be expected.

DRUG TREATMENT OF BEDWETTING

One drug, imipramine, has recently come into wide usage as a method of controlling bedwetting, and several studies have been conducted of its effectiveness. The evidence is clear that this drug does produce some benefit. The drug is taken each day by the child and is effective in stopping bedwetting for about half of the children, but only as long as the drug is taken. Of those children who stop taking it, only about 30 percent of them are cured, which is not much different, as we have seen, from the results obtained when no drug was used and one simply waited for the child to outgrow the problem. The drug has several undesirable side effects, especially at the higher doses at which the drug has more effect. Some medical authorities have criticized the use of this drug by children for periods of months and years since the child becomes dependent on its use as a substitute for learning nighttime bladder control. Nevertheless, the drug does have a fairly immediate effect and can be of great usefulness as a short-term relief for bedwetting for some children.

URINE-SIGNAL METHOD

The fourth current method of treating bedwetting is to provide an automatic signal to the child at the moment that he starts wetting his bed. The method is often called the pad-and-buzzer procedure, since a moisture-sensitive pad is placed under the bed sheet and a buzzer sounds when the pad becomes moistened by urine. The pad is put in place before the child goes to bed and the buzzer, which can be placed nearby on a dresser, will sound within a few seconds after wetting starts at any time during the night. When the child is awakened by the buzzer, he arises from bed to complete the urination in the toilet. The bed is remade with dry sheets, the alarm is reset, and the pad is replaced so that any additional wettings that night will again provide an awakening signal. Several companies manufacture this urine-signaling apparatus and it is available from some large mail-order companies at a cost of $25 to $50.

Many studies have tested the pad-and-buzzer method. The signaling procedure has been effective for about 90 percent of the children. The average child requires about two months of use of the apparatus. For about one-fourth of the children who were successful, bedwetting started again some time after the apparatus was discontinued. But, if the apparatus was used again, the bedwetting again stopped.

These results with the pad and buzzer are impressive indeed compared to the results obtained by the other forms of treatment. In fact, direct comparison tests have been made and show that the pad-and-buzzer method is far superior to either psychotherapy or to the drugs.

But, the pad-and-buzzer method is not without its

problems. Surveys show that about one-half of the parents say that they would rather not use the pad-and-buzzer method. Some of the problems mentioned are:

> The parent must awaken in the middle of the night to reset the apparatus and change the bed, often twice a night, for several weeks.
>
> The treatment is not usually effective immediately but rather requires several weeks for the average child, and months for some.
>
> The buzzer may awaken other children in the house.
>
> The buzzer may interrupt the parents at night at moments when they especially desire privacy.
>
> The child may deliberately disconnect the apparatus before going to sleep.
>
> The child's perspiration in hot weather sometimes causes the alarm to sound in the middle of the night even though the child had not urinated.
>
> The apparatus can become defective through use or abuse and fail to sound even though the child has wet.
>
> The cost of the apparatus and the replacement sensing pads is more than some parents can spend.
>
> The child sometimes becomes resentful at being awakened.

Because of the inconveniences and annoyances involved in the pad-and-buzzer method, many parents stop using it before success has been achieved. In some studies, as many as 40 percent of the parents discontinued the procedure. Had they continued, they might well have been successful, but they apparently became discouraged by the time, effort, and annoyance in this otherwise very effective method.

3 How the New Method Was Developed

Daytime Toilet Training

The origin of the new method of bedwetting treatment is similar to the origin of the new method of daytime toilet training which the senior author had designed earlier. Many readers may be familiar with the training manual entitled *Toilet Training in Less Than a Day* by N. H. Azrin and R. M. Foxx, which describes a rapid method of teaching young children how to toilet themselves. That book describes how toilet training was studied as part of a research effort to teach very severely retarded persons how to stop pants-wetting. When a method was discovered which was successful in one week, on average, with the severely retarded persons, the possibility seemed open that a modified version might be even more successful in teaching normal, nonretarded children to stop pants-wetting in even less time. The resulting research led to a method that was effective in one day for the average child. The results were published in a psychological journal, have since been repeated by other investigators, and were described in the book mentioned above so that parents could learn about the procedure.

Treating Bedwetting of Retarded Persons

Profoundly retarded persons usually continue to wet their bed during their entire lives. Only a small number, perhaps 30 percent, ever learn how to control their wetting at night. The pad-and-buzzer procedure, which is so effective with nonretarded persons, was almost totally ineffective for profoundly retarded persons. Under the direction of the senior author, N. H. Azrin, a new method was developed, therefore, based on learning principles which used the pad-and-buzzer method but also taught the persons to awaken at night when necessary, to be very aware of the wet or dry state of their bed, to take personal responsibility for bedwetting, to become well-practiced in toileting at night, and to be strongly motivated to remain dry at night. The results were very favorable in that all of the retarded persons stopped bedwetting. The bedwetting accidents were decreased by 91 percent during the very first week, and by 95 percent after one month. The speed of the training was especially impressive when one considers the degree of impairment of the trainees. They were unable to speak, or to dress themselves, or to eat normally, or to understand normal speech. Most had serious physical disabilities as well, including partial deafness, or blindness, or paralysis of an arm or leg. All had reached adulthood, the youngest being twenty-five and the oldest, sixty-three. Yet all were still wetting their bed until they were trained by the new method.

Extending the New Method to Normal Children

If the new training method was successful in teaching the profoundly retarded adults, might it not be at least as effective for normal, nonretarded children? The method was modified so that it would take advantage of the language, understanding, and motivation of normal children, and then a clinical test was conducted. The procedure still included the pad-and-buzzer apparatus, but now stressed having the child understand and rehearse the actions he should take when he had the urge to urinate while in bed. The instructor stayed up with the child all night, awakening the child each hour to focus his attention on his bladder sensations. After the one night of intensive training, the parents maintained a schedule of praise, practice, and teaching of personal responsibility by the child. Twenty-six children were in the study, their ages ranging from three years old to fourteen years old. The new method produced a rapid interruption of the bedwetting. The average child had only two bedwetting accidents before achieving two weeks of uninterrupted dryness. All twenty-six children stopped bedwetting; there were no failures. In contrast, those children in the experiment who received normal pad-and-buzzer training had a much higher frequency of accidents during the first weeks. The new method was faster than the pad-and-buzzer apparatus.

We attempted to improve the new method still further. Not much room was left for improvement in terms of speed since the average child who had been wetting almost every night had only two accidents after the intensive training and then enjoyed two consecutive weeks of dryness. But, we could try to improve the convenience of the method since it required the child to be awakened every hour during the one night of intensive training. Also, the new method used the pad-and-buzzer apparatus which, as we discussed earlier, caused reluctance and annoyance in many parents. To eliminate these inconveniences, we devised an improved method which did not include the pad-and-buzzer apparatus and did not require the parents to stay up throughout the intensive training night, but only up to their normal bedtime—about midnight. To compensate for the loss of effectiveness that would result from these omissions, we added several procedures. First, we had the child rehearse during the day, when it was convenient for the parent. Second, we had the child practice each day, increasing the capacity of the bladder. Third, we added one nightly awakening at a time convenient for the parent so the child would experience success at the start of the training.

The results of the field test with fifty-four children showed that the parents strongly preferred the new method to the pad-and-buzzer treatment, all parents having been given the choice of or experience with both methods. Specifically, 85 percent of the parents who had first tried the pad and buzzer chose to change to the improved method after two weeks. Conversely, none of the parents who tried the improved method initially changed to the pad and buzzer when given the choice at the same time. The improved method was much preferred and still very effective. The results showed that the average child had only four accidents before achieving the standard of two consecutive weeks of dryness. On the very first day after the one day of intensive training, bedwetting was reduced by 70 percent. After one week, accidents were reduced by 80 percent and by 90 percent after four weeks. Follow-up after one year showed that bedwetting was reduced by 98 percent. The improved method without the pad-and-buzzer apparatus was slightly less effective than when the apparatus was included, but was still effective for all of the children, and within a few days and more rapid than alternative treatments. The slight loss of effectiveness of the improvements was balanced by a considerable gain in convenience.

Teaching Parents to Use the New Method

In the controlled experiments that tested the new method, a counselor had gone to the child's home to conduct the intensive training on the first day. Would the new method still be effective if the parents did the training alone? To answer this question, parents and their bedwetting children were given instruction in the office for one session lasting about one and a half hours, after which they went home to try the new method. The results showed that parents could use the new method successfully and achieve their objective quickly. Of the forty-four bedwetting children, all of them stopped wetting. The average reduction after one day was 80 percent, after one week, 84 percent, and 96 percent after four months. The average child had only four accidents before reaching the standard of two weeks of uninterrupted dryness. These results are almost the same as were obtained when the counselor conducted the training. This clinical trial assured us that parents could use the procedure after they and their child received a description and written instructions.

Why Was This Book Written?

This book represents the latest phase in the attempt to provide help to bedwetting children and their parents. The results of the experiments with this new method have been published in psychological journals where they will be read and eventually used by psychologists and medical doctors. But, not all parents of bedwetting children seek out professional help since such assistance is costly and not always easily available. Also, we have described how embarrassed many parents and children are about the failure of the child to stop bedwetting, and their resulting reluctance to seek professional help. By describing the new procedure in detail in an easily available book, we hope that many more parents will learn how to solve the bedwetting problem. For those who do seek out professional help, this book can still be of assistance to parents and children in achieving a greater understanding of the bedwetting problem and the details of the treatment. We hope that this book will bring us closer to the ideal of eliminating bedwetting for all children.

The final step was to determine whether parents could train their children successfully with the new method if no professional counseling were available, using only an instructional manual. We, therefore, wrote the present book to describe the details of the new method as well as its general rationale. When parents requested treatment for their child's bedwetting, they were given the training manual and asked to read it and to try the new method on their own without the detailed description and practice which had been provided by the counselor in the previous studies. A brief test was given to the parents to assure that they understood the procedure before attempting training. The results of this effort have not yet been written up and published in a psychological research journal, as the other studies have been, but the general outcome was fairly favorable. About 80 percent of the parents were successful in training their child after having read the training manual and without professional assistance. The remaining parents requested, or required, assistance in order to be successful. These results, taken together with the results of the previous studies, indicate that the new method is effective in reducing bedwetting quickly and substantially and that most parents can be successful after having read about, and carried out, the procedures described in this book.

How Many Children Were Used in Testing the Method?

Twenty-six children were treated in the first published study which used the buzzer apparatus. Fifty-four were used in the second study which omitted the apparatus. An additional forty-four children and their parents were taught in the third study in the office setting. About fifty other children were treated in developing procedural improvements and who were not included in the published studies. The total is about 175 children who have been treated by this general method.

Here we have described only briefly the general rationale of the method. In the next chapter we now examine this rationale and general plan in more detail.

4 General Plan and Rationale of Treatment

The various procedures in the new treatment method are based on an analysis of the bedwetting problem in terms of learning principles. We assume that the child has learned to toilet properly during the day and no longer wets his pants, but still wets the bed.

Awareness During Sleep

The principal reason for bedwetting seems to be simply that when the child is sound asleep he is naturally not as aware of his bladder sensations as he is when awake. The problem is not that the child sleeps too soundly, but rather that he lacks sufficient awareness such as mothers have who will easily awaken from a very sound sleep as soon as their baby cries because of the unconscious concentration on the sounds the baby is making. To increase this awareness of his bladder sensations, several procedures are used. The child is awakened several times on the first night and asked to describe his need to urinate. During the day, he lies down on his bed, imagines he is sleeping, describes whether he has the need to urinate, and states what he should do about it. The pad-and-buzzer apparatus, if used, will also alert him immediately to his urinary urges during sleep.

Increasing Bladder Control

A second reason for bedwetting is that bladder control is insufficiently developed. During the day when the child is awake, the bladder control may be sufficient, but at night, the lack of attention during sleep means that this borderline degree of bladder control will not be sufficient. To increase voluntary bladder control, the child practices during the day how to start urination and how to hold it back. He also practices holding urination back as long as possible so that the bladder capacity will be increased. The child keeps a record of his bladder capacity, and the parent encourages his progress in increasing it.

Practice in Nighttime Toileting

Assuming that a child has become aware of the need to urinate at night but as yet has insufficient bladder control to hold it back, he should, of course, arise from his bed and go to the family toilet. Yet, he may well be reluctant to do so either because he does not wish to disturb his sleep, the effort seems too great, or he is somewhat uncertain as to how to reach the toilet in the darkened house. The solution is to give the child extensive practice in arising from the bed to go to the toilet until the action becomes a strong habit which will occur even in a state of extreme drowsiness.

Immediate Success

Learning is more pleasant and more assured when some success occurs from the very beginning. Several procedures are included to create this immediate success. The first day of training is made very intensive so that all of the skills are learned at the beginning. Also, the child drinks large amounts of fluids on this first day so that he can have many practice trials on the correct way to react to the nighttime urge to urinate. To help the child go through the entire night without wetting even though his bladder control is still borderline, he is awakened to toilet during the first few nights so that he need only hold back the urine for part of the night. These awakenings are gradually omitted as the child demonstrates bladder control.

Accepting Personal Responsibility for Correcting Bedwetting

Bedwetting is similar to any other undesired behavior in that it often persists because we have resigned ourselves to the inconvenience, or have forgotten about the benefits of changing it. This situation is especially true when some other person, such as the mother, takes on the responsibility of correcting the inconveniences. The result then is that the mother becomes very annoyed. The solution in the new method is to have the child take responsibility himself for the inconveniences of bedwetting, and for practicing the skills necessary to prevent future accidents. The child, not the parent, changes the bed sheets and makes up the bed. Also, before training, the child reviews the inconveniences bedwetting has caused him. To emphasize the benefits of staying dry, the parent and child decide on exactly what benefits he will obtain when dryness has occurred. When accidents do occur, the child practices as soon as possible the skills that will prevent future accidents. The child and not the parent has the primary responsibility for keeping the progress charts. By giving the child the responsibility for correcting and practicing, the parent no longer suffers the many inconveniences and has less reason to be angry with the child. Conversely, the child realizes how important it is for him and will try harder to practice the preventive procedures on his own with minimal reminders. The parent can now concentrate on encouraging the child in his efforts. This viewpoint was illustrated during the counseling sessions in which the counselor first taught the child what to do. The parents were then called in and the child explained to the parents what was to be done and asked the parents to assist and remind him.

5 Preparation for Training

How Old Should the Child Be?

Your child should be at least three years old. Children vary in their physical and mental development, but even if your two-year-old child seems advanced for his age, you should wait until the third birthday to give him an extra advantage.

Daytime Pants-wetting

If your child is still wetting his pants during the day, do not start bedwetting training. Wait until he has demonstrated perfect control during the day. Your child is definitely not ready if diapers are still being worn—in which case you should first toilet-train your child. A rapid

Before training for bedwetting, a child should be three years old and be able to stay dry during the day.

method for daytime toilet training is described in *Toilet Training in Less Than a Day*. If your child still has an occasional daytime pants-wetting, even once a month, delay starting the bedwetting training until at least a month has passed, and concentrate on teaching daytime control. Observe whether your child urinates very frequently during the day even if no pants-wettings occur, since a high frequency often indicates that the bladder capacity is not fully developed. If he must urinate every hour or two, start encouraging him to wait for longer periods, until he is able to wait easily for three hours or more. In summary, your child is probably ready if he is three years old, has not had a pants-wetting accident during the past month, and can easily wait about three hours between toiletings.

Medical Problems

If your child is ill, he should be treated for the illness before considering bedwetting training. Even if he has only a cold, wait until he has recovered, and do the same if he seems especially tired or listless or has any unusual physical complaints such as a headache or stomachache. Only a very small percentage—about 2 percent—of bed-wetting cases are caused by a medical problem, but if you suspect a medical cause, secure medical treatment, especially if urination is painful. If your child has epilepsy, you should not give excessive fluids, so omit that aspect of the procedure. Also, do not use drinks or snacks containing sugar if your child is diabetic. In general, exercise the same precautions you normally do regarding your child's medical needs and consult your physician if there is any doubt.

Drink and Snack Treats

If your child is young, three to eight years, you will be using snacks as part of your demonstration of approval. For children of all ages, you will be giving many drinks on the first day to create a strong desire to urinate so that your child will have more practice trials on the correct way to deal with these urges. For the younger children,

The child drinks lots of liquids so he will have a strong urge to urinate during training and be able to practice controlling that urge.

the drinks are also used as a reward. At the start of training, have several types of drinks available, selecting those that you know are his favorites, such as milk, soda, punch, cocoa, and juices—but not juice and milk too close together, since this combination upsets the digestion of some children. Similarly, have favorite snack treats such as potato chips, pretzels, raisins, pieces of fruit, dry cereal on hand for the younger child. Of course, include only those items that you feel that your child should have.

Have these snack items conveniently available, preferably in a large pocket, or if that is not feasible, on a high counter top near you.

Where to Train

Training will occur in the child's bedroom and in the toilet. Since your child will be traveling frequently between these two rooms, a special problem may occur for very young children when the bathroom is on a different level of the house and they cannot climb the stairs easily. One solution is to leave the child's potty-chair in his bedroom at night if he is still young enough to use one. A second solution is to give your child guided practice in using the stairs until you feel comfortable that he can do so safely by himself at night. If so, you will want to leave a light on at night to illuminate the stairs. For children of all ages, provide a dim night-light in the bedroom and in the hall leading to the bathroom so that your child can see well enough to find his way there. These lights should be very dim since the eye becomes sensitive during sleep and bright lights will be annoyingly intense upon awakening and will interfere with sleep.

Bed Arrangements

Your child should have his own bed and the bed should be arranged and located so that he can easily climb out of it and he can replace the sheets comfortably. If he is still in a crib type of bed, with a sliding side rail, lower the rail as far as possible so that it will not prevent him from climbing out. If your child is very young and you are concerned about him falling out, leave the rail just high enough to prevent this, but still low enough for him to climb over easily. Also, the mattress level must be low enough so that your child can step down easily to the floor. If you have an adjustable level for the spring and mattress, as is common on most cribs, lower the spring to the lowest level provided. If the mattress level is uncomfortably high and cannot be lowered, as in a regular bed, place a wide, stable stool, bench, box, or other object on the floor next to the bed so he can step down on it. Another consideration is that the bed should be at least a foot away from the walls on all sides to allow the sheets to be changed easily by your child when an accident has occurred. Some dry sheets should be in a location that your child can reach easily so he can obtain them without your assistance.

Ideally, your child should have his own bedroom so that his brothers and sisters will not be disturbed by his practicing. If he shares his bedroom with others, the disturbance will be reduced if his bed is the nearest to the door leading to the toilet.

More Than One Bedwetter in the Family

If two or more of your children are wetting their beds, start training with your oldest bedwetter. After your oldest child has stopped wetting for at least three weeks, you can start with your younger child. Your older child should then assist the younger one and will probably be eager to do so. Allow the younger bedwetting child to observe the older child's training since this promotes learning by imitation and he may become dry as a result of this observation.

One Child Is Wetting, but the Others Are Not

Children can be cruel to a brother or sister who is bedwetting when the other children do not have the problem. Accordingly, the brothers and sisters should be told about the training effort and their support should be encouraged. Otherwise, they may well interfere with your efforts. Tell them what you and their sibling will be doing beforehand, and have them tell you how they will react so you are sure that they understand.

Let Your Child Read About the Program

If your child is old enough to do so, have him read this book beforehand so that he also will be familiar with the details before you start the training. Ask him to put a written mark at any page or section he does not understand so that you can explain it to him later and discuss any other questions as well. Even if your child is fairly young and does not read too well, you can still use this book. Chapter 10 is a story about a boy who was taught to stop bedwetting. For a younger child, you should read this to him as a bedtime story.

Pad-and-Buzzer Apparatus

The pad-and-buzzer apparatus is included in the present procedure as an optional one. As was discussed in Chapter 2, this apparatus will make learning more rapid, but

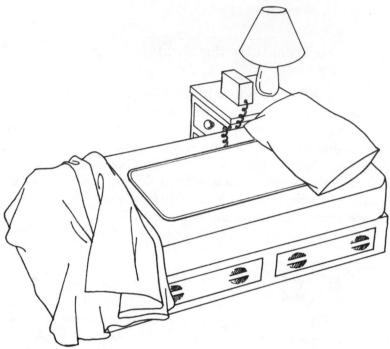

The pad-and-buzzer apparatus signals as soon as the bed is wet. This apparatus is slightly inconvenient but helps in learning to stay dry.

some parents say that they would rather not use it. The present method will take slightly longer if the pad and buzzer are not used, and consequently that is why the apparatus is recommended. Remember that the test results showed that the average bedwetter had only two instances of bedwetting, and accordingly there would be only two nights when the buzzer sounded, before two consecutive weeks of dryness occurred during which, of course, the buzzer never sounded. Because this method is so rapid, very few bedwettings will occur, and very few buzzer soundings, and very infrequent interruptions of the parents' sleep. On the other hand, you personally may still not desire to use the apparatus either because of this annoyance, or cost, or unavailability, or for any other reason.

If your decision is to omit the apparatus, skip all of the descriptions of its use in the remainder of this book.

If you have decided to use the apparatus, obtain one before starting this program. At the time of writing this book, the apparatus was advertised as available from the companies that are listed in Appendix 5. No endorsement is intended of either of these companies, the list being included to provide you with a choice and since the suppliers of this type of apparatus might be difficult for you to locate. No description will be given here as to how to operate the apparatus, since the operating procedure differs from one type to another and since each type of apparatus usually is accompanied by clear instructions specific to that model. The apparatuses have usually been certified as to safety and are probably no less safe than the electric blankets widely used for warmth.

There are some general rules for proper use of the pad-and-buzzer apparatus whatever model is obtained. You and your child should both examine the apparatus at each bedtime to be certain that it is connected properly. If the apparatus requires replacement pads, obtain an adequate supply beforehand. At each bedtime, locate the pad in the central area of the bed where your child's hips are most likely to be located. Locate the buzzer-off switch far enough from the bed so that your child will not simply reach out and shut off the buzzer while still half asleep. In hot weather, avoid excessive night clothing or blankets which will cause the buzzer to sound because of perspiration. If another child is in the same room, avoid use of a model that illuminates a lamp light in addition to sounding a buzzer. When the buzzer sounds, try to go to your child as soon as possible to help him awaken; otherwise he will become accustomed to sleeping through the buzzer.

Measuring Cup

Your child will be using a measuring cup in which to urinate as part of the program to increase the capacity of the bladder. Before training, obtain a widemouthed and transparent cup which is graduated in units of ½ ounces and has a total capacity of 16 ounces. The gradations should be clearly marked so that your child can read them easily, and the cup should be transparent so that small units of progress can be readily seen. The cup should be kept in the bathroom where your child can reach it easily.

Calendar Progress Chart

Post a chart of your child's progress in his room so that he can see at a glance how many dry nights he has had. Obtain beforehand a calendar which is large enough to be seen easily from a distance and post it on the wall at a height at which it is convenient for him to write—about shoulder-high for him. Instead of a calendar, you may use the calendar-type charts included in Appendix 7, which you can tear out. Alternatively, you may prefer to make up your own calendar form on a larger sheet of paper. Leave a pencil or pen near the chart, or preferably tied to a string and fastened nearby so that it will always be at hand.

What Day Should You Choose for Training?

If your child is attending school, it is possible to start the training when he returns from school if he comes home in the early afternoon. If you are a working parent and are not home during the day, training is best done on a weekend or a nonworking day. Most nonworking parents have preferred Friday afternoon and evening, whereas working parents have preferred Saturday or Sunday. The general guideline is to select a day when you can start training about 4:00 P.M. and have the entire evening free from visitors or competing activities. To avoid interruption of the new program, a date should be selected when the parents and child do not expect to take a vacation for at least a month. A vacation away from home during the first month would mean a change of bedtime and toileting schedules which could interrupt progress.

Both Parents

Both parents should be familiar with the training program and, if agreeable, both parents can participate in training although that is not necessary. If either parent does not desire to use the pad-and-buzzer apparatus, do not use it. If one parent is away from home for a few days, wait until both are present. If one parent is reluctant to use this training program, these doubts will probably be conveyed to the child, so such doubts should be resolved first so that each parent will be supportive of the efforts of the child and other parent.

Nightclothes

If your child is very young, he should wear loosely fitting training pants or pajamas which can be lowered easily for toileting. If your child is so young that he wears diapers in bed, discontinue the diapers since they are too difficult for him to remove himself.

Benefits of Being Dry at Night

About one day before training, review with your child the various benefits which will result from staying dry at night. Start by asking him what he doesn't like about wetting the bed and "What nice things could you do?" when he no longer wets at night.

As a reminder to your child, you may use the following list of reasons offered by many children of what they don't like about bedwetting. Review each item and check it off if it applies to your child.

_____ *Teasing* by brothers or sisters or friends.

_____ *Camp.* Can't go to summer camp.

_____ *Overnight at friend's house.* Afraid to wet their bed.

_____ *Friends overnight at my house.* Afraid they'll find out I wet.

_____ *Self-respect.* I feel ashamed of myself.

_____ *Parents annoyed.* Parents are disappointed and wetting causes work.

_____ *Camping overnight.* Can't have a sleeping bag for overnight camping.

_____ *Skin rash* from sleeping in wet pajamas and pants.

_____ *Visiting relatives overnight.* My parents are ashamed to let their relatives know.

_____ *Other.*

FOR VERY YOUNG CHILDREN

_____ *Bed instead of a crib.* Regular bed to replace the crib.

_____ *No diapers at night.* Training pants instead of diapers.

_____ *Grown-up.* Not be a baby anymore.

_____ *Other.*

Agreement for Benefits for Staying Dry

We want your child to enjoy immediately the natural benefits of staying dry at night. After you have reviewed the benefits in the previous list that your child desires, make a firm agreement the day before starting training about what specific benefits you will provide and when you will provide them. Use the benefits checked in the previous list as a guide. For example, if your child indicated he would like to have a friend overnight, make an agreement that you will allow him to have a friend overnight (specify whom), and on what day, and after how many consecutive days of dryness. The statement should be written out so that it will remind you and your child at the later date of the benefits to be received, since the details can easily be forgotten. A sample statement might be: Billy can call a friend up (Mike, Frank, or Charlie) to stay overnight on a Friday or Saturday night when five straight nights have passed without wetting. If too many straight dry nights are required, then the benefits will be too far away in time to seem possible, so you should choose a number of straight dry nights that is as small as possible, yet is reasonable. As to the selection of benefits, do not use only artificial rewards such as an increased allowance or movies which are not natural benefits for dryness. Only for young children, perhaps three to eight years of age, should many artificial benefits be used, since the natural benefits are not as real for them at that age.

To assist you in making these agreements, two sample agreement forms are presented, one for a four-year-old child and one for a thirteen-year-old child.

As noted in the agreement forms, artificial rewards such as the snacks and toys are used more for the younger child than for the older one, especially for the first few nights of dryness. Several other features of both contracts are important. Some benefits are scheduled for even one, two, or three nights of dryness so that the satisfactions will occur quickly. The exact number of nights of dryness is always specified to eliminate vagueness as to what is desired. The description of the benefit is always very specific so the child knows exactly what to look forward to. The agreements always specify an immediate action that the parent will take to schedule the benefit when the specified number of dry nights is achieved even if the benefit will occur later. Your child will be more successful and more motivated if the agreements you make with him contain these features.

SAMPLE AGREEMENT FORM
FOR A FOUR-YEAR-OLD GIRL—SANDRA

Special Treat No. 1: When Sandra has her first dry night, we
will buy her a banana split the next day.

Special Treat No. 2: When Sandra has two dry nights, we will
buy her the robot set she wants.

Special Treat No. 3: When Sandra has three dry nights, we
will bake her a cake the next day.

Diapers: When Sandra has had five days without wetting a
single night, we will throw all her diapers away and use
them as rags.

Bed: When Sandra has had two weeks without a single wetting, we will go to the furniture store and buy her a
grown-up bed like Mary's (her neighbor) and put the crib
away in the basement.

Visit Grandma: When Sandra has had three weeks without
wetting, we will call Grandma and ask her to have Sandra
visit overnight.

SAMPLE AGREEMENT FORM
FOR A FOURTEEN-YEAR-OLD BOY (BOBBY)

Special Treat No. 1: When Bobby has his first dry night, we
will treat him to any item of his choice at the ice cream
stand on the next day. .

Special Treat No. 2: When Bobby has three straight dry nights, we will get him the football he wants at the sports store the next day.

Sleeping Bag: After one week of dry nights, we will buy Bobby a sleeping bag like the one on p. 300 of the camping catalog.

Friends Overnight: After ten days of dry nights, Bobby can call his friends over for a pajama party the next weekend we are home.

Visiting Friends: After two weeks of dry nights, Bobby can call a friend (Mickey, Doug, Ray, Tom) to stay at his house the next weekend.

Camping: After three weeks of dry nights, we will arrange a family camping trip for our next holiday.

Summer Camp: After four weeks of dry nights, we will enroll Bobby in Boy Scout Camp for three weeks.

The various decisions and preparations for training should be made together with the child and in the spirit of a game. Do not decide by yourself or prepare by yourself. Instead, shop with your child for the measuring cup, snacks, etc., and have him assist with the Calendar Progress Chart, bed arrangement, and, of course the agreements. In this way, we are making him an active participant rather than a spectator.

6 | The Intensive Training Day

This first day of training should start in the early afternoon, about 3:00 to 4:00 P.M. for school-age children, and will end at about midnight or 1:00 A.M. The later you stay up, the more likely your child will be off to a good start. If your child is a preschooler, start the training shortly after lunch. Once training starts, your child should remain in the house and not go outdoors, since he will be practicing toileting at frequent intervals. He may, however, engage in some of his usual indoor activities so long as he understands and agrees that these activities will be regularly interrupted. Similarly, you can usually engage in some of your normal indoor activities, such as reading, meal preparation, household tasks, talking to family members, so long as you give priority to the practice trials and interrupt these activities at the scheduled times. Do not schedule any outside activities, visits by others, long telephone calls, shopping trips, or any other events that will occupy your attention for more than a few minutes. The reason is that on the first training day you should spend as much time as possible with your child between practice trials discussing with him what he will be doing in each of the steps in training.

Drinking to Create Frequent Desire to Urinate

Have your child drink as much as he comfortably can so that he will have a strong desire to urinate and will be able to have intensive practice in how to control this urge. Start giving extra drinks at the very start of training and continue until two hours before the end of training, which should be about 10:00 or 11:00 P.M. if training ends at midnight or 1:00 A.M. Use a graduated measuring glass to serve the drinks so that you can keep track of the amount. If your child is very young, try to have him drink about one glass (eight ounces) every hour for the first few hours. But, the older child should drink about two glasses (sixteen ounces) every hour for the first few hours. If he can comfortably drink more, have him do so and actively encourage him to drink by offering the drinks to him every fifteen minutes. Salty snacks (potato chips, popcorn, pretzels, peanuts, corn chips) should be freely available to him all the time, and you should remind him to eat some about every fifteen minutes.

For very young children, encourage them in addition by slightly sipping some of the drink yourself and by holding it up to touch their lips and by presenting it as a game or contest to see how much they can drink. After the first few hours, your child will probably be able to drink less than before. By getting only favorite drinks and snacks, and being encouraged to consider this drinking a humorous game, your child will view it as pleasant and fun. Older children and young adults who normally drink coffee or tea are especially advised to do so here since these drinks have the special characteristic of promoting the urge to urinate.

These extra drinks are given only during the first day and night of training.

Training in "Holding Back"

Children who wet their bed have been found to have a smaller bladder capacity and to urinate more frequently during the day than nonbedwetters. The holding-back procedure helps to increase the ability of the bladder to hold more urine and for a longer time. The procedure also teaches your child to be very sensitive to his bladder feelings, especially while in bed. The child is taught to strain until he has the urge to urinate, then to lie down on his bed where he practices holding back as long as he can.

The holding-back training starts about half an hour after the first large amount of drink has been taken, since that is about when the bladder should be somewhat filled. At this time, have your child go to the bathroom to strain and try to urinate. Use whatever terms are common for you and appropriate to the child's age. "Betty, try to go to the toilet," or "Billy, try to pee-pee." Have them try until they have a "full feeling." When he does "feel like I have to go," or, "I feel full now," or, "I feel like pee-pee," tell him to "hold it back," to try *not* to urinate and have him go quickly to lie down on his bed. There he is to lie quietly and pretend he is asleep by closing his eyes and breathing slowly and deeply. Have him lie down for two minutes while you encourage him to hold back his urine.

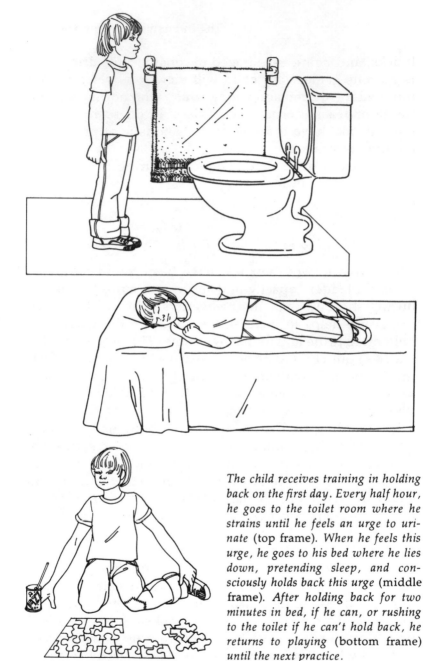

The child receives training in holding back on the first day. Every half hour, he goes to the toilet room where he strains until he feels an urge to urinate (top frame). When he feels this urge, he goes to his bed where he lies down, pretending sleep, and consciously holds back this urge (middle frame). After holding back for two minutes in bed, if he can, or rushing to the toilet if he can't hold back, he returns to playing (bottom frame) until the next practice.

If he is able to hold back for the two minutes and the urge is gone, he can return to his previous play activities. But if he says he cannot wait any longer, have him get up and rush to the toilet to urinate. If he is able to wait the two minutes but still has the urge at the end of that time, also have him get up then to go to the toilet. The sequence, in summary, is for the child to strain on the toilet every half hour until he has to urinate, at which time he goes to his bed and lies down and tries to hold back for two minutes. If the urge disappears, he returns to play. If the urge gets too strong, he rushes to the toilet. If the urge is still present after two minutes, he rushes to the toilet.

When the child is to arise from bed to go to the toilet, it is useful to prompt him with a phrase that emphasizes his active role, such as "Jump up and go."

Practice Every Half Hour

Repeat this holding-back practice every half hour from the start of training until bedtime. To help remind you and your child, it is more convenient to schedule it at the half hour and at the hour such as at 1:30, 2:00, 2:30, 3:00 . . . Another helpful reminder is to use a kitchen timer as a signal in which case your child will feel more personally responsible if you have him rather than you set it each time.

Unscheduled Toileting

Tell your child that if he has to go to the toilet before the next scheduled practice, he is to call you, at which time you will conduct the hold-back procedure in the same

way as if it were scheduled. Then, consider that practice
as a substitute for the next practice period.

Younger Children

Younger children usually require assistance in timing
how long they are to hold back. While they are holding
back in bed (eyes closed) have them count slowly to fifty,
or to say the alphabet slowly, whichever is within their
capability. Have them say it softly aloud at first so that
you can provide help if necessary.

Discussing Procedure

While your young child is holding back in bed, have the
child describe what should be done at the various stages
of urgency, prompting when necessary. For example, you
might say, "Marilyn, hold it back as long as you can.
Now, think about how your tummy feels. When you are
in bed and asleep and you have that full feeling, what will
you do?"

"I'll hold it back for as long as I can. Until it goes away."

"Good! If it doesn't go away, what will you do then,
Marilyn?"

"I'll get up out of bed, and I'll go fast to the bathroom
so I won't wet the bed."

"That's good; you know exactly what to do. Now pretend you are sound asleep, but think hard about how
your tummy feels. You have done beautifully! Only one
minute longer now."

When the child is holding back for two minutes in bed,
continually remind the child to think of his full feeling,

praise his success, and encourage him to continue. But do
not request any lengthy replies, since he is to be in a very
relaxed state.

As another example, the parent might say:

"Jimmy, think of your stomach. Think of how full it
feels. Are you thinking of how your stomach feels?"

"Mhmm."

"Good, keep thinking of it. You have just a little longer
to wait. I'm so happy you can wait so long. You can do it
at night, too, I'm sure of that."

"I finished counting."

"Do you still have to go?"

"Yes."

"OK, do what you will do at night when you still have
to go."

"I jump up out of bed and go to the bathroom so I won't
wet the bed."

"You know just what to do. Hurry. I've got the candy
and drinks waiting as soon as you finish. Jump up and
go."

By engaging in these descriptions, you are assuring
that your child is developing a heightened sensitivity to
the state of the bladder. These descriptions should continue during each of the practice periods every half hour.

Increasing the Duration of Holding Back

The duration of holding back should be lengthened gradually from one practice period to the next. Start with the
two-minute goal on the first trial and increase it by one
minute each time as the child succeeds. If the time goal
proves to be too long on a trial, keep it at the same dura-

tion, or even decrease it slightly, on the next trial until your child has been successful, treating the experience as a game in which you are trying to set a record. To keep track of the times, it is convenient to keep a paper and pen or pencil in the bathroom and write down the durations achieved on each effort so that you can know what goal to set next time as well as to be able to review the progress with your child at each practice period.

Early Bedtime

The holding-back practice will have been conducted several times, once every half hour. Bedtime on this training day should be set slightly earlier than usual, preferably no later than 7:00 P.M. for younger children and 8:00 P.M. for older children and young adults so that more time will be spent on actual sleep-time practice.

Changing Bed Sheets

Explain to your child that he will be taking personal responsibility for changing the bed sheets from now on and cleaning up when an accident occurs. One hour before bedtime, teach him how to change the bed sheets. First, demonstrate by doing it yourself while he observes, then have him do it while you watch him, being careful that he does all of it himself, including obtaining the fresh sheets and putting the old ones in the laundry hamper. For very young children, many parents have had doubts that their three- or four-year-old could change the sheets alone, but our experience has been that they can do so under patient, guided instructions. The general rule is to

The child is taught to make his bed so he can take responsibility for correct-ing any future bedwettings.

describe each move in detail when you demonstrate and to guide the child's hands manually as soon as he has difficulty in doing it himself, praising him continuously for his efforts. The younger children should be asked to make up the bed two or three times if great difficulty was experienced on the first attempt. Generally, even the youngest child has been delighted with this adult respon-sibility and pleased to be able to remove this source of annoyance for the parents.

Getting-Up Practice

The getting-up procedure consists of repeated practice in arising from bed to go to the bathroom and is intended to be an extension of the holding-back-in-bed procedure which has been practiced all afternoon. The procedure is to be used whenever bedwetting accidents have occurred. The reasoning is that the bedwetter has not yet sufficiently learned the habit of interrupting one's sleep to arise and go to the bathroom when the urge to urinate is too strong to hold back.

After your child has demonstrated his ability to make up the bed, have him put on his nighttime clothing—pajamas or training pants. Have your child lie down in bed as if asleep and, just as before, to count slowly to fifty to approximate a one-minute duration. The lights should be turned off, except perhaps for a very dim night-light. Soon after the count of fifty, the child arises and hurries to the bathroom where he attempts to urinate, then returns to bed and again counts to fifty while pretending to be asleep. This sequence is repeated twenty times; that is, he has lain in bed for twenty one-minute periods and practiced getting up from this imagined sleep to go to the bathroom. The total duration will be about one half hour.

Explain to your child the reasoning behind this getting-up practice beforehand, and explain that he will be doing this when an accident occurs so that more accidents will be prevented.

As your child does the getting-up practice, remain close by him, staying in the bedroom when he is in bed and walking directly behind him as he goes to the bathroom.

Bedtime Reminders

When your child goes to bed at the early bedtime, review the various features of the training program. Have your child describe to you what he is expected to do tonight if he feels the urge to urinate. "Hold it back. Or, jump up and go to the bathroom." Review what the agreed-upon benefits will be if he stays dry. Have him describe, say, who will change the bed if there is an accident and how he will do the getting-up practice. Explain to him that you will be waking him up a few times tonight to ask him about his need to toilet. Remind him to keep thinking about how his bladder feels. Have him touch and stroke the sheets and comment on their dryness. Strongly assure him of your confidence in his ability to stay dry on the basis of how well he has been able to hold back urination for long periods in his practice trials that day.

Hourly Awakenings During Sleep

After your child has gone to bed about 7:00 to 8:00 P.M. on this first training day, you will awaken him every hour until about midnight or 1:00 A.M. The purpose of these awakenings is similar to the holding-back practice trials he has been receiving that day prior to bedtime. Namely, he is learning to become very sensitive and alert to the full bladder feelings, to practice holding back, to practice getting up to go to the toilet but now doing so while actually in bed.

At each hourly awakening time, first feel the sheets to determine if they are dry. If they are dry, awaken him as gently as possible since we wish him to learn to awaken

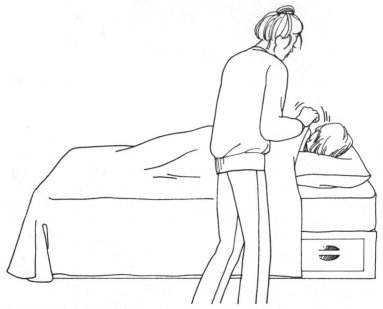

On the first training night, the child is awakened every hour until 1:00 A.M. to teach him to wake up easily.

with minimal prompting. First, call his name, then touch his shoulder while talking to him, then help him raise himself to a seated position until he is sitting without assistance. Ask him whether he has the full feeling in his stomach, and whether he must go to the toilet or whether he can wait until the next hour. If he says he can wait, praise him for his control, have him feel the sheets for their dryness, remind him to keep thinking about the full feeling, give him some more drinks, and have him return to sleep. As stated previously, the drinks are not given during the last two awakening trials, but are given during all of the earlier awakening trials.

If, upon being awakened, your child says he cannot

wait another hour, have him quickly jump up and go to the bathroom to urinate while you follow behind. When he has finished and returned to his bed, praise him for getting up, have him feel the sheets for dryness, remind him to keep thinking about the full feeling, give him some more drinks, and have him return to sleep for another hour.

Bedwetting Accident During Training Night

If you find the sheets are wet when you feel them at the hourly inspection, awaken your child so that he can change the sheets and do the getting-up practice. First, tell him that you are disappointed that the sheets are wet and have him feel them for wetness himself. Then have him obtain fresh nightclothes, put the wet clothing in the hamper himself, and dress himself. Then have him change the sheets just as he had practiced doing before bedtime. He removes the wet sheets himself, puts them in the laundry hamper, obtains the dry sheets, and puts them on the bed himself.

After the bed is remade, have him do the getting-up practice for twenty trials, just as he had done before bedtime. He lies down in his bed for about one minute, counting slowly to fifty, arises quickly, and rushes to the bathroom to try to toilet, and then returns to bed, repeating this sequence for twenty trials. When he has finished, he returns to bed. No further drinks are given. Ask him to feel the sheets for their dryness, remind him to think harder about his full feeling, and praise him for cleaning up and for the getting-up practice. Also remind him that he will be doing the getting-up practice again before bedtime tomorrow to help him prevent further accidents. Re-assure him of your confidence that he will be dry at the next inspection an hour later.

Keep conversation and praise to a minimum while your child is changing his clothes and the sheets and doing the getting-up practice. Otherwise, for the younger child especially, cleaning up and practicing after an accident can become so entertaining that he may be tempted to have accidents deliberately. Conversely, if there is continuing criticism and scolding, the child is likely to become very upset. The solution is to keep a middle ground and neutral attitude which is neither showing pleasure nor anger, but rather is an attitude that a problem has occurred about which you and your child have an understanding that he will correct. So, it is very important that you had discussed and he had agreed beforehand, prior to training, that he would take the responsibility willingly to change his clothing and sheets himself and practice the getting-up trials. So, when your child has an accident, you should first let him take the initiative. If he does not, give only a general reminder: "Timmy, the bed is wet. You know what to do now when it is wet." If he does not start or tell you what he is to do, make a simple informational statement, such as, "Put on dry clothes," or "Take off the wet sheets," or "When you wet, you change your clothes and sheets." Do not lecture or give long explanations.

Manual Guidance

For the younger child who is unsure of his skill in changing his clothes and sheets, gentle manual guidance is necessary. Within one or two seconds after giving your instruction, touch his hands and guide them through the correct actions. Release your touch after a second or two, and if he is making an effort, do not provide further manual guidance. If he stops, touch and, if necessary, guide briefly again. Stand next to, or right behind, your young child as he cleans up so that when you give an instruction you can touch and guide him immediately if he hesitates. Do not give an instruction if you are more than two feet away and certainly not from the other side of the room. For the older children, this manual guidance is usually not necessary or useful, but you should still stand close by the first time cleaning up is necessary so that you can give instructions if needed as to how you want the bed made. Also, during the getting-up practice, you may need to give instructions to him to count to the full count of fifty, to do so slowly, and to hurry to the bathroom rather than walking very slowly.

Bedwetting Signaled by Buzzer

If the pad-and-buzzer apparatus is properly functioning, a bedwetting accident would be signaled immediately by the buzzer. If the sheets were found to be wet at the hourly inspection, then the apparatus could not have been functioning properly and you should determine whether it has been hooked up correctly so that it will signal wetting next time. If a bedwetting is signaled by the buzzer, follow the same procedure described above for bedwettings discovered by inspection. That is, have your child change the bed, change his clothes, practice the getting-up actions for twenty trials, and give him all of the other reminders mentioned before.

Reset the apparatus following the instructions of the manufacturer.

The next awakening should be one hour after the bedwetting accident signaled by the buzzer.

Ending the First Training Night

The extra drinks will have been given all afternoon as well as during the period before bedtime, and at the hourly awakenings. Two hours before the last awakening, discontinue the drinks. Otherwise your child will have so much fluid that he will not be able to keep from bedwetting. So, if the last awakening is at 1:00 A.M., give drinks at the eleven o'clock awakening but not at the awakenings at midnight or at 1:00 A.M. Also, most children are not able to drink as much at the early awakenings as they had during the afternoon, so do not force the child to drink more than he can even if it is only a few ounces.

Awakening your child should become easier after he becomes accustomed to it. On the first or second awakening, you may need to hold him up in the sitting position for a few minutes until he is fully alert, but on successive awakenings, he should be able to awaken with only slight guidance.

After the last awakening, check that the buzzer apparatus, if you are using one, is set properly before you go to bed yourself.

In practice, almost none of the children have had an accident during the first night even though they have had so much to drink. The reasons are that they are awakened every hour and toilet themselves if they have the need, and also have their attention focused so strongly on their bladder sensations, the dry state of their bed sheets, and on the advantages of staying dry at night. All of these factors have come about because of the effort you and your child have made during the first day of intensive training. Your child is off to a good start, having been successful on this very first night even after having had more to drink than he has ever had before bedtime.

7 | Procedure After the First Training Day

General Plan

On the first day of training, your child learned about all of the procedures that he will now use on a less concentrated basis. Some of the procedures used on the first day will not be used again. The extra drinks are given only on the first day and not thereafter. Also, the awakenings every hour at night happen only on the first night, but thereafter only one awakening occurs each night, and even that one is eliminated after a short while as will be described shortly. The strain-and-hold procedure used every half hour on the first day will no longer be used. Instead, a modified procedure will be used to increase your child's bladder capacity whereby your child will attempt on his own to urinate less frequently in that he urinates only when his bladder is very full. Your child will continue to assume responsibility for his bedwettings by changing himself and the bed when an accident occurs and also to practice the getting-up procedure. If it was used initially, the pad-and-buzzer apparatus will continue to be used to help him become aware of the moment when his bladder lets go. Having given this overview, we will now consider the specific procedures to be used after the first day of intensive training.

Increasing Bladder Capacity

The day after training starts, begin bladder training procedure. Leave the transparent graduated cup in the bathroom in a place convenient for your child and have him urinate only into that container and not into the toilet. He is to use the graduated container whenever he urinates when at home. After each urination, read the number of ounces from the gradations on the container and write it down on a piece of paper which should also be located in the bathroom with a pen or pencil. If your child is an older child, or is a young adult, he can record this information himself. If your child is young, he should call you or your spouse at the time he urinates, or shortly thereafter, so that you can read the amount and write it on the piece of paper.

Compare the amount that he just urinated with the amount urinated on previous attempts and on previous days. If the amount is greater than ever before, tell him so. "Jimmy, that's eight ounces! Wow, that's more than you ever did! Your bladder is getting very big." Even if the amount is not the largest, provide him with encouragement and favorable comparisons. Imagine your child on Monday had six ounces, four ounces, and seven ounces, and now on his next urination had five ounces, you could say "Five ounces, Jimmy, that's more than you did the second time this morning. That's getting better."

Every day, the child urinates into a measuring cup instead of in the toilet and tries to increase his bladder capacity.

Or "Five ounces this time. That's more than you did any-time on the first day you started. You're really trying. Let's see if you can set a record next time." Even if the amount is the lowest ever, a positive attitude can be expressed. "Jimmy, it's only two ounces this time and that's not too high. But yesterday and this morning you had seven ounces, so I'd say you're doing great. Every day gets a little better. Let's try to make the next one extra big to make up for this one, OK?" Show this same positive attitude of encouragement for the older, as well as the younger child. Since the older child or young adult is recording himself, have him call you when he has finished urination to show you the container and to allow you to see the result compared with previous efforts.

The bladder control procedure is used until two weeks have passed without a single bedwetting accident. Then your child returns to urinating in the usual manner. As a way of reminding yourself and your child of this time requirement, you may add it to the list of agreements you had drawn up.

If your child is very young, be sure to give him a snack treat as well as praising him after any urination which is greater than the usual amount.

Allowance of Fluids

One of the most common methods of attempting to stop bedwetting is to prevent the child from drinking much fluid during the day and certainly none before bedtime. Yet, the evidence exists that this restriction of fluid is not helpful. When fluids have been restricted, the bladder capacity decreases and consequently the child is not able to retain as much fluid during the night. If the child is allowed, and encouraged, to drink freely during the day, the bladder capacity increases and the child is better able to sleep through the night without having to urinate. In the present method, large amounts of drinks were used during the first day only. After the first day, allow your child to drink fully and freely during the day, although do not encourage him to do so to the extent of the first day. Do not discourage him from drinking before bedtime either. Explain to your child that his bladder will get bigger and more used to holding liquids if he does drink freely during the day.

During the first week or two of training, the child gets up to toilet himself once during the early evening so he won't have to hold back the urine all night long. This is gradually phased out.

Nightly Awakening

On the second night of training, you will awaken your child once at your normal bedtime. So, if your normal bedtime is midnight, awaken your child then. Use the same gentle method of awakening you used for the hourly awakenings on the first training night. Tap your child on the shoulder and ask him, "Bobby, what should you do?" and wait about five seconds before repeating this, if necessary. Again, praise him for arising if he does so, but, if he doesn't, gently assist him in sitting up, removing the blanket, with his legs over the side of the bed. As before, ask him, "How does your stomach feel? It's time for you to go to the bathroom." Be sure that he's fully awake by talking with him and having him look you in the eye. When he does go to the bathroom, continue the conversation and praise him for his effort in getting up to prevent a bedwetting. Before he gets up, have him feel the sheets and comment on their dryness and again when he returns to bed. Have him describe what he will do if he has the need to urinate and tell him how confident you are in his ability. If your child has gone to bed at, say, 8:00 P.M., then he had only to hold back his urine until midnight when you awakened him. Since he toileted at midnight, then he had only to hold back his urine until 7:00 A.M., when he normally woke up, a period of seven hours. Had he not been awakened to toilet himself he would have to hold his urine from 8:00 P.M. to 7:00 A.M., a total of eleven hours.

Adjusting the Awakenings

The interval for which your child must hold back his urine is gradually increased each night that he is dry by awakening him a half hour earlier each night. So, in the above example, he is awakened at 11:30 the next night, then 11:00 the next, then 10:30, 10:00, 9:30, and so on. When the awakening time is only one hour after his bedtime, discontinue the nightly awakenings entirely. So, in the present example, when the awakening time reaches 9:00 P.M., omit the awakening since he had gone to bed only an hour previously and will not benefit appreciably by the awakening. Move the awakening time one half hour earlier as described each night for which your child was dry. But, if he was wet the previous night, keep the time of awakening the same until the next dry night occurs. So, if your child had been awakened at ten o'clock the night before and had a bedwetting that night, then tonight you will again awaken him at ten o'clock, not at nine thirty, and continue at ten o'clock until a dry night occurs. This adjusting schedule gradually increases the duration for which he must stay dry as long as he is successful. But when he has an accident, the duration does not increase. This schedule gradually moves the nightly awakening from the parents' normal bedtime closer to the child's normal bedtime.

Happy Clock

Use the "Happy Clock" as illustrated as a way of keeping track of the time that you should give the nightly awakening. A blank Happy Clock is included in Appendix 6, which you can tear out for use with your child, or draw your own on a larger sheet of paper which will be more clearly visible. Post the Happy Clock next to your child's bed so that both of you can look at it each bedtime to determine what time he should be awakened that night and to praise him for the progress toward eliminating the nightly awakening entirely.

The Happy Clock in the illustration has two hands penciled in. The lower hand should be drawn to point to the time when the awakenings will be discontinued. For the child in this example, the normal bedtime is 8:30 P.M., so the awakenings will have been discontinued, according to our rule, one hour after that, which is 9:30 P.M. Accord-

ingly, the hand in the illustration is drawn to point at 9:30. The other hand should be drawn to point to the parents' normal bedtime, which in this example is 12:30 A.M.

Each night that the child is dry, the time of awakening moves over one half hour and the space for that half-hour period should be shaded with the pencil. So, in the example shown, the child has been dry for three nights and is to be awakened at 11:00 P.M. The area between 11:00 P.M. and 12:30 A.M. is shaded in. If that child is again dry that night, the area from 10:30 to 11:00 P.M. will be shaded in to show that awakening will occur at 10:30. This representation allows the younger children to see their progress at a glance. When the space between the two hands is entirely filled, the awakenings will be discontinued, and this fact can be pointed out to the children at each bedtime. Each morning after a dry night, have your young child shade in the new area. By having your child do it, you are assuring your child's awareness of the progress being made. Using a colored crayon will make the progress still more evident as the area in color grows progressively larger. This method of representation is especially useful for children who have not yet mastered time-telling, but is also very useful for somewhat older children as a more vivid indication of progress than would be the case by simply writing down the scheduled hour of awakening.

In this example, the clock shows that the parents' bedtime is 12:30 A.M., that the child will be awakened at 11:00 P.M. the next night, and that the awakenings will be discontinued when the shaded area reaches 9:30 P.M.

Changing Sheets and Clothing

Your child will continue to be required to change his clothing and to remake the bed whenever he has had an accident. The procedure he is to follow has been described in the previous chapter for the intensive training day. He is to take off his wet nightclothes, put them in the designated dirty laundry container, obtain clean clothing, and dress himself. He is then to remove the wet sheets, also put them in the dirty laundry, obtain fresh sheets, and remake the bed as it was before the accident. This correction should be done as soon as you have detected the accident, which would normally be at the once-a-night awakening, or at the early-morning inspection one half hour before his normal awakening. Do not change his clothes or remake the bed yourself even though you could certainly do it more quickly. The pur-

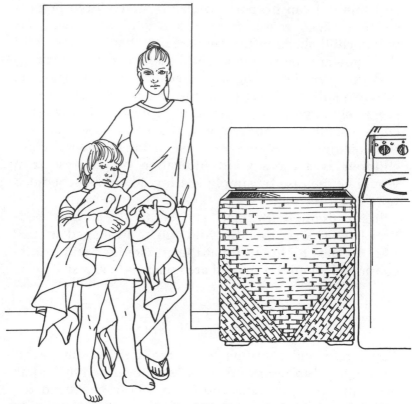

Whenever an accident occurs, the child changes the bedsheets and remakes the bed on his own.

pose of this procedure is to have your child take personal responsibility for his accident and its correction, and this can only come about if he does it all by himself.

Children are quite willing, and usually pleased, to take on this responsibility providing that they have been shown how to do it and if the requirement is communicated without anger. If the accident has been detected at the nightly awakening, your child may be reluctant to remake the bed because he is not fully awake. By gradually awakening him, and explaining the need for correction, he will usually do so quite readily. It is preferable to spend a few minutes awakening the child than to rush him before he is fully awake and perhaps irritable. The first few times he remakes the bed you should stand by to assure that he is doing it in the correct manner, but once having assured yourself, you should ask him to call you when he is finished. Changing the bed is now his responsibility, and you will be able to be more objective about his problem now that this chore is removed from you.

If the wet bed was not detected early enough in the morning, your child may not have enough time to remake the bed without being late for school, if he is of school age. In such circumstances leave the bed unmade until he returns from school.

Keep the clean bed sheets in a location easily accessible to the very young child, so that he can obtain them without your assistance.

Getting-up Practice

The getting-up practice was described briefly in the previous chapter concerning the intensive training day. Your child should have performed this practice before going to bed on that training night. The getting-up procedure will be performed from now on whenever your child has an accident. On the first training night, your child performed the getting-up practice simply as a demonstration of his ability to do the procedure even though he may not have had an accident. But now he will practice getting up whenever he has an accident. If the accident is detected at the morning inspection, he will do the practice at that time as well as that night before he goes to bed. If the

Whenever bedwetting has occurred, the next night the child does twenty trials of the getting-up practice, in which he rushes to the bathroom after imagining that he is asleep and had the urge to urinate.

accident was detected at the nightly awakening, he will do the practicing at the time he was awakened and again before he goes to bed the next night. The purpose of the getting-up practice, you will recall, is to establish the act of arising from bed as a very strong habit so that your child will be able to do so automatically at night, even when he is sound asleep, whenever he has the need to urinate. If he has no accident, then he has learned how to handle the problem and there is no need for him to have to practice. But, whenever he has an accident, this indi-cates that he has not yet learned to get up easily in response to his bladder signals and needs more practice in doing so. By arranging for the practice only when accidents have occurred, it will be done only when it is needed.

The reason that the practicing is done at the two scheduled times is to associate the act of getting up closely in time with the bedwetting. For the practice to be most effective, it should be done under circumstances that resemble most closely those existing during sleep. In the morning when the child is awakened after an accident, he is still sleepy, so the situation is fairly similar to the situation during actual sleep, and practicing at that time can be expected to be more effective than at other times when he is fully awake. The second practice period is given at bedtime, even though the child is fairly awake at that time, since the child can be expected to remember best during his sleep those actions that took place immediately before falling asleep. As with the morning practice period, this bedtime practice is closely associated in time with the sleep period and can be expected to be more effective for that reason as well.

The getting-up practice, you will recall, consisted of the child lying down in bed for about one minute while pretending to be asleep, and then arising quickly to rush to the bathroom where he briefly tried to urinate. He then returned to the bed and repeated this sequence for a total of twenty trials. To make this practice most effective, try to arrange the situation so that it is as similar as possible to the situation that exists during actual sleep. Have the lights dimmed or shut off just as they normally are at night. Have your child close his eyes as they will be during actual sleep. Have him breathe slowly and deeply and lie in the posture that he usually adopts when asleep, such as curling up on his side. Tell him to relax his body and to pretend that he is sleeping.

To provide sufficient time to create the sensations of sleep, the child should lie in bed for about one minute. This duration need not be exact and should not be timed. However, to give the younger child an approximate idea of what a one-minute duration is, you should have him count slowly to fifty or to recite the alphabet slowly during the first few trials as he rests in bed. If the interval seems much too short, have him recite aloud at first so that you can show him how to recite more slowly. But, discontinue this recitation as soon as your child has learned to approximate a one-minute duration, since that is not a natural thought sequence during sleep.

During this pretended sleep, we wish to have the child concentrate on his bladder sensations. When he is very relaxed, tell him to think about the feelings in his stomach and whether it feels as if he has to go to the toilet. Tell him to strain slightly, and when he feels as if he has to go even just a little bit, have him quickly jump out of bed and rush to the bathroom. If he does not have any feeling whatsoever that he has to urinate, then tell him to pretend that he has to go by thinking what it has felt like in the past. As he lies in bed, softly instruct him to direct his thoughts to this imagined need to urinate. For example, you might say,"Larry, remember to jump up just as soon as you feel like you have to go. Think about how it feels when you have to go. Think hard. . . ." If you have the time to remain with your child throughout the twenty practice trials, you should do so to assure that he is performing them correctly, and you can continue to prompt your child on several of the trials to direct his thoughts to his need to urinate. But, if your time is limited, then try to be present during at least the first one or two trials to assure that he has started off correctly. When he is performing the rest of the trials on his own while you are doing something else, have him call out from the bathroom which practice trial he has just completed so that you can follow his progress at a distance.

The getting-up practice is probably the single most important procedure in this training program. The procedure teaches the child to be aware of his bladder sensations while asleep, and teaches him a positive alternative response that will prevent wetting. It is true that the procedure requires about one half hour of the child's time and at least a few minutes of the parent's time for each practice period, but it will be recalled that the results of the studies showed that the average child required this practice on only four days before two consecutive weeks of dryness occurred, since the average child had only four accidents before achieving that goal. Consequently, this procedure should be carried out very conscientiously on the few occasions when it is needed. The child should be given a thorough explanation of the need for the procedure: It is a skill that must be overlearned since it must be carried out when he is asleep. Under no circumstances is the procedure to be presented to the child as a punishment for wetting, but rather as something constructive that he can do to prevent wetting. Should your child begin to show reluctance to perform the procedure, repeat your explanation of why the procedure is needed. To encourage him, spend as much time with him as he practices as you can conveniently spare and praise him for his efforts.

The getting-up practice is to be carried out after the child has remade his bed after an accident, and then again the next night before bedtime. The sequence, then, is that when a wetting has been detected, the child first remakes his bed and then does the getting-up practice. The next night, he again does the practice at bedtime. Each acci-

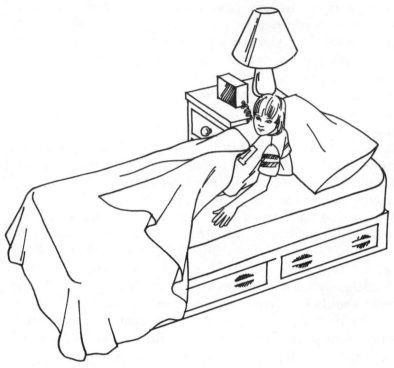

Before going to bed each night, the child feels the sheets to make him aware of their dry feeling and he rehearses what he will do if he has the need to urinate.

dent therefore results in two separate half-hour periods of getting-up practice, one period being spent right after the accident and the other being spent at the next bedtime.

Early Bedtime Practice in Getting Up

If your child had an accident the night before, he should practice the getting-up procedure before going to bed the next night. Since this practice will take about a half hour, the normal bedtime would be delayed unless he started earlier. Accordingly, have your child do the getting-up practice one half hour before his normal bedtime if he had a bedwetting the night before. Explain beforehand to your child that people remember during their sleep, such as in dreams, those thoughts they had right before going to sleep and that is why the getting-up practice is needed right before he goes to bed. Some children complain that the practice keeps them from some other activity, such as playing or television viewing. Explain to him that his bedtime would be delayed unless the practice is started earlier.

Bedtime Reminders

When your child goes to bed at night, you will perform several procedures designed to help focus his attention on the need to stay dry. Several of these procedures were also used at the end of the intensive training day. You will continue to use them now every night at bedtime.

AWARENESS OF BED SHEETS

When your child is asleep, he will only have a dim awareness that his bed is wet. To increase this awareness, you will have him touch and stroke the bed sheet to "feel its dryness," and to concentrate on how it feels. Ask him to close his eyes momentarily as he runs his hands along the sheet and to tell you whether he can remember this dry feeling.

BEDTIME REMINDER OF HOW TO DEAL WITH URGE TO URINATE

At bedtime, you want to be reassured that your child remembers what he is to do if he has the urge to urinate. Simply telling him not to wet the bed is a negative statement which does not tell him what positive actions he should take. The positive action which he can take, of course, is to arise quickly from the bed and hurry to the bathroom. The other positive action is to hold back just as he had done so successfully on the intensive training day. As he goes to sleep, you want to be sure he remembers these two reactions and is carrying these thoughts into his sleep. Ask him what he will do when he has the urge, rather than telling him, so that you can tell from his answer that he really does know. If he gives a partial answer, such as, "I'll hold it back until I don't have to go anymore," then ask him what else he must do, rather than you providing the missing information. In response to the above partial answer, you might ask, "And what else should you do? Run to the toilet? That's right. I'm sure you can do it. Are you thinking hard about how you will do it? Good, that will help you remember when you're asleep."

BEDTIME AWARENESS OF "FULL FEELING"

You also want your child to be very aware of his bladder sensations and any urge to urinate at this crucial moment before falling asleep so that he will also carry that thought with him into sleep. To help him have this awareness, have him describe how his stomach feels as he is lying down in bed and ask if he feels any need to urinate. "Do you feel you have to go at all?" If he does, ask him what he should do. "Jump up and go to the toilet." Tell him to do so. If he says he has no need, ask him to strain to try to create the urge. If he can, then again ask him what he should do, and have him go to the bathroom, reminding him to do the same thing at night.

BEDTIME REVIEW OF PROGRESS

You do not wish your child to fall asleep with fear and doubts in his mind. Accordingly, do not threaten or warn. Such threats are to be avoided at any time and bedtime is especially important. Instead, concentrate on his positive achievements and review them at this time so that he will fall asleep feeling proud of himself and assured that he will once again be successful. Remind him of his previous dry nights. "I know you can do it again; you've been dry for four nights in a row." Even if he had an accident recently, stress the positive, such as by saying, "You've been dry for four nights out of the last seven, looking at your Progress Calendar. That's fantastic! Before we started you couldn't do it at all. At this rate, you'll be dry almost every night. I know you can do it." Even if this is the first day after the intensive training day, you can stress the positive by reviewing his achievement on the intensive training day. "Yesterday, you were dry all night, even with all of that drinking. That's amazing. That shows you can control yourself now, and I'm proud of how well you did! Let's make it another dry night." Also, as part of this progress review, comment on his success in increasing his bladder control by the holding-back practice. "Today you filled the cup to at least six ounces every time. That's more than ever, so I know you can hold it back now. You sure are learning fast in solving this problem." In addition, you can point out his progress

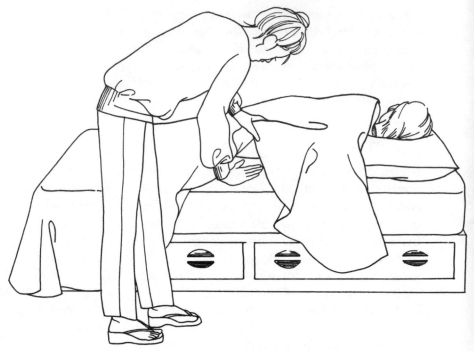

Each morning, one half hour before the child normally wakes up, the bed is inspected for wetness. If it is wet, the child changes the sheets at that time and does the getting-up practice.

in the getting-up practice and tell him how that is becoming a well-practiced habit.

Morning Inspection

If you have not used the buzzer apparatus, you will not have known whether a bedwetting occurred until the morning. Since we wish your child to remake the bed if it is wet, allow enough time for him to do so by inspecting the bed one half hour before the normal time for getting up. If the bed sheets are felt to be dry, allow your child to continue sleeping for the additional half hour. But if by touching the sheets, the bed is found to be wet, awaken your child immediately so that the next half hour can be spent in changing the sheets and in practicing the getting-up trials.

If you have used the buzzer apparatus, then these early-morning inspections theoretically are not necessary, since any bedwetting will have been signaled during the night at the moment that wetting occurred and your child would have already changed his clothes and the sheets. Nevertheless, the buzzer apparatus does not always operate properly so it is possible that wetting has occurred but the buzzer did not sound. It is advisable, therefore, to check your child's sheets for wetness a half hour before your child's normal wake-up time even if the buzzer was used.

What If You Do Use the Pad-and-Buzzer Apparatus?

The method has been described up to now under the assumption that you have decided not to use the buzzer apparatus. Some slight changes will occur if you do decide to use it.

The principal difference in the procedure when using the apparatus is that the changing of the bed sheets and the getting-up practice are done when the buzzer sounds rather than when you inspect the bed. The pad-and-buzzer apparatus provides constant inspection and a loud signal when bedwetting occurs. Otherwise, the inspections are made only in the morning and at the scheduled nightly awakening. So, if the buzzer sounds at 3:00 A.M., then you will arise, awaken your child, have him change

The pad-and-buzzer apparatus makes learning faster by giving an immediate signal when the bed is wet. It is inconvenient because it wakes everybody up in the middle of the night.

the sheets, and engage in the getting-up practice before he returns to bed. In the infrequent event that two bed-wettings occur during one night, you should have your child remake the bed and perform the getting-up practice after each wetting. The apparatus is reset by you after a wetting so it is capable of detecting a second wetting that might occur that night.

Because wettings are detected automatically, there is theoretically no need to inspect the bed for wetting, either at the nightly awakening or early in the morning. But, no apparatus is foolproof, and some bedwettings do fail to activate the apparatus. Perhaps the apparatus was not plugged in, or the pad is in the wrong position, or the apparatus is internally defective, or the child unplugged it. Or, the buzzer may have sounded but the child then disconnected it and went back to sleep before you noticed it. All of these possibilities are relatively rare, but they do occur and will slow down the learning. Therefore, as an extra precaution, check the bed for wetness at the nightly awakening and also in the morning even though the apparatus theoretically should make these inspections unnecessary.

The apparatus manufacturers usually supply detailed instructions for the proper use of the apparatus, and these directions should, of course, be followed. A few aspects of the proper use should be stressed. First, the child should be given a thorough explanation of the purpose of the apparatus and its operation. A trial demonstration beforehand is useful during the day in which you pour some water on the pad so that he can know what the buzzer sounds like. Also, it is advisable to have the child sleep without nightclothes below the waist so that the urine will flow freely onto the pad and not be absorbed in large part by the nightclothes. Before bedtime, and again at the scheduled nightly awakening, check the apparatus for proper connection and position. When the buzzer sounds, try to arise as soon as possible to help the child awaken and supervise his cleaning up and his practice.

For some of the pad-and-buzzer apparatuses, one change can be made in the procedure which makes its usage more economical. These apparatuses usually consist of a sandwich-like arrangement in which a large sheet of absorbent paper is inserted between an upper and lower metal sheet. The upper metal sheet is porous to allow urine to flow through it into the absorbent sheet of paper. When this paper becomes wet, the buzzer sounds. When the apparatus is purchased, several sheets of paper are enclosed, since they must be replaced after each wetting; more sheets of paper must be purchased for continued use of the apparatus. To reduce this expense and inconvenience, absorbent cloth may be used instead of the absorbent paper. An ordinary cloth bed sheet can be cut into several small sections, each of them being the same size as and used instead of the sheet of paper. Since the cloth sheets are reusable after being washed and dried, additional paper sheets need not be purchased. Parents have generally preferred to use the cloth sheets, especially if the bedwetting of their child persists for a longer time than is usual. Since this substitute of cloth sheets may not be possible with all types of pad-and-buzzer apparatuses, it is suggested that the new arrangement be tested beforehand by dripping water on the pad.

Calendar Progress Chart

Each morning at wake-up time, have your child mark the Dry-Bed Calendar which is posted next to the bed. If the bed was dry that night, mark it as "D" for dry or simply

DRY-BED CALENDAR

MON	TUES	WED	THURS	FRI	SAT	SUN
	1	2	3	4	5	6
7	8	9 *Dry*	10 *Dry*	11 *Wet*	12 *Dry*	13 *Dry*
14 *Dry*	15 *Wet*	16 *Dry*	17 *Dry*	18 *Dry*	19 *Dry*	20 *Dry*
21 *Dry*	22 *Dry*	23 *Dry*	24 *Dry*	25 *Dry*	26 *Dry*	27 *Dry*
28 *Dry*	29	30	31			

write "Dry," using large letters. Or if the bed was wet, mark it "W" for wet or simply "Wet." A sample filled-in Dry-Bed Calendar is shown in the illustration. In that example, the child was wet on the third night, Friday, then had three dry nights before the next accident on the following Tuesday, after which he was dry for the next thirteen nights. Blank forms that can be used for this calendar are printed on separate pages in Appendix 7, and they can be torn out and used if you do not have a separate calendar. The blank calendars have the days of the week listed, such as Sunday, Monday, and so forth, but not the dates, such as Oct. 1, 2, 3, and so forth, since they differ for each month, so fill in the numbers for the month in which you are starting. Continue to record on the Dry-Bed Calendar until at least one month has passed without an accident. At wake-up time and at bedtime have your child look at the Dry-Bed Calendar and you make some comments about the progress being shown, praising him for it. This calendar will enable you and your child to determine at a glance when he can receive the benefits you had agreed upon after different numbers of dry nights, such as having his brother sleep with him after four dry nights. Also, when you wish to inform any of your friends or his friends of his progress you can do so easily by showing them the Dry-Bed Calendar. Even when an occasional accident occurs, the calendar shows how minor the accident is in the long-term view.

Keeping the Agreement of Benefits

Before training started, you made an agreement with your child as to several benefits that you would provide as he achieved dryness. You should now enthusiastically pro-

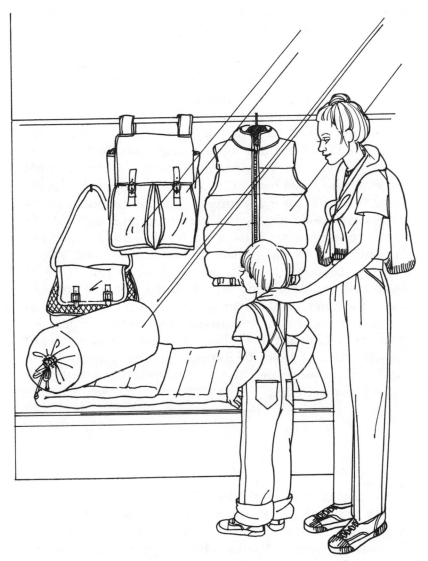

When the child starts staying dry at night, give him the promised rewards, such as the sleeping bag and overnight trips.

vide those benefits as scheduled. The written agreement is best kept next to the Calendar Progress Chart so that you and your child can conveniently observe when the next benefit is due. As a reminder to yourself, review the Progress Calendar with your child each morning when the results of the previous night are recorded, and look at the written agreement as to whether a scheduled benefit has been earned for that day. If, say, a visit to a friend has been earned because the agreed-upon two weeks of dryness has been achieved, congratulate him warmly for his success. And have him call up his friend that day to arrange the visit. Or if a younger child is scheduled to receive a sundae for his second straight night of dryness, be certain to arrange for him to receive the sundae that very day, and with proud praise for his achievement. Whatever the scheduled benefit, do not delay in providing it. As an additional reminder of scheduled benefits, you and your child can look at the Progress Calendar and the written agreement at each bedtime and see whether dryness that night will result in a scheduled benefit. Since most of the scheduled benefits are natural benefits of dryness, the child will be motivated to continue practicing as he receives these benefits.

Family Help

The entire family should help in supporting the child's efforts. We have previously emphasized that both parents must agree beforehand to the desirability of attempting the new procedure. Further, both parents should be familiar with the procedure so that one can supervise when the other is too busy or away. The child will make more of an effort when he sees that both parents are involved

The child should receive encourgement from both parents and other members of the family for his progress in staying dry.

and will not fall into the pattern sometimes seen in other areas of playing one parent off against the other.

If there are other children in the family, they, too, should be informed of the reasons for the various procedures in this training program so that they will understand why the child is doing these things. Ask the other children to help the child by telling him to keep trying. Show them the Happy-Face Clock and the Progress Calendar and the progress being made. If they are not actively encouraged to praise the child, then, instead, they may tease or criticize. One of the rewards for the younger child may be to sleep with a brother or sister, and this should be encouraged to promote their mutual involvement.

At breakfast each morning, the parents should comment on whether the child has been dry and if so, prompt the other children to praise the child for his success. Even if an accident occurred, comment on his having cleaned up, practiced, and on the successes he has had previously.

At supper, again the parents should mention their confidence that the child will be dry that night and, similarly, prompt the other children to do the same.

In combination, this praise and reassurance from the entire family will create an enthusiasm about practicing and maintaining awareness of his urinary habits.

Telling Friends and Relatives

Bedwetting is a problem which is generally known only to family members; usually only one or two other persons may know about it, such as a grandmother, aunt, babysitter, or next-door neighbor. The very young child often places great importance on the approval of these persons. If so, the child will be motivated by informing them of his successes, and this provision should be considered for inclusion in the benefits agreement. Call these persons on the phone and have them speak to the child, expressing their pleasure at the progress being achieved. If one of these persons visits the house, have him or her look at the Progress Calendar and tell the child how well he is doing. Older children are likely to feel ashamed to discuss the problem with others, but young children are usually encouraged by this support from outside the immediate household family.

Rewards for Younger Children

In addition to your enthusiastic praise you should also give rewards to young children, since such rewards carry

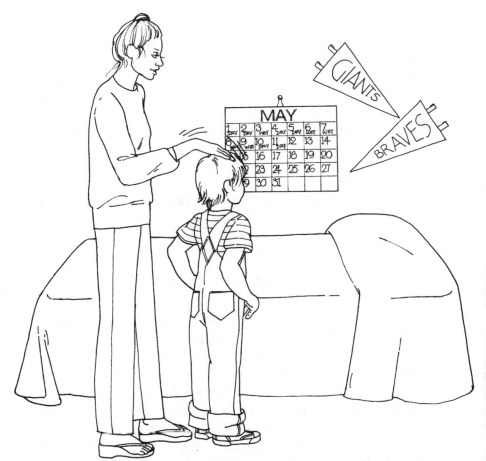

Show your pride in your child by encouraging him for every small indication of progress.

more of a meaning for them that you really do approve. So, for young children, give them a small piece of candy, a favorite drink, a trip to the shopping center, a ride, or whatever else you know the child likes very much, and do this whenever you praise. The size or amount of the reward can be very small since the important feature is that the reward is a visible and concrete indication of approval. For example, you might say, "Thelma, you filled the glass way up this time, twelve ounces! Come with me, I'm going to give you a potato chip." Or "You had two dry nights, Walter; let's celebrate by having a picnic today."

Positive Attitude Toward Your Child's Efforts

Throughout training try to maintain a positive attitude toward all of your child's efforts even when your child is not doing as well as he might seem to be able to do. Your child will be trying to control an action in his sleep, a task which is a great challenge whatever the action might be. This program teaches the skills of bladder control, bladder awareness, rapid awakening, and toileting, but in addition your child will require great motivation to persist in his efforts in spite of an occasional accident at first. Praise your child for everything he does in connection with his training. Praise your child throughout the holding-back trials on the first day, such as, "Wanda, you waited the whole two minutes. That's a long time," or, "Sammy, you held back for the whole two minutes on the bed. You should do very well tonight, too." Praise your child for getting up by himself when the buzzer sounds. "Allen, I'm so pleased you got up to change even before I got here. I'm glad you're taking care of things by yourself."

And, of course, every night without an accident should result in praise. "You did it, Betty! You went the whole night without wetting! That's the first time and I am so proud of you." Or, "Carl, imagine that, two nights in a row with no accidents! I think you licked the problem with your trying so hard."

What If My Child Has a Temper Tantrum and Won't Practice?

Occasionally, a child becomes upset after an accident and refuses to change his sheets or do the getting-up practice and may even have a temper tantrum. This refusal is more likely to occur at night when the child was awakened by the sounding of the buzzer after an accident or at one of the scheduled awakenings. The child is sleepy and one can sympathize with his reluctance.

The child is less likely to refuse to change the sheets or practice getting up by your being certain before the training starts that the child fully understands why these activities must be carried out. The nightclothes and the sheets were wet by him, not by the parent, so he should change them. That when he changes them, rather than the parent, the parent will not get annoyed. That they must be changed right away so that the bed will be a clean place to sleep in, and he will not get a skin rash, and he won't get used to sleeping in a wet bed. The getting-up practice must be done in order to get into the habit of getting up in his sleep when he is wet. That it wasn't learned well enough; otherwise the accident wouldn't have occurred. That it must be done for twenty trials, rather than just one, because it isn't enough to know what to do, but to have it become a habit so he will do it even when asleep. Explain that you want him to be proud of himself when he has a dry bed and to know that it happened because of how hard he tried. These explanations should be given before the first training day and discussed until the child understands the reason for them in every way. Ask him if he agrees to do these things and provide additional discussion until he does agree.

Refusals will also be minimized by repeating the explanations at every opportunity as to why the changing of sheets and getting-up practice are needed. During the first training day when he does these activities without having had an accident, repeat the reasons. "Wilma, you made the bed all by yourself. Now Mommy won't get so mad, because now you're taking care of it," or, "Charlie, you ran so fast to the toilet. That's good. I'm sure you'll get to the bathroom fast enough when you really have to go."

Whenever an accident occurs again, repeat the reasons to the child as to why he must change his sheets and do the practice trials. "David, you had an accident, but you changed the sheets so now you won't get a rash or get used to sleeping in a wet bed." Or, "Evelyn, you did the whole twenty practices by yourself. I'm proud. Now you know how to get up much better than you did before this accident."

If the child has a tantrum, or refuses to change sheets or practice in spite of the prior explanations and agreements, do not become angry. Instead calm him down first. Perhaps he is not fully awake so talk to him for a few minutes, reassuring him of your love for him and telling him you'll talk to him about the reasons for doing the corrections until he has awakened and feels better. Have him sit on the toilet or a chair until he is calmed down and is willing to continue. It is important that the sheet changes and practice be done, but reassure him until he is calmed, and wait a few minutes until he is ready. He will realize that you are not punishing him, that you are sympathetic with the inconvenience involved for him, and that you will wait as long as is necessary, but he must start eventually.

While the child is sitting in a chair to "think about it" and to calm down, remove any distractions such as watching TV or playing or reading. He should concentrate on the need for practicing.

If the refusal occurs in the morning when the child is scheduled to leave for school, do not allow him to be late. Instead, have him do the cleaning up and practicing as soon as he returns from school.

To show your understanding, tell your child how sleepy he must be at being awakened at that hour, that you know it takes efforts to make the bed up, that you can understand how he gets tired getting up so many times to go to the toilet. By sympathizing with his annoyances, you are telling him you are looking at the situation just as he is and are not blaming him for his reluctance.

When he eventually does start to change the sheets or practice, you should immediately praise him for making the effort and remind him once again of how his efforts will prevent future accidents and will make him proud of himself.

What If My Child Wets When He Is Not Feeling Well?

We have already mentioned that training should not be started if your child is not feeling well. What should you do later when your child has been dry for many weeks but then becomes ill and starts wetting? These circumstances occur occasionally. When young children become ill, bedwetting sometimes starts again. If your child is too ill to make the bed himself or do the getting-up practice, you should not require him to do so. Yet, he may ask to be excused from the agreed-upon changing of the bed and practicing even though he feels only minimally ill and can easily do those things. A good general rule to follow if your child is going to school is that if he is too sick to attend school that day and must remain in bed, he should also be excused from cleaning up and practicing. Similarly, if your child is a preschooler, and is too ill to play outside or be involved in his usual activities, he also should be excused from cleaning up and practicing. Of course, if your doctor says his condition does not permit these activities, also excuse him. As soon as your child is able to go to school or resume his usual play activities or the doctor gives his permission, have your child clean up and practice after each accident once again.

8 Ending the Training

Ending the Training

The present training program was designed to be effective in a short period of time and proved to be so when the various procedures were conscientiously and consistently carried out. The question, then, is when to end the training. When your child has remained dry for the first night, you may understandably feel that he has learned how to control the problem and that the training procedures are no longer needed. The evidence shows, however, that many nights of dryness must pass before we can be assured that the problem is solved. Your child is learning a new and difficult skill, and one night of dryness does not mean that he has reversed years of wetting. How many dry nights must pass?

When two weeks, that is fourteen consecutive days of dryness, have occurred, the chances are very good that your child has acquired nighttime control. The statistics show that most children will stay dry once they achieve fourteen straight dry nights. The others will have a brief return of bedwetting, but as we will discuss later, they will quickly become dry again when some of the procedures are temporarily reintroduced. So about two weeks of dryness is the cutoff duration that you will use in ending most of the procedures.

After two weeks of uninterrupted dryness, discontinue the pad-and-buzzer apparatus if you have been using it.

After two weeks of uninterrupted dryness, discontinue the bladder-control procedure. Your child no longer need urinate in the measuring cup. Encourage him to continue to hold back his urine as long as he can, but have him do so on his own.

After two weeks of uninterrupted dryness, you can discontinue the early-morning inspections of the bed. You no longer need to examine the bed for wetness one half hour before your child's normal time of arising. You should, however, continue to examine it at some time after he has awakened in the morning when it is convenient for you, just to be certain.

The nightly awakenings are discontinued according to the Happy Clock procedure already described. You will recall that your child is awakened one half hour earlier after each dry night. When the awakening was scheduled to occur within one hour of the normal bedtime, you discontinued it entirely. Your child will now sleep through the entire night without being awakened by you to toilet himself.

The continual praise and rewards for dryness are gradually decreased and, again, by the end of two weeks of uninterrupted dryness, are eliminated entirely as a formal procedure. Occasional spontaneous compliments are, however, natural and desirable.

The Progress Calendar Chart should continue to be

used until one month (thirty days) of uninterrupted dryness has elapsed. This procedure takes but a few seconds. You will continue to check the bed each morning. By having your child mark the chart each day with you, he will be reminded of your continued concern that he should try to stay dry.

The requirement that your child change the sheets should be permanent. Your child now understands that correcting the wetness is his responsibility and that he is responsible for remaking the bed if an occasional accident should ever happen again.

Similarly, the getting-up practice should be a permanent requirement. If an accident occurs after several weeks or months of dryness, that indicates that more practice is needed before going to bed that night.

The two permanent procedures are, therefore, the remaking of the bed and the getting-up practice. Since accidents will now rarely, if ever, occur, these two activities will be correspondingly infrequent since they are necessary only if an accident occurs.

What If Wettings Start Again?

For about one-fourth of the children, wetting may start again even though the child had been dry for several weeks or months before that. When such a wetting occurs, have your child change his clothes and the bed in the usual manner by himself and do the getting-up practice. As soon as the accident is discovered in the morning, have him change the bed sheets in the usual way and remind him of the need to practice that evening. A half hour before bedtime, have him do the getting-up practice for twenty trials and, at bedtime, have him feel the sheets and remind him of the need to stay dry, assuring him of your confidence in his ability to do so. Check the bed a half hour earlier the next morning so that if it is wet, time will be available for changing the sheets. Continue checking for a few days until no further wetting occurs. This simple and brief renewal of the getting-up practice and the bed changing should prevent further bedwettings. So when a bedwetting occurs after you thought they had been eliminated, treat the situation in a calm, problem-solving manner. On the one hand, do not ignore it and hope that it will not appear again. On the other hand, do not become angry with your child, nor assume that the bedwetting problem is as great as ever. Rather, consider the bedwetting as a signal that a little more practice is needed and that if the practice is carried out at the very first accident, no further accidents are likely to occur for a very long time.

9 Some General Questions About Bedwetting Training

What Should I Do if the Procedure Does Not Work?

The results obtained in the studies with this method showed that all of the children who continued using the procedures stopped wetting their beds. So you should be strongly assured that your child, too, will be successful if the procedure is carried out in the same manner. But, we should realize that every child is different and that there is probably a very small number of children with whom the procedure might not be effective. Also, a misunderstanding may occur as to how to do the present training. If benefits are not seen within the first week, read over the description of the procedures once again to discover any such misunderstanding. If this review does not lead to successful training, consult a behavior therapist since they are the persons who are most likely to be familiar with this new method and can clarify misunderstandings or try to adapt the procedure to some special needs of your child. A list of some behavior therapists may be obtained from:

Association for Advancement of Behavior Therapy
420 Lexington Avenue
New York, New York 10017

Or you may prefer to seek professional help from a psychologist, medical doctor, or pediatrician.

Should I Try to Rely Only on This Book?

This book describes a program that has been successful when it was carried out by parents who, along with their child, were given an explanation of the procedure by a counselor. In addition, the counselor asked and answered questions and had the parent and child act out some of the procedures. This book is intended to be a partial substitute for a counselor in that it relies on a written explanation rather than spoken instructions and demonstrations. The extent to which you will be successful depends greatly on how well you understand and follow the instructions here. The best teacher of any new skill is someone who has had successful experience in teaching that skill previously, and the same is true of teaching a child to control his bladder at night. You might well make an effort, therefore, to obtain the assistance and advice of any other parents you know who have used this method successfully with their own child, or a professional behavior therapist, counselor, psychologist, doctor, or pediatrician who can explain the method and answer questions. Their instructions, plus the information you have obtained from this book, will make you better prepared to proceed.

Which Children Have More Difficulty Learning?

We might expect large differences in the ease of training children to stop bedwetting because of differences in age, in sex, in the prior frequency of bedwetting, and so forth. Surprisingly, studies have found little difference caused by most of these factors. Boys seem to learn at about the same rate as girls. Younger children, from three to six years, do learn more slowly than the older children of twelve to fourteen years, but the difference is fairly slight. Children who had wet every night learn about as fast as those who were wetting on only some of the nights. Similarly, not much difference is found between children with a high IQ and those with a low IQ, except perhaps when the IQ is so low as to indicate substantial mental retardation. One factor that seems to be important is whether the child has mastered toileting during the day. Those children who are still having daytime accidents require more training than those who are no longer having accidents. Consequently, the present procedure stresses that the child first be thoroughly trained in his daytime toileting. One might expect that bedwetting is associated with deep sleep, but this has not been found to be the case. What is important is whether the child learns to awaken to go to the bathroom. Children who do awaken to go to the toilet are more successful. For this reason, the present method emphasized teaching the child to awaken to toilet himself in response to his full bladder sensations.

Is Bedwetting a Sign of a Personality Disorder?

As embarrassing and troublesome as bedwetting is, one may wonder whether bedwetting is a signal of an underlying emotional disturbance or personality disorder. It has been found that bedwetting occurs for children who are well-adjusted as well as for those who are emotionally upset. So, you should not conclude that your child's bedwetting is necessarily evidence that your child has unusual emotional problems. The bedwetting does often cause emotional problems. It has been found that when bedwetting has been cured, the child generally shows an improvement in his attitude and adjustment. Emotional adjustment is also related to bedwetting in a different way. For some children who have been dry at night for months or years, a sudden emotional shock, such as the death of a parent or family member, may result in a return of bedwetting. In such instances, the emotional upset does seem to cause the bedwetting, but training such as is described in the present program will correct this bedwetting in the same way as it corrected that which had been present from early childhood. So, if bedwetting suddenly occurs again after an emotional disturbance, deal with the problems separately. Give your child the reassurance and support necessary to reduce the emotional problem as you normally would. Simultaneously, reintroduce the training procedures for bedwetting just as you would have done had the bedwetting reappeared without any emotional disturbance causing it. Bedwetting is a problem that occurs with or without a state of emotional disturbance and seems to cause emotional upset as much as it is caused by emotional upset. Staying dry should be viewed as a skill to be learned rather than as a sign of a healthy or unhealthy personality.

Mental Retardation

If your child is mentally retarded, the present method may still be used if the retardation is fairly mild. In that case, you definitely should use the buzzer apparatus to help him develop sensitivity to his bladder signals. You should also use the snack rewards especially frequently since he will then understand better that he has done something well and that you approve. Because of the retardation he may have difficulty understanding what you desire when you ask him to strain at the toilet and to hold back, so this procedure on the first day should be omitted if he has difficulty in comprehending it. Also because of the retardation, he may be unable to count to himself in bed during the getting-up practice so you should then time the period (about one minute) yourself, and not ask him to do so.

If your child is profoundly or severely retarded, the present program requires extensive modification, but bedwetting training is still possible. As mentioned earlier, the present program of research began with teaching retarded persons. A separate book has been published which deals specifically with toilet training and bedwetting training of severely retarded persons and is listed in the References at the back of this book.

Reminder Outline and Questions

To assist you in remembering the various procedures, outlines are included in the various Appendixes.

In Appendix 1 there is a list of questions that serve as reminders of the preparations you make before starting training.

Appendix 2 is an outline of the training procedures to be used only during the intensive training day.

Appendix 3 outlines the procedures to be used regularly after the intensive training day, and Appendix 4 describes when each of the procedures should be discontinued. Each of these outlines is used at a different stage of training. By having these outlines before you, they will serve as a reminder of the procedures and the sequence in which they are to be used.

Appendix 8 is a self-test to help you determine how well you remember the procedures described in this book. It is recommended that you take this self-test after reading the book. If you have difficulty in answering some questions, you will benefit from reading again those sections of the book that deal with those questions. Also, the answers to the questions on the self-test are given on the page following the questions.

10   A Bedtime Story About a Boy Who Stopped Bedwetting

The following story about Timmy describes the common thoughts and actions of young bedwetters who have used this training procedure. The names are fictitious and the events do not describe one actual person's experiences, but are a composite of those of children who have been trained by our method.

Consider using this story to be read to your child at bedtime to help inform him about the training procedure. Of course, if your child is older and can read well, have him read this story himself or even, as was noted earlier, he might read the rest of the book as well. Your child should read the story or have it read to him a few days before you start the training so that he will know what to expect. As you read the story, feel free to interrupt to comment on how Timmy, the hero of this story, has had experiences similar to those of your child.

Timmy was eight years old and was in the third grade at school. Sandler was his last name, Timmy Sandler. His friends sometimes called him Sandy and he liked that nickname because it reminded him of the sandy beach where he always had so much fun.

Timmy smiled and laughed a lot so the other children liked to play with him because he was so much fun to be with. At school, the other children liked to play with him at recess. And when there was no school, the other boys often came by the house to ask him to play and to be on their team.

But Timmy had a problem that his friends didn't know about. He wet his bed at night.

Almost no one knew he wet his bed except, of course, his mother and his father and his big sister, Betty, and a few people who found out about it by accident, like when his sister told her friends one day. He found out because all of a sudden Betty's friends came over to him at school and began calling him terrible names like "Baby," "Pee-Baby," and "Water-Bucket."

And Betty wasn't always very nice about it, either. They liked to play together and Betty taught him many new things. But when they had a quarrel and Betty became angry, she started calling him "Baby," too. So now he was afraid to play with her anymore. Mom told Betty to stop teasing and never again to tell any of her friends about the bedwetting, that Timmy would stop soon by himself if people didn't nag him about it. Timmy was very glad to hear his mother say that. He didn't want anybody in the world to know.

Timmy's mother knew, of course. Every morning she would look at the bed and say, "Oh, no!" "Again?" or, "Won't this ever end?" or something like that. Then she would make up the bed and sound upset and talk about all the work and all the laundry she was doing and kept talking like that all the while that she was putting away the wet sheets and making the bed. When she acted like that, Timmy went to another room to hide so he wouldn't hear her. For the last few months, though, she didn't say anything except, "Don't worry Timmy, you'll outgrow it. Just keep trying." But you could tell she wasn't happy.

Timmy's father didn't say too much about it. In fact, he acted a little surprised when Timmy's mother told him not long ago that maybe the bedwetting would stop if Timmy had more blankets to keep him warm. "Is my big man still wetting?" he asked, and patted Timmy on the head, but didn't say anything else about the bedwetting or the blankets.

A few other grown-ups knew about the bedwetting. Uncle Jack and Auntie Susan knew because Timmy wet one of their beds when he was visiting them two years ago. Grandma knew because his mother asked her once for help and now she asked about it almost every time she called. Some of his mother's friends knew about it because his mother had once asked them at her bridge club and now they always asked him, "Have you stopped wetting yet?" when the bridge club met at his house.

But Timmy usually didn't answer when people asked him about it. He didn't want to talk about it and never told anybody, even if someone did ask.

What could he do about it? He was asleep when it happened. Sometimes he dreamed that he was going in the toilet, or behind a tree or a bush, but that was all he could remember. He thought about it a lot, but what did everybody expect him to do? "I can't help it, I try," he told his mother. "Please don't be mad at me."

Timmy and his mother had tried many different things. They went to the doctor who asked him many questions and said Timmy was very healthy and that there was nothing wrong with him, that he would outgrow it soon. That was a very long time ago.

Then they tried not drinking. No milk or Cokes at supper. And never any drinks after supper, even when they went out to eat or to the ice cream store. Timmy felt left out, although he hoped it would help. It didn't.

The hardest thing his mother did was wake him up every hour all night long for about two weeks. He didn't mind it so much after a while. He would do anything that would help, but his mother got very angry after the first few nights and complained about being sleepy all the time. A few times her alarm clock didn't wake her up and she didn't awaken Timmy and he wet his bed, so she gave up on that.

Then she told him to sleep on his back and went into the bedroom to turn him over if he wasn't. That didn't work either. So she had him sleep on his stomach for a few nights. Still, the wettings went on. Someone else said that a hard bed was good, so a hard board was put under the mattress. Still no change.

They went back to the doctor and he gave them some pills for Timmy to take. But the pills made him so sleepy that he had to stop taking them.

"I give up," his mother had said after the pills. Now she never said anything about wetting. She had heard that bedwetting might be happening because Timmy was unhappy. So she tried even harder to make him happy and never scolded him, especially about bedwetting.

One day his mother came home with another idea. She just heard from a friend in the bridge club about a way of stopping bedwetting that had worked for her friend's daughter who was only four years old. Mrs. Golden, her friend, had gone to a psychologist who showed Mr. and Mrs. Golden and their girl, Cindy, a new training program. He had them practice it in the office for about an hour and gave them some papers which described the procedure to take home with them. Cindy had started two weeks ago and had only two accidents since then. Mrs. Golden suggested that Timmy's mother try it, too, even though she had "given up." So Timmy's mother read the report and asked Mrs. Golden to tell her about the new method.

Mrs. Golden said that she did not believe it either, herself, at first, but decided to give it a try. She was told by the psychologist that the average child who used this method had only one or two wettings on the very first week and had only four wettings before being dry for two straight weeks. And sure enough, her girl Cindy did even better so far. The way she described it, Cindy was given exercises to help increase her bladder control so she wouldn't have to go to the bathroom so often. Cindy was taught to get up in her sleep automatically when she had to go, and she was taught how to concentrate on this at night and to get up quickly when she had to. One of the nicest things was that now Cindy made up the bed and her mother didn't have to. Mrs. Golden said many other things, but Timmy's mother had heard enough to know that she was going to try it.

She called the number Mrs. Golden gave her and made an appointment at a time when Timmy and her husband could come with her, since all three had to be there: Timmy, his mother, and his father. When they arrived, the psychologist, who was a woman, took Timmy into a room alone after she had talked to him and his parents and had given them some papers to fill out. She told Timmy that from now on he was in charge of stopping the bedwetting. She had him practice "holding back" when he had to go to the bathroom and also had him practice getting up quickly at night, using a sofa in the office as if it were Timmy's bed. She had Timmy practice feeling his bed sheets at night and thinking hard about how his tummy felt when he had to go to the toilet. Timmy answered questions about what he should do when he had an accident from now on. It all sounded so easy to Timmy that he was sure he could do it. Then she called Timmy's mother and father in and asked Timmy to explain to them what he was going to do and to ask them to help him.

Timmy told his mother and father that his mother wouldn't have to change the sheets anymore, that he would take care of it. And that he was going to do lots of practicing to stop from wetting. He would practice getting up over and over and over until he was able to get up even when he was asleep. And he would practice waiting when he had to go to the toilet so that he could wait at night, too. In the beginning, until he practiced enough, he would get up once each night to go to the toilet so he wouldn't have to hold back for so long. And every night at bedtime he would think real hard about whether he had to go to the toilet and about getting up if he had to.

Timmy also told his parents how they could help him. On the first day, which would be a very busy practicing day, they would give him lots of Cokes and nice drinks and remind him every half hour to practice holding back. Every night his parents would help him to think about getting up. He wanted his mother to teach him how to change the sheets and make up the bed. When he practiced his getting-up exercises, he would ask them to watch him so that they could know how hard he was practicing. He would like them to tell him nice things when they saw him practicing the right way. When he stayed dry, he hoped they would give him something that he couldn't have before because he was wetting. And they would talk to Betty, his sister, to stop teasing him and ask her to help him, too.

Timmy's mother and father were delighted at how well Timmy understood the new training idea and how excited he was at helping himself. They told Timmy that they would do all of these things for him and that they felt sure he would be a success because he was so excited about it.

Before Timmy and his parents left the office, they made some promises about what Timmy should get to do once he started being dry. This is what they decided.

AGREEMENT

A BIG MILK SHAKE

When Timmy has been *dry for one night,* Dad will take him the next day after dinner for the biggest milk shake the store has. (Timmy was afraid to drink before bedtime so this was something special he could do if he didn't have to worry about wetting.) And a sundae the next night, too, if he's dry.

TELL GRANDMA

When Timmy has been *dry for three nights* in a row, we will call Grandma and let you tell her how you have learned how to stop wetting.

PLASTIC SHEET

When Timmy has been *dry for five nights,* he can take the plastic sheet off his bed. (Timmy hated that plastic sheet because it reminded him that he was still wetting.)

PAJAMAS

When Timmy is *dry for six nights,* we'll go to the store and buy him nice new pajamas.

HAVE FRIEND OVER

When Timmy is *dry for seven nights,* he can call a friend —either Larry, Bill, or Dick—and have him sleep over the next Friday or Saturday night that we are at home.

SLEEPING BAG

When Timmy has been *dry for ten nights,* we'll buy him a sleeping bag the next time we go shopping that's less than $20.

VISITING RELATIVES OVERNIGHT

When Timmy has been *dry for twelve nights,* we'll call Auntie Susan and Uncle Jack and arrange for an overnight visit to their house in the country with the apple trees. (Remember, Timmy had wet one of their beds during his last visit there.)

CAMP

When Timmy has gone for *fifteen nights dry,* we'll send the money to the summer camp so he can go this summer.

In addition, according to the training plan, Timmy will not be awakened to toilet at night after he had had *six dry nights.*

And when *two weeks of straight dryness* with no accidents has passed, Timmy will not use the measuring cup anymore when he goes to the toilet.

After *one month of straight dryness*, Timmy will not use the Calendar Chart anymore and will not do the bedtime practice of feeling the sheets. And Mom and Dad will not check the bed each morning anymore.

Timmy's father wrote out the agreements. Before they left, the psychologist told Timmy to call every day to tell her how he did the night before and that she would be calling him, too, in case he had any questions. She gave Timmy's mother some pages to look at at home to help remind them of the things they were to do.

Mr. Sandler was eager to start. He hadn't realized how much Timmy really wanted to stay dry but just hadn't known what to do. He told Timmy's mother that he wanted to help in the training, too.

Timmy's mother had tried so many other ways before that she couldn't be sure anything would work until she actually saw it happen. But this training did seem different in so many ways. Instead of cutting out drinks, it gave more drinks. Instead of waking Timmy up every hour all night long for weeks, she only had to wake him up once each night, and always before she went to bed herself. And making Timmy's bladder bigger, that seemed like such a good idea. She remembered that he went to the toilet so often during the day, too, and couldn't wait once he had to go. As to practicing getting up at night, that made more sense than just telling him to get up or not to wet. She wondered why she hadn't thought of that herself. As for Timmy making his own bed, that part of it was worth the effort even if he never did stop wetting. Seeing is believing, she thought.

Timmy's thoughts were different. Now he could do something about wetting instead of being told over and over again to try. Try what? Now he could practice holding back so his bladder in his tummy could hold more. That made sense. And now he could practice getting up at night so he could do it automatically, like riding a bike, without having to think about it. And now he could practice thinking how his tummy felt when he had to go. That was like learning to pay attention to his stomach when it started "growling," and he learned that meant it was mealtime and he should hurry home so he wouldn't be late for dinner.

Timmy and his mother and father talked on the way home about when they should start. Timmy wanted to start tomorrow, which was Friday. Dad wanted to start Saturday when he could help. But Timmy was so eager, they decided to start the next day right after Timmy came home from school. Dad would help when he came home from work at 5:30.

Mrs. Sandler looked at the reminder list she had been given as soon as they came home. She went over it with Timmy.

The first question on the reminder list was whether Timmy was old enough. Yes, he was over three years old.

Had Timmy stopped pants-wetting during the day? Yes, about five years ago. Yes, he had been given a medical exam already. But, what about the drinks and snacks? Timmy helped her get the soda, the kind without sugar, and some potato chips.

Was there a light in the hall and a night-light in the bedroom? They checked, and the one in the bedroom had burned out so they replaced it. Was his bed in a convenient location? They decided to move it away from the wall so he could make it up more easily, and closer to the bedroom door so he could get to the bathroom faster. Have the other children been informed? His sister, Betty, was all full of questions when they had come home, and they told her what Timmy was going to do.

What about the pad-and-buzzer apparatus? Mr. Sandler didn't like that idea and neither did Mrs. Sandler because they didn't want to get up in the middle of the night. Timmy didn't like the idea of a gadget in his bed. But they all agreed that if the buzzer was needed, they wouldn't mind too much if it helped. They decided to wait one week. If the wetting didn't stop at all, they would use it. Mrs. Sandler remembered seeing them for sale in mail-order catalogs and other places.

What about a measuring cup for Timmy to use when he went to the toilet? Mrs. Sandler had a Pyrex measuring cup that was big enough. It held 16 ounces and had the numbers marked on the side. Timmy got a note pad and put it in the bathroom with a pencil for writing down the numbers.

The next thing was a calendar for marking whether Timmy was wet or dry each night. Betty said she had a calendar in her room they could have. Everyone thanked her for being so helpful.

The next reminder was to choose a day to start training. Now that they had everything, they decided for sure to start tomorrow. Timmy would come home from school as early as he could so he could start right away. And tonight he would go to sleep early since he would be waking up a lot tomorrow on the first day of training.

Had both parents agreed on a training plan? Mrs. Sandler checked with Mr. Sandler. They both thought all of the procedures made sense. The next question was whether Timmy's pajamas were loose enough. They checked and realized that Timmy had grown a lot. The pajamas were very tight. Betty offered to let him use her pajamas, which she had outgrown, until he got new ones.

Had a written agreement been made about special treats for staying dry? Yes, they had done that at the psychologist's office. Dad got some thumbtacks and put the agreement on the wall next to Timmy's bed along with the Progress Calendar so they could see quickly what special treat was due.

Had the child been told all about the training? Yes, they had talked about it at the office and on the way home.

Had some special treats been promised for even one or two dry nights? Yes, the milk shake and sundae.

"That's it," said Timmy. "We're all set to go tomorrow. Thanks, Betty, for helping, and you, too, Mom and Dad. I'm going to sleep now so I won't be too tired to practice tomorrow. Good night." He went to bed thinking about all of the special things he would soon be getting.

The next day Timmy returned home early from school so that he could start training. This was the first day of training.

Timmy's mother found the reminder sheet that listed the things to do on this first training day and put it on the table where she could look at it. As soon as Timmy came home, she told him they would get started right away. The first thing to do was to talk about what Timmy would do that day. Betty, his sister, asked if she could watch. Timmy's mother said, "Sure, and you can help, too." Betty was happy to help.

Timmy told his mother he would be drinking a lot and would practice going to the toilet. That he would lie down in bed and pretend he was asleep and practice holding back while lying down. That he would practice rushing to the bathroom when he couldn't hold back anymore. That, before he went to bed, he would learn how to make his bed and to do the getting-up practice. And after he went to bed, he would get up every hour when his mother awakened him to see if he had to go to the bathroom. He forgot to say anything about what he would do if he had an accident, so his mother asked him about that. He knew exactly. He said he would change the sheets and do the getting-up practice.

The first thing to do was for Timmy to start drinking a lot. Timmy's mother had his favorite drinks ready in the refrigerator—milk and Coke. Timmy drank a big glass of milk and then asked if he could go out and play. His mother told him that he should stay inside the house today so that it would be easier to call him every half hour to practice. Betty said she'd help by calling him and offered to go to the store to buy some more milk just in case. Timmy went to the family room to watch TV and play until she got back. Then he would play Monopoly with her. His mother started making dinner. She decided to make something simple today that did not need too much watching so she could interrupt it easily to spend time with Timmy. The time was 3:30.

About fifteen minutes later she went to the family room and offered Timmy some potato chips and peanuts which he ate. That made him thirsty so he had some more milk.

At 4:00 she called Timmy, and he came over right away to the bathroom. She asked Timmy to try to urinate and to tell her when he felt he had to do it. Timmy strained until he felt as if he were going to urinate and told his mother. "OK," she said, "that's good that you have to go. Now rush to your bed and practice holding it back while you are lying down." Timmy still felt that he had to go, but he held his stomach in and held back. His mother followed right behind him as he lay on his bed. She looked at her watch so she could time the two minutes and told Timmy, "You're holding back beautifully. Now, pretend you're asleep and count very, very slowly to fifty, wait a while after each number, and I'll tell you when it's time to get up." Right before Timmy lay down, she asked him, "What will you do if you can't hold it back?" Timmy answered, "I'll get up and rush to the bathroom so I won't wet the bed." "That's right," his mother said.

As Timmy lay on the bed, he closed his eyes and made himself feel very loose and relaxed, and curled up on his side with his legs bent just the way he did when he went to bed at night. Timmy still felt he had to go to the bathroom when he had counted to twenty. But he held back as hard as he could. When he had counted to thirty, though, the feeling was gone. That was about when his mother said, "One more minute to go, you can do it." And he did, because a short while later after he finished counting, his mother told him the time was up and he got up out of bed.

She talked with him about how this holding back would make his bladder stronger, why he should continue drinking, how she would teach him to make his bed, and all the other things he would do. She kept telling him how pleased she was that he held back for so long. She gave him some peanuts and another big glass of milk. He went back to the family room.

Betty had come home and so Timmy started playing Monopoly with her. Mrs. Sander gave him some potato chips about ten minutes later, and again, a few minutes after that. Each time, Timmy also had another drink.

At 4:30, Betty told Timmy it was time to practice again, and she came to the bathroom with Timmy even before their mother reminded them. Again, Timmy was asked to strain until he felt like going. He only strained a little before he felt he was about to go. So quickly, they went to his room where he lay down in bed and again pretended he was asleep. After about one minute he said he couldn't wait. "What should you do then?" his mother asked. Timmy quickly got up and rushed to the bathroom where he urinated. His mother praised him for holding back so long and also for getting up from bed so quickly.

Timmy was proud of himself as he returned to playing with Betty after his mother gave him another drink. She also praised Betty for being so helpful.

Every half hour Timmy was called to the toilet to try to go. Each time, he lay down on his bed and tried some more to hold back. Once he had to go even before he was called by his mother. She had him go to his bed and lie down there again while he tried to hold back. He did hold back and pretty soon didn't have to go anymore.

Timmy's father came home before six o'clock, just in time to see Timmy practicing to hold back in the toilet. He told Timmy he was doing really well.

Dinner was ready soon, and while they ate, they all talked about how well Timmy was holding back and how fast he rushed out of bed to go to the bathroom. Timmy ate hungrily and had another glass and a half of milk during the meal.

Just a few minutes after the meal was over, Timmy's father saw that it was 6:30 and time for the next practice. Timmy went to the bathroom and strained. He had been drinking so much that now it was easy. He felt his tummy feel hard and heavy, and he tried very much to hold back the urine. Again he went to his bed and lay down and tried to wait still longer. When he couldn't wait, he rushed to the bathroom and "went."

Timmy usually went to bed at eight o'clock. At seven o'clock he had another practice in holding back and again he was able to hold it back for the whole two minutes. It was now getting close to bedtime.

Timmy's mother told him that now they would practice what he should do in case he had an accident. First she asked Timmy to tell her once again what he should do. Timmy told her that if he had an accident he would change his pajamas, change the sheets, and do the getting-up practice. Timmy's mother told him how pleased she was that he knew what to do. She gave him more drinks and told him they would then practice cleaning up.

Timmy's mother had him lie down in bed and close his eyes and then she said, "Pretend. Pretend that you had an accident and I just woke you up." She touched him on the shoulder and said, "Timmy, the bed is wet. Show me what you will do." Timmy told her that he would change his clothes. He jumped out of bed. He took off his pajamas and put them in the dirty laundry basket. Then he took his other set of clean pajamas from his dresser and put them on.

Timmy's mother was pleased and told him that was exactly right. "Now I'll show you how to change the bed," she said.

She told Timmy to take off the blanket and sheets and to put the sheets into the dirty laundry basket. Then she told him where the clean sheets were and went with him while he took the clean sheets out of the closet and went back to the bed. She told Timmy that first he would watch her do it, then she would let him make up the bed.

She started putting the sheets on and described out loud to Timmy what she was doing. "First, you spread the sheet on the bed. Then walk around the bed, pulling the sheet so that it hangs down the same on all sides and the bottom. Then, tuck the sheet under the mattress. Walk around the bed, tucking it in and pulling the sheet so it is nice and smooth. Make the corners neat by tucking in one side, then lift the mattress to fold the other side without making the sheet 'bunch up.' " She had him do one side of the bed and two of the corners. Then she put on the top sheet and then the blanket, explaining everything while she did it. And she let him do part of it.

When she was finished, she said, "Now, you do it, Timmy." Timmy did it very slowly since he was not sure, but his mother told him he was doing it just fine and reminded him what to do next. She was so proud. He was doing it slowly, and so she started to do it for him, but he said, "Let me do it myself, please, Mommy," and she readily agreed. When he had some trouble with the corners and with making the sheet smooth, instead of doing it for him, she told him how to do it and guided his hand for a moment.

Finally, Timmy was finished. Timmy's mother called his sister and father in to see what he had done. They all told him how smooth and neat the bed looked and what a good job he had done. Timmy was very pleased with himself.

"Now," his mother said, "let's do the getting-up practice. Remember how you are supposed to do it? You lie down in bed and pretend you are asleep. Then you will try to make yourself feel like you have to go even just a little bit. You'll jump up very, very quickly. If you can't make yourself feel like you have to go, then think real hard and try to remember what it feels like. As soon as you can remember, then quickly jump up. Go to the bathroom fast and try to go to the toilet. Then come back to bed and start all over again. How many times do you do this, Timmy?" Timmy told her, "Twenty times." "That's right," Timmy's mother said as he lay down on the bed for the first practice.

"Now, Timmy, I want you to count out loud so I can hear you—softly, but just loud enough for me to hear," Timmy's mother told him. "Close your eyes; that's right. And you can be on your side with your legs pulled up a little, the way you usually do. And breathe real deep and slow just the way you see me do when I'm asleep." Timmy did as he was told and began counting, "One, two, three, four," and so on. "A little more slowly and that will be perfect," his mother said softly. Timmy

continued more slowly, "Eleven . . . twelve . . . thirteen . . ." and so on much more slowly until he reached
the number fifty. Then he stopped.

Timmy tried to make himself feel as if he had to go to
the bathroom. In a few seconds he started feeling like it
and immediately jumped up and ran to the bathroom
where he really did go. When he came back, his mother
told him he did it perfectly and to start the second practice.

On the next few practices he counted quietly to himself,
and pretty soon he didn't have to count at all because he
could tell how long he had to wait. Also, on the next few
practices, he couldn't make himself feel as if he had to
urinate. So he thought about some other times when he
really felt like going, and jumped up as soon as he
thought of how it felt.

Timmy's mother stood near the door of the bedroom all
the time and told Timmy how well he was doing on each
practice. Timmy counted the number of practices. Each
time he came back to his bed from the bathroom he would
call out, "One," or "Two," or "Three." Finally, on the last
practice, he called out "Twenty," and said, "Boy, I'm
tired." Betty and his father also told Timmy how well he
had done.

By now it was close to Timmy's bedtime. As he climbed
into bed, his mother sat on the edge of the bed to talk to
him and to give him the bedtime reminders.

First, she asked him to repeat what he should do if he
had an accident tonight. Timmy told her that he would
change his clothes, change the bed, and do the getting-up
practice.

Then she reminded him that she would be waking him
up every hour for him to go to the toilet if he had to.
Timmy told her he would wake up right away as soon as
she asked him to.

Timmy then drank some more, about half a glass of milk. Then Timmy felt the sheets, running his hands over them and thinking about how dry they felt. His mother talked with him about the milk shake and sundae and other nice things he would be receiving if he was dry. She reminded him to think about how his tummy felt and asked him what he would do if he felt as if he had to urinate. "I'll get up real fast," he said, "and I'll run to the bathroom." His mother gave him a kiss, said good night, and left the room. As she left, she started to close the door but left it open when she realized that Timmy would have an easier time getting to the bathroom if it was not closed as it usually was.

An hour later, Timmy's mother came into the bedroom and saw him sound asleep. She felt the blanket and was delighted to find that the bed was dry. She softly said, "Timmy, Timmy," but he didn't answer. She touched his shoulder, but still Timmy didn't move. So she started to raise him, but he opened his eyes and sat up. She talked to him until he looked her in the eye and seemed awake and attentive. "What are you supposed to do now, Timmy?" she asked. "Can you hold it another hour or do you want to go to the bathroom?" Timmy felt as if he'd better go, and said so as he quickly got out of bed and went to the bathroom. His mother told him that he did the right thing if he felt as if he had to.

When Timmy returned, he drank some more, then got into bed where he again felt the sheets and thought how dry they were. Again, his mother told him to think about his tummy and asked him what he would do if he felt he had to go. He told her, and then fell asleep as he thought about how he should get up.

At the next awakening an hour later, Timmy woke up as soon as his mother touched his shoulder and the time after that he sat up as soon as he heard his name called.

The first two times he was awakened he got up and went to the bathroom. The next time he didn't feel as if he had to go so he said he would wait even after his mother asked if he was sure. She told him she was glad he was able to hold back so long.

At the eleven o'clock awakening, Timmy's mother did not give him any more drinks. He was so sleepy anyhow that he didn't feel too thirsty now. She thought that the last awakening would be at one o'clock, but then Timmy's father said that he would stay up until two o'clock and give Timmy another wake-up just to make sure.

Timmy's bed was dry at each of the awakenings. He had gotten up to go to the bathroom on all but two of them. After the last awakening at two o'clock, his dad went to sleep, too. His sister had gone to sleep much earlier and his mother just an hour ago. The first day of training was over.

Timmy's mother was very nervous when she went to check his bed the next morning to see if it was dry. She thought to herself that with all those drinks it would be a miracle. She checked while Timmy was still asleep at 7:00 A.M., a half hour before his usual wake-up time at 7:30.

Timmy's bed was dry! She quickly woke up Betty and Timmy's father and told them the good news. She made an extra-special breakfast of pancakes and sausages, which was Timmy's favorite.

This was the first dry night that Timmy had ever had and that called for a celebration.

They all went into Timmy's bedroom at 7:30 to wake him up and tell him the good news. When he was awake, they all clapped their hands and hugged him. Then they clapped again as Timmy wrote "Dry" in big letters on his Calendar Progress chart. That meant a big milk shake today.

At breakfast, they all talked about how Timmy had finally learned to stay dry and all because he had tried so hard and practiced so hard. Timmy's father said he would like to take Betty along to the ice cream store, too, and get her something for being such a big help.

It was Saturday and no school. After breakfast Timmy had to go to the bathroom and almost forgot that now he was supposed to hold back as long as he could. He was able to wait about twenty minutes. Then he did it in the measuring cup when he couldn't wait much longer. Timmy's mother showed him how to read the number on the cup and they wrote it down. He had held back a long time and his mother and father told Timmy he was starting off very nicely.

Timmy played outside during most of the day. Each time that he felt that he had to go to the bathroom he told himself to wait. He found that if he could make himself wait for even a little while, then he didn't have to go. Each time he did go to the bathroom, he did it in the measuring cup and showed it to his mother. She was pleased at how much he did and wrote it down on the paper in the bathroom. Then she emptied the cup.

When Timmy did a very big amount in the cup, his mother always gave him something special like a cookie or ice cream. In fact, even when he didn't do an extra amount in the cup, she was pleased that he was trying so hard and always told him.

At dinner they all again told Timmy how proud they were of him. Then they went to the ice cream store where Timmy got his big milk shake. Dad gave Betty a milk shake, too.

At bedtime that night, Timmy looked at the Happy Clock. He drew the hand in to point at twelve o'clock. That was when his mother would wake him up tonight to go to the toilet. That was the time when she usually went to sleep. She and Dad were going out to a party tonight and would be back about eleven o'clock.

After Timmy "set" the Happy Clock, his mother reminded him about getting up if he had to go at night and also what he should do if he found the bed wet. He felt the sheets and thought hard about his tummy. He decided he felt a little bit like going to the bathroom so he got up right then and went even before his mother asked him to.

At twelve o'clock, when his mother and father checked his bed, it was dry. They awakened Timmy then and had him go to the bathroom.

Timmy was dry the next morning, too. That was two nights in a row. They all looked at the written agreement and saw that meant a sundae for him today. Timmy wrote down "Dry" again on his Calendar Progress Chart in the morning, and also penciled in the Happy Clock to show 11:30.

He was dry again the next night. That was three dry nights in a row. That meant a call to Grandma. Timmy's mother called her and said she had some wonderful news to tell her about Timmy's bedwetting. She would let Timmy tell her himself. Timmy was bubbling with excitement as he told her. Grandma kept telling him how excited she was, too, and said she would come over and visit soon to see him.

Timmy was dry the next night, too. All this time he was using the measuring cup and trying very hard to hold back as long as he could so that he could get as much in the cup as he could. And every day, especially at each meal, his mother and dad told him he was doing great. Betty helped, too, by reading from the cup when his mother wasn't there when he went to the bathroom. Each night before he went to bed he penciled in a bigger part of the Happy Clock. So, after the fourth dry night he now would be awakened at nine o'clock, just one hour and a half after he went to bed.

On the fifth night, when Timmy was awakened, the bed was wet. Timmy was so upset he almost started to cry. But his mother told him not to cry. She was sad that the bed was wet, but now he knew what to do to correct it. As his mother watched, he changed his clothes and then remade the bed, putting the clean sheets on. Then he did the getting-up practice. It was about ten o'clock and he was sleepy, but he knew that this practice would help him to stay dry the rest of the night. When he finished, his mother told him that she was sure his practice would help him to stay dry and she gave him the same reminders as before. That night, when everyone was asleep, he got up all by himself when he started dreaming about going to the toilet. In the morning, his bed was dry.

Before breakfast, he sadly wrote "Wet" on his calendar, but his mother and dad and Betty all told him that just one "Wet" after four dry nights was wonderful and they were sure he would be dry again. That night he missed part of his playtime because he had to start his getting-up practice a half hour before bedtime. Timmy didn't like stopping the playing with his friend, but he knew that by practicing he would be able to keep dry that night. At bedtime he didn't color in the Happy Clock since the clock should be colored only if the bed was dry the night before. Timmy did his getting-up practice and tried real hard. Each time he lay on his bed he thought to himself, Tonight if I have to go even a little bit I'm going to hold it back no matter what! And I'll get up so fast!

And he was right. That night he was dry. He was dry when his mother woke him up to go to the bathroom. And he was still dry in the morning. "We knew the other night was just an accident and that you could do it, Timmy," his mother said. And Betty and Dad agreed. He wrote "Dry" in big letters on his calendar that morning. And that night, before bedtime, he was smiling when he colored in the Happy Clock earlier by another half hour.

That was five nights he had been dry. His agreement was that when he was dry for five nights, he could throw away the plastic sheet on his mattress. When he took it off, he asked his mother if he should save it just in case. She said, "No, Timmy, let's throw it away. You might have one or two more wettings by accident, but I don't think we really need it." Timmy put the sheet in the trash can.

The next night he was dry again. That was six nights and the agreement said that now he could have a new pair of pajamas. That afternoon he went with his mother to the store and Timmy picked out a pair of pajamas with big stripes just like the ones he saw his friends wear.

And the next night he was dry again. Seven nights. That meant he could call Larry to come sleep over next Friday or Saturday. He called and Larry was glad to come. He had never stayed over with Timmy before. No one had.

Three more nights Timmy was dry and that meant he got a sleeping bag. Dad had said no more than $20. But when Dad saw one sleeping bag on sale for $30 that had down feathers in it, he told Timmy to get it anyhow. He had been dry for six nights in a row now!

But, then, another accident. That happened soon after the awakening at night had stopped. And now he had to hold back all night long. So, the next morning he changed the bed and did the getting-up practice. And the next night he did the practice again a half hour before bedtime. It worked and he was dry again.

Timmy's mother knew that the getting-up practice was

a lot of work for Timmy. So, she was surprised when Timmy told her the next night that he wanted to do the practice before he went to bed even though he didn't have to. He wanted to be sure that he would be dry that night.

During the daytime he tried very hard to hold back and to go to the bathroom as few times as he could. So, each time he used the measuring cup he was able to see that he could hold more and more.

Two weeks went by without any wettings since Timmy had that last accident. When twelve days had passed, the agreement said that he could go to Auntie Susan's to visit overnight. Mom called and she set a date. Mom told her not to worry about Timmy wetting the bed because now he was dry every night.

Two weeks of dryness was when Timmy didn't have to use the measuring cup anymore. But he decided that he would still hold back as long as he could so he would be able to hold back easier at night, too.

The next night he was dry again. That was fifteen nights and that was extraspecial. Timmy's father called the camp director and told him that Timmy was going to go to camp that summer. His father wrote out a check and a letter for the summer camp and Timmy put it in the mailbox. "I'm going to have so much fun!" he shouted.

Timmy had one more accident three days later and then another one three weeks after that. He was very sad each time he had one. But he knew what to do each time. He changed the sheets and did the twenty getting-up practices. And his mother did not get angry or look so sad anymore.

Betty stopped teasing him. And Dad was so proud of him. His mother and father told him one day as they looked at the Progress Calendar, "Timmy, we want to buy you a new bed, a bigger one. You are getting to be a young man now and we're not worried about the bed being ruined anymore. So this weekend we'll go to the furniture store and we'll choose a new bed together." Timmy wondered if that new bed was in the agreements. "No," his mother said, "that's an extra thing we want you to have."

Timmy kept on writing on the Progress Calendar each morning. But, after one whole month went by, he stopped. He soon forgot that he ever had wet his bed.

One day, one of the friends who had teased him before said, "Say, Timmy, do you still wet your bed?"

"Of course not," Timmy answered quickly. "That was a long, long, long time ago!"

Appendix 1

REMINDER LIST OF PREPARATIONS FOR TRAINING

	(Circle Answer)	
1. Is the child old enough?	Yes	No
2. Has the child stopped pants-wetting during the day?	Yes	No
3. If the problem seems medical, has a physician been consulted?	Yes	No
4. Do you have ample amounts of the child's favorite drinks and snack treats?	Yes	No
5. Is there a night-light in the hall and enough light in the bedroom for the child to be able to find the way to the toilet?	Yes	No
6. Has the child's bed been placed in a location convenient for him to get to the toilet and for making his bed?	Yes	No

7. Have the other children at home been informed of the training effort and told how to help?   Yes   No

8. If you have decided to use a pad-and-buzzer apparatus, have you obtained one and learned how to use it?   Yes   No

9. Have you obtained a measuring cup for your child?   Yes   No

10. Do you have a Calendar Progress Chart?   Yes   No

11. Have you chosen a convenient day for training?   Yes   No

12. Have both parents agreed on the training plan?   Yes   No

13. Are the child's nightclothes easy to remove for toileting?   Yes   No

14. Has a written agreement been made with the child regarding the benefits the child will receive?   Yes   No

15. Has the child been told about all of the training procedures and the reasons for each of them?   Yes   No

16. In the written agreement, have benefits been arranged for even one or two dry nights as well as for longer-term dryness?   Yes   No

Appendix 2

OUTLINE OF THE TRAINING PROCEDURES ON THE INTENSIVE TRAINING DAY

I. DURING THE AFTERNOON
   A. Parent reviews the procedures with the child and asks child to repeat them to show his understanding.
   B. The child is encouraged to drink large amounts of his favorite drinks.
   C. Every half hour the child is requested to attempt urination.
      1. If the child feels the need to urinate, he is encouraged to hold it back as long as he can until the urge goes away.
      2. If the urge to urinate remains, the child lies on his bed as if asleep, then arises and goes to the bathroom, to urinate in the cup, acting out what he should do at night.
      3. The child is praised for his efforts, whether or not he urinated, and is given more drinks.

II. ONE HOUR BEFORE BEDTIME
   A. Parent reviews with the child the procedures of correcting accidents.
   B. Parent continues to encourage the child to drink.
   C. Child acts out the procedures to be followed after an accident.
      1. Child is required to change his own nightclothes.
      2. Child removes sheets and puts them back on himself.
   D. Child acts out the getting-up practice.
      1. Child lies down in bed as if asleep.
      2. Child counts to self.
      3. Child arises and hurries to the bathroom.
      4. Child attempts to urinate in the measuring cup.
      5. Child returns to bed.
      6. Child repeats above steps—1, 2, 3, 4, and 5—twenty times while parent counts the trials.

III. AT BEDTIME
   A. Bedtime scheduled earlier than usual.
   B. The parent reviews the procedure to be followed on accident correction and scheduled awakenings and the child restates these requirements.
   C. Child continues to drink.
   D. The parents review with the child the benefits promised for dryness and express their confidence in the child.
   E. The child feels the sheets and comments on their dryness.
   F. The child retires for the night.

IV. AFTER THE CHILD IS IN BED
   A. Awaken the child every hour until midnight or 1:00 A.M.
   B. Use a minimal prompt to awaken the child.

C. Determine whether the bed is wet.

D. If the bed is dry:

    1. Ask the child whether he can wait or whether he must urinate.

        a) If the child is able to wait another hour:

            (1) Praise his urinary control.

        b) If the child feels he must urinate:

            (1) Child goes to bathroom to urinate in the cup.

            (2) Praise child for his preventive action.

            (3) Child returns to bed.

        c) Child feels the bed sheets and comments on dryness.

        d) Praise child for having a dry bed.

        e) Give child more drinks (discontinue after 10:00 or 11:00 P.M.).

        f) Child returns to sleep.

E. If the bed is wet:

    1. Awaken the child and mildly reprimand for wetting.

    2. Child feels wet sheets and comments on wetness.

    3. Child goes to bathroom to finish urinating.

    4. Child changes into dry nightclothes.

    5. Child removes wet sheets and places in dirty laundry.

    6. Child obtains dry sheets and remakes the bed.

    7. Child performs getting-up practice for twenty trials.

    8. Remind child to awaken half hour earlier in morning and to do getting-up practice before bedtime tomorrow.

    9. Child feels bed sheets and comments on dryness.

   10. Praise child for correcting the wetness.

   11. Child returns to sleep.

V. INSPECT THE BED FOR DRYNESS ONE HALF HOUR EARLIER THE NEXT MORNING.

Appendix 3

OUTLINE OF
THE CONTINUING PRACTICE
AFTER THE INTENSIVE
TRAINING DAY

I. HOLDING-BACK PRACTICE
   A. Child uses measuring cup for every urination.
   B. Write down the amount of urination.
   C. Praise the child for his short-term and long-term progress at each urination.
      1. If younger child, give small snack treat as reward.

II. NIGHTLY AWAKENING
   A. Awaken child once during night.
      1. Use minimal prompt when awakening.
      2. Inspect bed for wetness.
      3. Child feels sheets and comments on dryness or wetness.
      4. Child goes to the bathroom, urinates in the cup, and returns to bed.
      5. Child feels sheets again.

  6. Child states what he will do if he feels urge to uri-
     nate.
  7. Express confidence to child as child returns to sleep.
 B. Adjust time of the nightly awakening (see Happy
    Clock).
  1. On first night, awaken child at parents' bedtime.
  2. If child is dry, awaken him one half hour earlier the
     next night.
  3. If child is wet, awaken him at the same time the next
     night.
 C. If child is wet at the nightly awakening:
  1. Gently reprimand child and have child feel wet
     sheets.
   a) Child changes nightclothes, changes sheets.
   b) Child performs getting-up practice for twenty
      trials.
   c) Child returns to sleep after feeling dry sheets and
      describing what he will do if he has the urge to
      urinate.
   d) Praise child for practice and express confidence in
      future success.
   e) Remind the child to perform the getting-up prac-
      tice again before his bedtime the next day.

III. CALENDAR PROGRESS CHART
 A. Each morning have child record previous night's wet-
    ness or dryness.
  1. Discuss with child the progress made.
  2. Both parents discuss progress with child.
  3. Relate the progress to the benefits and rewards listed
     in the agreements.

IV. AT BEDTIME
 A. Child feels sheets and comments on their dryness.
 B. Child describes what he will do if he has urge to urinate.

C. Child describes his current need to urinate.

D. Express confidence in child and review his progress.

E. Discuss how the child's progress is related to the rewards listed in the agreements.

V. MORNING BED INSPECTION—one half hour earlier than usual awakening

A. If bed is dry, do not awaken child.

B. If bed is wet, child performs usual changing and getting-up practice.

C. Calendar Progress Chart and Happy Clock are marked as to wet or dry.

VI. ONE HALF HOUR BEFORE USUAL BEDTIME

A. If child was wet previous night, child performs getting-up practice.

VII. DURING DAY

A. Child and parents describe progress to relevant friend or family members.

B. Parents repeatedly express confidence in child and praise him.

C. Review written agreement of benefits and provide them as promised.

Appendix 4

OUTLINE FOR
PHASING OUT
THE TRAINING PROGRAM

I. NIGHTLY AWAKENINGS
   A. Nightly awakening occurs one half hour earlier after each dry night.
      1. When nightly awakening is within one hour of bedtime, discontinue the nightly awakenings entirely.
      2. Eliminate Happy Clock when nightly awakenings are discontinued.

II. HOLDING-BACK PRACTICE
   A. After *fourteen straight nights of dryness,* discontinue need for child to urinate in measuring cup.
   B. Encourage child on his own to hold back urine as long as possible.

III. CALENDAR PROGRESS CHART
   A. Discontinue recording on Calendar Progress Chart after *one straight month of dryness.*

IV. MORNING INSPECTIONS OF BED
   A. Discontinue early-morning inspections after *one straight month of dryness.*

V. BEDTIME AWARENESS PROCEDURE
   A. Discontinue feeling of sheets and thought rehearsal after *one straight month of dryness.*

VI. PRAISE FOR BEING DRY
   A. Gradually decrease after the first two weeks of dryness.

VII. PAD-AND-BUZZER APPARATUS (IF USED)
   A. Discontinue apparatus after two weeks of dryness.

VIII. PROCEDURES WHICH WILL NOT BE PHASED OUT
   A. Child changes clothes and remakes bed after an accident.
   B. Child does getting-up practice before bedtime if there was an accident the night before, as well as doing the practice when the accident was discovered.

Appendix 5

SUPPLIERS OF
THE PAD-AND-BUZZER
APPARATUS

1. Sears, Roebuck, Catalog No. 8G1164 (Wee-Alert Buzzer). Approximate cost, $28.
2. Montgomery Ward, Catalog No. 53B21530 (Wet-Guard Kit). Approximate cost, $28.

Appendix 6

DRY-BED
HAPPY CLOCK

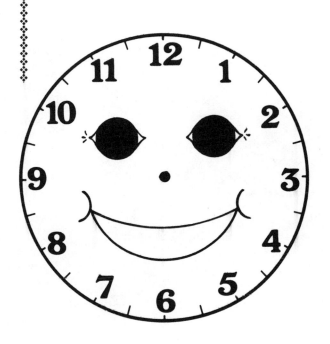

Appendix 7

DRY-BED CALENDAR

MON	TUES	WED	THURS	FRI	SAT	SUN

Appendix 7 (*continued*)

DRY-BED CALENDAR

MON	TUES	WED	THURS	FRI	SAT	SUN

Appendix 8

SELF-TEST
QUESTIONS

Circle the correct answer for each question. The correct answers can be found on page 177.

1. How old should the child be before training?
   a) 2 yrs. b) 3 yrs. c) 6 yrs.

2. Should training be started if the child has many accidents during the day?
   a) Yes b) No

3. Should a physician be consulted before training if there seems to be a medical problem?
   a) Yes b) No

4. If the child has a slight cold, should training be started?
   a) Yes b) No

5. Should training be started if the husband and wife do not agree with the need for this method of training?
   a) Yes b) No

6. The family is going on a vacation in 2 weeks. Can training start now anyhow?
   a) Yes b) No

7. Should the child continue to wear diapers at night during training?
   a) Yes b) No

8. If the child is still using a potty chair, and not the regular toilet, can training still be started?
   a) Yes b) No

9. Should the other children in the family be told about the training?
   a) Yes b) No

10. What should the other children in the family be asked to do about the training? Should they
    a) Stay out of it? b) Help? c) Watch, but not talk about it?

11. If the toilet is on a different floor, and the child can't walk the stairs, should training start anyhow?
    a) Yes b) No

12. How far should the child's bed be from the walls?
    a) Doesn't matter b) A foot or more c) Touching wall

13. The hallway from the bedroom to the toilet should
    a) Be dark b) Have some light

14. If 2 children are bedwetting, should training be started for both at the same time?
    a) Yes b) No

15. If 2 children are bedwetting, which child should be trained first?
    a) The older b) the younger

16. If another child sleeps in the same room, can training be started anyhow?
    a) Yes b) No

17. If the child is about 15 or 16 years old, should this training procedure be used?
    a) Yes b) No

18. If the child is 6 years old, about what are the chances that he will outgrow the bedwetting problem during the next year?
    a) 9 chances out of 10   b) 5 out of 10   c) 2 out of 10

19. How much should the child be told about the details and reasons for the training?
    a) Very little b) What to do, but not why c) What to do and why

20. When should the child be told about the training?
    a) Once training starts b) Beforehand

21. Will the trainer have to get up in the middle of the night to do this training?
    a) Yes b) No

22. Should all of the training procedures be started
    a) On the same day? b) Can they be added one day at a time?

23. Should
    a) All of the recommended procedures be used? b) Can some be omitted?

24. Is the pad and buzzer
    a) Required? b) Recommended? c) Not useful?

25. Should the parent schedule any other activities during the first training day?
    a) Yes b) No

26. What supplies are needed before starting training?
    a) Drinks, snacks, measuring cup b) Measuring cup
    c) None

27. When giving drinks on the first day should one use
    a) Different types of drinks? b) One type?

28. On the first training day should the snack treats be
    a) Salty? b) Sweet?

29. On the first afternoon that training starts, should the child play
    a) Outdoors? b) Indoors?

30. On the first night of training should the child have extra drinks up until
    a) Suppertime? b) His bedtime? c) 2 hours before the parents' bedtime?

31. On the first training night, how often should the child be awakened?
    a) Every hour b) Every half hour c) Every 2 hours

32. Is awareness development during sleep one of the basic objectives of treatment?
    a) Yes b) No

33. Is increasing bladder control a basic objective of treatment?
    a) Yes b) No

34. Is practice in nighttime toileting optional?
    a) Yes b) No

35. Recording on a Calendar Progress Chart is
    a) Optional b) Required

36. On the first day of training, should a contract of benefits for staying dry at night be made just for
    a) Long-term success? b) Even 1 or 2 days' success?
    c) Both long- and short-term success?

37. On the first day of training, should the list of inconveniences of being wet at night be
    a) Discussed with your child? b) Ignored?

38. On the first day of training, should
    a) The child make his own bed? b) The parent?

39. On the first day of training should the urine be measured
    a) Once? b) Each time the child urinates?

40. On the first training day, when the child has the urge to go, should one encourage the child
    a) To toilet immediately? b) To hold back?

41. On the first training day, should the child return to play if the urge to urinate is gone?
    a) Yes b) No

42. On the first training day should the holding-back procedure be practiced
    a) Until suppertime? b) Until bedtime?

43. On the first training day after lying down, if the urge persists after 2 minutes should the child jump up and go?
    a) Yes b) No

44. Should the child look at a clock to time his holding-back duration?
    a) Yes b) No

45. When should measuring of urine be done?
    a) Only on the first day of training b) Until the child is dry for 2 weeks

46. On the first day of training should the parent be
    a) Next to the child? b) In a different room?

47. On the first night of training should the child be awakened
    a) Only at midnight? b) Each hour until midnight?

48. If the child is very slow to awaken, should the parent
    a) Persist? b) Let him sleep?

49. If on the hourly inspection on the first night of training, the child is wet, shall the parent
    a) Let him sleep? b) Change his sheets? c) Let him change his sheets?

50. On the hourly inspection on the first night of training, if the child is wet should he do the getting-up practice
    a) As soon as he changes the sheets? b) Wait until the next day?

51. If the pad and buzzer is used and it signals an accident, should the parent
    a) Let the buzzer awaken the child? b) Help the child awaken?

52. When should the bedtime story about bedwetting be read?
    a) Before the first night of training b) After the first night

53. Should the child be spanked for having an accident?
    a) Yes b) No

54. On the first night should bedtime be set
    a) Earlier by one half hour? b) At usual bedtime? c) One half hour later?

55. Should the child stroke the sheets and comment on their dryness before going to bed
    a) Each night? b) Only on training night?

56. Should the getting-up practice be used
    a) Only on the first training night? b) Whenever a bed-wetting accident is discovered?

57. If there has been an accident, should the getting-up procedure be used
    a) Again before bedtime the next night? b) Only after the accident?

58. Should the snacks and drinking of liquids be given
    a) On the second night after training? b) Only on the first night of training? c) The rest of the week?

59. Should the child be praised when the measured amount of urine
    a) Sets a record? b) Is very large? c) For every attempt?

60. During the day should the child's drinking be
    a) Restricted? b) Not restricted?

61. If the child becomes upset and refuses to do the getting-up practice, should the child
    a) Be allowed to skip it? b) Think about it and then do it? c) Be forced to do it immediately?

62. If the child is upset and refuses to do the getting-up practice after an accident, even after thinking about it for several minutes, should he be allowed to
    a) Skip it? b) Think about it some more and then do it? c) Be spanked and forced to do it?

63. While the child is "thinking about it" after having an accident, should he be
    a) Watching TV? b) Playing? c) Sitting and thinking alone?

64. Should the bed be inspected each morning a half hour before waking-up time?
    a) Yes b) No

65. Should the nightly awakening be discontinued when
    a) The Happy Clock is pointed at the child's bedtime? b) 1 hour after the child's bedtime? c) At the parents' bedtime?

66. Should the Happy Clock nightly awakening time be moved
    a) Toward bedtime? b) Away from it?

67. Should the child's wetness or dryness each day be recorded on the Progress Chart
    a) By the child? b) By the parent?

68. Should the parent discuss the Progress Chart with the child
    a) When there has been an accident? b) Every night?

69. After the first training night, is the nightly awakening done
    a) Once a night? b) Several times each night?

70. After the training day, should the child continue to use the measuring cup for
    a) Every urination? b) Just before bedtime? c) Only when the parent is at home?

71. Who should write down the amount of measured urine in the cup?
    a) The parent b) The child

72. Should snack treats be given as a reward for
    a) Each large amount of measured urine? b) Only when a record is set?

73. After the first training day, when the child is awakened at the nightly awakening, should he
    a) Stroke sheets? b) Go urinate in bathroom? c) Describe his future actions if he has the urge later? d) All of the above—stroke sheets, go urinate, describe intentions?

74. If the child is wet, is the time of nightly awakening the next night
    a) Moved one half hour later? b) Kept at the same time?
    c) Moved one half hour earlier?

75. If the child is dry, is the time of awakening the next night
    a) Moved one half hour later? b) Kept at same time?
    c) Moved one half hour earlier?

76. When the child is found to have an accident, how many getting-up practice trials does he do?
    a) 1 b) 5 c) 20

77. When the child is doing the getting-up practice and changing the sheets after an accident, the parent should stay next to the child
    a) Only on the first few days b) After every accident

78. After an accident, the child
    a) Strokes the sheets? b) Changes the sheets? c) Strokes and changes the sheets?

79. After an accident, the parent shows
    a) Disapproval of wetness? b) Confidence in future efforts with no disapproval? c) Disapproval of wetness and confidence in future efforts?

80. If the bed is found dry at the morning inspection, the child is
    a) Awakened and praised b) Allowed to sleep c) Awakened, praised, and returned to sleep

81. After an accident, the child practices the getting-up exercise the next night
    a) At his usual bedtime b) A half hour before the usual bedtime

82. The morning inspections are made by the parent until the child has
    a) 1 dry night b) 1 week of dryness c) 1 month of dryness

83. After one straight month of dryness, discontinue
    a) The morning inspections b) The bedtime feeling of sheets and thought rehearsal c) Progress Calendar recording d) all of the above

84. The measuring cup records of urination should be discontinued after
    a) 1 night of dryness b) 2 weeks of dryness c) 3 months of dryness

85. The changing of sheets by the child after an accident should be discontinued
    a) After 1 week of dryness b) 1 month of dryness c) Never discontinued

86. The getting-up practice after an accident should be discontinued
    a) After 1 month of dryness b) After 3 months of dryness c) Never discontinued

87. The list of agreed-upon benefits for dryness should be posted
    a) In the bathroom b) Next to the Progress Chart c) In the kitchen

88. The Calendar Progress Chart is posted in the
    a) Bedroom b) Kitchen c) Bathroom

89. The rewards and benefits listed in the agreement should be
    a) Saved up and given when it is convenient b) given one at a time as soon as each one is earned

90. If an accident occurs after 2 months of dryness, should one
    a) Omit the practice unless wetting persists? b) Reintroduce the cleaning up and practice right away?

SELF-TEST ANSWERS

1) b.	24) b.	47) b.	69) a.
2) b.	25) b.	48) a.	70) a.
3) a.	26) a.	49) c.	71) b.
4) b.	27) a.	50) a.	72) a.
5) b.	28) a.	51) b.	73) d.
6) b.	29) b.	52) a.	74) b.
7) b.	30) c.	53) b.	75) c.
8) a.	31) a.	54) a.	76) c.
9) a.	32) a.	55) a.	77) a.
10) b.	33) a.	56) b.	78) c.
11) b.	34) b.	57) a.	79) c.
12) b.	35) b.	58) b.	80) b.
13) b.	36) c.	59) c.	81) b.
14) b.	37) a.	60) b.	82) c.
15) a.	38) a.	61) b.	83) d.
16) a.	39) b.	62) b.	84) b.
17) a.	40) b.	63) c.	85) c.
18) c.	41) a.	64) a.	86) c.
19) c.	42) b.	65) b.	87) b.
20) b.	43) a.	66) a.	88) a.
21) b.	44) b.	67) a.	89) b.
22) a.	45) b.	68) b.	90) b.
23) a.	46) a.		

References

I. REVIEW OF STUDIES OF THE OCCURRENCE OF BEDWETTING
Lovibond, S. H. *Conditioning and Enuresis*. Elmsford, N.Y.: Pergamon Press, 1964.

II. BEDWETTING IN INSTITUTIONALIZED POPULATIONS
Baller, W. R., and Giangreco, J. C. "Correction of Nocturnal Enuresis in Deaf Children," *The Volta Review*, 7 (1970):545–47.

Jehu, D.; Morgan, R. T. T.; Turner, R. K.; and Jones, A. "A Controlled Trial of the Treatment of Nocturnal Enuresis in Residential Homes for Children." *Behavior Research and Therapy* 15 (1977):1–16.

Kaffman, M. "Enuresis Among Kibbutz Children." *Harefuah* 62 (1962):251–53.

———. Toilet-Training by Multiple Caretakers: Enuresis Among Kibbutz Children." *Israel Annals of Psychiatry and Related Disciplines* 10 (1972):341–65.

Mowrer, O., and Mowrer, W. M. "Enuresis: A Method for Its Study and Treatment." *American Journal of Orthopsychiatry* 8 (1938):436–47.

Thorne, F. C. "The Incidence of Nocturnal Enuresis After Age Five." *American Journal of Psychiatry* 100 (1944):686–89.

III. HISTORY OF TREATMENTS FOR BEDWETTING

Glicklich, L. B. "An Historical Account of Enuresis." *Pediatrics* 8 (1951):859–75.

IV. INVENTION OF THE PAD-AND-BUZZER METHOD

Mowrer, O., and Mowrer, W. M. "Enuresis: A Method for Its Study and Treatment." *American Journal of Orthopsychiatry* 8 (1938):436–47.

V. COMPARISON OF DRUG TREATMENT AND PAD-AND-BUZZER TREATMENT OF BEDWETTING

McConaghy, N. "A Controlled Trial of Imipramine, Amphetamine, Pad-and-Bell Conditioning and Random Awakening in the Treatment of Nocturnal Enuresis." *The Medical Journal of Australia* (1969):237–39.

Shaffer, D.; Costello, A. J.; and Hill, I. D. "Control of Enuresis with Imipramine." *Archives of Disease in Childhood* 43 (1968):665–71.

VI. REVIEWS OF STUDIES OF THE PAD-AND-BUZZER TREATMENT OF BEDWETTING

Collins, R. W. "Importance of Bladder-Cue Buzzer Contingency in the Conditioning Treatment for Enuresis." *Journal of Abnormal Psychology* 82 (1973):299–308.

Jones, H. G. "The Behavioural Treatment of Enuresis Nocturna." In *Behaviour Therapy and the Neuroses*, edited by H. J. Eysenck, Elmsford, N.Y.: Pergamon Press, 1960, pp. 337–403.

Lovibond, S. H. *Conditioning and Enuresis.* Elmsford, N.Y.: Pergamon Press, 1964.

Yates, A. J. *Behavior Therapy*. New York: John Wiley, 1970.

VII. COMPARISONS OF PSYCHOTHERAPY WITH THE PAD-AND-BUZZER TREATMENT OF BEDWETTING

DeLeon, G., and Mandell, W. "A Comparison of Conditioning and Psychotherapy in the Treatment of Functional Enuresis." *Journal of Clinical Psychology* 22 (1966):326–30.

Werry, J., and Cohrssen, J. "Enuresis—An Etiologic and Therapeutic Study." *The Journal of Pediatrics* 67 (1965):423–31.

VIII. NONTECHNICAL DISCUSSION OF MEDICAL ASPECTS OF BEDWETTING

Rowan, R. L. *Bed-Wetting, A Guide for Parents*. New York: St. Martin's Press, 1974.

IX. BLADDER CAPACITY INCREASED BY TRAINING

Hagglund, T. B. "Enuretic Children Treated with Fluid Restriction or Forced Drinking." *Annals Paediatriae Fenniae* 11 (1965):84.

Muellner, S. R. "Development of Urinary Control in Children." *Journal of the American Medical Association* 172 (1960):1256.

Paschalis, A. P.; Kimmel, H. D.; and Kimmel, E. "Further Study of Diurnal Instrumental Conditioning in the Treatment of Enuresis Nocturna." *Journal of Behavior Therapy and Experimental Psychiatry* 3 (1972):253–56.

Starfield, B., and Mellits, E. D. "Increase in Functional Bladder Capacity and Improvements in Enuresis." *The Journal of Pediatrics* 72 (1968):483–87.

X. RETARDED PERSONS TREATED FOR BEDWETTING BY THE PRESENT METHOD

Azrin, N. H., and Foxx, R. M. "A Rapid Method of Toilet Training the Institutionalized Retarded." *Journal of Applied Behavior Analysis* 4 (1971):89–99.

Foxx, R. M., and Azrin, N. H. *Toilet Training the Retarded: A Rapid Program for Day and Nighttime Independent Toileting*. Champaign, Ill.: Research Press, 1973.

XI. DAYTIME TOILET TRAINING

Azrin, N. H., and Foxx, R. M. *Toilet Training in Less Than a Day*. New York: Simon and Schuster, 1974.

Foxx, R. M., and Azrin, N. H. "Dry Pants: A Rapid Method of Toilet Training Children." *Behavior Research and Therapy* 11 (1973):435–42.

Butler, J. F. "The Toilet Training Success of Parents After Reading 'Toilet Training in Less Than a Day.' " *Behavior Therapy* 7 (1976):185–91.

XII. THE PRESENT METHOD OF TREATING BEDWETTING

Azrin, N. H.; Hontos, P. T.; and Besalel-Azrin, V. B. "Elimination of Enuresis Without a Conditioning Apparatus: An Extension by Office Instruction of the Child and Parents." *Behavior Therapy*. In press.

————; Sneed, T. J.; and Foxx, R. M. "Dry Bed Training: Rapid Elimination of Childhood Enuresis." *Behavior Research and Therapy* 12 (1974):147–56.

————, and Thienes, P. M. "Rapid Elimination of Enuresis by Intensive Learning Without a Conditioning Apparatus." *Behavior Therapy* 9 (1978):342–54.

Besalel, V. B.; Azrin, N. H.; and Thienes-Hontos, P. "Evaluation of a Parent's Manual for Training Enuretic Children." *Behavior Therapy*. In press.

Bollard, R. J., and Woodroffe, P. "The Effect of Parent-Administered Dry-Bed Training on Nocturnal Enuresis in Children." *Behavior Research and Therapy* 15 (1977):159–65.

Doleys, D. M.; Ciminero, A. R.; Tollison, J. W.; Williams, C. L.; and Wells, K. C. "Dry-Bed Training and Retention Control Training: A Comparison." *Behavior Therapy* 8 (1977):541–48.

Index

[Page numbers in *italics* indicate illustrations.]